SHORTLISTED • EMMA HUMPHREYS MEMORIAL PRIZE

SHORTLISTED • BROKEN FRONTIER AWARDS: BEST GRAPHIC NOVEL

PRAISE FOR *BECOMING UNBECOMING*

'Unflinching, heartbreaking and utterly compelling. Una's story explores how the public silencing of women's voices too often creates a private hell.'
– Emma Jane Unsworth

'Touching, moving and tackling a really serious subject. A wonderful, wonderful book.' – Jenni Murray, BBC Radio 4 *Woman's Hour*

'My favourite graphic novel this year… incredibly powerful, insightful… a very unapologetic call for the importance of listening to other women's lives.'
– Anna James, BBC Radio 4 *Open Book*

'A brilliant, brave and fiercely intelligent book.'
– Kerry Hudson, *Herald Scotland*

'Poignant, powerful, astute.' – Paul Gravett, Top Ten British Graphic Novels

'Una somehow manages to render everything beautifully with a high concept visual style.' – *Tech Times*, Best Comics of 2015

'Brilliantly controlled and compelling… It joins the dots between the personal and political with breathtaking ease and manages to rewrite the rules of visual storytelling in the process. A profoundly important book that everyone, particularly men, should read immediately.'
– Gareth Brookes, *Forbidden Planet International*, Best of the Year

'A very brave, important and thought-provoking book.' – *Savidge Reads*

'Hugely powerful… The words and images are woven together beautifully.'
– *Elle*

'A beautiful, haunting, take on Peter Sutcliffe's reign of terror, and the women and communities he destroyed. The bare fact is, as Una beautifully explores, that females are living under a reign of patriarchal power that requires us to take the rough with the rough. Except we don't. Consume this book, and be prepared to join the revolution.' – Julie Bindel

'This game-changing graphic novel… marks a major new feminist voice.'
– *Guardian*

'Male violence against women is a major problem – for all of us. This exploration of blame and shame brings home that fact in an immediate way, but also with great delicacy.' – Mary Talbot

'A fantastic graphic novel. The denouement is just astounding.'
– Kieron Gillen

'Read the wonderful, beautiful and powerful *Becoming Unbecoming* in one jetlagged gulp.' – Sarah Savitt

'Make no mistake, this is one of the most important comics works of 2015.'
– *Broken Frontier*, Comic of the Week

'Honest, matter-of-fact and absolutely gut-wrenching… shows what happens when women refuse to be silent. When our voices are heard. When we start to shout back. Read this. Get angry. Start shouting.' – *Emerald Street*

'A sensitively rendered yet powerful exploration of the blame and shame culture that surrounds sexual violence… *Becoming Unbecoming* should be read by everyone… heartbreakingly tender. One of the most important novels published in 2015.' – *Pamreader*

'Packed with sobering statistics and personal anecdotes, B*ecoming Unbecoming* is not an easy read, but it's a relevant and important one.'
– *Library Journal*

'This challenging debut graphic novel is dense with facts, figures, and exposition, but the issues it explores—sexual violence and the public response to it – are what make it truly difficult to read… It's as well crafted as it is difficult – and an important document of the lingering effects of male violence against women.' – *Publishers Weekly*, starred review

'It is beautiful to handle, with inky images you want to touch and narrative that falls into prose. It is also a harrowing and politically sharp book.'
– *Feminist Intelligence*

BECOMING
UNBECOMING

Una

myriad m∞

First published in 2015
Reprinted 2016

Myriad Editions
59 Lansdowne Place
Brighton BN3 1FL, UK

www.myriadeditions.com

Second printing

3 5 7 9 10 8 6 4 2

A CIP catalogue record for this book is available from
the British Library.

ISBN: 978-1-908434-69-2
E-ISBN: 978-1-908434-70-8

Printed by Jelgavas Tipografija in Latvia on paper sourced from
sustainable forests.

Dedicated to all the others.

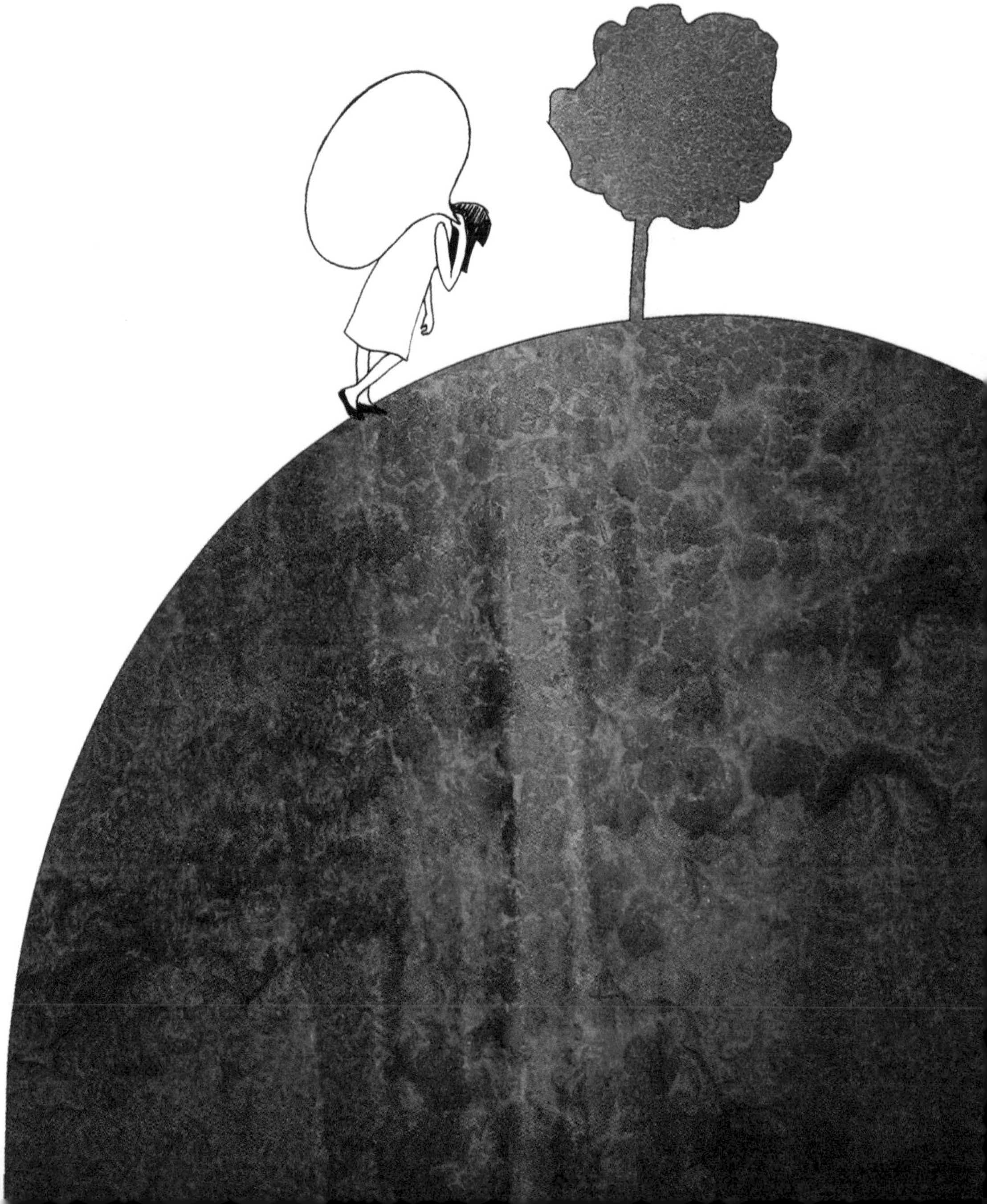

MY NAME IS UNA.

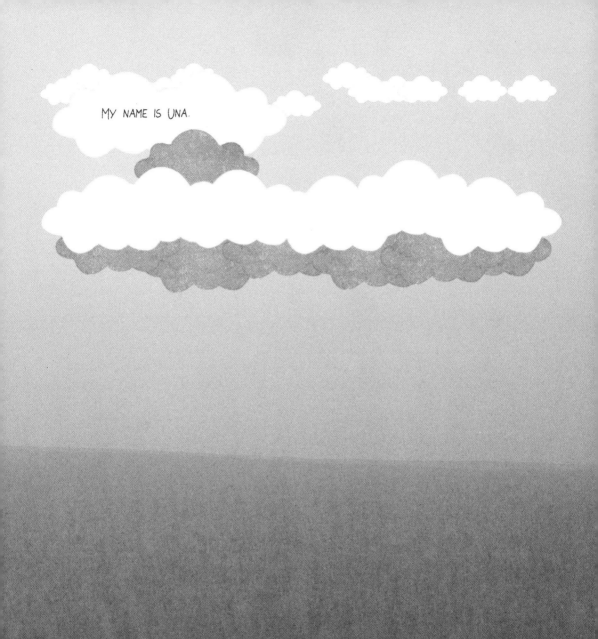

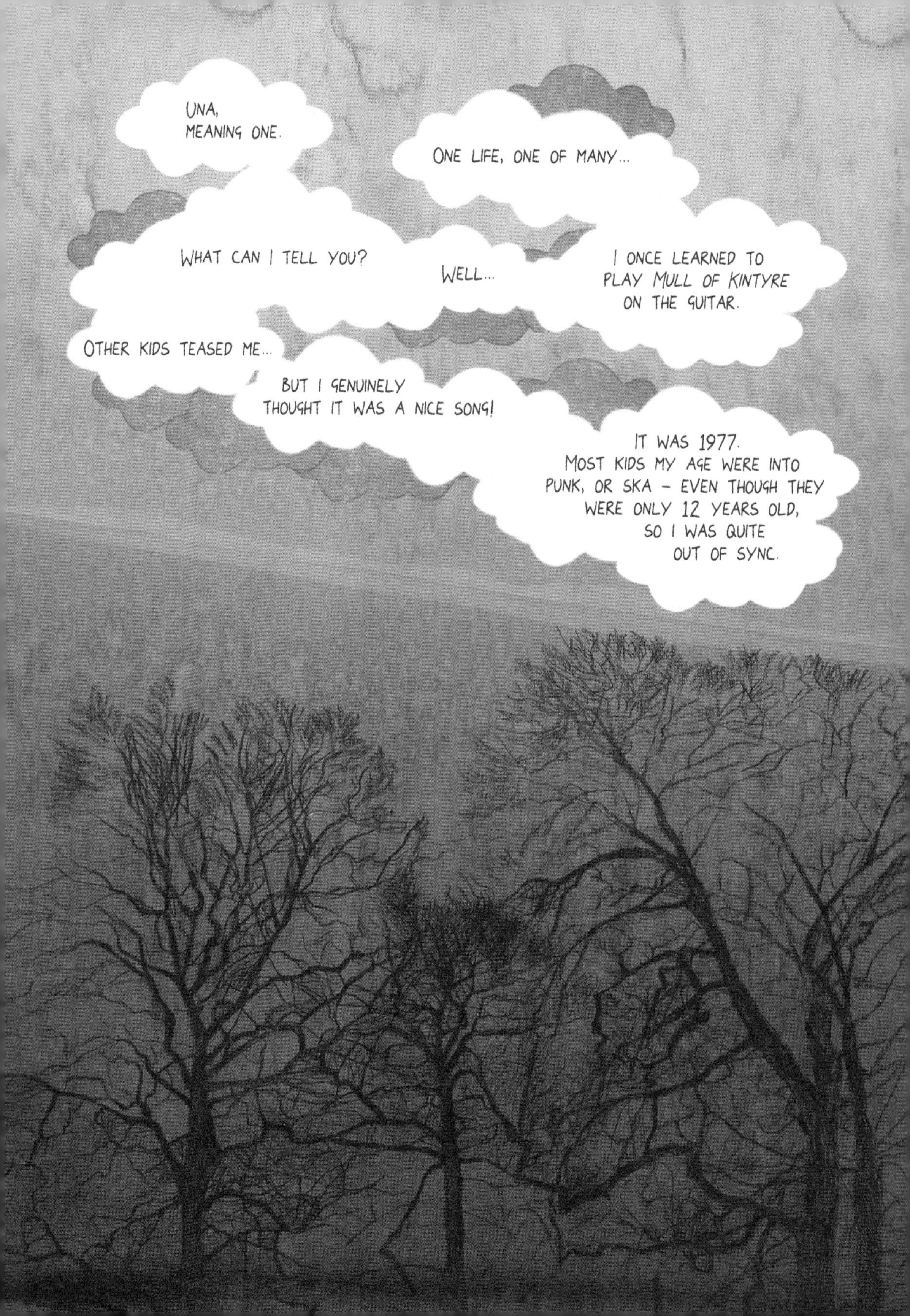
UNA,
MEANING ONE.
ONE LIFE, ONE OF MANY...
WHAT CAN I TELL YOU?
WELL...
I ONCE LEARNED TO PLAY MULL OF KINTYRE ON THE GUITAR.
OTHER KIDS TEASED ME...
BUT I GENUINELY THOUGHT IT WAS A NICE SONG!
IT WAS 1977. MOST KIDS MY AGE WERE INTO PUNK, OR SKA - EVEN THOUGH THEY WERE ONLY 12 YEARS OLD, SO I WAS QUITE OUT OF SYNC.

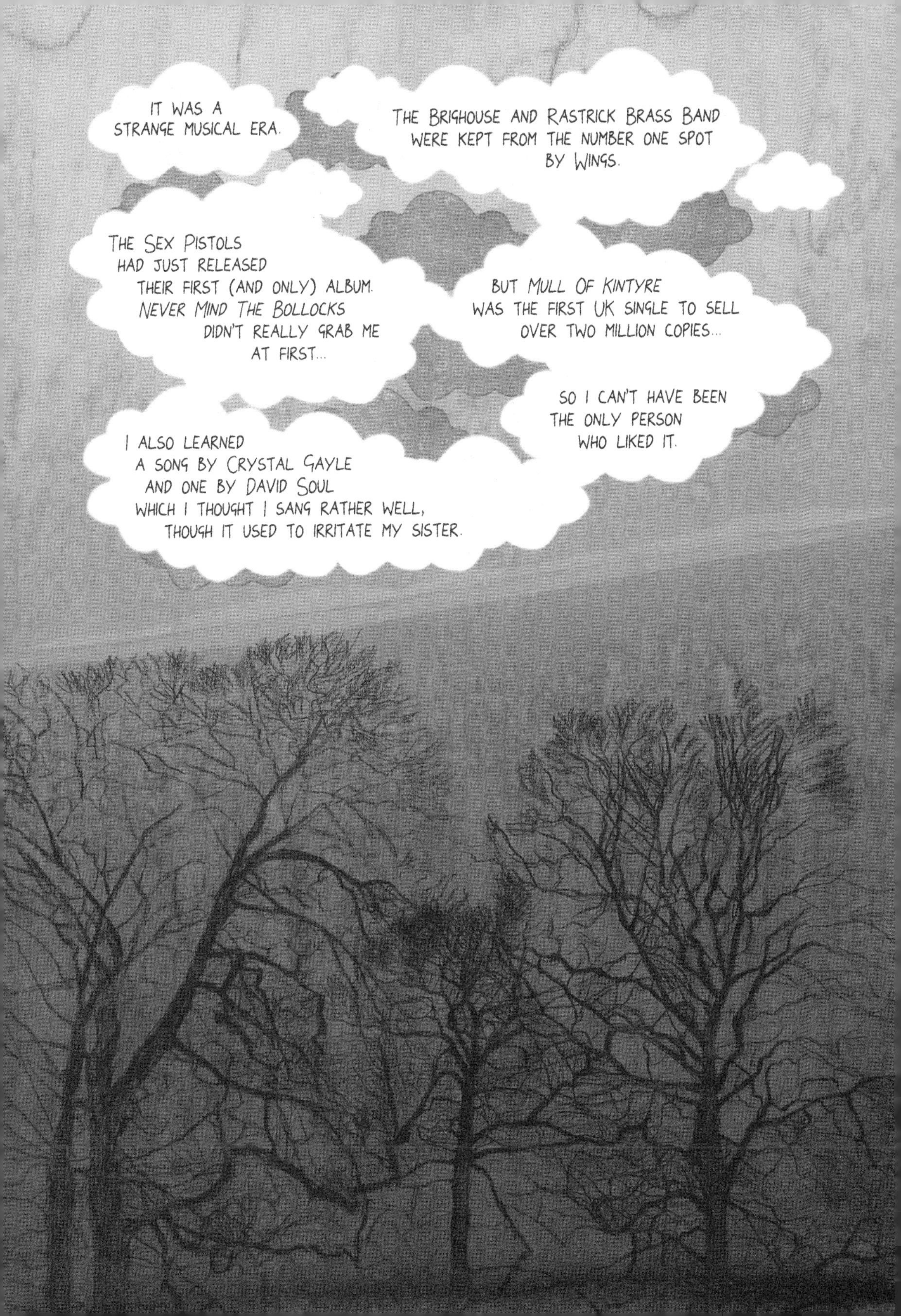
IT WAS A STRANGE MUSICAL ERA.
THE BRIGHOUSE AND RASTRICK BRASS BAND WERE KEPT FROM THE NUMBER ONE SPOT BY WINGS.
THE SEX PISTOLS HAD JUST RELEASED THEIR FIRST (AND ONLY) ALBUM. *NEVER MIND THE BOLLOCKS* DIDN'T REALLY GRAB ME AT FIRST...
BUT *MULL OF KINTYRE* WAS THE FIRST UK SINGLE TO SELL OVER TWO MILLION COPIES...
SO I CAN'T HAVE BEEN THE ONLY PERSON WHO LIKED IT.
I ALSO LEARNED A SONG BY CRYSTAL GAYLE AND ONE BY DAVID SOUL WHICH I THOUGHT I SANG RATHER WELL, THOUGH IT USED TO IRRITATE MY SISTER.

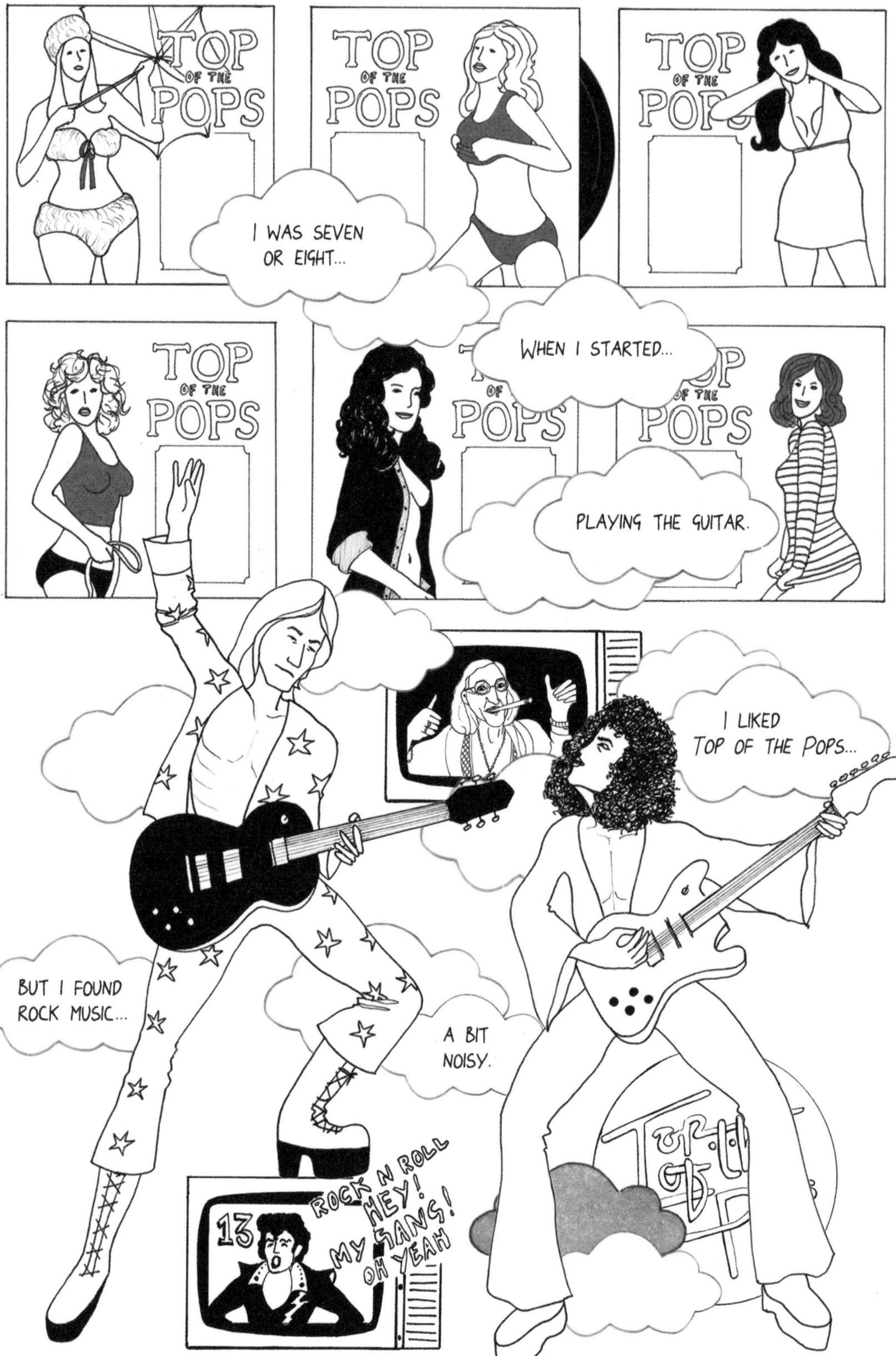
TOP OF THE POPS
I WAS SEVEN OR EIGHT...
WHEN I STARTED...
PLAYING THE GUITAR.
I LIKED TOP OF THE POPS...
BUT I FOUND ROCK MUSIC...
A BIT NOISY.
13
ROCK N ROLL
HEY!
MY GANG!
OH YEAH

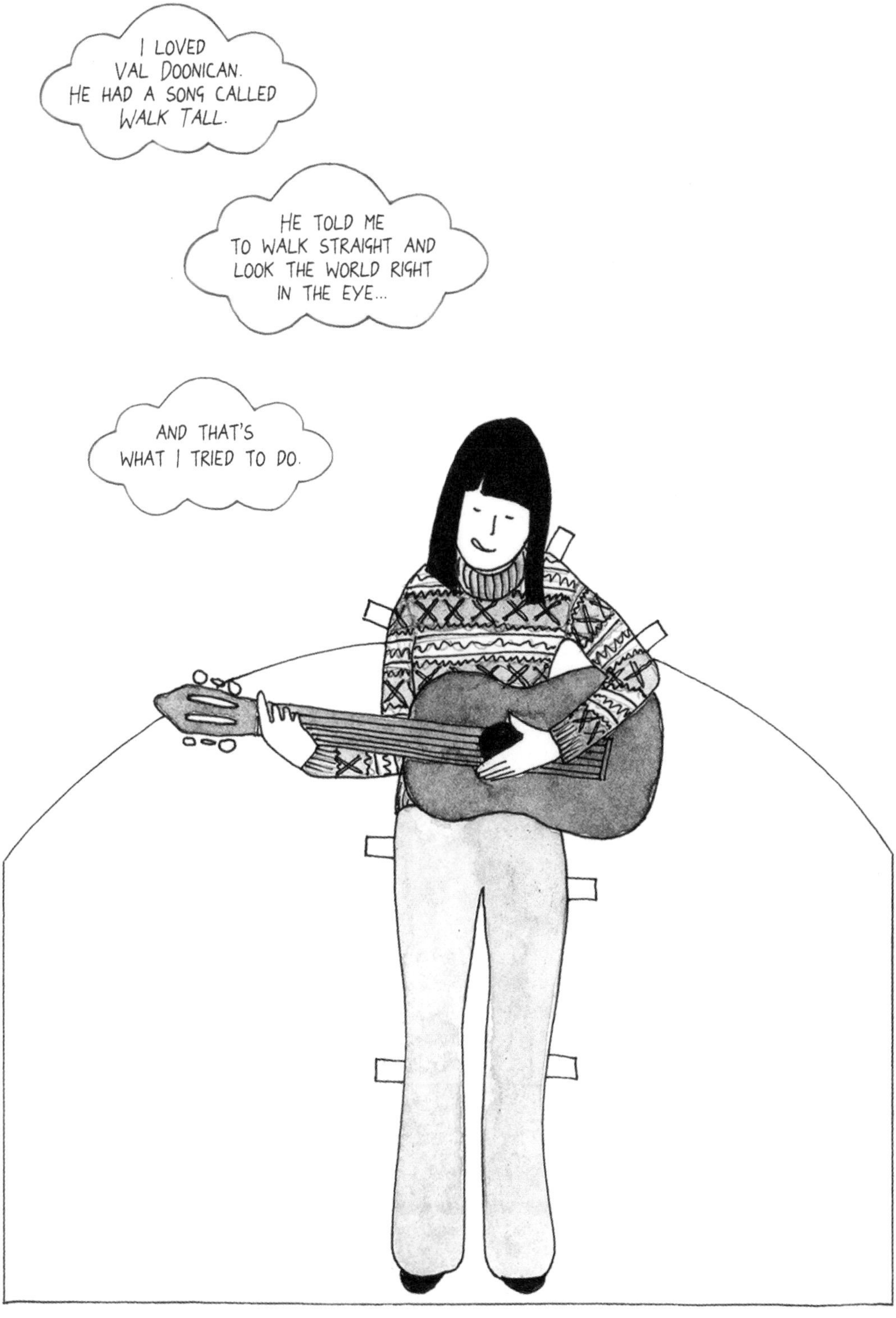
I LOVED VAL DOONICAN. HE HAD A SONG CALLED WALK TALL.
HE TOLD ME TO WALK STRAIGHT AND LOOK THE WORLD RIGHT IN THE EYE...
AND THAT'S WHAT I TRIED TO DO.

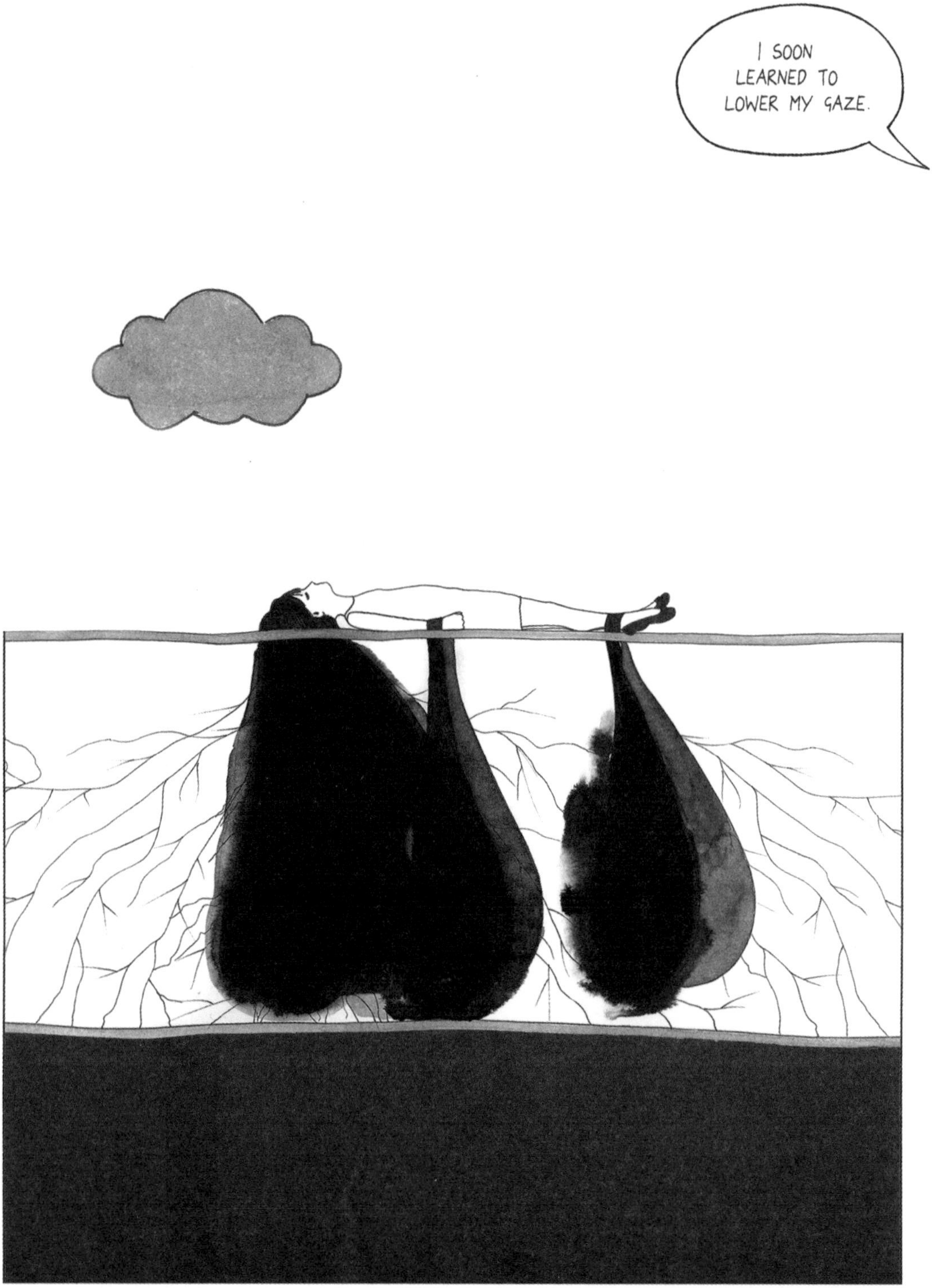
I SOON LEARNED TO LOWER MY GAZE.

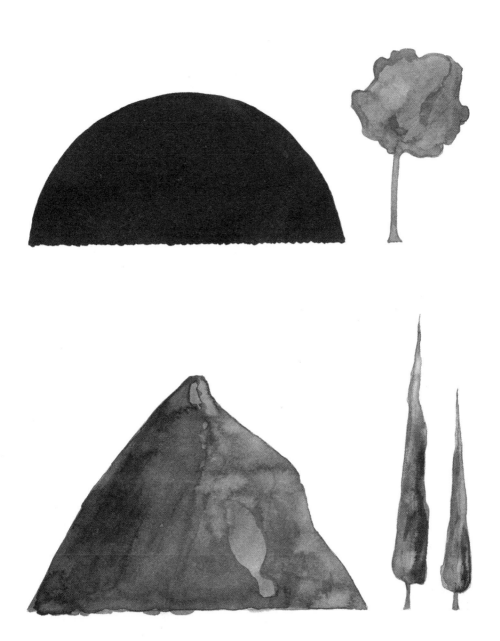

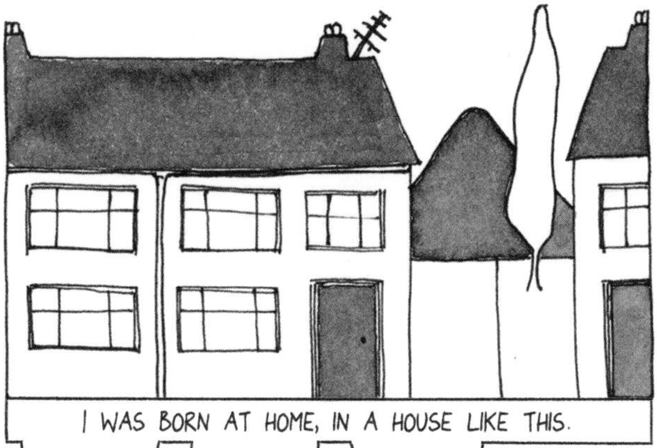
I WAS BORN AT HOME, IN A HOUSE LIKE THIS.

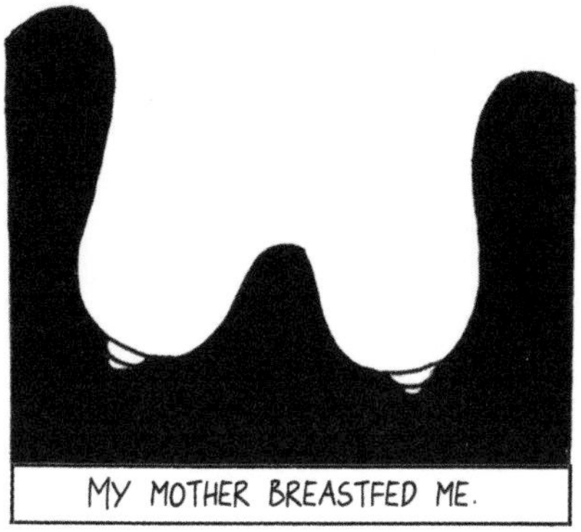
MY MOTHER BREASTFED ME.

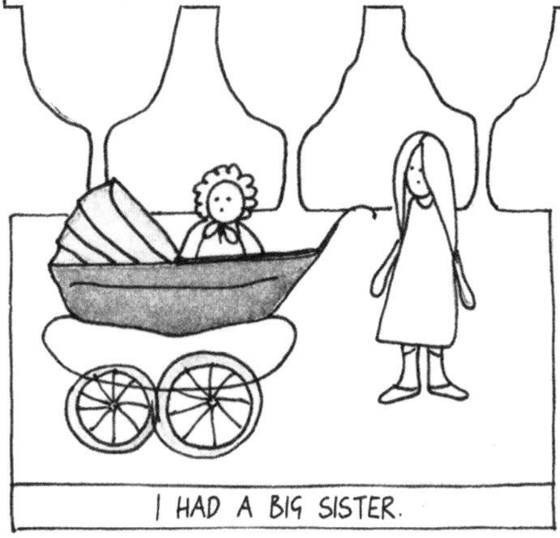
I HAD A BIG SISTER.

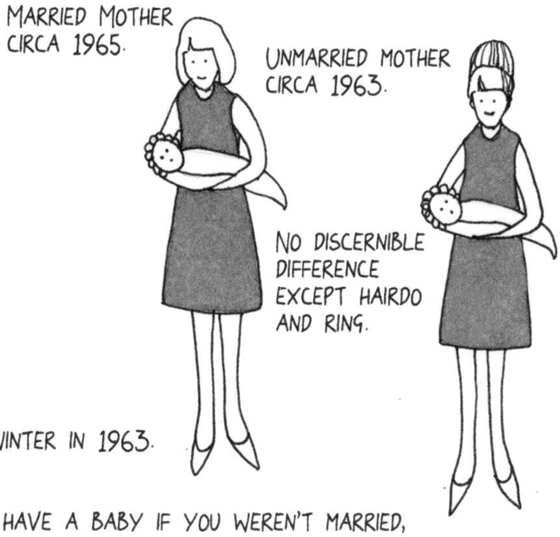
MARRIED MOTHER CIRCA 1965.
UNMARRIED MOTHER CIRCA 1963.
NO DISCERNIBLE DIFFERENCE EXCEPT HAIRDO AND RING.

MY SISTER WAS BORN JUST BEFORE A HARSH WINTER IN 1963.
OUR MOTHER WASN'T MARRIED THEN.

IN 1963, IT WAS AN EXTRAORDINARY THING TO HAVE A BABY IF YOU WEREN'T MARRIED,
SO MY SISTER'S MOTHER WAS AN UNMARRIED MOTHER.
WHAT WAS MY SISTER?
AND WHAT WAS HER FATHER? I WONDER.

NO ONE TOLD HER ABOUT THIS, SHE LEARNED IT FROM A BOY AT SCHOOL.
OUR MOTHER HAD BETTER LUCK WITH ME AS MY FATHER MARRIED HER BEFORE I POPPED OUT.

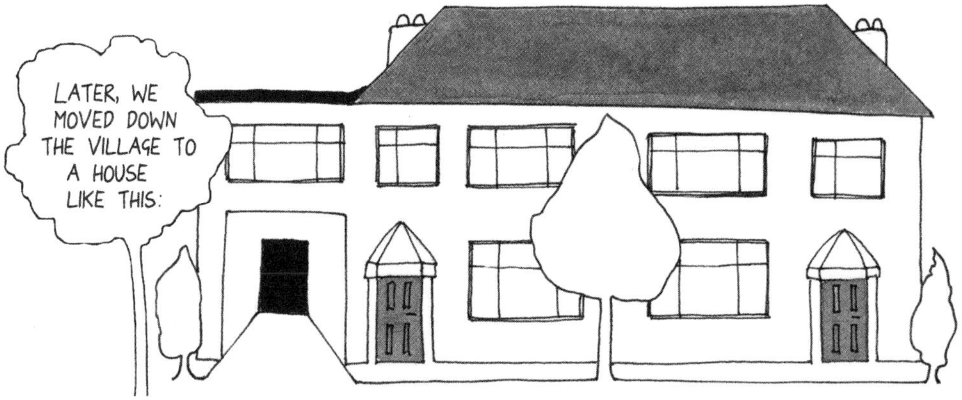
LATER, WE MOVED DOWN THE VILLAGE TO A HOUSE LIKE THIS:

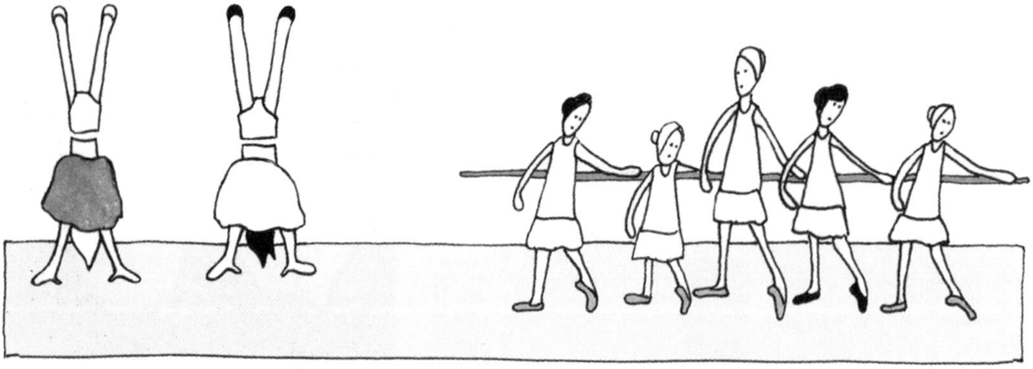

I WENT TO THE LOCAL SCHOOL.

I HAD BALLET CLASSES.

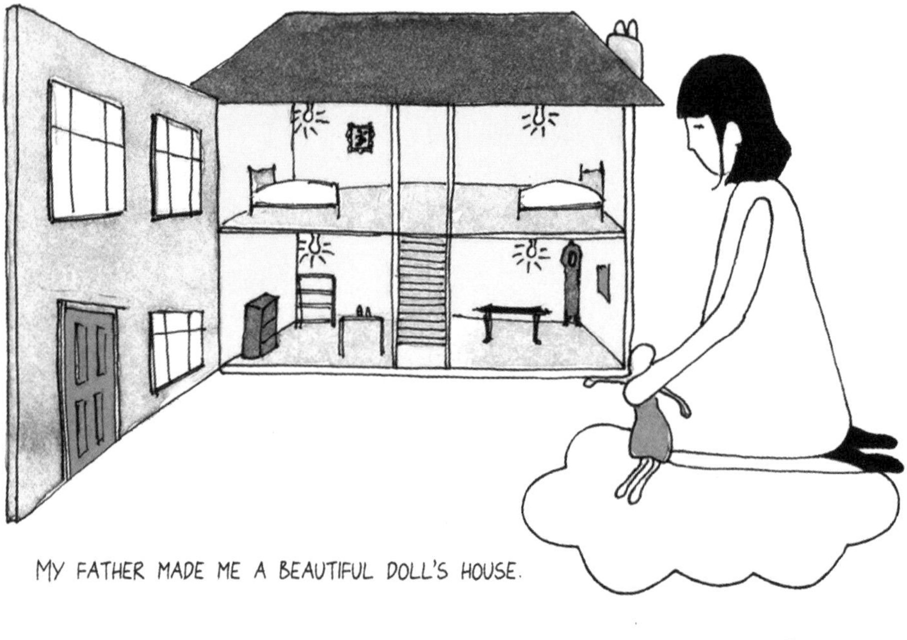

MY FATHER MADE ME A BEAUTIFUL DOLL'S HOUSE.

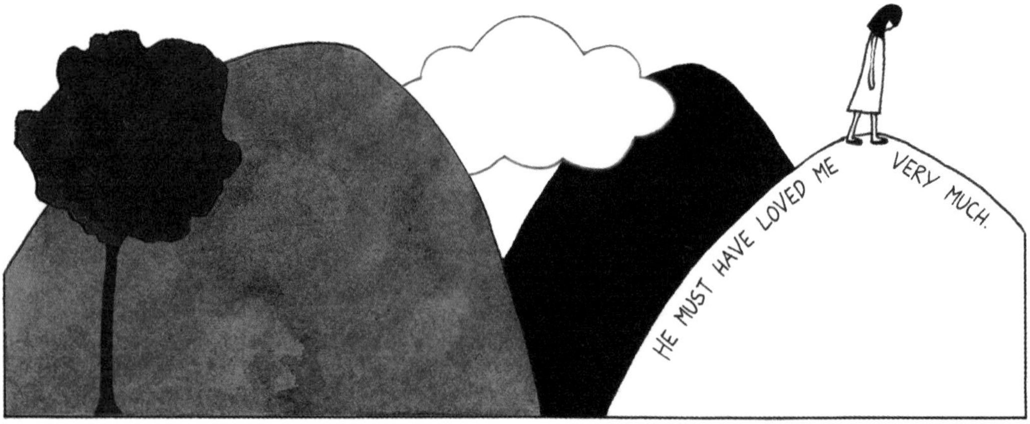
HE MUST HAVE LOVED ME VERY MUCH.

MY FAVOURITE TIMES WERE CHRISTMAS AND SUMMER HOLIDAYS...

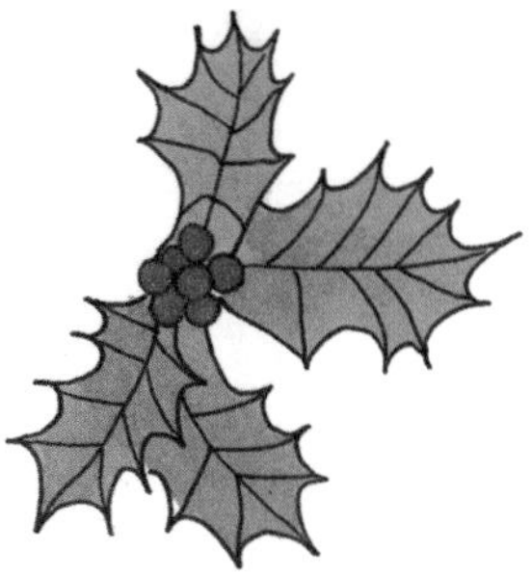

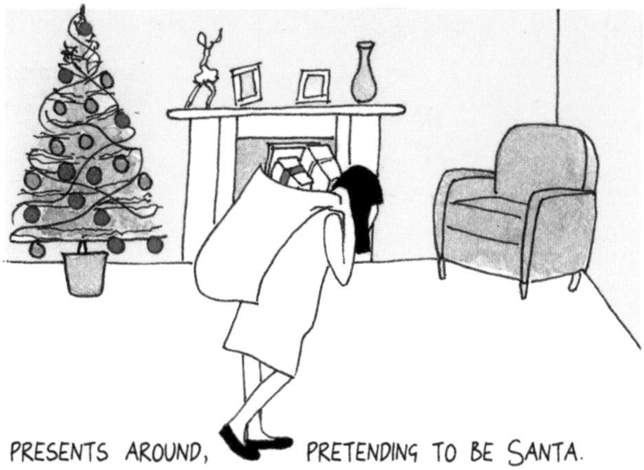

AT CHRISTMAS I CARRIED A PILLOWCASE OF PRESENTS AROUND, PRETENDING TO BE SANTA.

ON HOLIDAY IN THE SUMMER I'D WANDER SLOWLY ALONG THE BEACH, IMAGINING I WAS A CHARACTER IN A BOOK: A PIRATE'S WIFE, A DRAGON HUNTER, AN ORPHANED GIRL IN A STORY OF THIEVES AND SMUGGLERS, OR AFTERNOON TEA AND BOARDING SCHOOL.

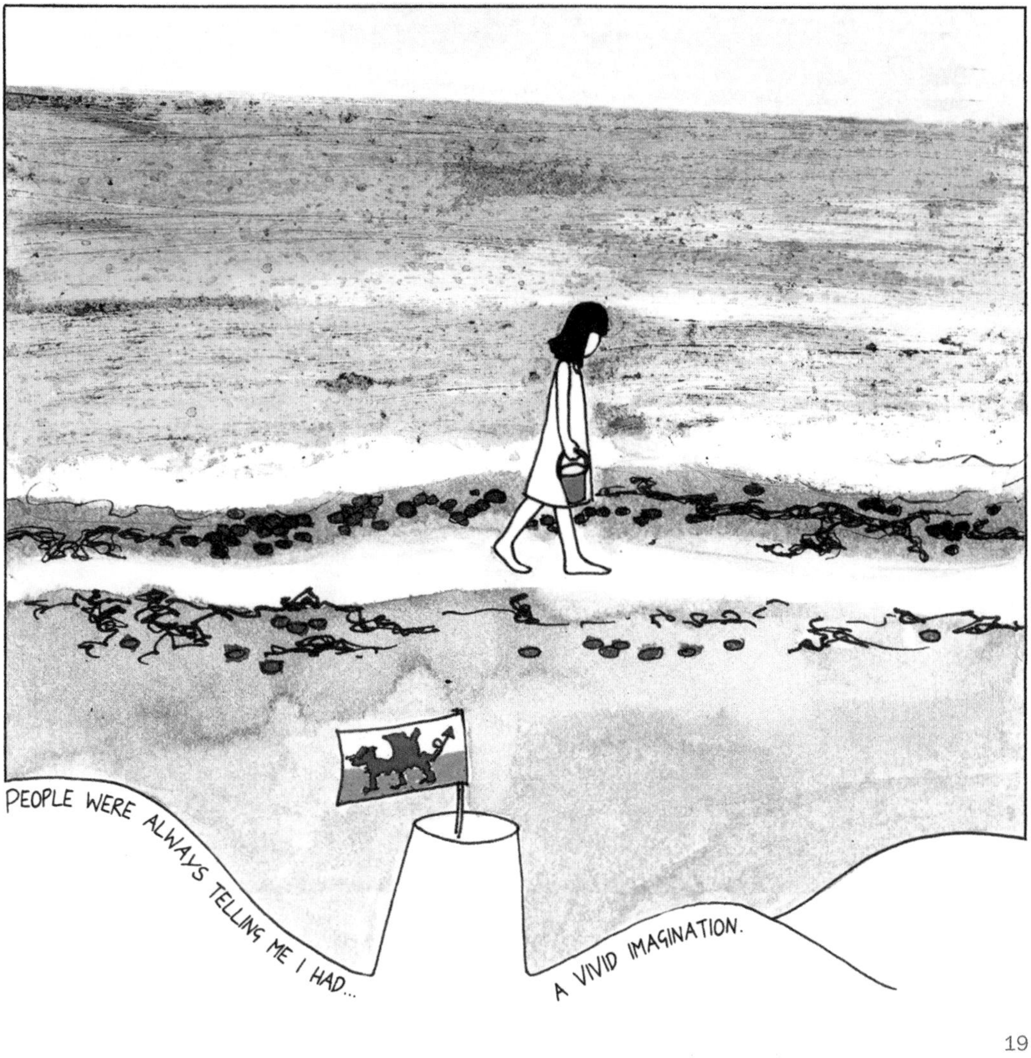

PEOPLE WERE ALWAYS TELLING ME I HAD... A VIVID IMAGINATION.

FOR A WHILE, THE SEVENTIES SEEMED LIKE A COSY, ROSY WORLD, BUT IT WAS A TURBULENT DECADE. THERE WERE:

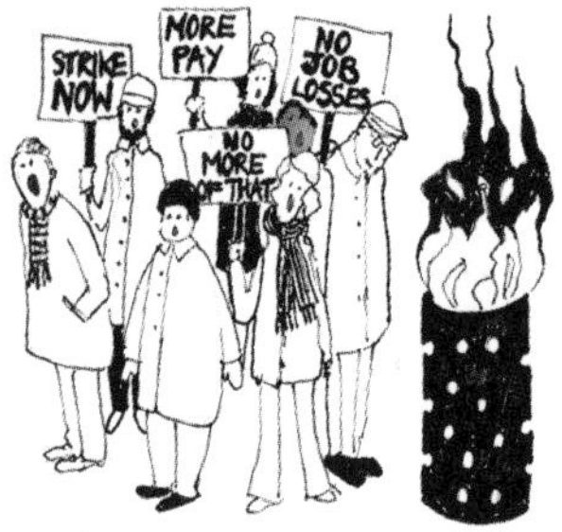
STRIKE NOW
MORE PAY
NO JOB LOSSES
NO MORE OF THAT

STRIKES

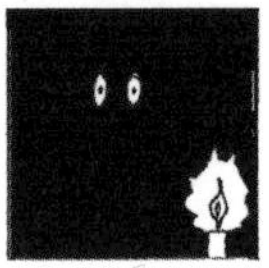

POWER CUTS

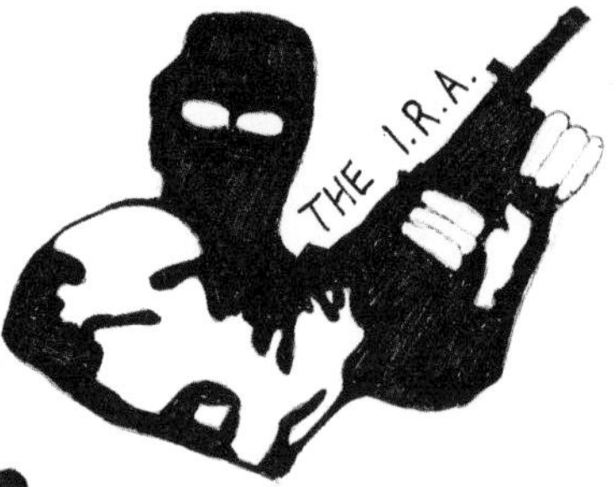
THE I.R.A.

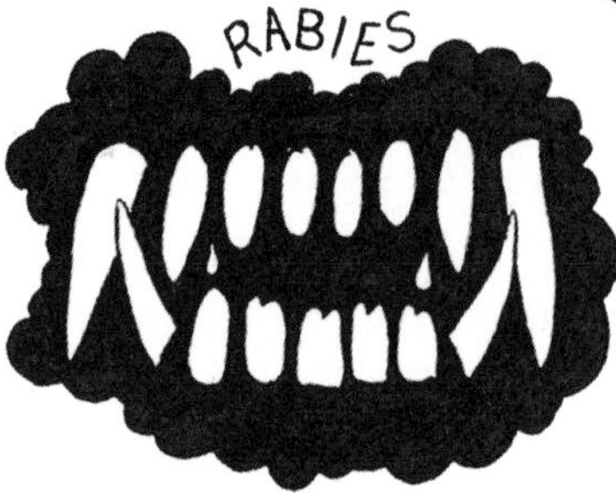
RABIES

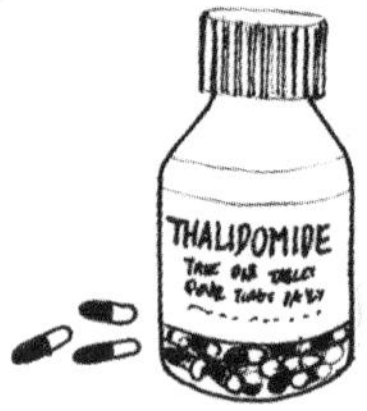
THALIDOMIDE

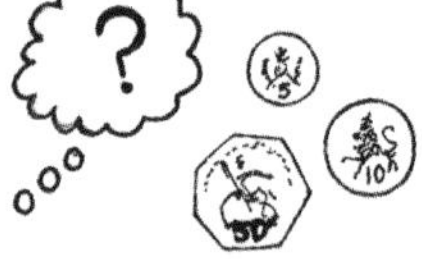
?

DECIMALISATION

IT WASN'T ALL BAD. THERE WAS ALSO THE EQUAL PAY ACT, THE SEX DISCRIMINATION ACT, *PINK FLOYD* AND *FAWLTY TOWERS*.

I WASN'T PAYING ATTENTION TO ANY OF THIS AT THE TIME. MY SEVENTIES WORLD CONSISTED OF WATCHING *BLUE PETER* AND EATING SHERBET OUT OF A PAPER BAG, WITH A LOLLY.

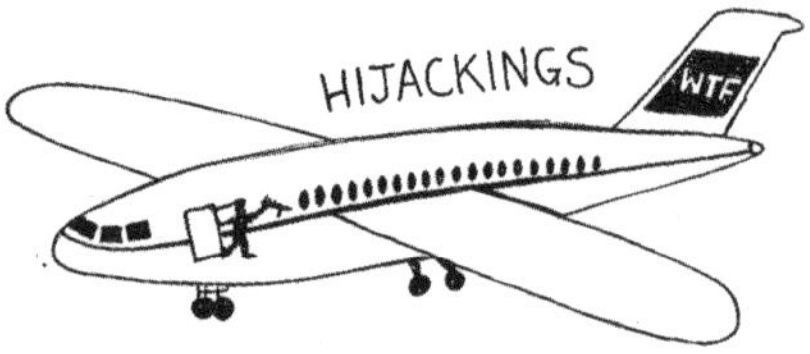
HIJACKINGS
WTF

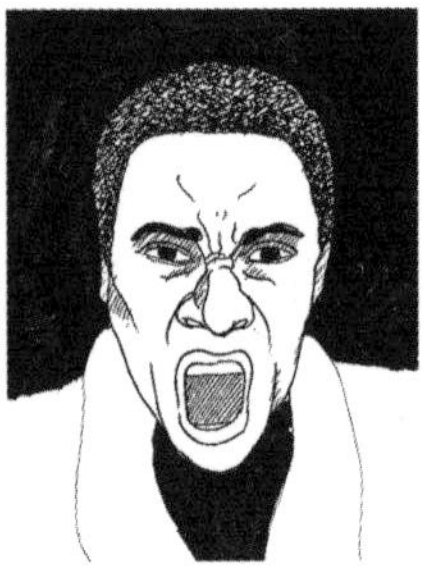

RACE RIOTS

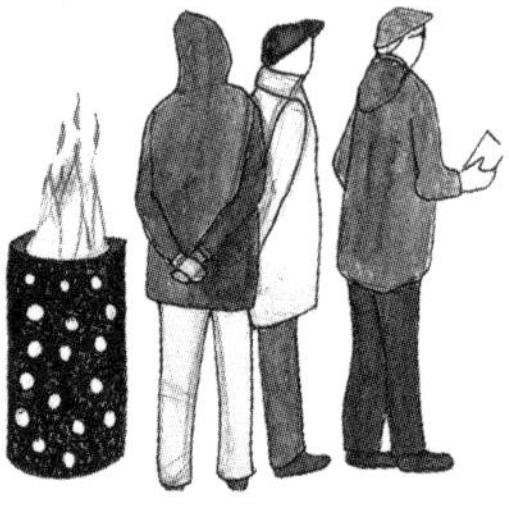

STRIKES AGAIN

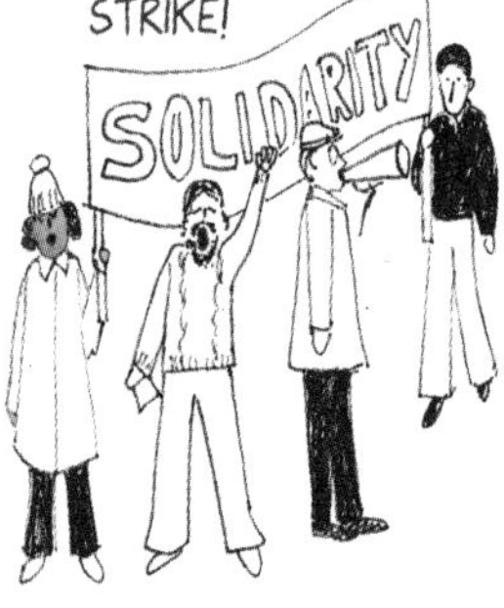
STRIKE!
STRIKE!
STRIKE!
SOLIDARITY

FOOTBALL HOOLIGANS

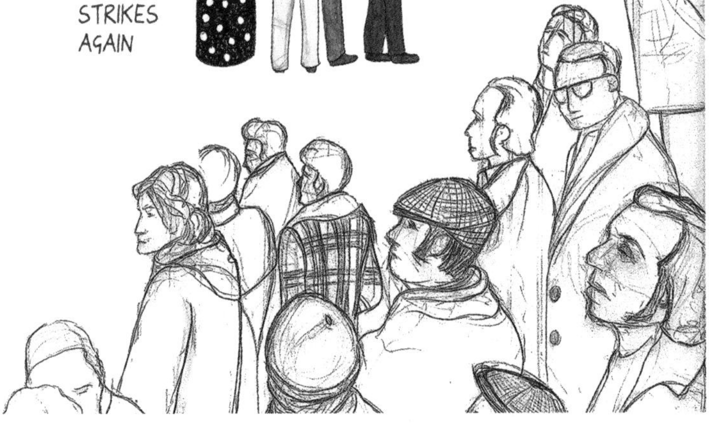

I LIVED IN THE WEST OF THE BIGGEST COUNTY IN THE UK.

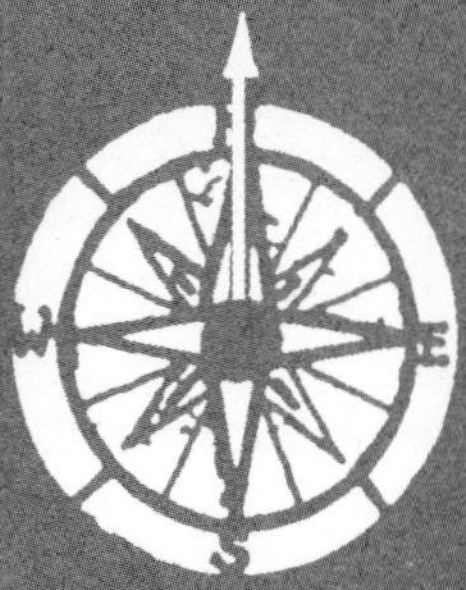

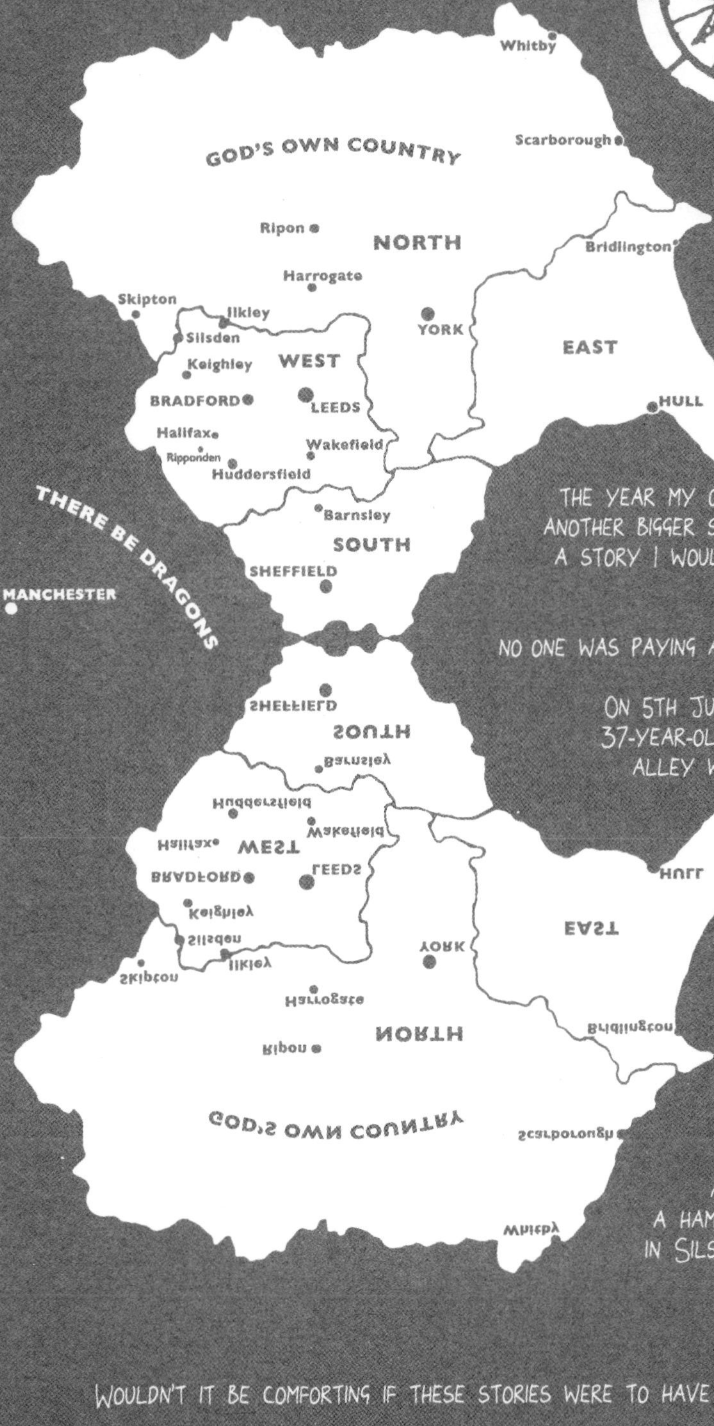

Whitby
Scarborough
GOD'S OWN COUNTRY
Ripon
NORTH
Bridlington
Harrogate
Skipton
Ilkley
YORK
Silsden
EAST
Keighley
WEST
BRADFORD
LEEDS
HULL
Halifax
Ripponden
Wakefield
Huddersfield
THERE BE DRAGONS
Barnsley
SOUTH
SHEFFIELD
MANCHESTER

IN 1974 THERE WAS A LOT OF ARGUING ABOUT YORKSHIRE. BOUNDARIES WERE BEING REARRANGED. PEOPLE WERE NOT HAPPY ABOUT IT.

IN 1975, THE YEAR MY OWN *SMALL* STORY BEGINS, ANOTHER BIGGER STORY WAS TAKING SHAPE. A STORY I WOULD LISTEN TO THROUGHOUT MY FORMATIVE YEARS.

NO ONE WAS PAYING ATTENTION TO IT AT FIRST.

ON 5TH JULY, SOMEONE ATTACKED A 37-YEAR-OLD KEIGHLEY WOMAN IN AN ALLEY WITH A HAMMER AND KNIFE. SHE SURVIVED.

ON 15TH AUGUST, SOMEONE ATTACKED A 46-YEAR-OLD HALIFAX WOMAN IN THE STREET WITH A HAMMER AND KNIFE. SHE WAS SERIOUSLY INJURED.

AND ON 27TH AUGUST, SOMEONE ATTACKED A 14-YEAR-OLD GIRL WITH A HAMMER, IN A COUNTRY LANE IN SILSDEN, BADLY INJURING HER.

WOULDN'T IT BE COMFORTING IF THESE STORIES WERE TO HAVE HAPPY ENDINGS?

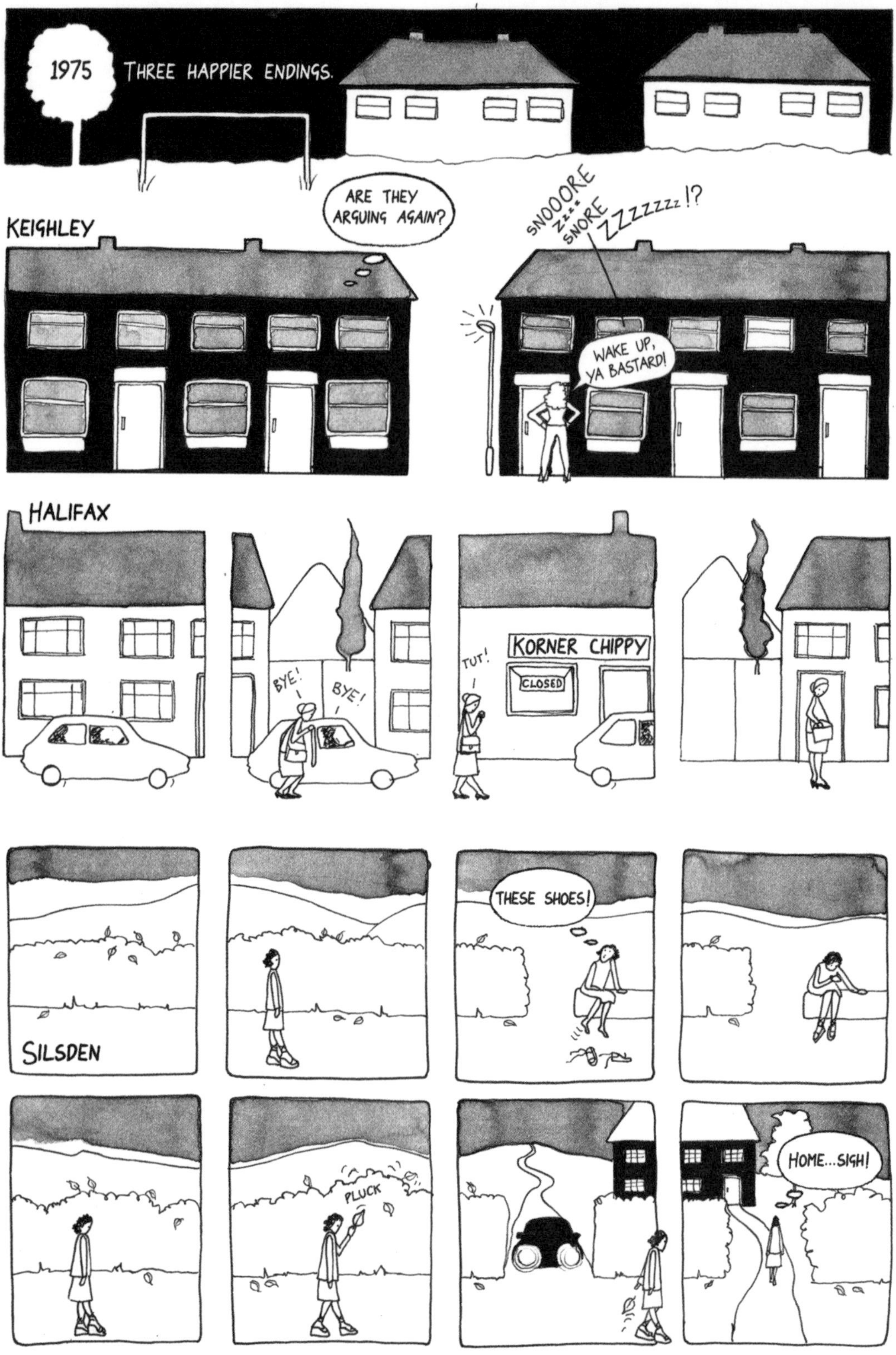
1975
THREE HAPPIER ENDINGS.
KEIGHLEY
ARE THEY ARGUING AGAIN?
SNOOOORE Zzzz SNORE ZZZzzzz !?
WAKE UP, YA BASTARD!
HALIFAX
BYE!
BYE!
TUT!
KORNER CHIPPY
CLOSED
SILSDEN
THESE SHOES!
PLUCK
HOME...SIGH!

1975 WAS A BUSY YEAR FOR YORKSHIRE.

AMONG OTHER THINGS...

ON 7TH MARCH, THE BODY OF TEENAGE HEIRESS
LESLEY WHITTLE WAS FOUND AT THE BOTTOM OF
A DRAINAGE SHAFT. DONALD NEILSON, WHO KILLED HER,
WAS NICKNAMED BY THE PRESS AS 'THE BLACK PANTHER'.
HE TURNED OUT TO BE FROM BRADFORD. LATER THAT YEAR,
ON 5TH OCTOBER, THE BODY OF AN 11-YEAR-OLD GIRL NAMED
LESLEY MOLSEED WAS FOUND ON A MOOR NEAR RIPPONDEN.
SOMEONE HAD SEXUALLY ASSAULTED AND KILLED HER. THEN ON
30TH OF OCTOBER, SOMEONE ATTACKED A FOURTH WOMAN WITH
A HAMMER, IN A SUBURB OF LEEDS. MOTHER TO FOUR YOUNG
CHILDREN, SHE DIED OF HEAD INJURIES AND MULTIPLE STAB WOUNDS.
TEN WEEKS LATER, SOMEONE KILLED ANOTHER WOMAN IN THE SAME
WAY, OUTSIDE A LEEDS CLUB.

BY DECEMBER OF THAT YEAR, WEST YORKSHIRE POLICE STILL HADN'T MADE
ANY PROGRESS WITH INVESTIGATIONS INTO THE HAMMER ATTACKS AND NO ONE
IN THE MEDIA HAD THOUGHT OF AN EXCITING NICKNAME FOR THE KILLER YET, BUT
POLICE *HAD* CHARGED THE WRONG MAN WITH THE MURDER OF LESLEY MOLSEED.
STEFAN KISZKO,[1] WHO WAS REPORTED TO BEHAVE IN ODD WAYS, CONFESSED AFTER BEING
QUESTIONED FOR TWO DAYS WITHOUT A SOLICITOR PRESENT. HE WAS JAILED FOR LIFE, SPENDING
16 YEARS IN PRISON BEFORE HE WAS ACQUITTED, DEVELOPING SCHIZOPHRENIA WHILE HE WAS INSIDE.
MEANWHILE, THE MAN WHO *ACTUALLY* KILLED LESLEY, RONALD CASTREE, AN ORDINARY MARRIED MAN
WHO RAN A COMICS SHOP IN ASHTON-UNDER-LYNE, DIDN'T GO TO PRISON TILL 2007 – 32 YEARS LATER,
WHEN FORENSIC DNA EVIDENCE PROVED HE DID IT.

1975 WAS ALSO A BUSY YEAR FOR ME. IT WAS THE YEAR I MET A MAN WHO TOLD ME HIS NAME WAS
DAMIAN. IT WAS THE START OF A LONG, HOT SUMMER...

I WAS WEARING ONE OF MY BIG SISTER'S DRESSES, PRETENDING TO BE A PRINCESS. IT WAS A WHITE HALTER NECK WITH SMALL BLUE FLOWERS. I USED TO BORROW IT WITHOUT ASKING HER.

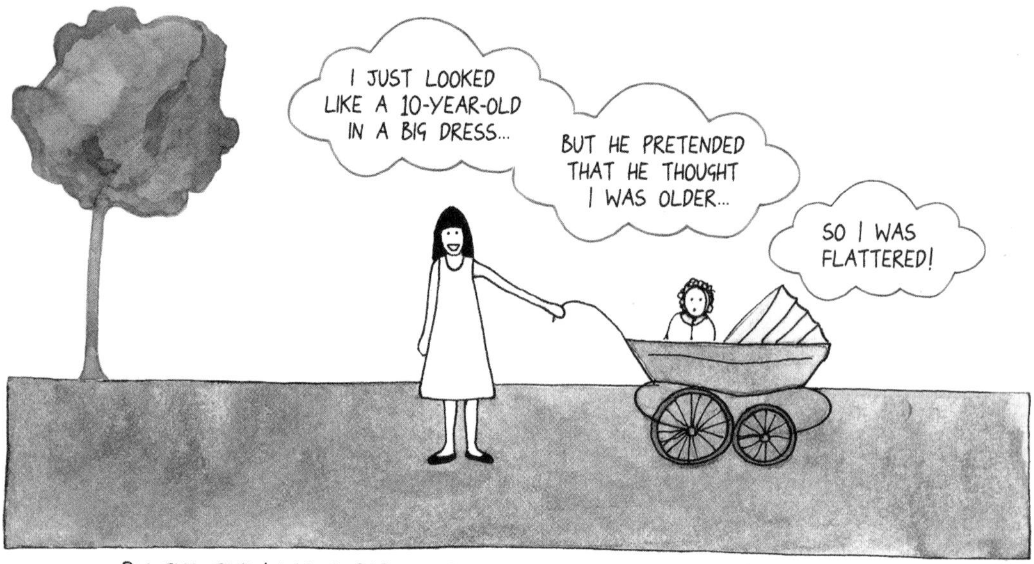
I JUST LOOKED LIKE A 10-YEAR-OLD IN A BIG DRESS...
BUT HE PRETENDED THAT HE THOUGHT I WAS OLDER...
SO I WAS FLATTERED!

BY THIS TIME I HAD A BABY SISTER TOO AND ALTHOUGH I DIDN'T KNOW IT YET...

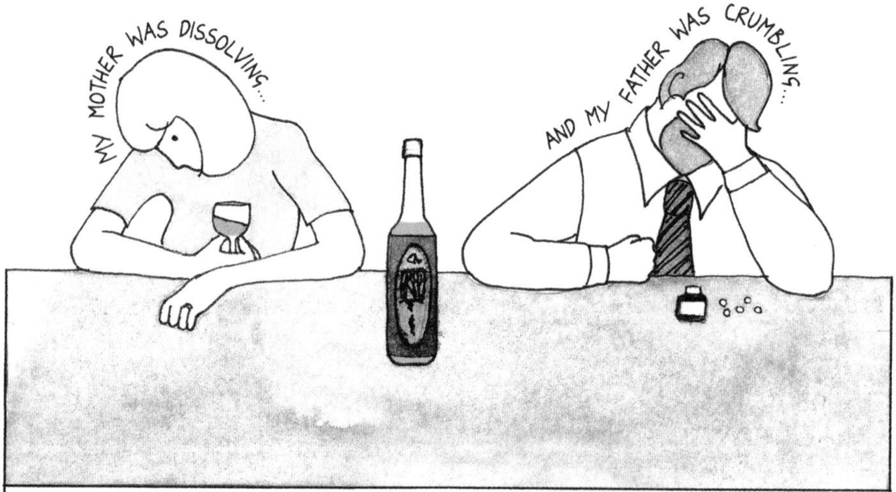
MY MOTHER WAS DISSOLVING...
AND MY FATHER WAS CRUMBLING...

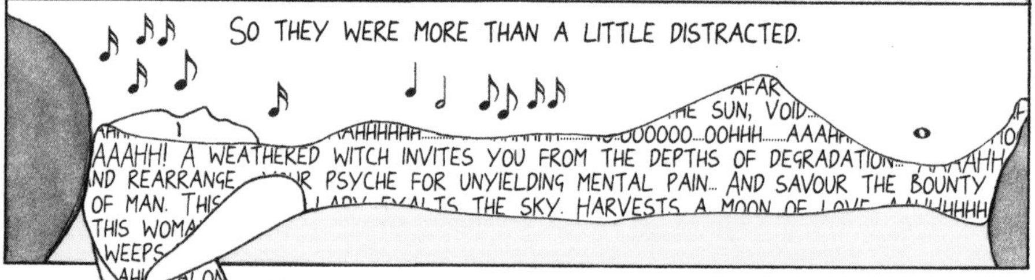
SO THEY WERE MORE THAN A LITTLE DISTRACTED.
AAAHH! A WEATHERED WITCH INVITES YOU FROM THE DEPTHS OF DEGRADATION...
YOUR PSYCHE FOR UNYIELDING MENTAL PAIN... AND SAVOUR THE BOUNTY
THE SKY. HARVESTS A MOON OF LOVE

MY BIG SISTER WASN'T EXACTLY HAPPY EITHER.

I DIDN'T TELL ANYONE ABOUT THE MAN CALLED DAMIAN AND THEY DIDN'T ASK. UNFORTUNATELY, IF YOU DON'T TELL... NO ONE NOTICES.

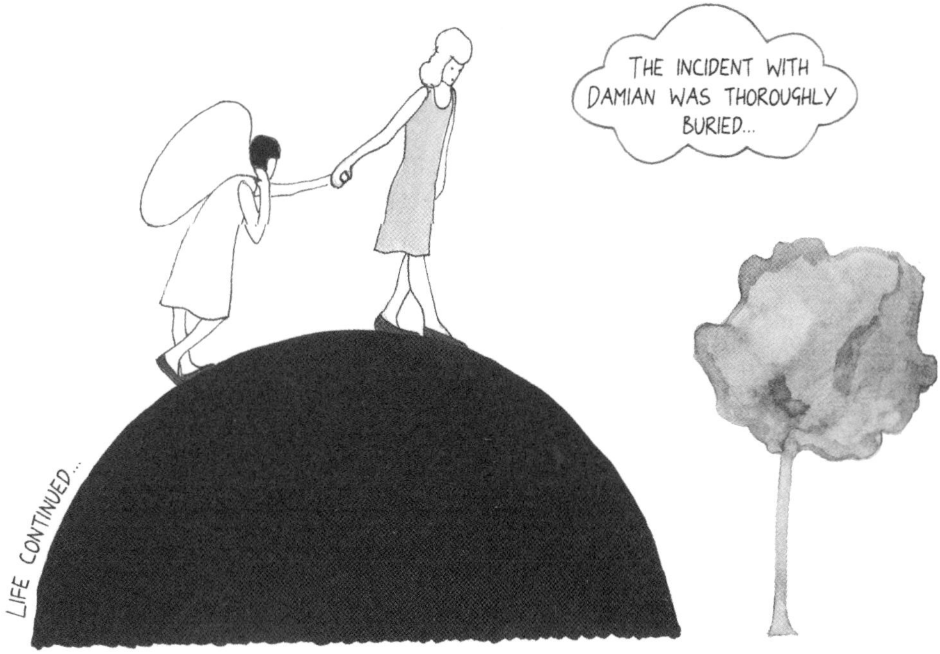
THE INCIDENT WITH DAMIAN WAS THOROUGHLY BURIED...
LIFE CONTINUED...

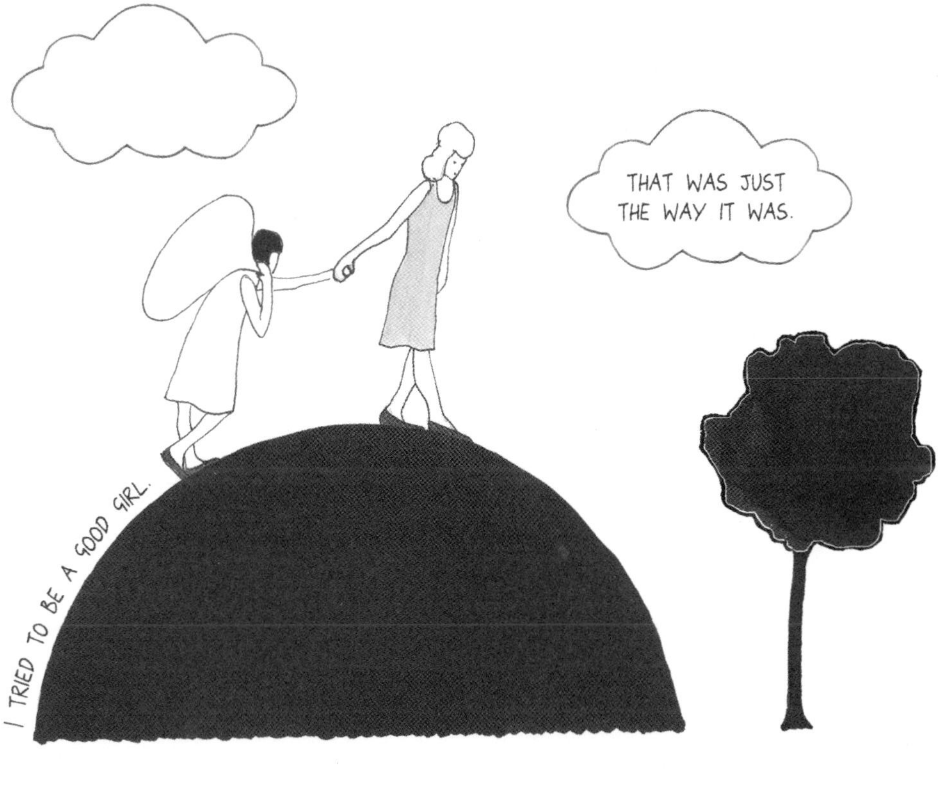
THAT WAS JUST THE WAY IT WAS.
I TRIED TO BE A GOOD GIRL.

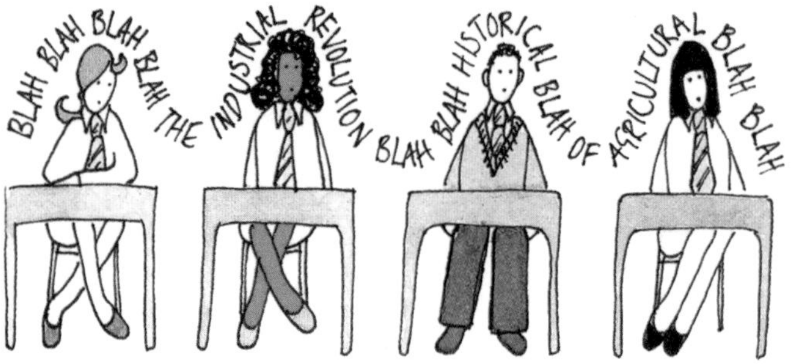
BLAH BLAH BLAH BLAH THE INDUSTRIAL REVOLUTION BLAH BLAH HISTORICAL BLAH OF AGRICULTURAL BLAH BLAH

IN THE AUTUMN I STARTED HIGH SCHOOL.

I ALSO STARTED WETTING THE BED.

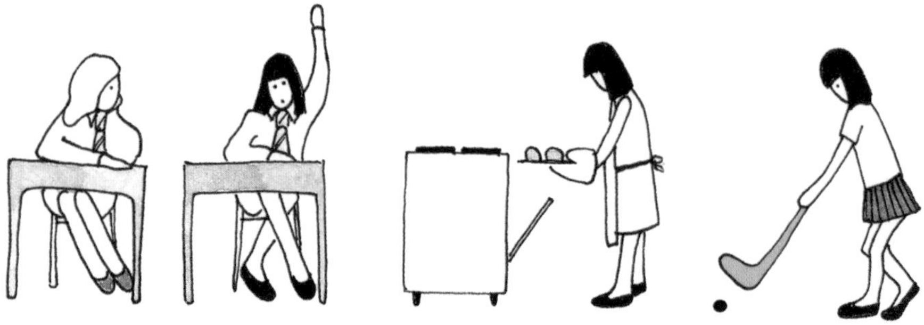

SCHOOL WAS OK. I LIKED IT AND DID WELL QUITE EASILY AT FIRST.

I MADE SOME FRIENDS.

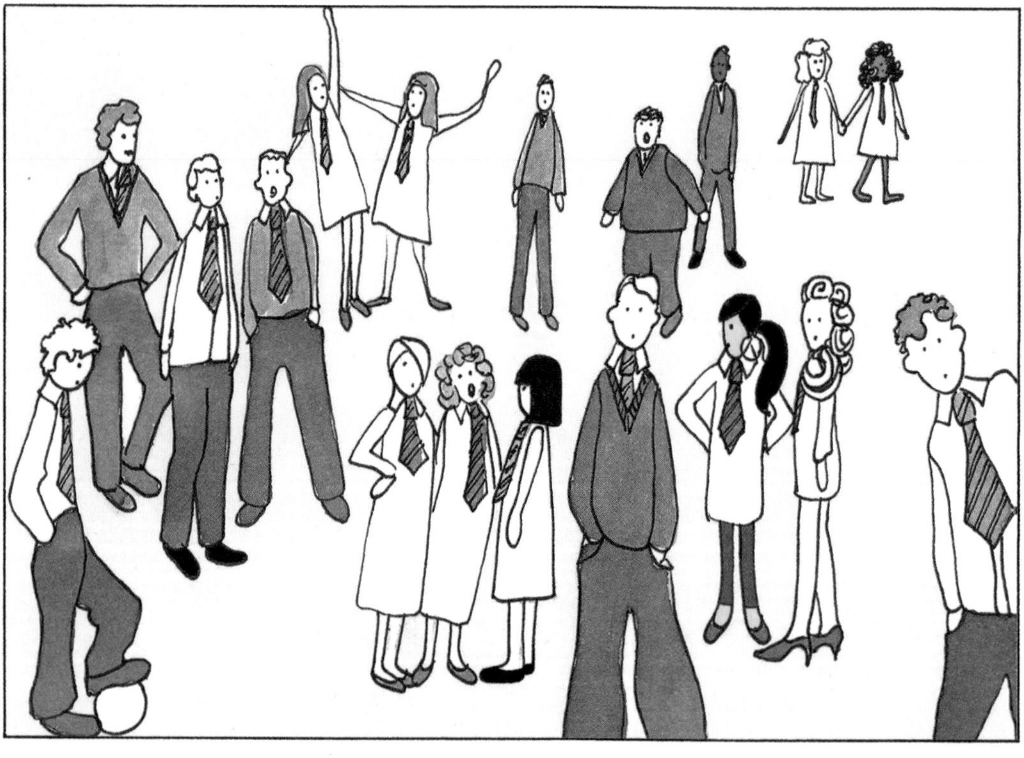

I ENJOYED ART, BUT OTHER KIDS SEEMED TO THINK IT WAS A WASTE OF TIME.

ONCE, IN CLASS, I DREW A PICTURE OF A BOY I FANCIED. THE TEACHER LIKED IT AND DISPLAYED IT IN THE CORRIDOR. EVERYONE RECOGNISED HIM. YOU CAN IMAGINE HOW THE OTHER KIDS LAUGHED...

I WAS SO EMBARRASSED! NEEDLESS TO SAY HE DIDN'T ASK ME OUT, EVEN THOUGH I WAS REALLY GOOD AT DRAWING.

SOME OF THE OTHER GIRLS AT SCHOOL HAD BOYFRIENDS. THEY WERE SOPHISTICATED TYPES, WHO WORE TIGHTS AND HAD HAIRDOS.

MY FRIENDS AND I DIDN'T HAVE HAIRDOS OR BOYFRIENDS, AND WE MOSTLY WORE SOCKS.

BY 1977 EVERYONE WAS TALKING ABOUT ALL THE HORRIBLE MURDERS THAT WERE HAPPENING AROUND LEEDS AND BRADFORD.

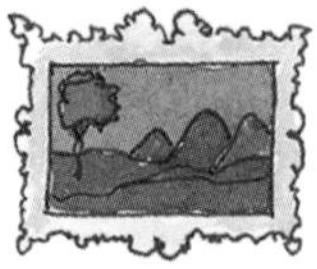

I DIDN'T KNOW WHAT A PROSTITUTE WAS, BUT I WONDERED ABOUT THESE WOMEN... WHO WERE THEY?

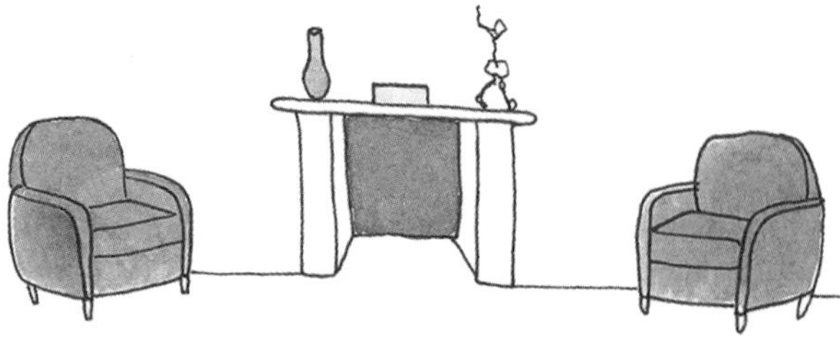

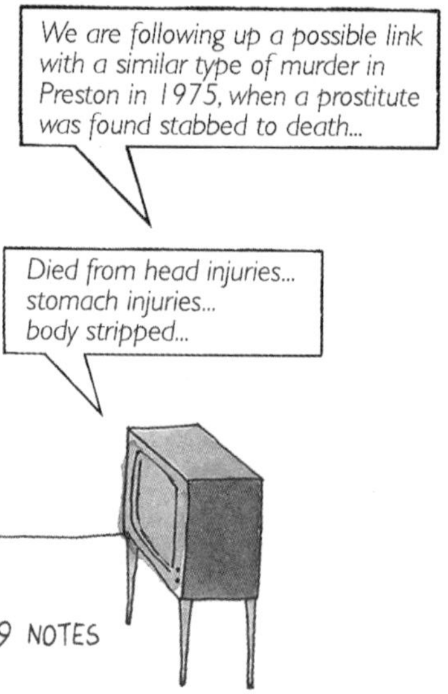

We are following up a possible link with a similar type of murder in Preston in 1975, when a prostitute was found stabbed to death...
Died from head injuries... stomach injuries... body stripped...

THE KILLER HAD GIVEN ONE OF THEM A FIVE POUND NOTE – ONE OF 69 NOTES WITH CONSECUTIVE NUMBERS THAT COULD BE TRACED TO ONE BANK.

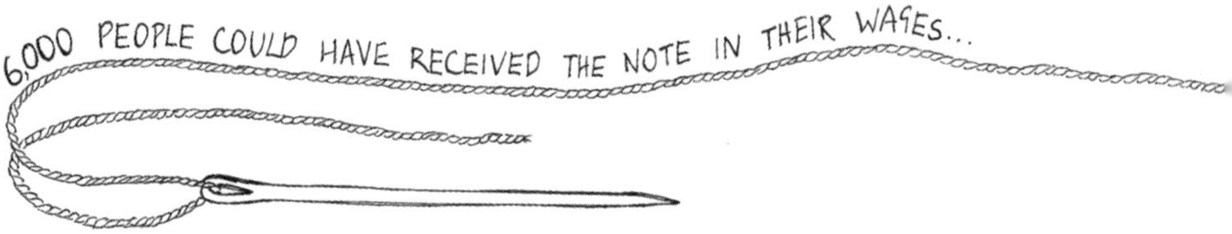

6,000 PEOPLE COULD HAVE RECEIVED THE NOTE IN THEIR WAGES...

LIKE FINDING A NEEDLE IN A HAYSTACK![2]

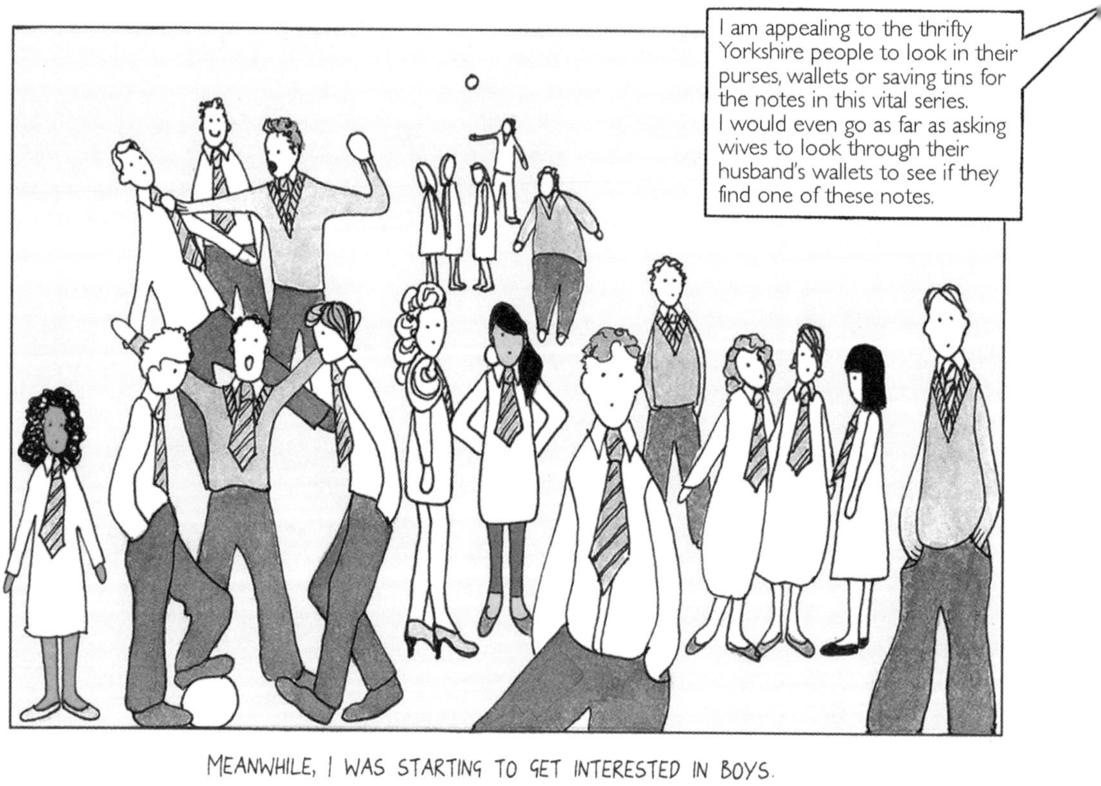

I am appealing to the thrifty Yorkshire people to look in their purses, wallets or saving tins for the notes in this vital series. I would even go as far as asking wives to look through their husband's wallets to see if they find one of these notes.

MEANWHILE, I WAS STARTING TO GET INTERESTED IN BOYS.

PARK VICTIM WAS YOUNG MOTHER OF TWO

'I have found no indication at this stage that she had been acting as a prostitute, but our inquiries are being directed to see whether she had this mode of life'

Link with 'Jack the Ripper' style deaths?
Police chief keeps open mind

HEARTBREAK OF 5 A.M. SEARCH BY CHILDREN

Murder in fog

Killer is a maniac, says CID chief

Dramatic murder plea to crowds

Savage and sadistic sex attack on Leeds 'mother in fear'

Mr Hobson, head of Leeds CID, said they were keeping an open mind about whether her murder was connected with the unsolved 'Jack the Ripper' murders of two prostitutes in Leeds

Woman battered: 'Killer may strike again' warning

WE LIVED LIFE TO THE FULL

Victim's husband speaks

Heartbreak four are told 'Mummy's dead'

GIRLS WARNED IN RIPPER HUNT

GIRL, 14, BRUTALLY BEATEN IN LANE

BY 1978 MORE THAN 200 WEST YORKSHIRE POLICE OFFICERS WERE WORKING PERMANENTLY ON THE RIPPER INQUIRY. THE MANY FAILURES OF THIS INVESTIGATION ARE WELL DOCUMENTED. THE POLICE MADE NO MEANINGFUL PROGRESS AND WERE UNDOUBTEDLY OUT OF THEIR DEPTH.

THEY WEREN'T COMPLETELY STUPID; A SENIOR DETECTIVE DECLARED ON NATIONAL RADIO THAT THE RIPPER MUST BE SOMEBODY'S HUSBAND, SOMEBODY'S SON... BUT SOMEBODY'S DAUGHTER HAD BEEN TRYING TO TELL THEM WHAT THE RIPPER LOOKED LIKE SINCE 1975. SHE GOT A GOOD LOOK AT HIM DURING THE LONG CONVERSATION THEY HAD, THE EVENING SHE WALKED HOME ALONE, ALONG A QUIET COUNTRY LANE, WEARING SHOES UNSUITABLE FOR THE PURPOSE.

HE WAS UNASSUMING, CALMING EVEN, WHILE THEY WALKED ALONG, CHATTING. HE DIDN'T MAKE HER FEEL NERVOUS OR UNCOMFORTABLE. THEY TALKED ABOUT THE WEATHER AND HE TOLD HER HE LIVED AT HOLROYD HOUSE, NEARBY. THEN WHEN THEY REACHED THE END OF HER DRIVEWAY, AS SHE TURNED TO SAY GOODBYE, HE HIT HER ON THE HEAD WITH A HAMMER SEVERAL TIMES, MAKING A LOUD GRUNTING SOUND. SHE THOUGHT HE MUST BE THE BLACK PANTHER SHE'D HEARD SO MUCH ABOUT ON THE NEWS.

BY A 'DARK STRANGER'

AS HE WAS INTERRUPTED BY A PASSING CAR, HE DIDN'T MANAGE TO KILL HER.
HE PICKED HER UP, THREW HER OVER A FENCE AND RAN OFF.

THE PHOTOFIT THAT SOMEBODY'S DAUGHTER PROVIDED IN 1975 TURNED OUT LATER TO BE AN
ALMOST EXACT LIKENESS. WHEN SHE SAW THE PHOTOFITS MADE BY OTHER WOMEN, SHE
RETURNED TO THE POLICE STATION WITH HER MOTHER, TO EXPLAIN THAT THE RIPPER WAS
THE SAME MAN THAT ATTACKED HER.

BUT OFFICERS EXAMINING HER CASE DECIDED NOT TO INCLUDE IT IN THE INQUIRY ON THE
GROUNDS THAT SHE WAS NOT A PROSTITUTE AND COULDN'T HAVE BEEN MISTAKEN FOR ONE.

SO IF THEIR LINE OF THINKING WAS, WHY WOULD ANYONE WANT TO KILL HER, IF SHE WASN'T
A PROSTITUTE, WHY *DID* THEY THINK SOMEONE HAD TRIED TO KILL HER?

'THEY DIDN'T TAKE ME SERIOUSLY,' SHE SAID, LATER.
'I DON'T KNOW WHY, MAYBE IT WAS MY AGE?'[3]

We are
having fun and
games today,
aren't we?

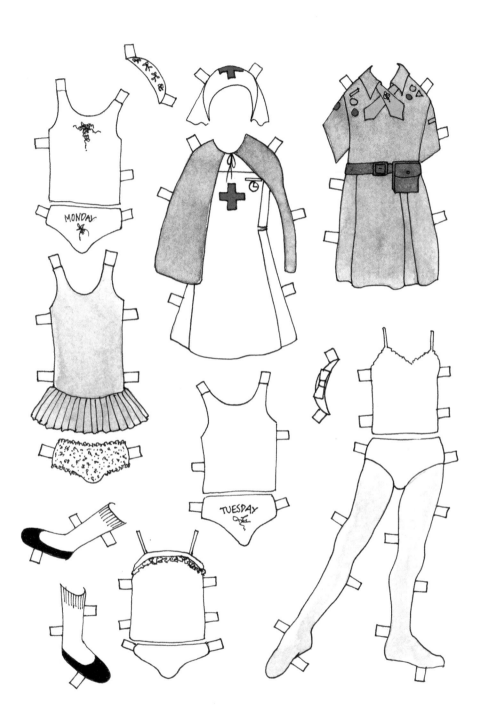

MONDAY

TUESDAY

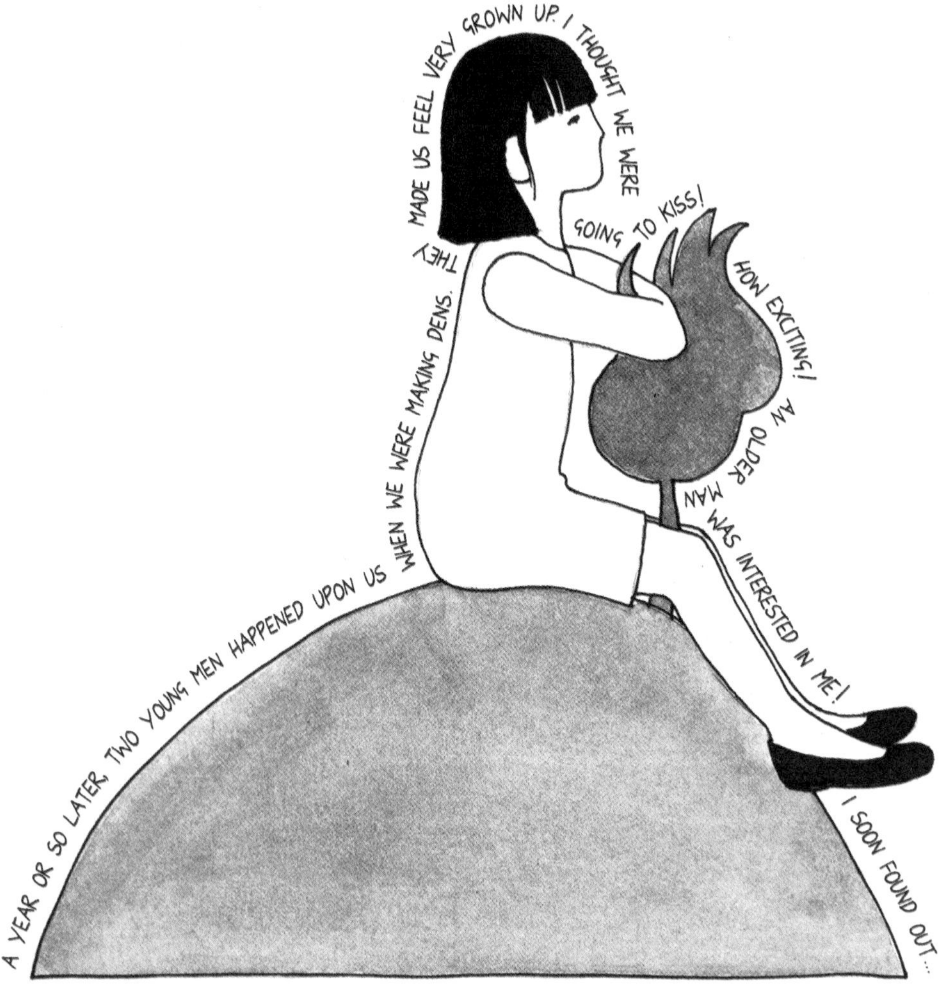
A YEAR OR SO LATER, TWO YOUNG MEN HAPPENED UPON US WHEN WE WERE MAKING DENS.
THEY MADE US FEEL VERY GROWN UP. I THOUGHT WE WERE GOING TO KISS!
HOW EXCITING! AN OLDER MAN WAS INTERESTED IN ME!
I SOON FOUND OUT...
I HADN'T REALLY UNDERSTOOD THE SITUATION.

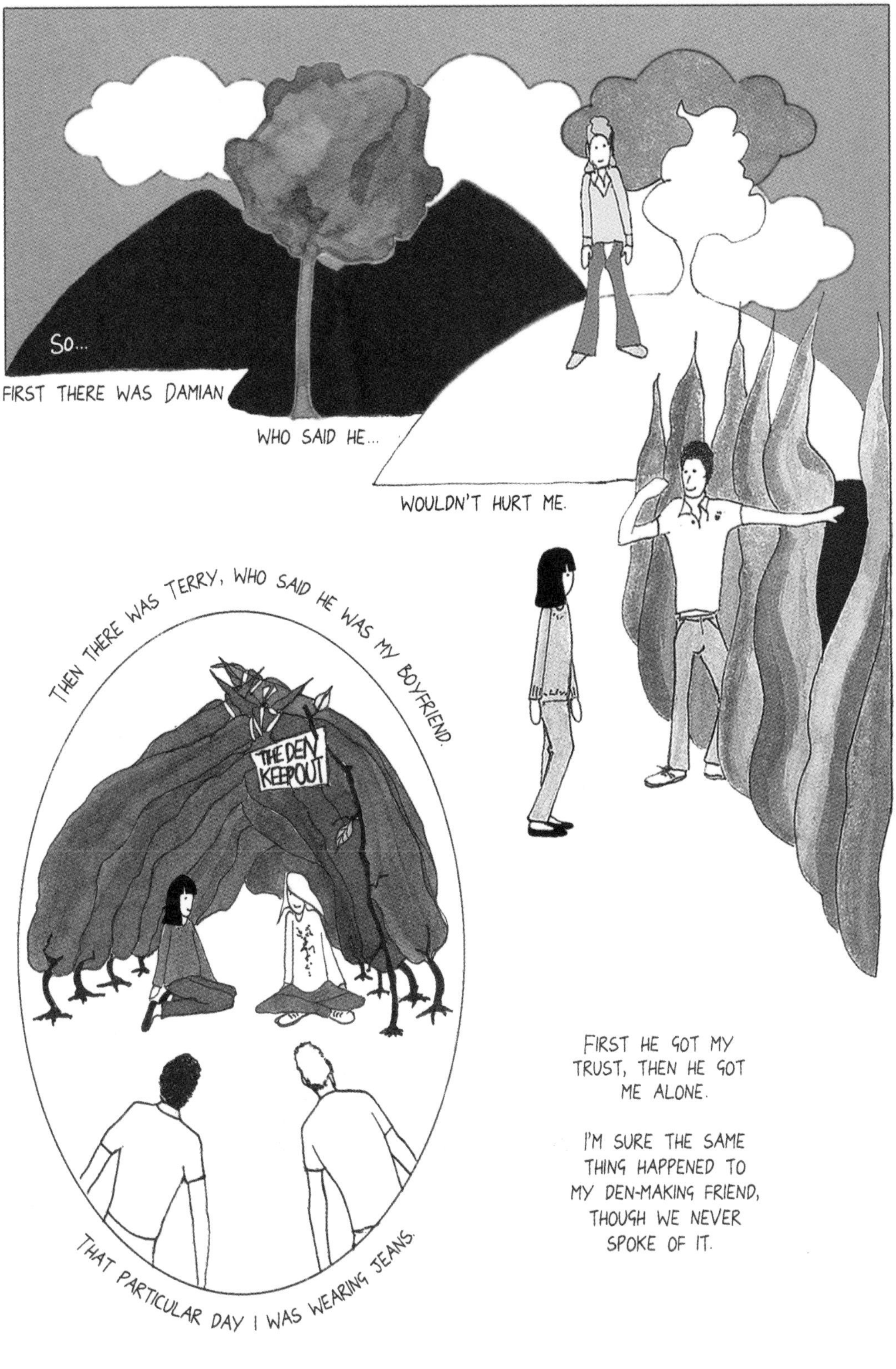
So...
FIRST THERE WAS DAMIAN
WHO SAID HE...
WOULDN'T HURT ME.
THEN THERE WAS TERRY, WHO SAID HE WAS MY BOYFRIEND.
THE DEN KEEPOUT
THAT PARTICULAR DAY I WAS WEARING JEANS.
FIRST HE GOT MY TRUST, THEN HE GOT ME ALONE.
I'M SURE THE SAME THING HAPPENED TO MY DEN-MAKING FRIEND, THOUGH WE NEVER SPOKE OF IT.

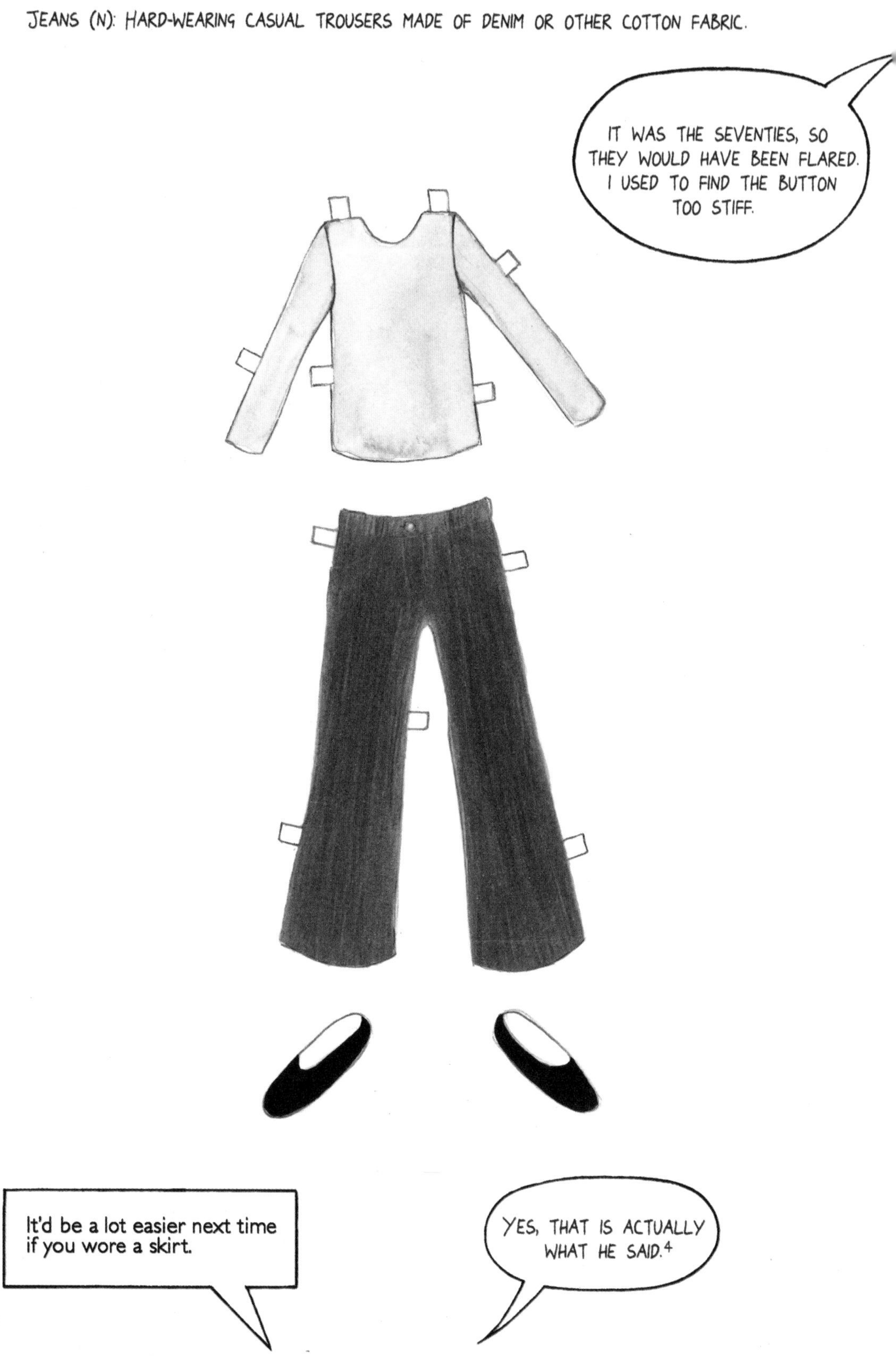
JEANS (N): HARD-WEARING CASUAL TROUSERS MADE OF DENIM OR OTHER COTTON FABRIC.
IT WAS THE SEVENTIES, SO THEY WOULD HAVE BEEN FLARED. I USED TO FIND THE BUTTON TOO STIFF.
It'd be a lot easier next time if you wore a skirt.
YES, THAT IS ACTUALLY WHAT HE SAID.[4]

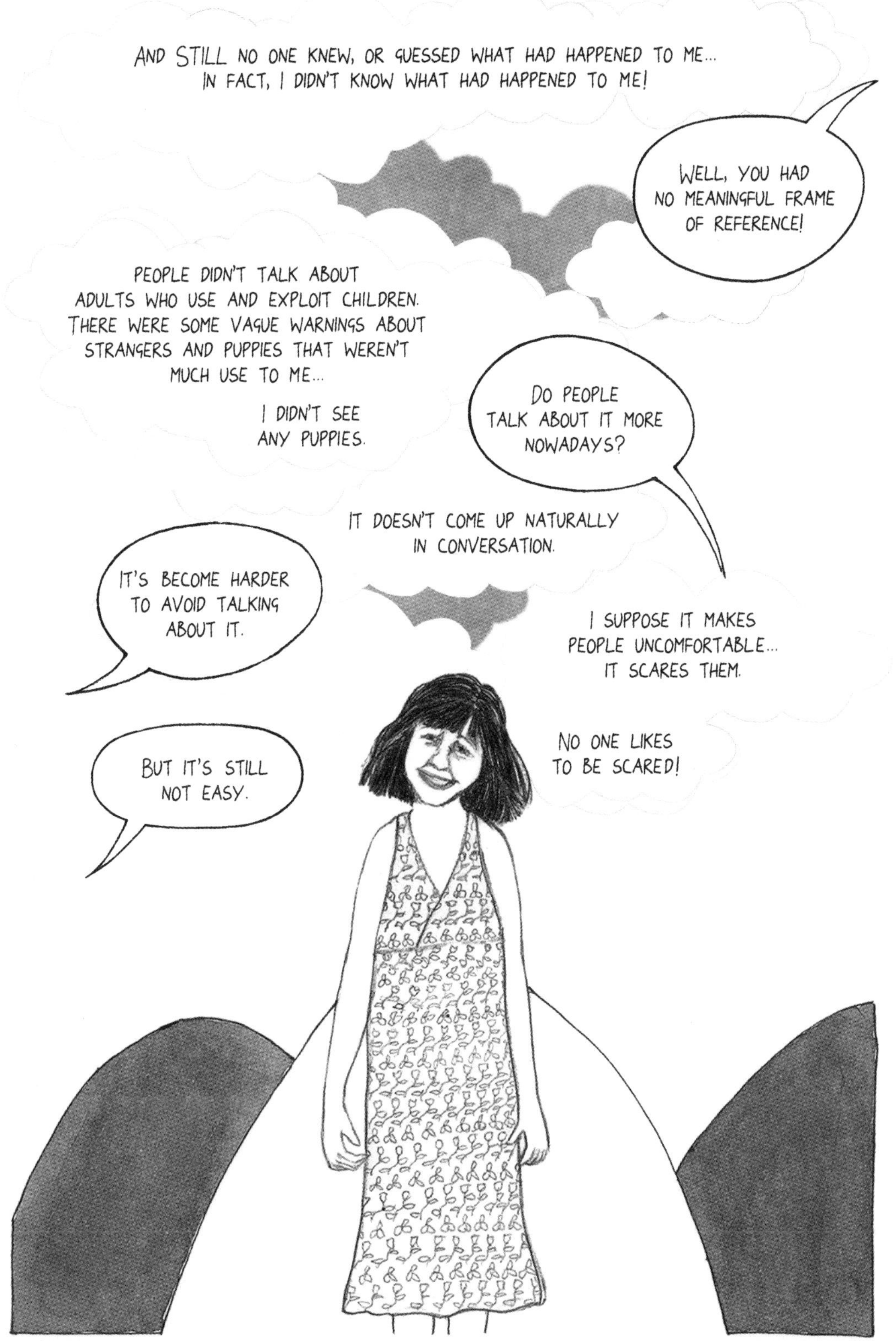
AND STILL NO ONE KNEW, OR GUESSED WHAT HAD HAPPENED TO ME... IN FACT, I DIDN'T KNOW WHAT HAD HAPPENED TO ME!
WELL, YOU HAD NO MEANINGFUL FRAME OF REFERENCE!
PEOPLE DIDN'T TALK ABOUT ADULTS WHO USE AND EXPLOIT CHILDREN. THERE WERE SOME VAGUE WARNINGS ABOUT STRANGERS AND PUPPIES THAT WEREN'T MUCH USE TO ME...
I DIDN'T SEE ANY PUPPIES.
DO PEOPLE TALK ABOUT IT MORE NOWADAYS?
IT DOESN'T COME UP NATURALLY IN CONVERSATION.
IT'S BECOME HARDER TO AVOID TALKING ABOUT IT.
I SUPPOSE IT MAKES PEOPLE UNCOMFORTABLE... IT SCARES THEM.
BUT IT'S STILL NOT EASY.
NO ONE LIKES TO BE SCARED!

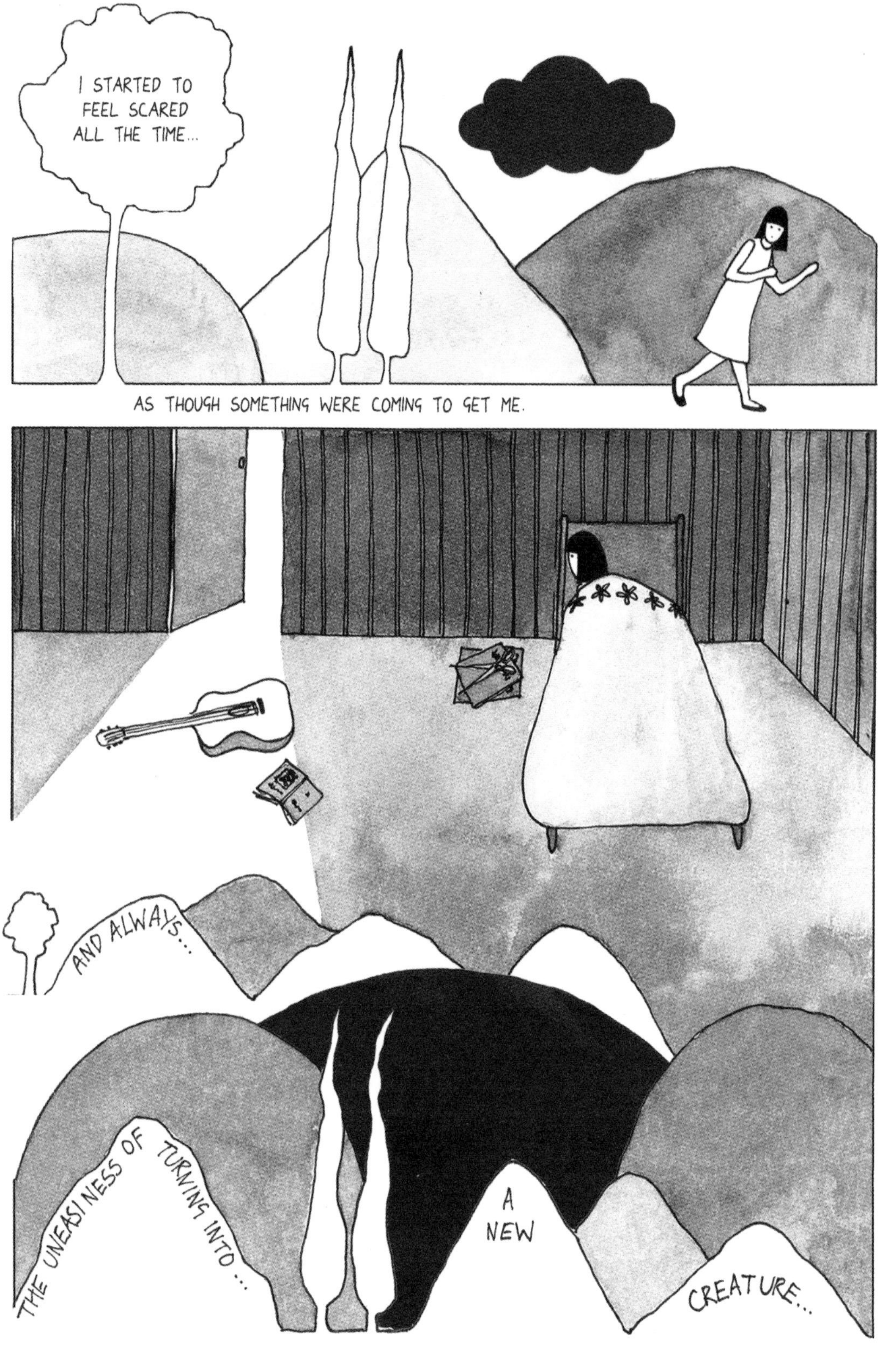
I STARTED TO FEEL SCARED ALL THE TIME...
AS THOUGH SOMETHING WERE COMING TO GET ME.
AND ALWAYS...
THE UNEASINESS OF TURNING INTO...
A NEW
CREATURE...

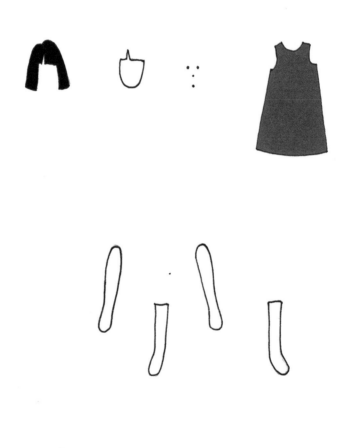

MY BODY WAS CHANGING.

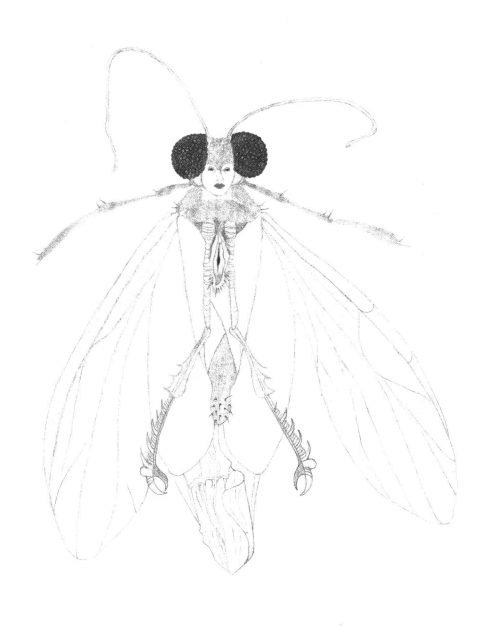

MY WINGS DIDN'T SEEM TO WORK VERY WELL. PERHAPS THEY WERE JUST DECORATIVE?

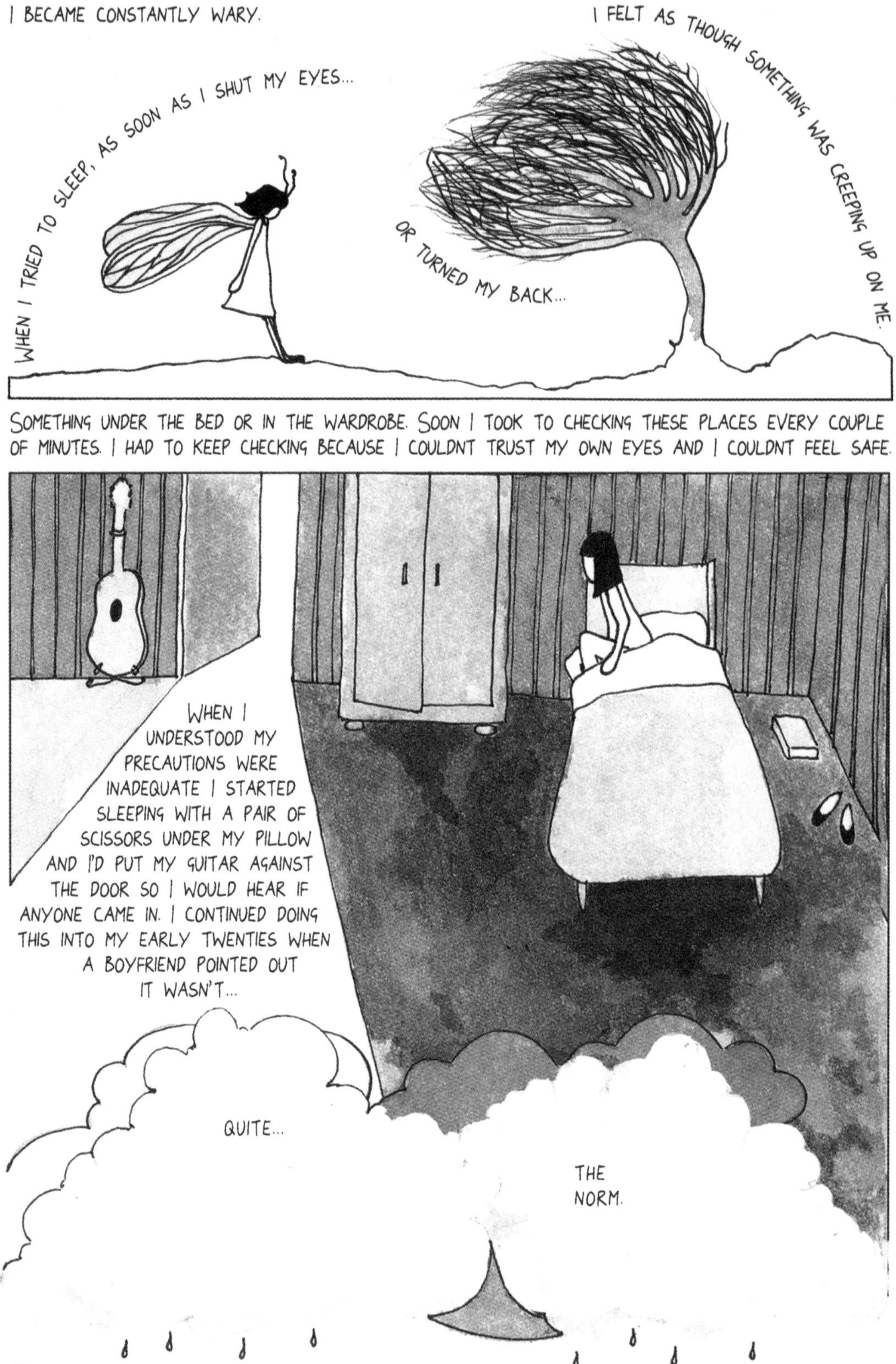
I BECAME CONSTANTLY WARY.
WHEN I TRIED TO SLEEP, AS SOON AS I SHUT MY EYES...
OR TURNED MY BACK...
I FELT AS THOUGH SOMETHING WAS CREEPING UP ON ME.
SOMETHING UNDER THE BED OR IN THE WARDROBE. SOON I TOOK TO CHECKING THESE PLACES EVERY COUPLE OF MINUTES. I HAD TO KEEP CHECKING BECAUSE I COULDNT TRUST MY OWN EYES AND I COULDNT FEEL SAFE.
WHEN I UNDERSTOOD MY PRECAUTIONS WERE INADEQUATE I STARTED SLEEPING WITH A PAIR OF SCISSORS UNDER MY PILLOW AND I'D PUT MY GUITAR AGAINST THE DOOR SO I WOULD HEAR IF ANYONE CAME IN. I CONTINUED DOING THIS INTO MY EARLY TWENTIES WHEN A BOYFRIEND POINTED OUT IT WASN'T...
QUITE...
THE NORM.

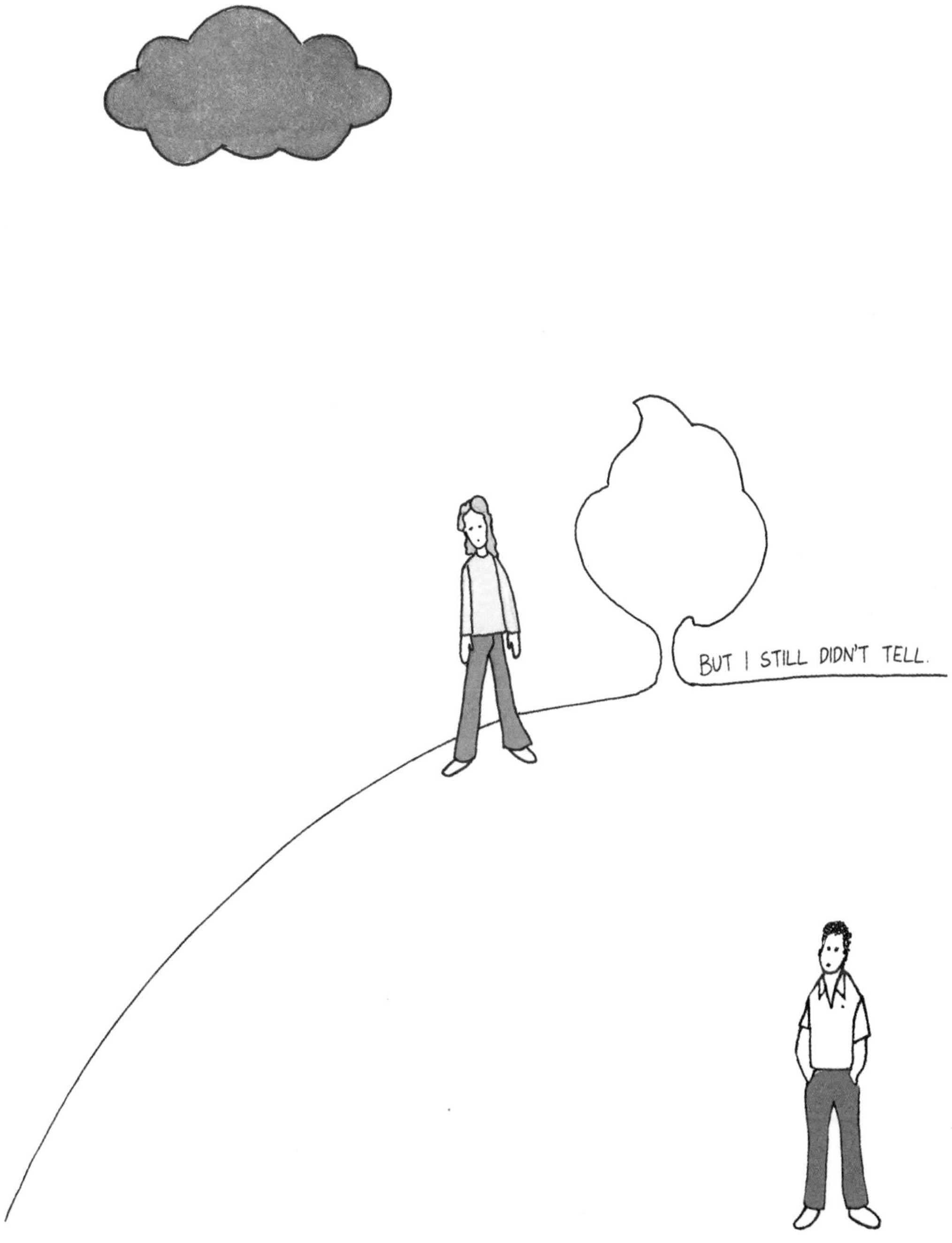
BUT I STILL DIDN'T TELL.

I HADN'T BEEN ALARMED AT FIRST. WHEN DAMIAN HAD WANDERED UP, IT WAS CASUALLY, AS THOUGH HE WAS JUST PASSING. HE DIDN'T MAKE ME FEEL NERVOUS OR UNCOMFORTABLE.

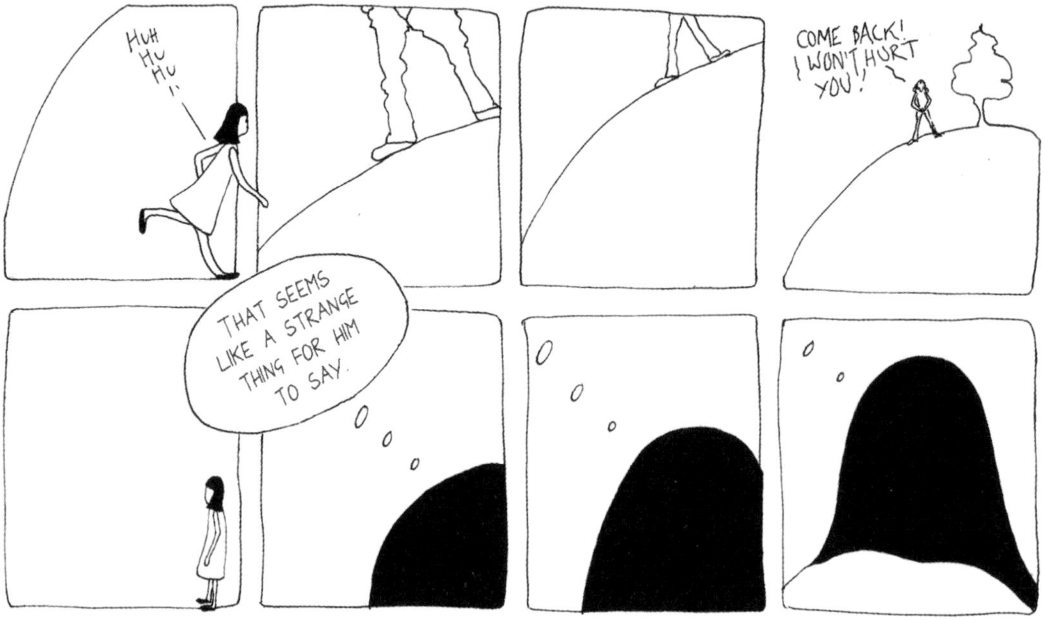
HUH HU HU !!
COME BACK! I WON'T HURT YOU!
THAT SEEMS LIKE A STRANGE THING FOR HIM TO SAY.

HE LOOKED IN AMUSEMENT AT THE GAME I WAS PLAYING, AS ADULTS DO, THEN ASKED ME QUESTIONS I DIDN'T UNDERSTAND, AS THOUGH HE THOUGHT I WAS MUCH OLDER THAN I WAS. HE TOLD ME HE LIVED ON CHAPEL STREET NEARBY.

HE WAS PRACTISED AT SOOTHING ME THROUGH THE SHOCK OF WHAT HE DID NEXT.

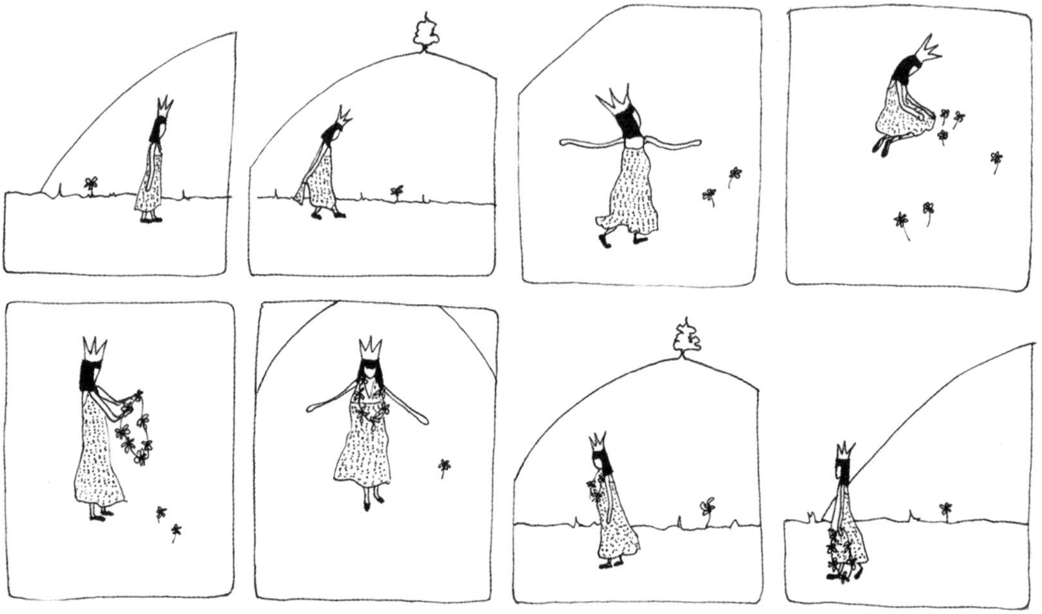

WHEN I BECAME ALARMED ENOUGH TO BREAK THROUGH MY FEAR AND WRIGGLE AWAY, I RAN QUICKLY TO WITHIN SIGHT OF THE HOUSES. HE COULDN'T FOLLOW AS HE DIDN'T WANT TO BE SEEN AND I REALISE NOW, HE HAD HIS TROUSERS DOWN, SO COULDN'T RUN.

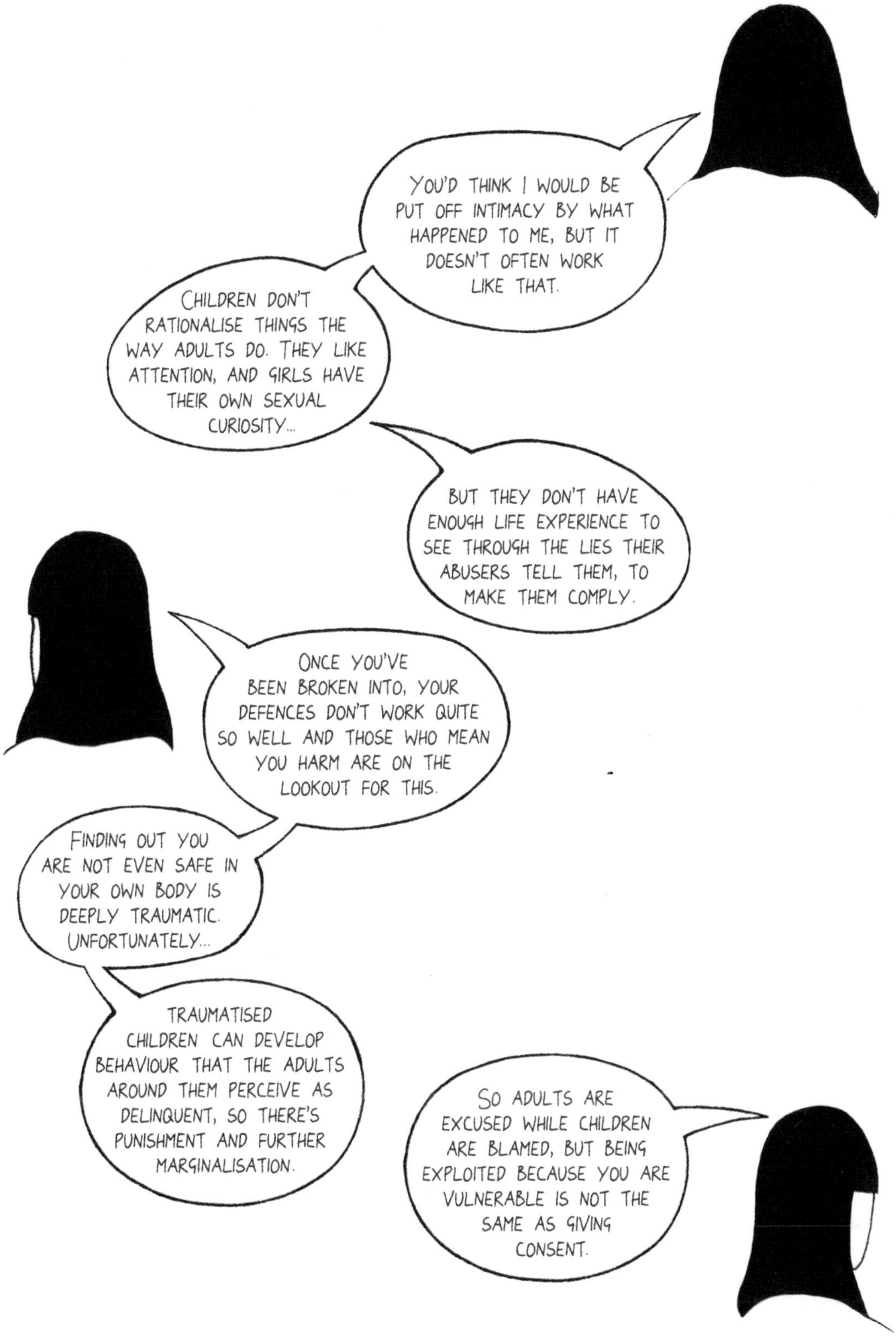
YOU'D THINK I WOULD BE PUT OFF INTIMACY BY WHAT HAPPENED TO ME, BUT IT DOESN'T OFTEN WORK LIKE THAT.
CHILDREN DON'T RATIONALISE THINGS THE WAY ADULTS DO. THEY LIKE ATTENTION, AND GIRLS HAVE THEIR OWN SEXUAL CURIOSITY...
BUT THEY DON'T HAVE ENOUGH LIFE EXPERIENCE TO SEE THROUGH THE LIES THEIR ABUSERS TELL THEM, TO MAKE THEM COMPLY.
ONCE YOU'VE BEEN BROKEN INTO, YOUR DEFENCES DON'T WORK QUITE SO WELL AND THOSE WHO MEAN YOU HARM ARE ON THE LOOKOUT FOR THIS.
FINDING OUT YOU ARE NOT EVEN SAFE IN YOUR OWN BODY IS DEEPLY TRAUMATIC. UNFORTUNATELY...
TRAUMATISED CHILDREN CAN DEVELOP BEHAVIOUR THAT THE ADULTS AROUND THEM PERCEIVE AS DELINQUENT, SO THERE'S PUNISHMENT AND FURTHER MARGINALISATION.
SO ADULTS ARE EXCUSED WHILE CHILDREN ARE BLAMED, BUT BEING EXPLOITED BECAUSE YOU ARE VULNERABLE IS NOT THE SAME AS GIVING CONSENT.

HINDSIGHT

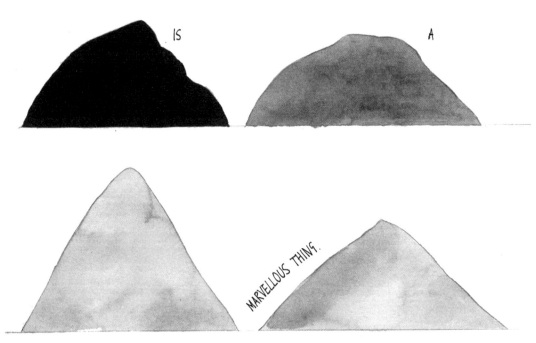

IS

A

MARVELLOUS THING.

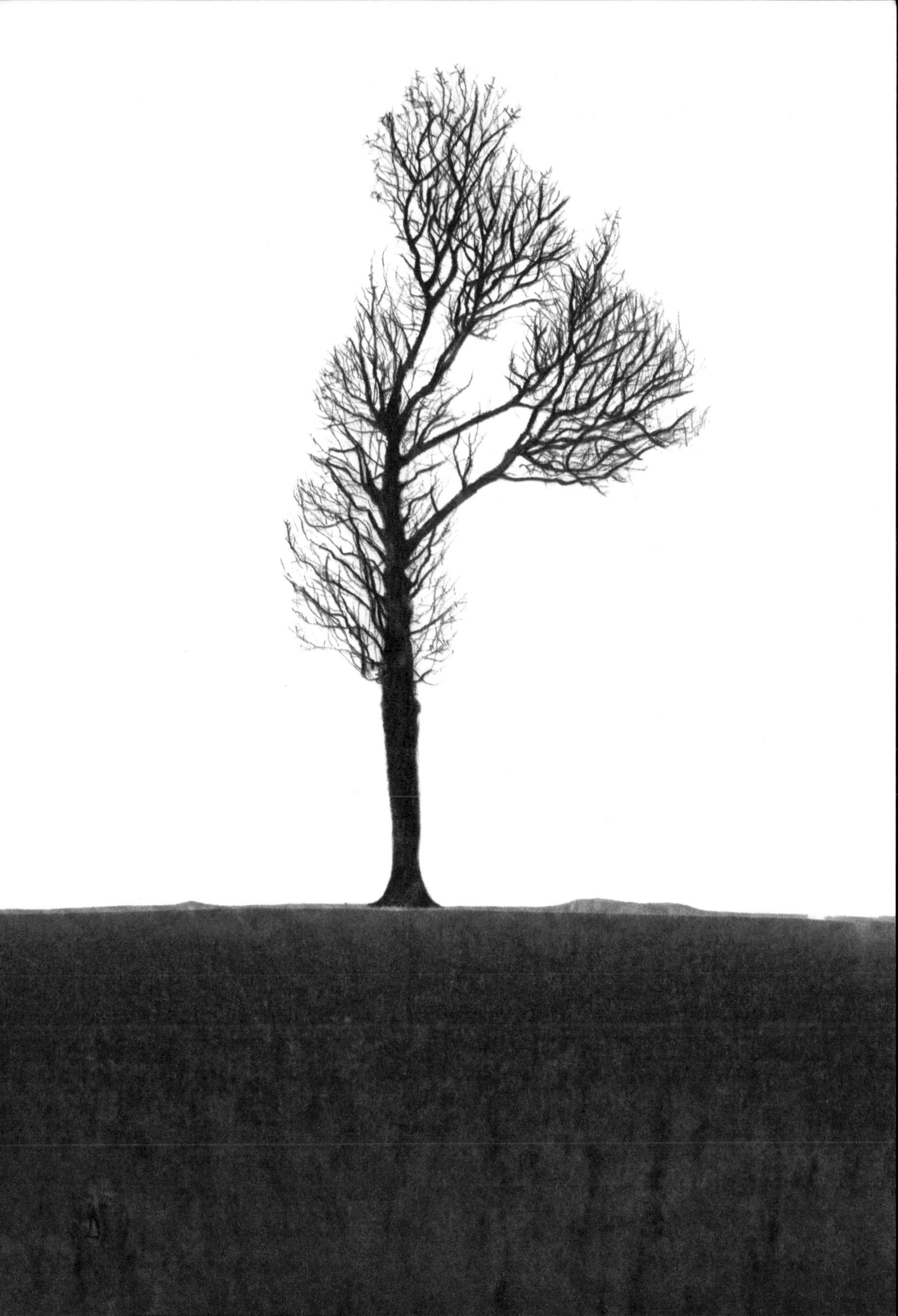

Yorkshire Evening Post, 30th June 1977

An open message to the Ripper...

You have killed five times now.

In less than two years you have butchered five women in Leeds and Bradford.

Your motive, it's believed, is a dreadful hate for prostitutes – a hate that drives you to slash and bludgeon your victims.

But inevitably, that twisted passion went terribly wrong on Sunday. An innocent 16-year-old lass, a happy respectable working class girl from a decent Leeds family, crossed your path.

How did you feel yesterday when you learned that your bloodstained crusade against streetwalkers had gone so horribly wrong?

That your vengeful knife had found so innocent a target?

Sick in mind though you undoubtedly are there must have been some spark of remorse as you rid yourself of Jayne's bloodstains.

Is it not time for you to seek help, to call a halt to your slaughter, before another Jayne falls to your knife?

Someone, somewhere in this city probably knows your secret, a wife, a mother a sister. People whose love for you keeps their lips sealed.

Now they too carry your burden.

Your infamous predecessor, Jack the Ripper, carved his victims in London's gas-lit streets in the 1880s.

Unlike the Ripper, no rope awaits you – only understanding treatment in spite of the ghastliness of your crimes.

If there are to be no more Jayne MacDonalds on your growing list of victims, now is the time to end your vengeance and seek help for yourself.

If you wish to unburden yourself, to free both yourself and possibly your family from the frightening shadows you have cast, you need only to pick up a telephone.

The numbers to ring are Leeds 454297 or Leeds 454173. Talk to the police, they are ready to help.

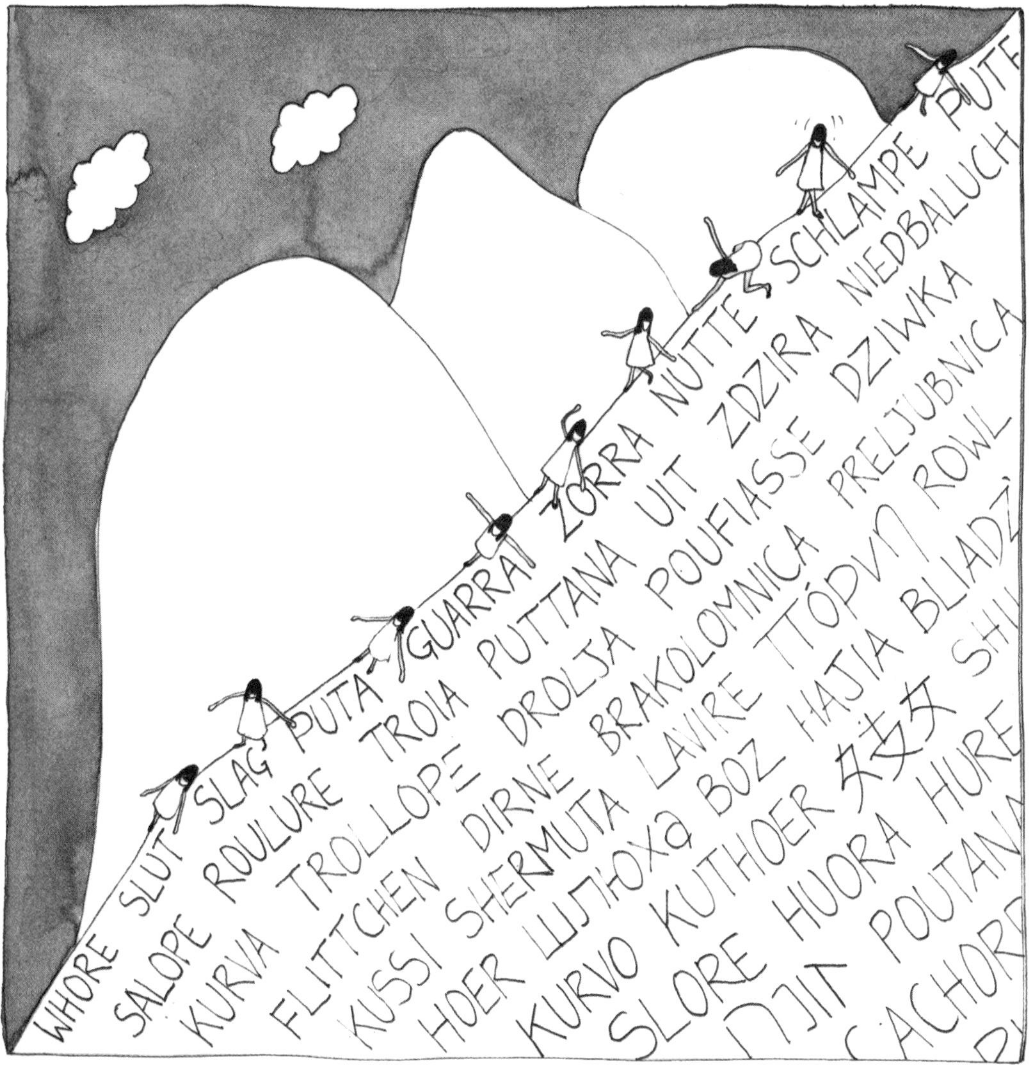
WHORE SLUT SLAG PUTA GUARRA ZORRA NUTTE SCHLAMPE
SALOPE ROULURE TROIA PUTTANA UIT ZDZIRA NIEDBALUCH
KURVA TROLLOPE DROLJA POUFIASSE DZIWKA
FLITTCHEN DIRNE BRAKOLOMNICA PRELJUBNICA
KUSSI SHERMUTA LAVIRE
HOER BOZ
KURVO KUTHOER
SLORE HUORA HURE
POUTANA

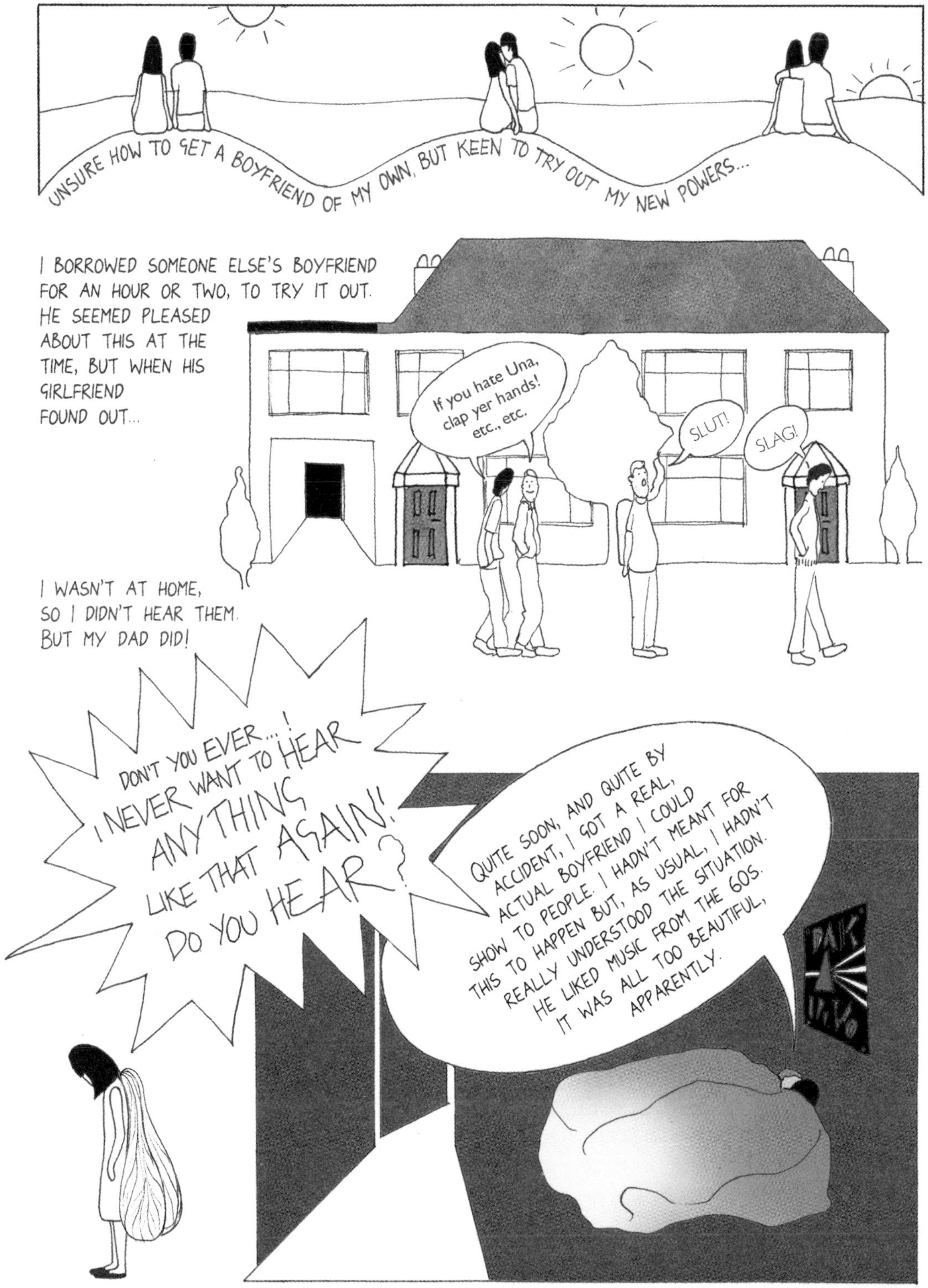
UNSURE HOW TO GET A BOYFRIEND OF MY OWN, BUT KEEN TO TRY OUT MY NEW POWERS...
I BORROWED SOMEONE ELSE'S BOYFRIEND FOR AN HOUR OR TWO, TO TRY IT OUT. HE SEEMED PLEASED ABOUT THIS AT THE TIME, BUT WHEN HIS GIRLFRIEND FOUND OUT...
If you hate Una, clap yer hands! etc., etc.
SLUT!
SLAG!
I WASN'T AT HOME, SO I DIDN'T HEAR THEM. BUT MY DAD DID!
DON'T YOU EVER...! I NEVER WANT TO HEAR ANYTHING LIKE THAT AGAIN! DO YOU HEAR?
QUITE SOON, AND QUITE BY ACCIDENT, I GOT A REAL, ACTUAL BOYFRIEND I COULD SHOW TO PEOPLE. I HADN'T MEANT FOR THIS TO HAPPEN BUT, AS USUAL, I HADN'T REALLY UNDERSTOOD THE SITUATION. HE LIKED MUSIC FROM THE 60S. IT WAS ALL TOO BEAUTIFUL, APPARENTLY.

HE WAS OLDER THAN ME AND HE WAS REPULSIVE, EVERYONE THOUGHT SO. IT USED TO MAKE ME FEEL QUITE SICK. OTHER KIDS LAUGHED AT ME BUT I WAS HAPPY, BECAUSE I WAS LONGING TO BE LOVED.

MY MUM FOUND OUT ABOUT REPULSIVE ROBERT AND TOOK ME TO THE DOCTOR TO BE PUT ON THE PILL. SHE DIDN'T WANT ME TO SUFFER THE WAY SHE HAD.

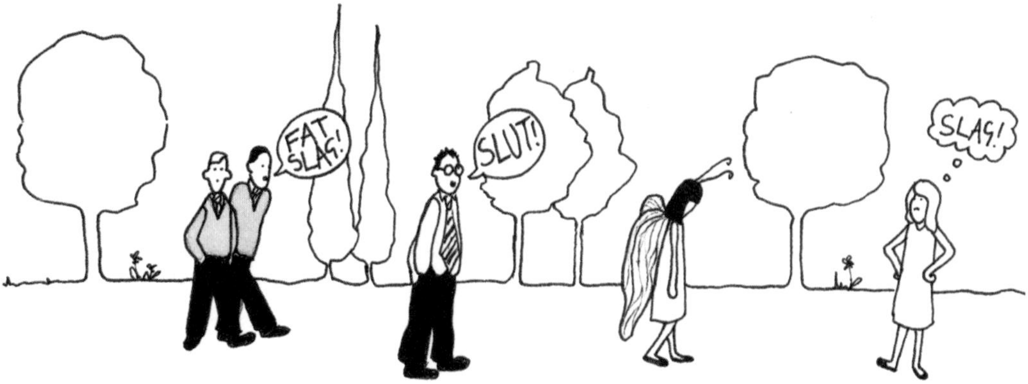
FAT SLAG!
SLUT!
SLAG!

AN UNFORTUNATE SIDE EFFECT OF THE CONTRACEPTIVE PILL WAS THAT, WHEN THEY FOUND OUT I TOOK IT, BOYS FELT EVEN MORE ENTITLED TO MY BODY.

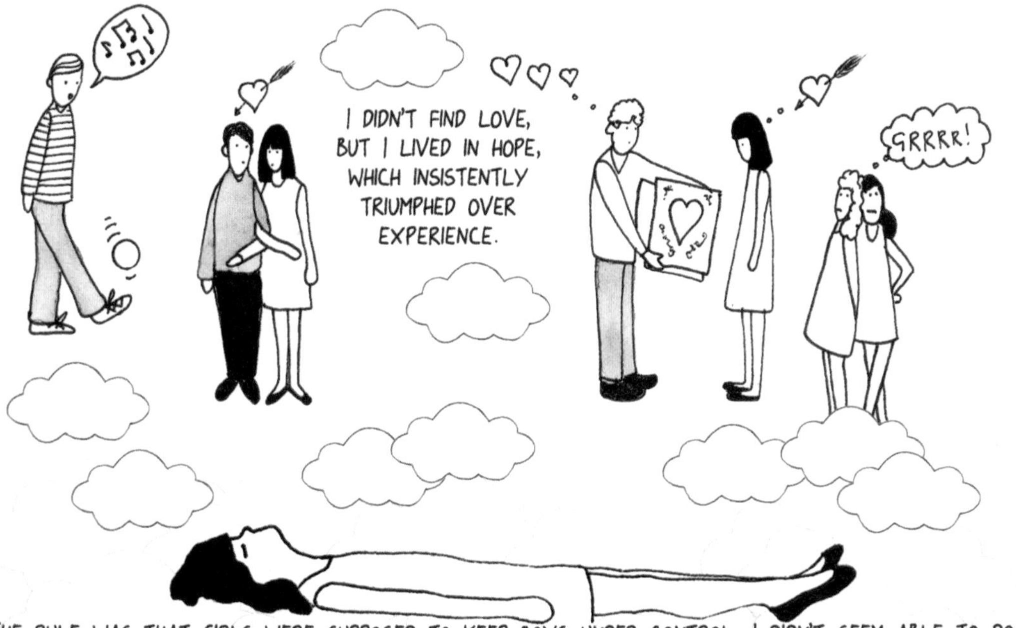
I DIDN'T FIND LOVE, BUT I LIVED IN HOPE, WHICH INSISTENTLY TRIUMPHED OVER EXPERIENCE.
GRRRR!

THE RULE WAS THAT GIRLS WERE SUPPOSED TO KEEP BOYS UNDER CONTROL. I DIDN'T SEEM ABLE TO DO THIS. BOYS WERE NOT EXPECTED TO CONTROL THEMSELVES. GIRLS HAD TO BE SEXY, BUT NOT TOO SEXY AND, ALTHOUGH THE RATE AT WHICH GIRLS GREW WAS COMPLETELY BEYOND THEIR CONTROL, THEY HAD TO BE CAREFUL NOT TO LET THEIR BREASTS AND THIGHS ALARM PEOPLE. GIRLS WERE REQUIRED TO DO SEXUAL THINGS TO BE THOUGHT DESIRABLE, BUT THEY HAD TO DO THESE THINGS WITHOUT REVEALING THEIR OWN NEEDS. THEY WERE EVEN ALLOWED TO 'DO IT' SO LONG AS THEY KEPT 'IT' A SECRET. BOYS WERE REQUIRED TO BE PROUD OF BEING SEXUAL, SO IT WASN'T SECRET FOR LONG. SLUT WAS THE WORST THING A GIRL COULD BE. GIRLS WHO COULD RECOGNISE A SLUT IN THEIR MIDST COULDN'T POSSIBLY BE SLUTS THEMSELVES SO THIS WAS A POPULAR LINE OF DEFENCE. ONCE YOU'VE BEEN BRANDED, NOTHING YOU DO OR SAY MAKES ANY DIFFERENCE. THERE WAS ANOTHER SLUT IN MY SCHOOL, I HEARD SOME BOYS SHOUT IT AT HER IN THE CORRIDOR. I NEVER GOT TO TALK TO HER ABOUT IT, BUT I THOUGHT SHE WAS BEAUTIFUL.

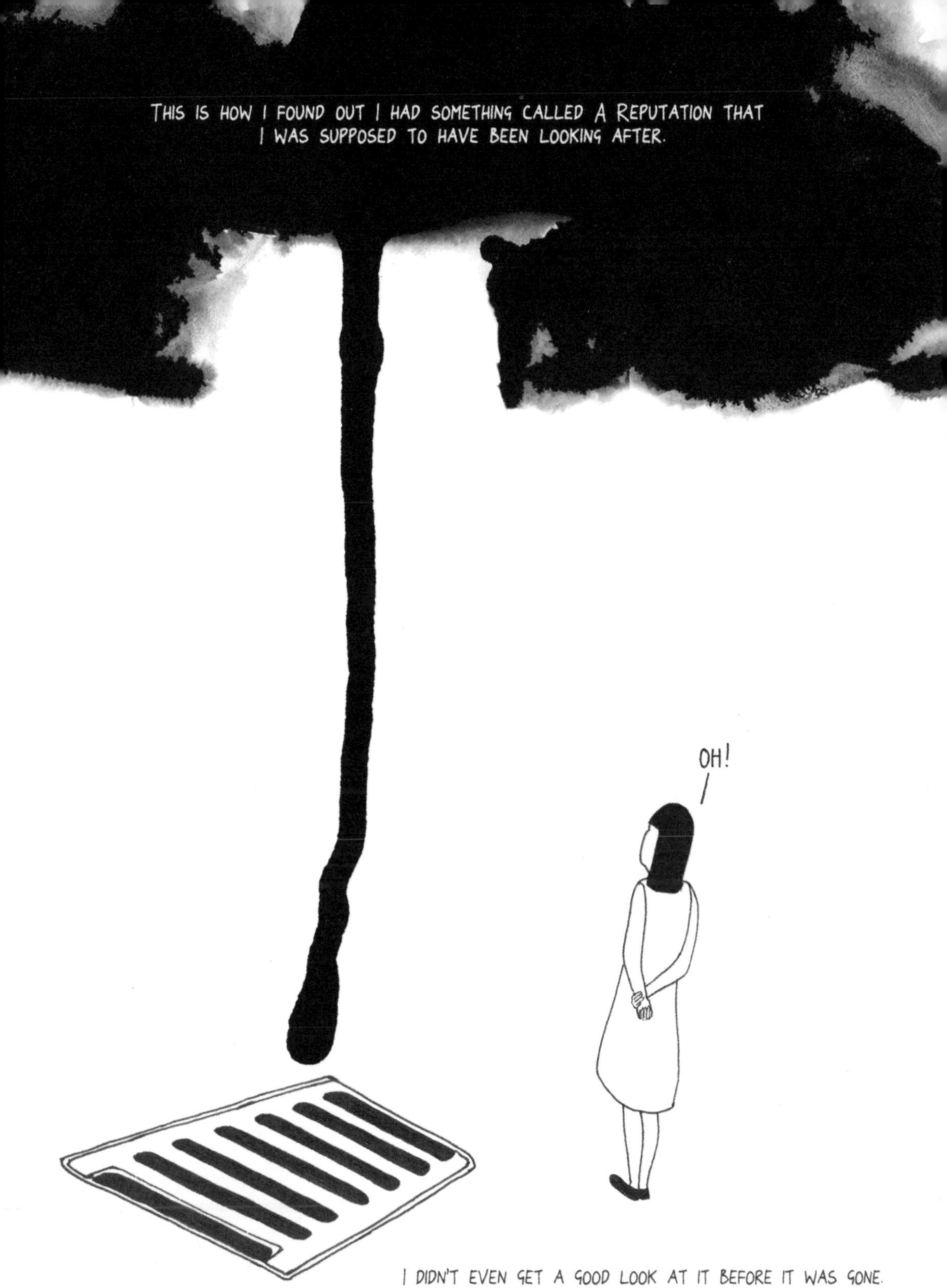
THIS IS HOW I FOUND OUT I HAD SOMETHING CALLED A REPUTATION THAT I WAS SUPPOSED TO HAVE BEEN LOOKING AFTER.
OH!
I DIDN'T EVEN GET A GOOD LOOK AT IT BEFORE IT WAS GONE.

I WAS IN A DIFFERENT CATEGORY OF FEMALE (NO, NOT A PRINCESS).

I CARRIED ON AS IF EVERYTHING WERE PERFECTLY NORMAL...

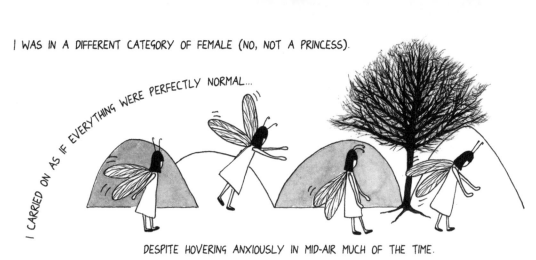

DESPITE HOVERING ANXIOUSLY IN MID-AIR MUCH OF THE TIME.

WHEN PEOPLE SHOUTED THINGS...

^#**!?%!
SLAG!

?#*&!

*#¿?^!!

I PRETENDED NOT TO NOTICE.

WHEN FRIENDS WERE TOLD BY THEIR PARENTS TO STOP HANGING OUT WITH ME, I SWALLOWED MY SHAME AND SPENT MORE TIME ALONE.

LUCKILY I LIKED READING.

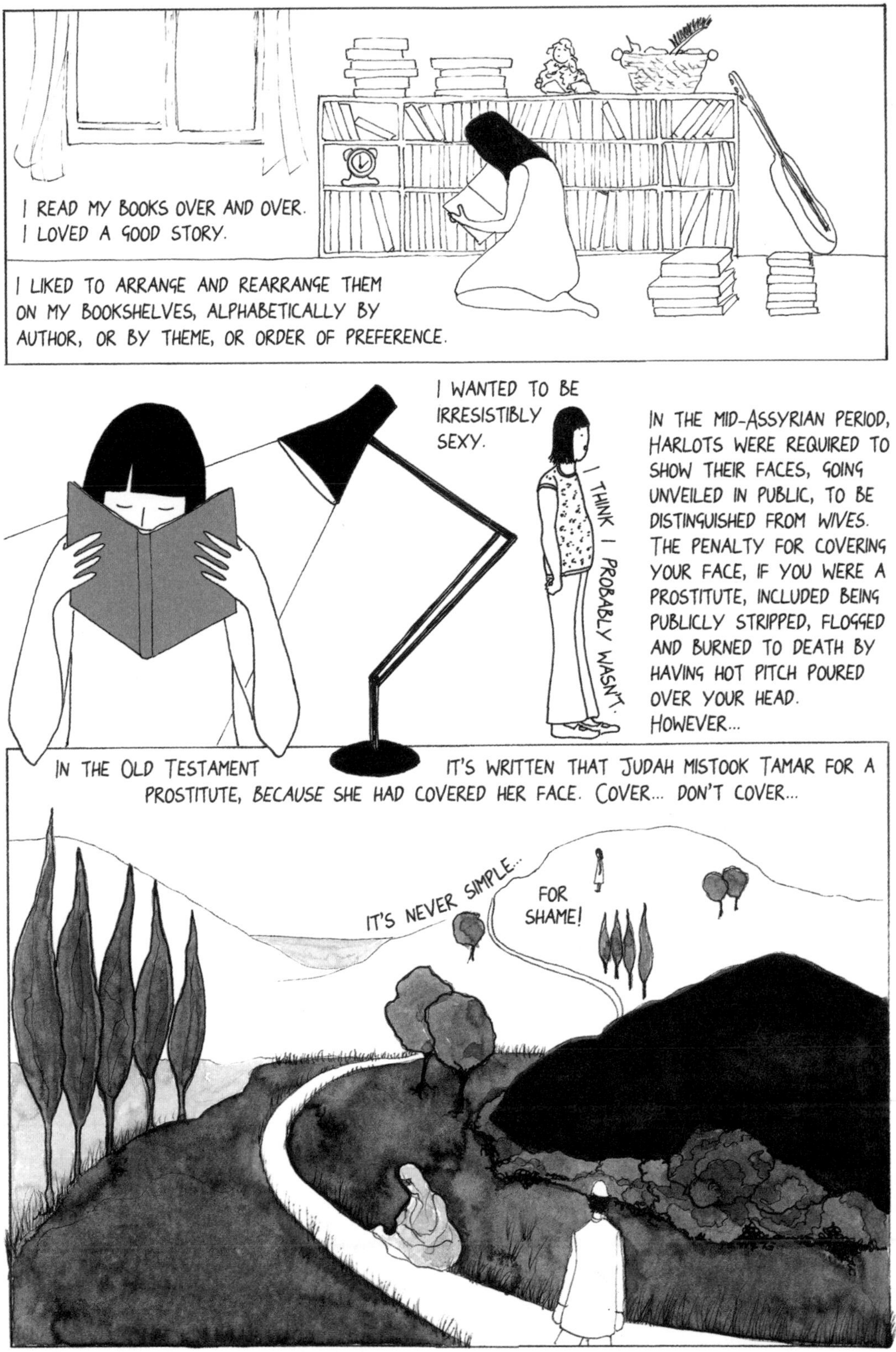
I READ MY BOOKS OVER AND OVER. I LOVED A GOOD STORY.
I LIKED TO ARRANGE AND REARRANGE THEM ON MY BOOKSHELVES, ALPHABETICALLY BY AUTHOR, OR BY THEME, OR ORDER OF PREFERENCE.
I WANTED TO BE IRRESISTIBLY SEXY.
I THINK I PROBABLY WASN'T.
IN THE MID-ASSYRIAN PERIOD, HARLOTS WERE REQUIRED TO SHOW THEIR FACES, GOING UNVEILED IN PUBLIC, TO BE DISTINGUISHED FROM WIVES. THE PENALTY FOR COVERING YOUR FACE, IF YOU WERE A PROSTITUTE, INCLUDED BEING PUBLICLY STRIPPED, FLOGGED AND BURNED TO DEATH BY HAVING HOT PITCH POURED OVER YOUR HEAD. HOWEVER...
IN THE OLD TESTAMENT IT'S WRITTEN THAT JUDAH MISTOOK TAMAR FOR A PROSTITUTE, *BECAUSE* SHE HAD COVERED HER FACE. COVER... DON'T COVER...
IT'S NEVER SIMPLE...
FOR SHAME!

‘Go home before it’s too late!’

‘Good time’ girls’ warning

Canon Gordon Croney, vicar of Leeds, considers police-controlled houses of prostitution to be impractical. ‘I know it’s an easy answer, but I believe it could make the problem worse.’ he says.

‘If prostitutes came under police protection, then it could make a psychopath like the Ripper prey on innocent women.’

*

Feb 13th 1978

Shadows of the Ripper

‘The Twilight Girls’

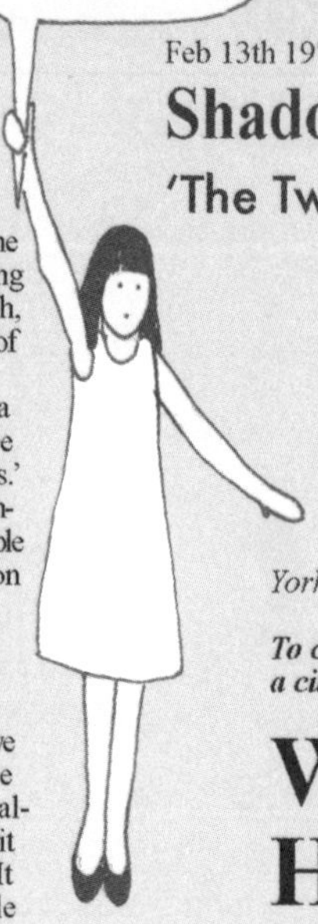

Leeds magistrate for the past 35 years had, during his career on the bench, dealt with hundreds of cases of prostitution.

‘As a person and as a magistrate I would be against legalised brothels.’ he says. ‘It would be offensive to the majority of people who hold strong views on prostitution.’

*

‘And at a time when we are supposed to be approaching sexual equality I would have thought it even more unacceptable. It is denigrating the whole dignity of women.

‘It may reduce the number of sexual offences but I don’t see that to do something good one should do something bad.’

‘Shame? It’s just a job’

Yorkshire Evening Post, Thursday 16th February 1978

To conclude our series ‘The Twilight Girls’ we take a look at Amsterdam, a city where brothels have police blessing.

Whores’ Law: How a big city is coping

14th February 1978

Maria is nineteen... ‘on the game for three and a half years’ our reporter on the second of our series ‘The Twilight Girls’

MARIA – THE PREGNANT HUSTLER

Maria’s mother was Spanish and died when she was a child. She says her father has disowned her. ‘I’m not ashamed of what I do. I’m a hustler and I do a job and get paid for it.’

With her noticeable pregnancy, her days in business must be numbered? Apparently not. ‘Some men really like pregnant women, they tell me they like me this way. I’ll carry on until I get too big’ she says. She’s hazy about life after the birth but sees herself hustling for a long time yet.

‘Wouldn’t you like to settle down and have a family?’ I wondered. ‘I am having a family,’ she said.

Like all hookers, Maria knows violence. She knows death can be part of the job. She’s been battered and attacked, dumped out in the country in just her bra and pants, and once almost ended up as another murder statistic on the files. A punter turned vicious in a hotel room and tried to strangle her.

‘He didn’t like women – like the Ripper – and he grabbed me round the throat. If I hadn’t have screamed I’m sure he would have killed me.’

DESPITE THE OBVIOUS LACK OF SUCCESS WEST YORKSHIRE POLICE WERE HAVING CATCHING HIM...

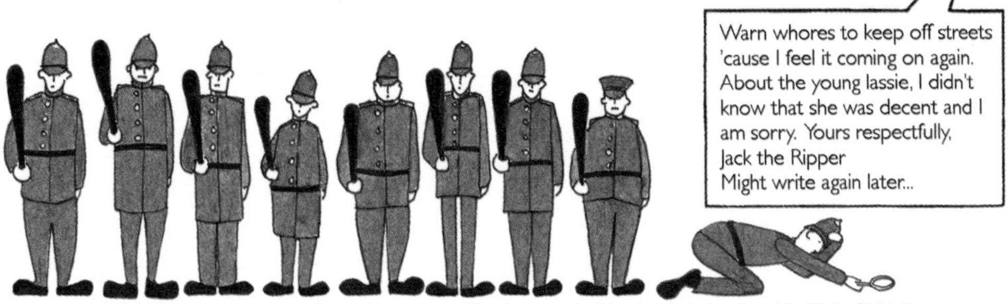
Warn whores to keep off streets 'cause I feel it coming on again. About the young lassie, I didn't know that she was decent and I am sorry. Yours respectfully,
Jack the Ripper
Might write again later...

A MAN FROM SUNDERLAND DECIDED IT WOULD BE A LAUGH TO PRETEND TO BE THE RIPPER.

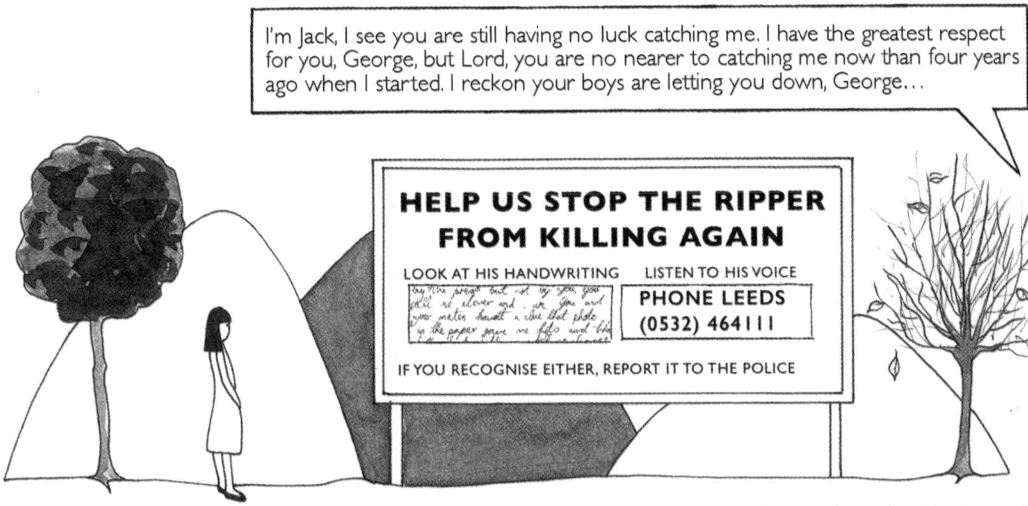
I'm Jack, I see you are still having no luck catching me. I have the greatest respect for you, George, but Lord, you are no nearer to catching me now than four years ago when I started. I reckon your boys are letting you down, George...
HELP US STOP THE RIPPER FROM KILLING AGAIN
LOOK AT HIS HANDWRITING
LISTEN TO HIS VOICE
PHONE LEEDS (0532) 464111
IF YOU RECOGNISE EITHER, REPORT IT TO THE POLICE

HE'D ADAPTED LETTERS THE OTHER RIPPER WAS SUPPOSED TO HAVE SENT, 100 YEARS BEFORE. NO ONE NOTICED THE SIMILARITY. HE MADE A RECORDING OF HIS VOICE, MOCKING THE POLICE, LIKE A PROPER VILLAIN IN A THRILLER. EXPERTS IDENTIFIED HIS ACCENT AS BEING FROM CASTLETOWN, 100 MILES AWAY.

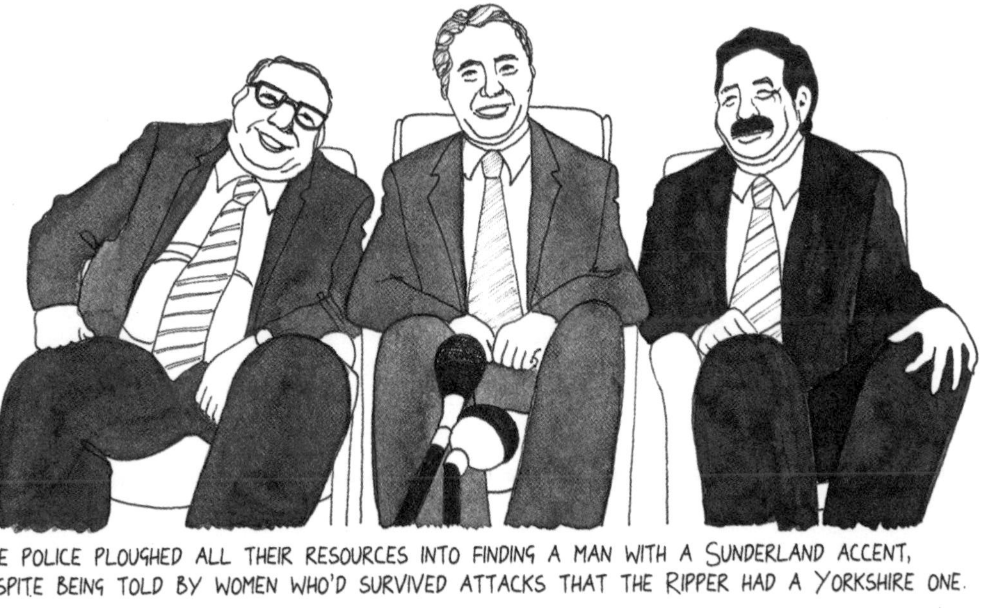

THE POLICE PLOUGHED ALL THEIR RESOURCES INTO FINDING A MAN WITH A SUNDERLAND ACCENT, DESPITE BEING TOLD BY WOMEN WHO'D SURVIVED ATTACKS THAT THE RIPPER HAD A YORKSHIRE ONE.

March 8 1978

Dear sir, I am sorry I cannot give my name for obvious reasons, I am the Ripper. I've been dubbed a maniac by the press but not by you, you call me clever and I am...

Dear sir
I am sorry I cannot give my name for obvious reasons I am the Ripper. I've been dubbed a maniac by the press but not by you, you call me clever and I am. You and your mates haven't a clue that photo in the paper gave me fits and that stuff about killing myself no chance I've got things to do. My purpose to rid the streets of them sluts me regret his that young jaosie Mcdonald didn't know cause changed routine that nite. Up to number 8 now you say

My purpose to rid the streets of them sluts...

you ton 75 Get about
You me in Sunderland
dont bother I am not daft not posted letter there on one of my trips Not a bad place improvement on Chapeltown and

56

YOU HAVE KILLED FIVE TIMES NOW... YOUR MOTIVE, IT IS BELIEVED, IS A DREADFUL HATRED OF PROSTITUTES, A HATE THAT DRIVES YOU TO SLAS[H] AND BLUDGEON YOUR VICTIMS. BUT INEVITABLY, THAT TWISTED PASSION WENT HORRIBLY WRONG ON SUNDAY NIGHT. AN INNOCENT SIXTEEN-YEAR-OLD LASS, A HAPPY, RESPECTABLE WORKING CLASS GIRL FROM A DECENT LEEDS FAMILY, CROSSED YOUR PATH. HOW DID YOU FEEL YESTERDAY WHEN YOU LEARNED THAT YOUR BLOODSTAINED CRUSADE HAD GONE SO HORRIBLY WRONG? ... SICK IN MIND THOUGH YOU UNDOUBTEDLY ARE, THERE MUST HAVE BEEN SOME REMORSE AS YOU RID YOURSELF OF JAYNE'S BLOODSTAINS. YORKSHIRE EVENING POST, 28TH JUNE 1977. I AM CONVINCED THINGS COULD HAVE WORKED OUT DIFFERENTLY HAD PETER MARRIED A GIRL MORE ON HIS OWN LEVEL WHO DIDN'T HAVE SO MANY PROBLEMS OF HER OWN. PETER EXCHANGED A LOVING, WARM AND CARING FAMILY BACKGROUND FOR A CLAUSTRO-PHOBIC AND RIGID EXISTENCE IN SONIA'S WORLD. SUNDAY MIRROR, 24 MAY 1981. 'IF WE HAD TWENTY OR THIRTY SUSPECTS IN ONE ROOM WE WOULD KNOW VERY QUICKLY WHICH ONE WAS THE RIPPER'. GEORGE OLDFIELD, ASSISTANT CHIEF CONSTABLE OF WEST YORKSHIRE, SUNDAY TELEGRAPH, 23 NOVEMBER 1980. DETECTIVES FAILED TO UNCOVER AN ALMOST PERFECT PHOTOFIT LIKENESS AND DESCRIPTION OF SUTCLIFFE DATING BACK TO AUGUST 1975, SOON AFTER HIS ATTACKS BEGAN. A 14 YEAR OLD SCHOOLGIRL, TRACEY BROWNE, SURVIVED THE HEAD INJURIES SHE RECEIVED IN AN UNSOLVED ATTACK WHICH BORE ALL THE HAILMARKS OF WHAT LATER WAS CLEARLY IDENTIFIED AS RIPPER

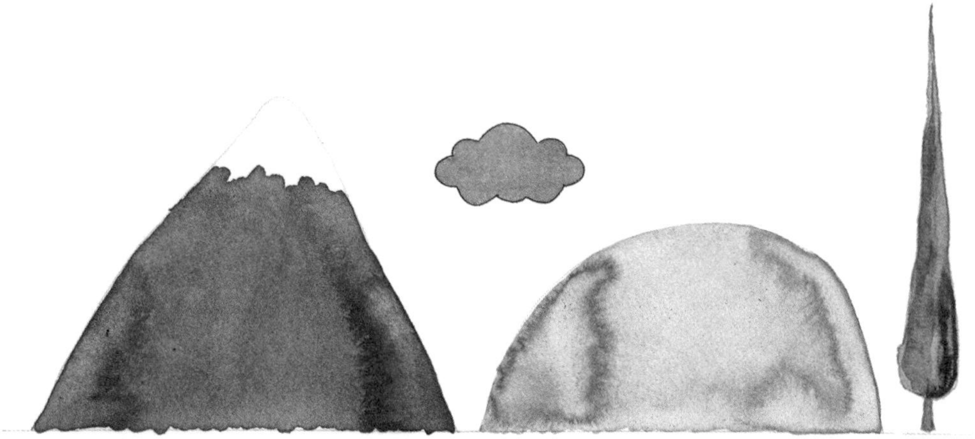

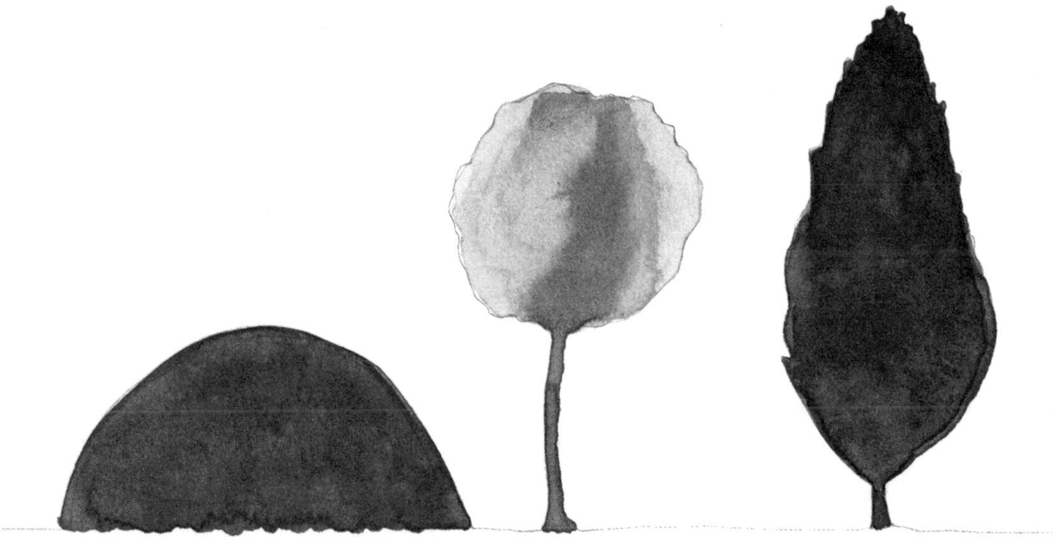

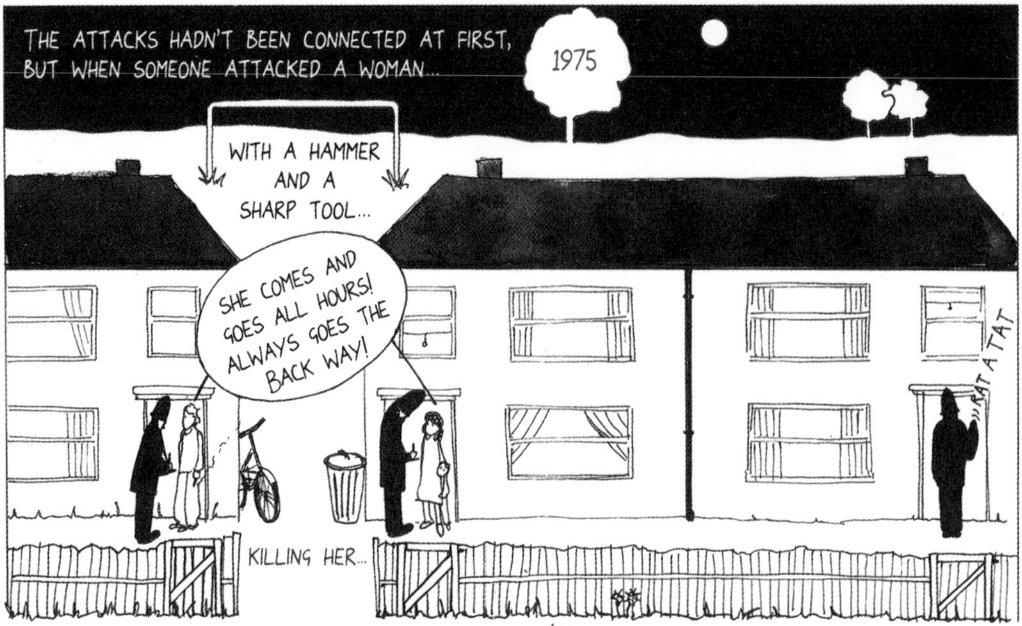
THE ATTACKS HADN'T BEEN CONNECTED AT FIRST, BUT WHEN SOMEONE ATTACKED A WOMAN...
1975
WITH A HAMMER AND A SHARP TOOL...
SHE COMES AND GOES ALL HOURS! ALWAYS GOES THE BACK WAY!
RAT A TAT
KILLING HER...

THE DETECTIVE IN CHARGE OF THE INQUIRY WANTED TO FIND OUT AS MUCH AS HE COULD ABOUT HER LIFE.

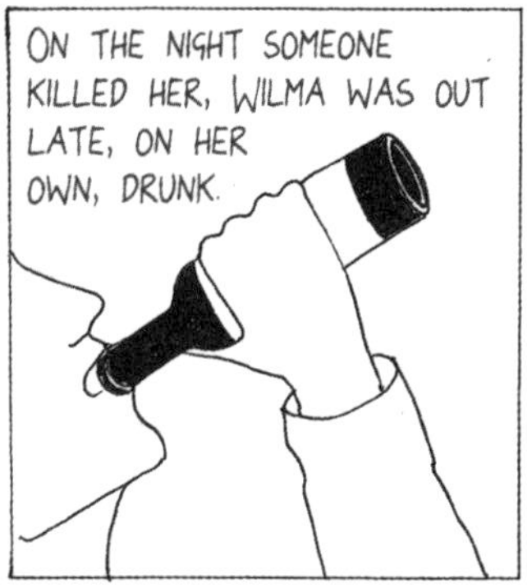
ON THE NIGHT SOMEONE KILLED HER, WILMA WAS OUT LATE, ON HER OWN, DRUNK.

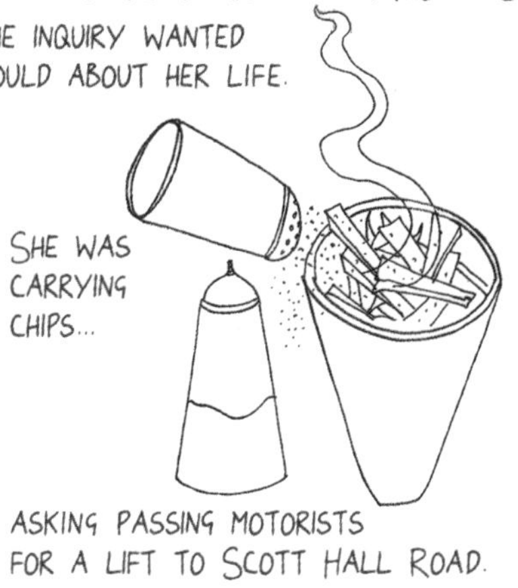
SHE WAS CARRYING CHIPS...
ASKING PASSING MOTORISTS FOR A LIFT TO SCOTT HALL ROAD.

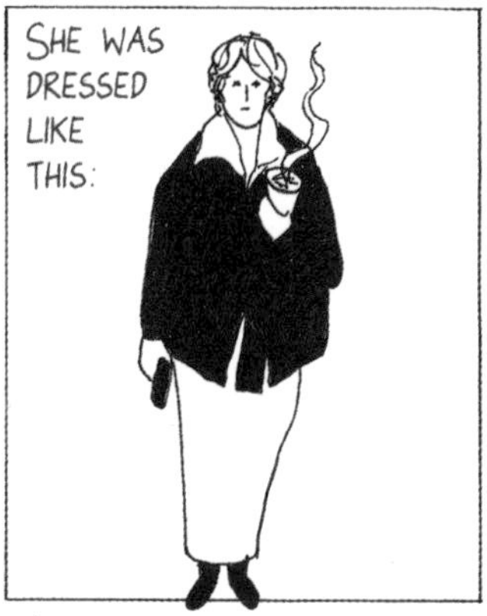
SHE WAS DRESSED LIKE THIS:

TEN WEEKS AFTER SOMEONE KILLED WILMA, DETECTIVES WERE LISTENING CAREFULLY TO EMILY'S HUSBAND.

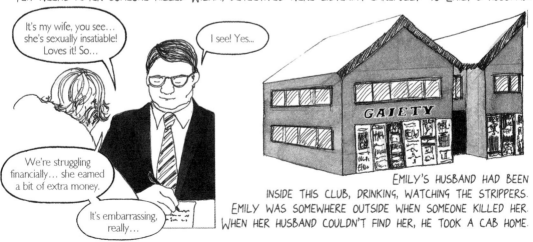

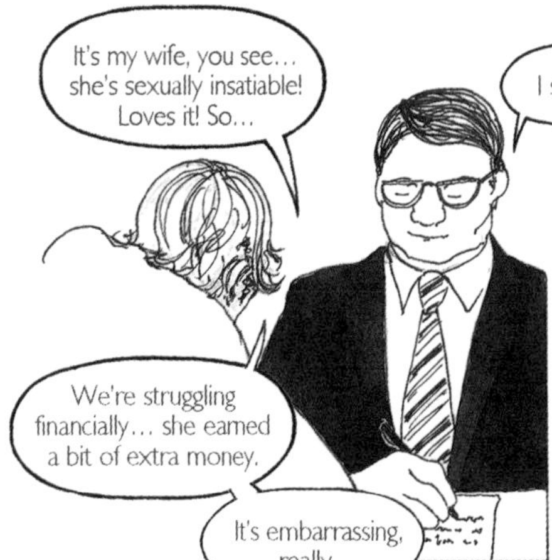
It's my wife, you see... she's sexually insatiable! Loves it! So...
I see! Yes...
We're struggling financially... she earned a bit of extra money.
It's embarrassing, really...

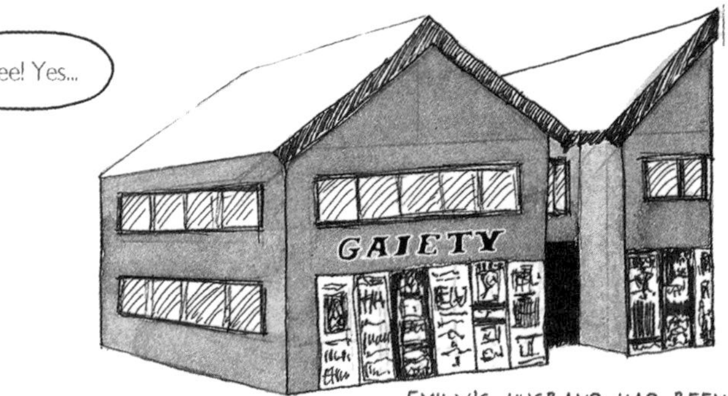
GAIETY

EMILY'S HUSBAND HAD BEEN INSIDE THIS CLUB, DRINKING, WATCHING THE STRIPPERS. EMILY WAS SOMEWHERE OUTSIDE WHEN SOMEONE KILLED HER. WHEN HER HUSBAND COULDN'T FIND HER, HE TOOK A CAB HOME.

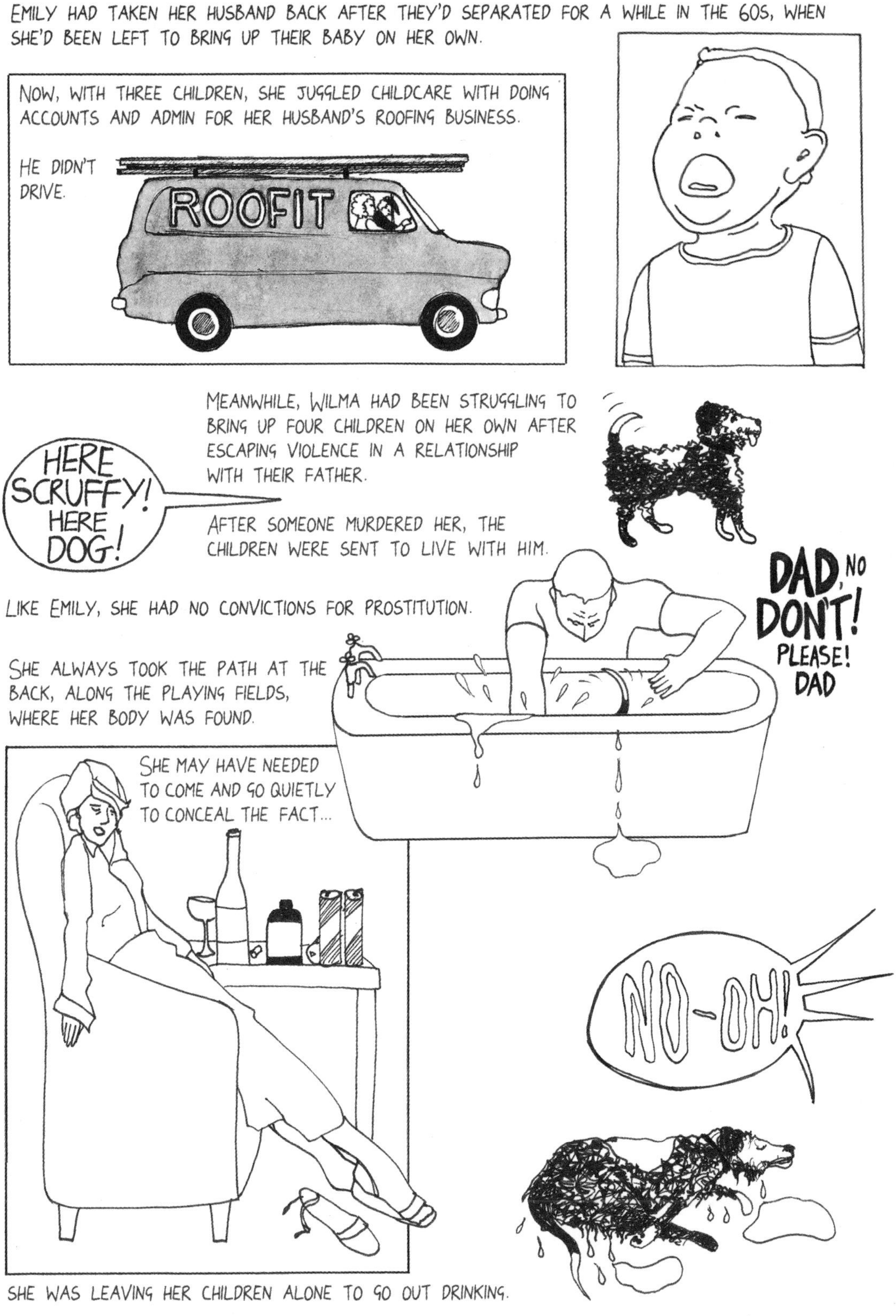
EMILY HAD TAKEN HER HUSBAND BACK AFTER THEY'D SEPARATED FOR A WHILE IN THE 60S, WHEN SHE'D BEEN LEFT TO BRING UP THEIR BABY ON HER OWN.
NOW, WITH THREE CHILDREN, SHE JUGGLED CHILDCARE WITH DOING ACCOUNTS AND ADMIN FOR HER HUSBAND'S ROOFING BUSINESS.
HE DIDN'T DRIVE.
ROOFIT
MEANWHILE, WILMA HAD BEEN STRUGGLING TO BRING UP FOUR CHILDREN ON HER OWN AFTER ESCAPING VIOLENCE IN A RELATIONSHIP WITH THEIR FATHER.
HERE SCRUFFY! HERE DOG!
AFTER SOMEONE MURDERED HER, THE CHILDREN WERE SENT TO LIVE WITH HIM.
DAD, NO DON'T! PLEASE! DAD
LIKE EMILY, SHE HAD NO CONVICTIONS FOR PROSTITUTION.
SHE ALWAYS TOOK THE PATH AT THE BACK, ALONG THE PLAYING FIELDS, WHERE HER BODY WAS FOUND.
SHE MAY HAVE NEEDED TO COME AND GO QUIETLY TO CONCEAL THE FACT...
NO-OH!
SHE WAS LEAVING HER CHILDREN ALONE TO GO OUT DRINKING.

SO, THE FIRST TWO WOMEN TO DIE FROM THEIR INJURIES LED COMPLICATED LIVES. WAS THAT WHAT MADE THEM PROSTITUTES?

BEFORE THEM, THE FIRST THREE WOMEN TO SURVIVE ATTACKS WERE:

A WOMAN IN THE MIDDLE OF AN ARGUMENT WITH A BOYFRIEND.

A WOMAN ON HER WAY HOME FROM THE PUB.

A TEENAGER IN UNSUITABLE SHOES.

TWO OF THESE WOMEN WERE DESCRIBED BY POLICE AS HAVING LOOSE MORALS.[5] THE OTHER WAS IGNORED.

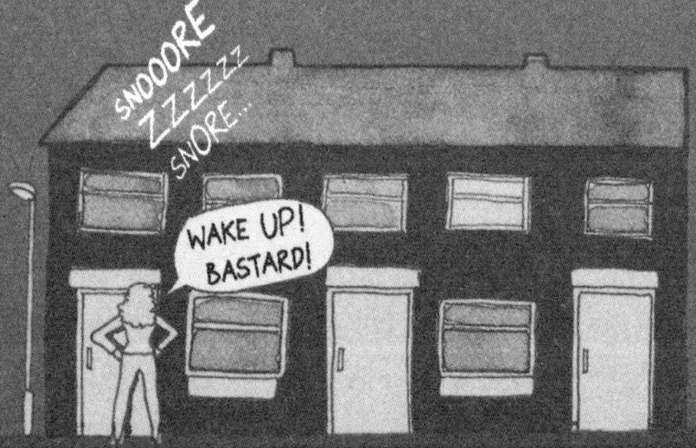
SNOOORE
ZZZZZZ
SNORE...
WAKE UP! BASTARD!

EVEN IF EVERY ONE OF THEM HAD BEEN WALKING DOWN THE STREET STARK NAKED, SHOUTING, 'A TENNER TO TOUCH MY BEAUTIFUL ARSE' AT THE TOP OF HER VOICE, THIS WOULDN'T BE A REASON TO ATTACK HER – OF COURSE.

THE IDEA THAT THERE WAS A PROSTITUTE KILLER ON THE RAMPAGE WAS, IT SEEMS, SIMPLY PLUCKED FROM THE AIR.

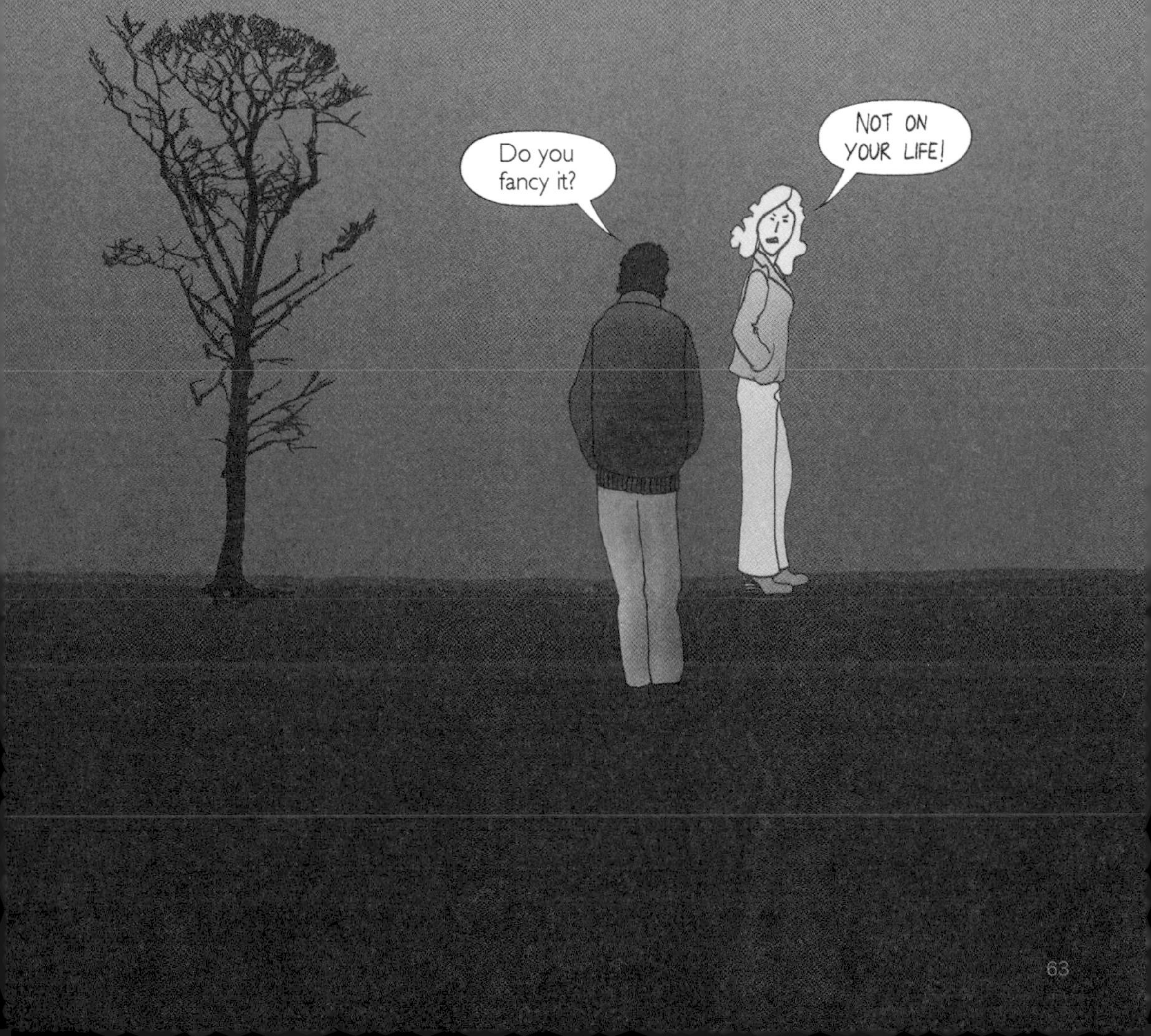

Do you fancy it?
NOT ON YOUR LIFE!

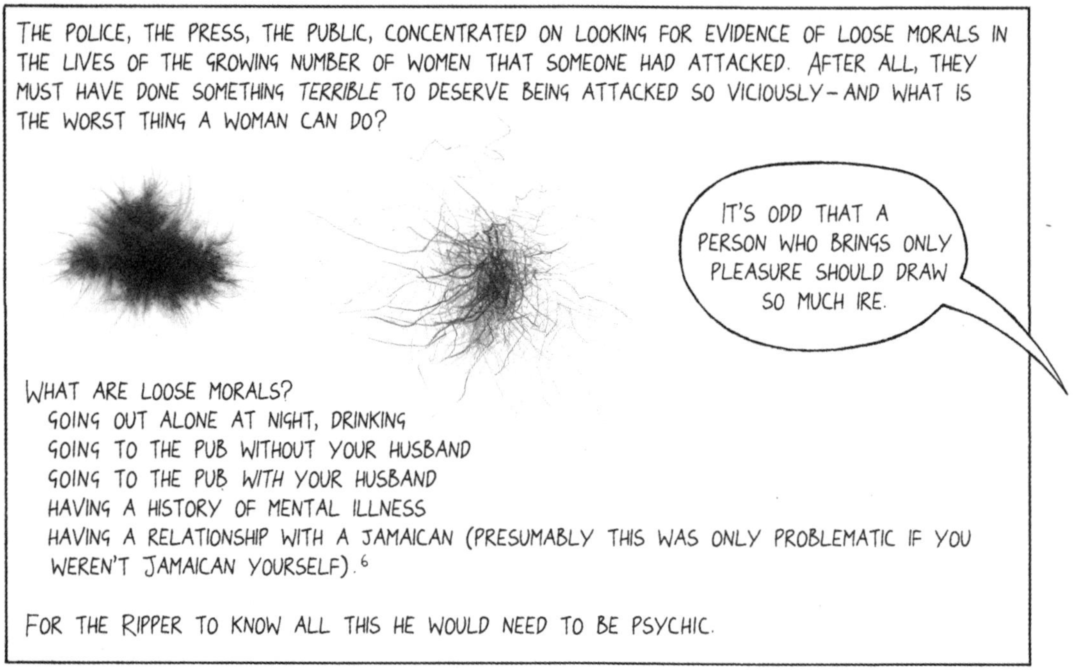
THE POLICE, THE PRESS, THE PUBLIC, CONCENTRATED ON LOOKING FOR EVIDENCE OF LOOSE MORALS IN THE LIVES OF THE GROWING NUMBER OF WOMEN THAT SOMEONE HAD ATTACKED. AFTER ALL, THEY MUST HAVE DONE SOMETHING *TERRIBLE* TO DESERVE BEING ATTACKED SO VICIOUSLY – AND WHAT IS THE WORST THING A WOMAN CAN DO?
IT'S ODD THAT A PERSON WHO BRINGS ONLY PLEASURE SHOULD DRAW SO MUCH IRE.
WHAT ARE LOOSE MORALS?
GOING OUT ALONE AT NIGHT, DRINKING
GOING TO THE PUB WITHOUT YOUR HUSBAND
GOING TO THE PUB *WITH* YOUR HUSBAND
HAVING A HISTORY OF MENTAL ILLNESS
HAVING A RELATIONSHIP WITH A JAMAICAN (PRESUMABLY THIS WAS ONLY PROBLEMATIC IF YOU WEREN'T JAMAICAN YOURSELF).[6]
FOR THE RIPPER TO KNOW ALL THIS HE WOULD NEED TO BE PSYCHIC.

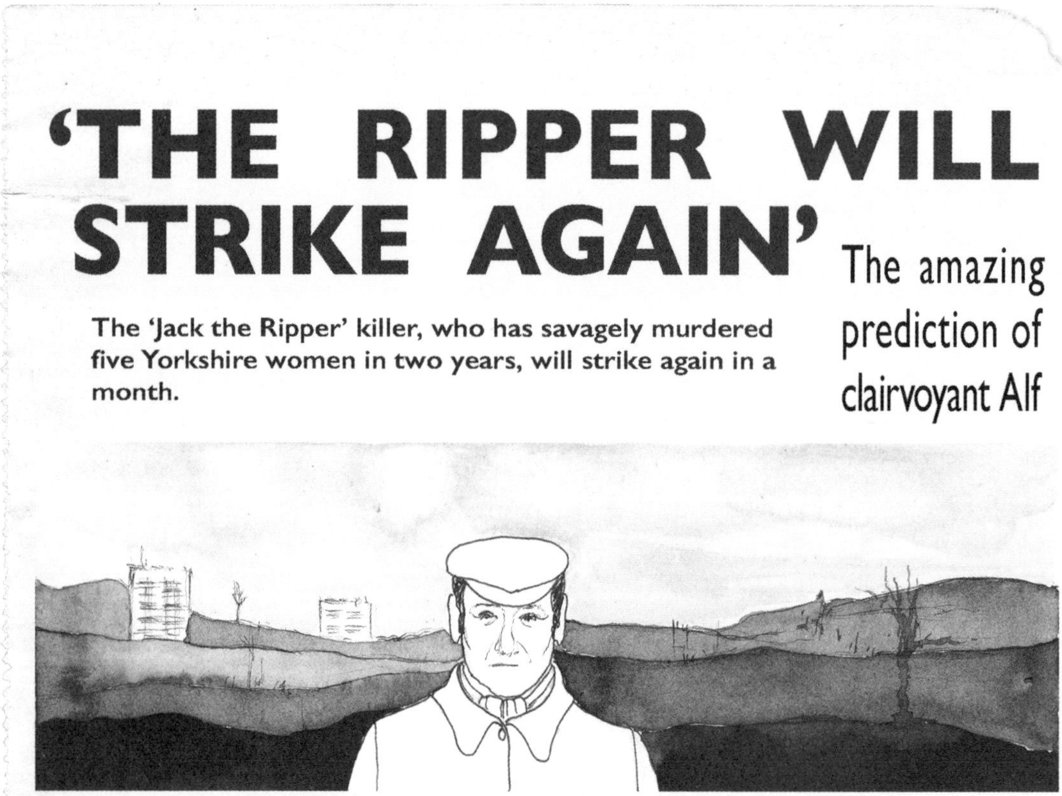

'THE RIPPER WILL STRIKE AGAIN'

The amazing prediction of clairvoyant Alf

The 'Jack the Ripper' killer, who has savagely murdered five Yorkshire women in two years, will strike again in a month.

Clairvoyant Alfred Cartwright at the scene of the murder.

A PERSON WHO LACKS MORAL FIBRE IS UNABLE TO DO THE RIGHT THING IN A DIFFICULT SITUATION.

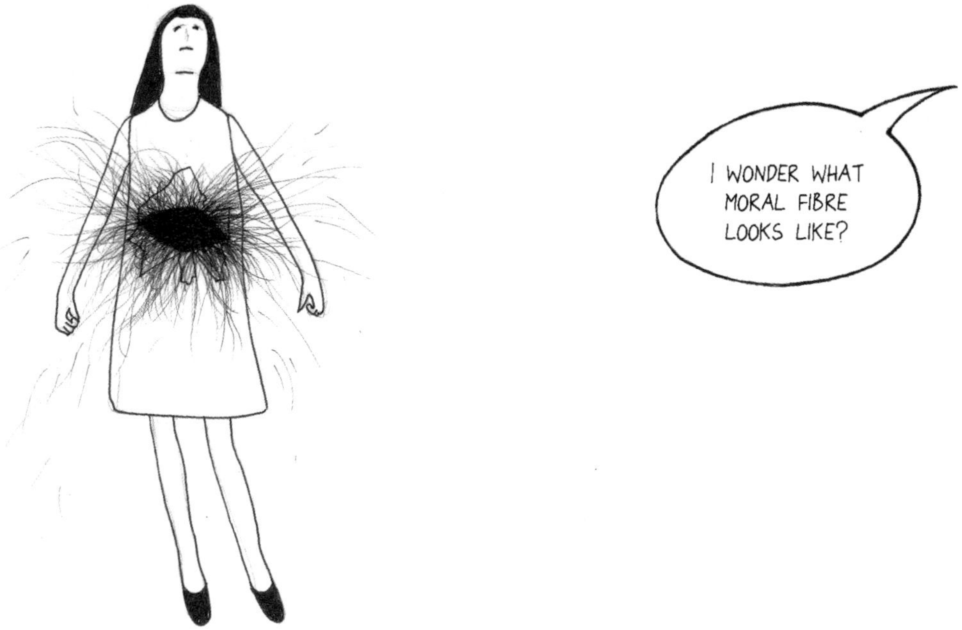
I WONDER WHAT MORAL FIBRE LOOKS LIKE?

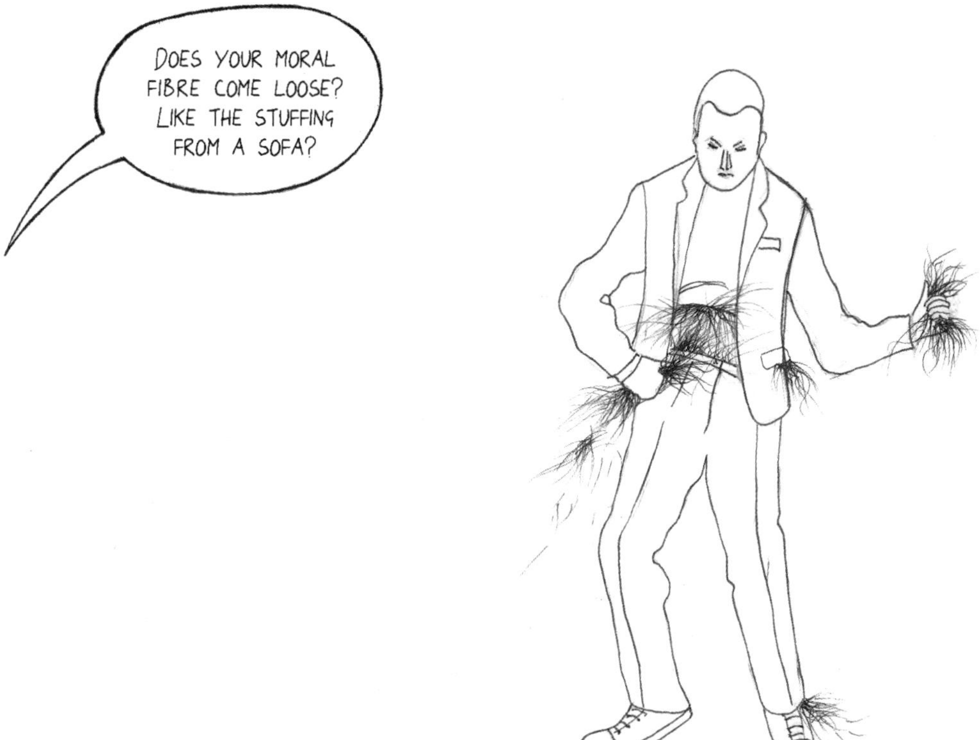
DOES YOUR MORAL FIBRE COME LOOSE? LIKE THE STUFFING FROM A SOFA?

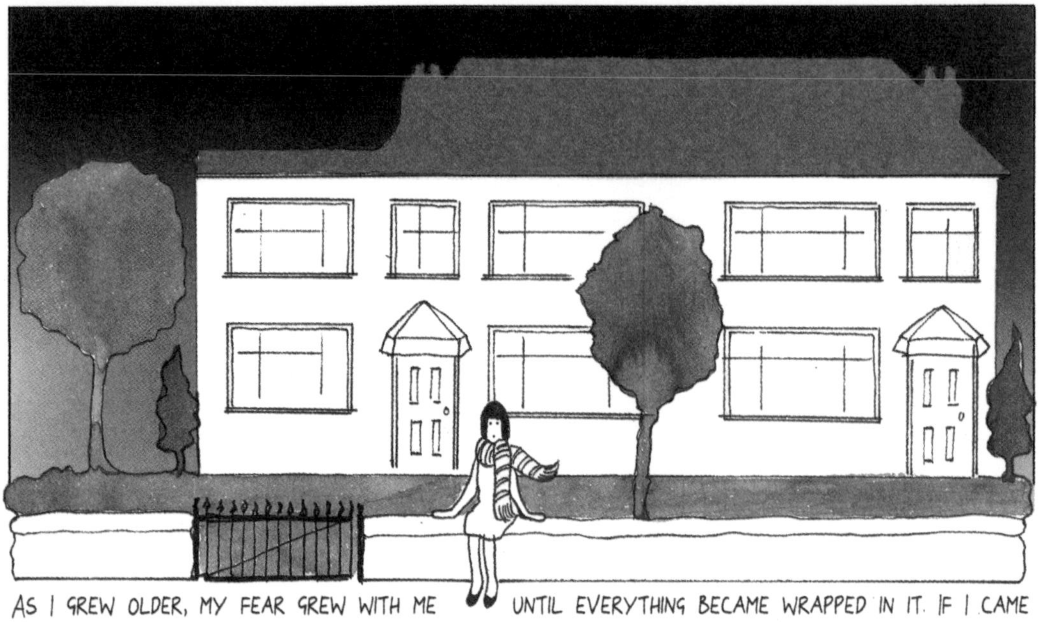

AS I GREW OLDER, MY FEAR GREW WITH ME UNTIL EVERYTHING BECAME WRAPPED IN IT. IF I CAME HOME TO FIND THE HOUSE EMPTY, I WAS TOO FRIGHTENED TO GO INSIDE, SO I WOULD SIT ON THE GARDEN WALL UNTIL MY MOTHER CAME HOME.

AROUND THIS TIME, GROUPS OF WOMEN WERE DEMONSTRATING THEIR ANGER AT BEING TOLD TO BE EXTRA CAREFUL WHEN OUT AT NIGHT, OR MAYBE TO JUST STAY IN, WHEN THEY WEREN'T THE ONES DOING ALL THE RAPE AND MURDER. I WISH I HAD KNOWN ABOUT THEM AT THE TIME...

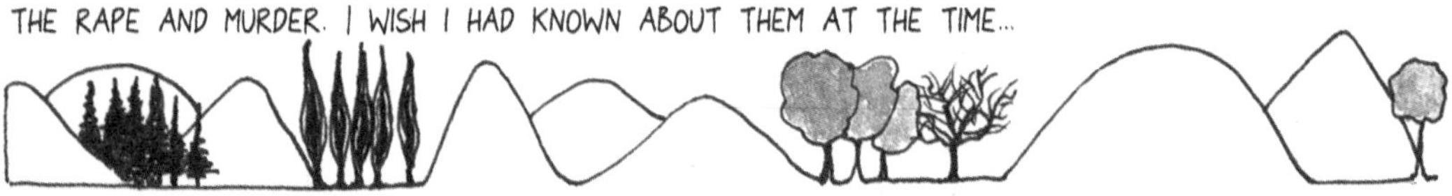

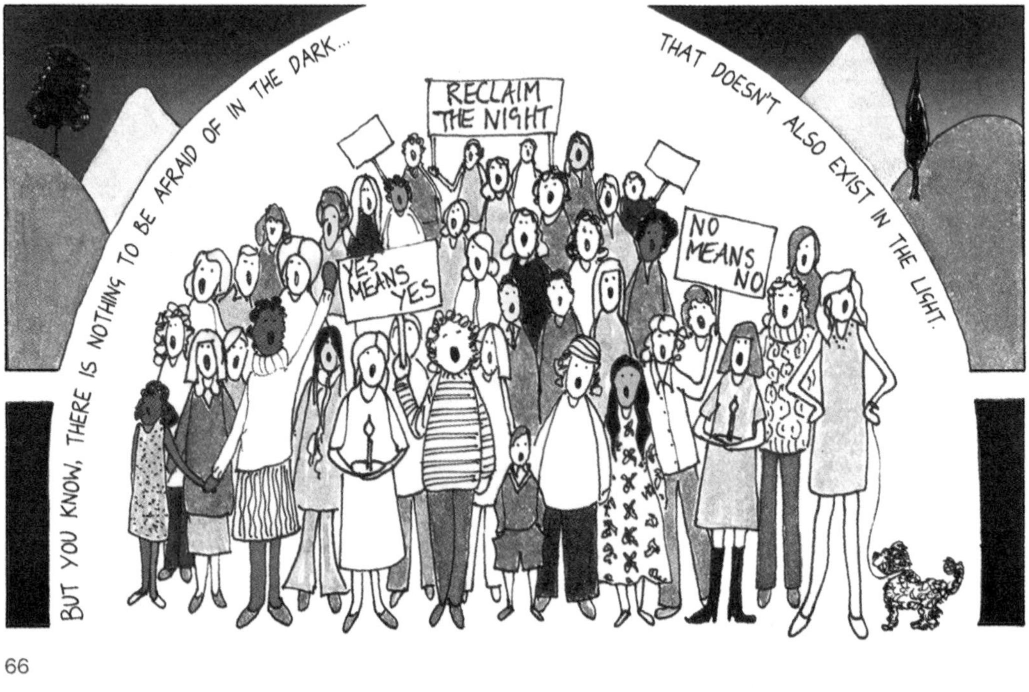
BUT YOU KNOW, THERE IS NOTHING TO BE AFRAID OF IN THE DARK...
THAT DOESN'T ALSO EXIST IN THE LIGHT.
RECLAIM THE NIGHT
YES MEANS YES
NO MEANS NO

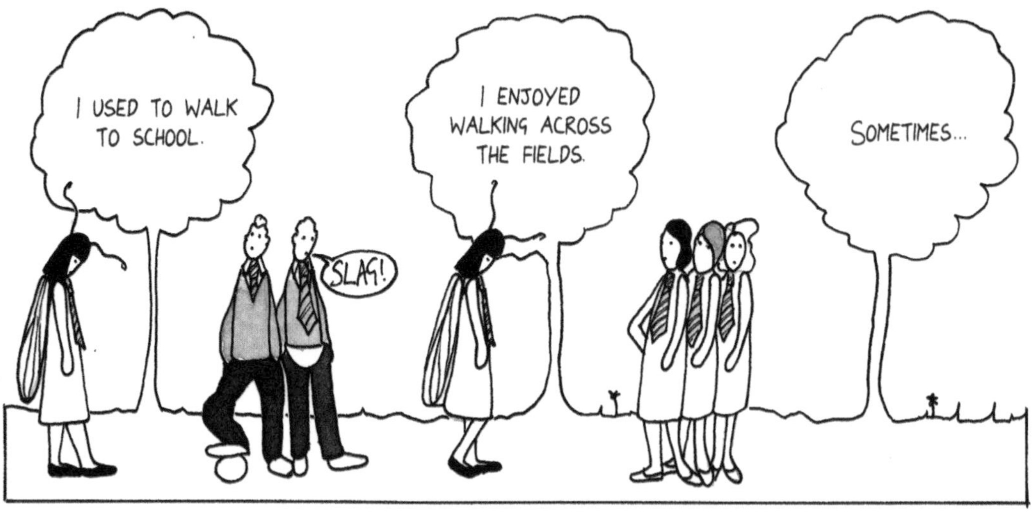
I USED TO WALK TO SCHOOL.
SLAG!
I ENJOYED WALKING ACROSS THE FIELDS.
SOMETIMES...

ONE DAY, THE GIRLS WERE TOLD NOT TO WALK TO SCHOOL ANY MORE, BUT TO CATCH THE BUS INSTEAD, AND NEVER ALONE. BOYS WERE NOT GIVEN ANY INSTRUCTIONS. ALL GIRLS, EVERYWHERE, HAD NOW TO BE CAREFUL, BECAUSE THE RIPPER HAD KILLED ANOTHER YOUNG WOMAN. THIS TIME, PEOPLE WERE OUTRAGED! THE POLICE ISSUED A STATEMENT.

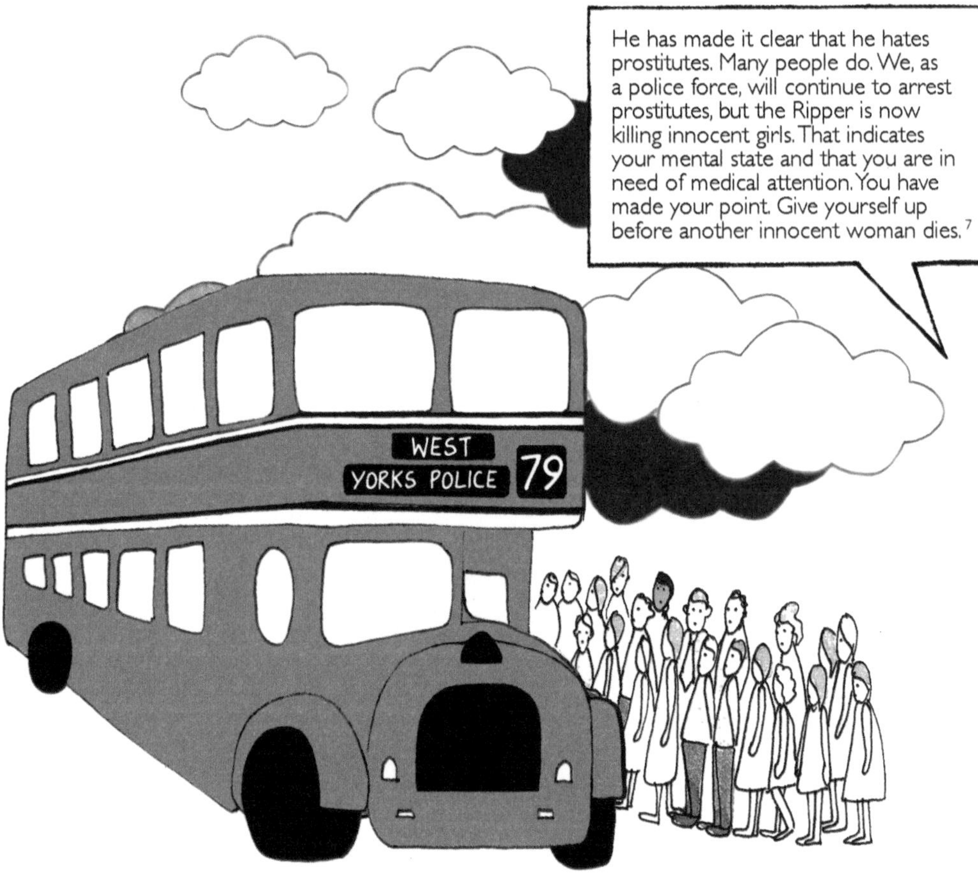
He has made it clear that he hates prostitutes. Many people do. We, as a police force, will continue to arrest prostitutes, but the Ripper is now killing innocent girls. That indicates your mental state and that you are in need of medical attention. You have made your point. Give yourself up before another innocent woman dies.[7]
WEST YORKS POLICE
79

IT SEEMED IT WAS REASONABLE TO WANT TO KILL SOME WOMEN, BUT NOT OTHERS.

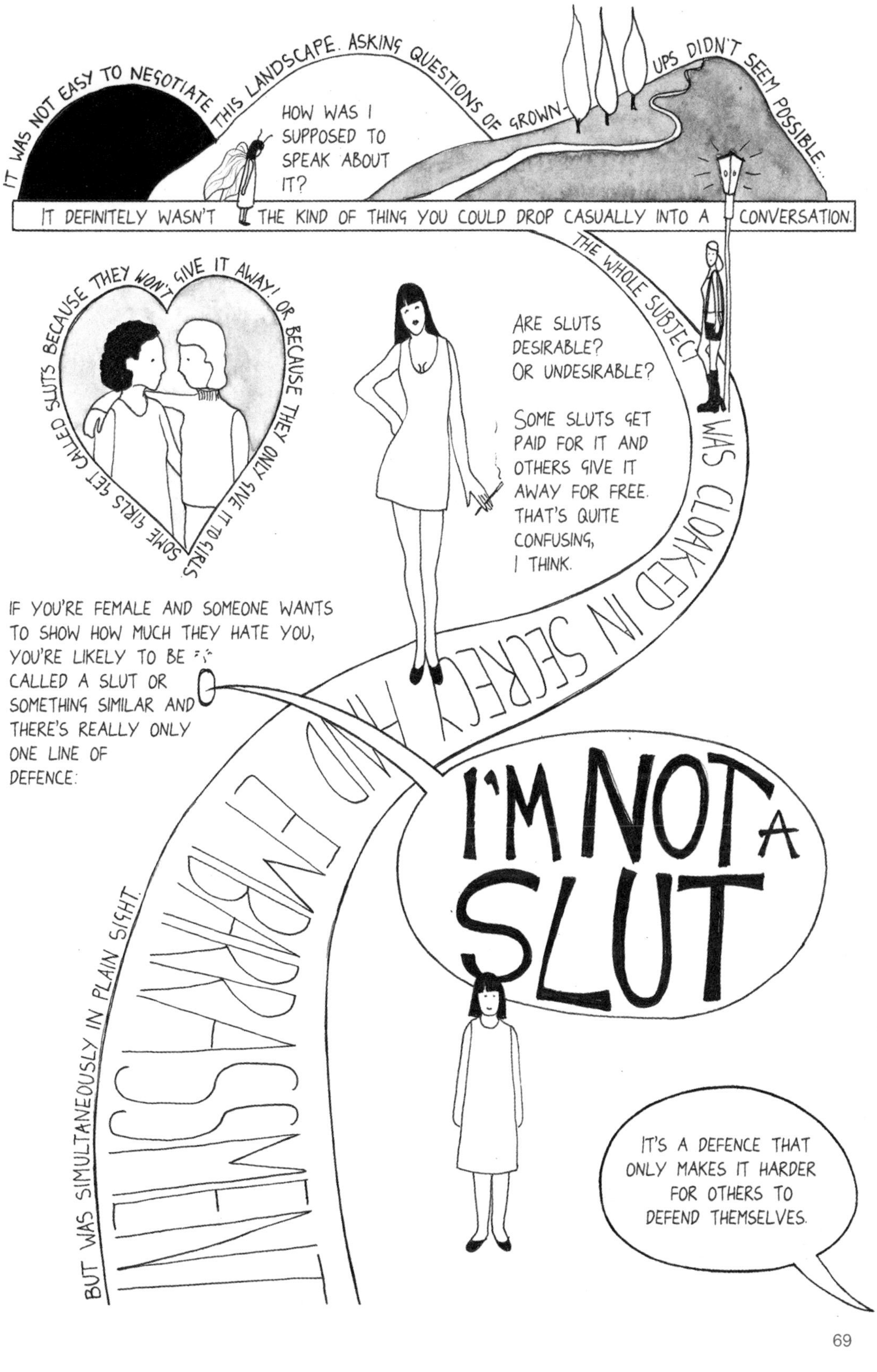
IT WAS NOT EASY TO NEGOTIATE THIS LANDSCAPE. ASKING QUESTIONS OF GROWN-UPS DIDN'T SEEM POSSIBLE...
HOW WAS I SUPPOSED TO SPEAK ABOUT IT?
IT DEFINITELY WASN'T THE KIND OF THING YOU COULD DROP CASUALLY INTO A CONVERSATION.
SOME GIRLS GET CALLED SLUTS BECAUSE THEY WON'T GIVE IT AWAY! OR BECAUSE THEY ONLY GIVE IT TO GIRLS
ARE SLUTS DESIRABLE? OR UNDESIRABLE?
SOME SLUTS GET PAID FOR IT AND OTHERS GIVE IT AWAY FOR FREE. THAT'S QUITE CONFUSING, I THINK.
THE WHOLE SUBJECT WAS CLOAKED IN SECRECY AND EMBARRASSMENT
BUT WAS SIMULTANEOUSLY IN PLAIN SIGHT.
IF YOU'RE FEMALE AND SOMEONE WANTS TO SHOW HOW MUCH THEY HATE YOU, YOU'RE LIKELY TO BE CALLED A SLUT OR SOMETHING SIMILAR AND THERE'S REALLY ONLY ONE LINE OF DEFENCE:
I'M NOT A SLUT
IT'S A DEFENCE THAT ONLY MAKES IT HARDER FOR OTHERS TO DEFEND THEMSELVES.

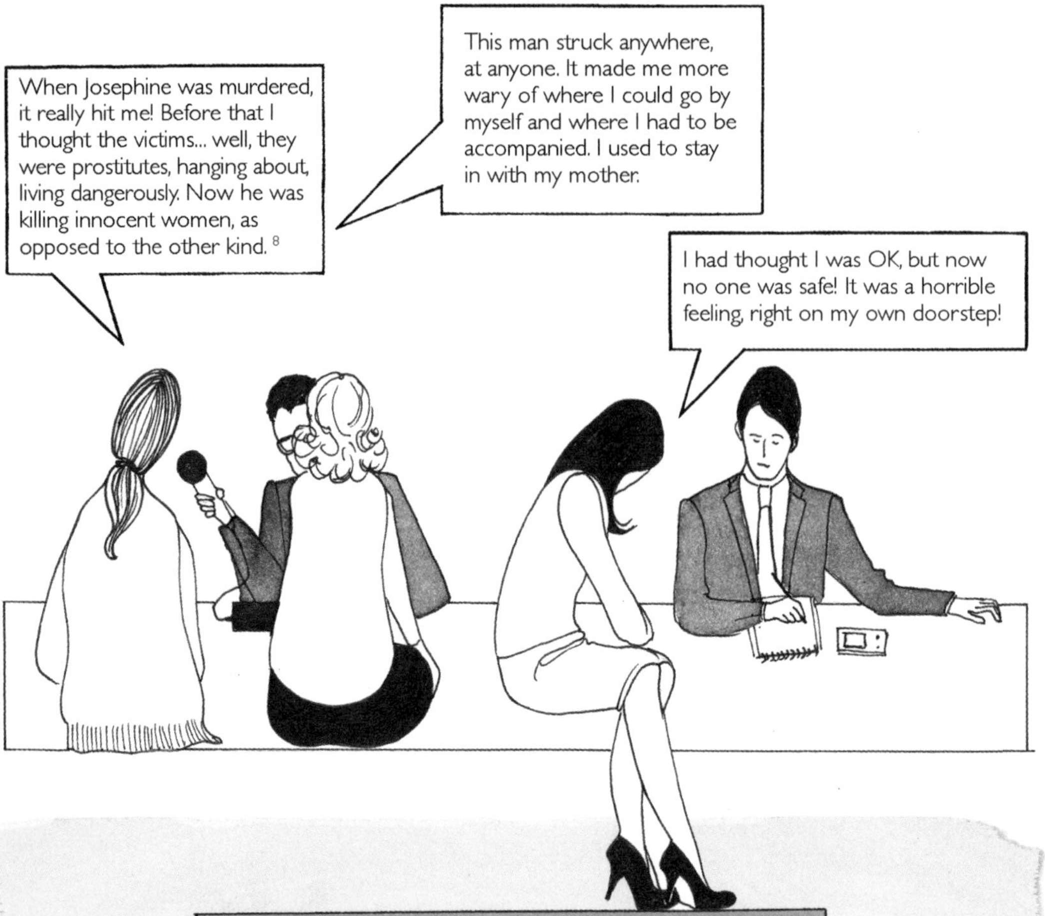
When Josephine was murdered, it really hit me! Before that I thought the victims... well, they were prostitutes, hanging about, living dangerously. Now he was killing innocent women, as opposed to the other kind. [8]
This man struck anywhere, at anyone. It made me more wary of where I could go by myself and where I had to be accompanied. I used to stay in with my mother.
I had thought I was OK, but now no one was safe! It was a horrible feeling, right on my own doorstep!

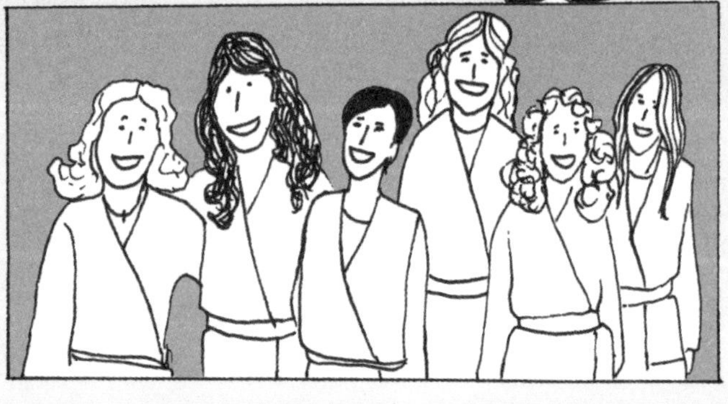

Fear that they might be attacked by the Yorkshire Ripper has prompted these Leeds girls to join a karate club. They are from the left: Sarah Cook (16), Naomi Horseman (15), Emma Baker (15), Louise Butcher (16), Sandra Butcher (15) and Angela Driver (16)

While the killer, who has already claimed ten victims, is at large, many women feel afraid to walk alone at night. 'There is no doubt the girls first joined us because they were frightened of the Ripper,' said instructor Mr Mick Green (29). Within a few weeks, the girls have been taught how to throw an opponent much bigger and stronger than themselves and also how to withstand a knife attack. 'Now they find that at the same time as teaching them self defence, it gives them a general feeling of confidence.'

WE ARE LOOKING FOR A VERY STRANGE MAN

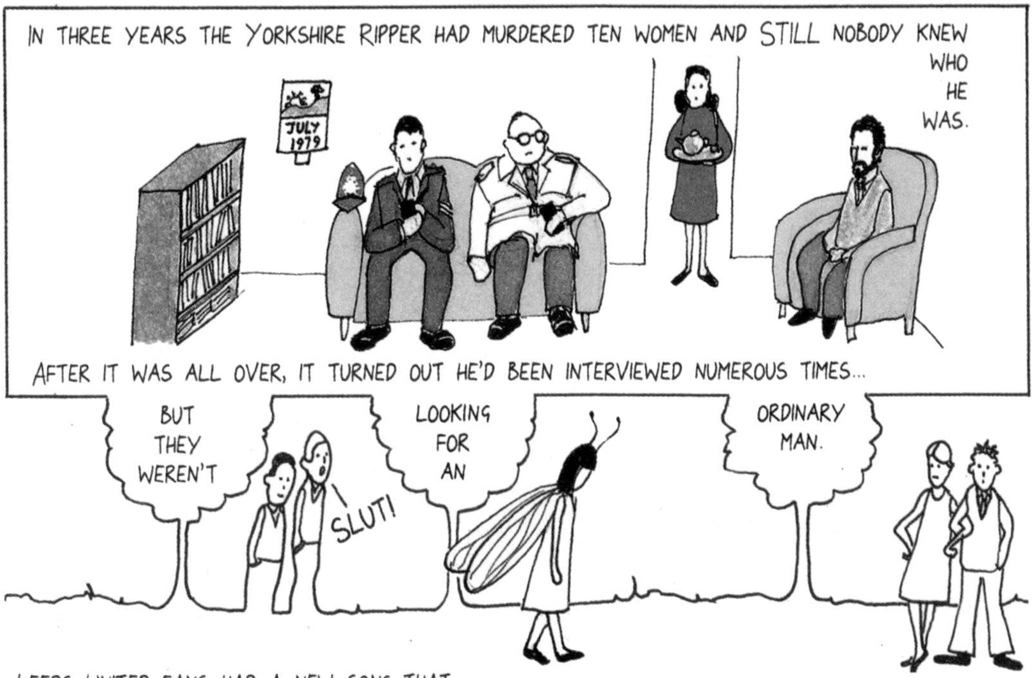
IN THREE YEARS THE YORKSHIRE RIPPER HAD MURDERED TEN WOMEN AND STILL NOBODY KNEW WHO HE WAS.
JULY 1979
AFTER IT WAS ALL OVER, IT TURNED OUT HE'D BEEN INTERVIEWED NUMEROUS TIMES...
BUT THEY WEREN'T
SLUT!
LOOKING FOR AN
ORDINARY MAN.

LEEDS UNITED FANS HAD A NEW SONG THAT BOYS USED TO SING ON THE WAY TO SCHOOL. TRY IT TO THE TUNE OF *GUANTANAMERA*! IT'S QUITE CATCHY!

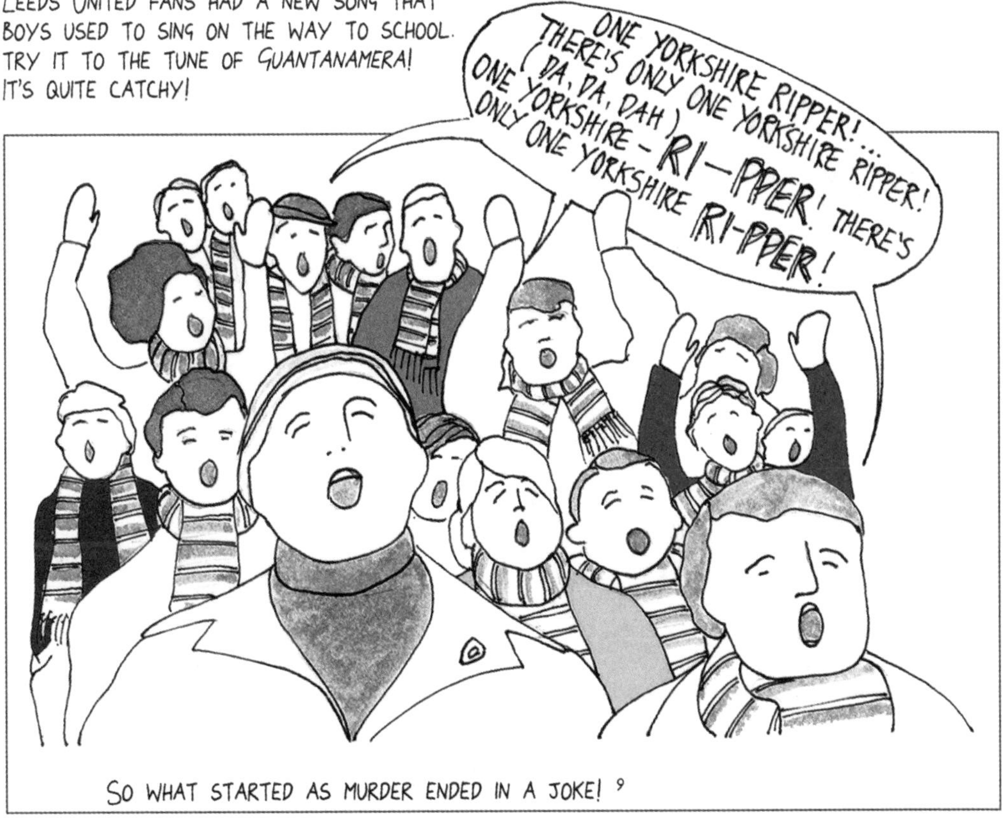
ONE YORKSHIRE RIPPER!... THERE'S ONLY ONE YORKSHIRE RIPPER! (DA, DA, DAH) ONE YORKSHIRE - RI-PPER! THERE'S ONLY ONE YORKSHIRE RI-PPER!
SO WHAT STARTED AS MURDER ENDED IN A JOKE! [9]

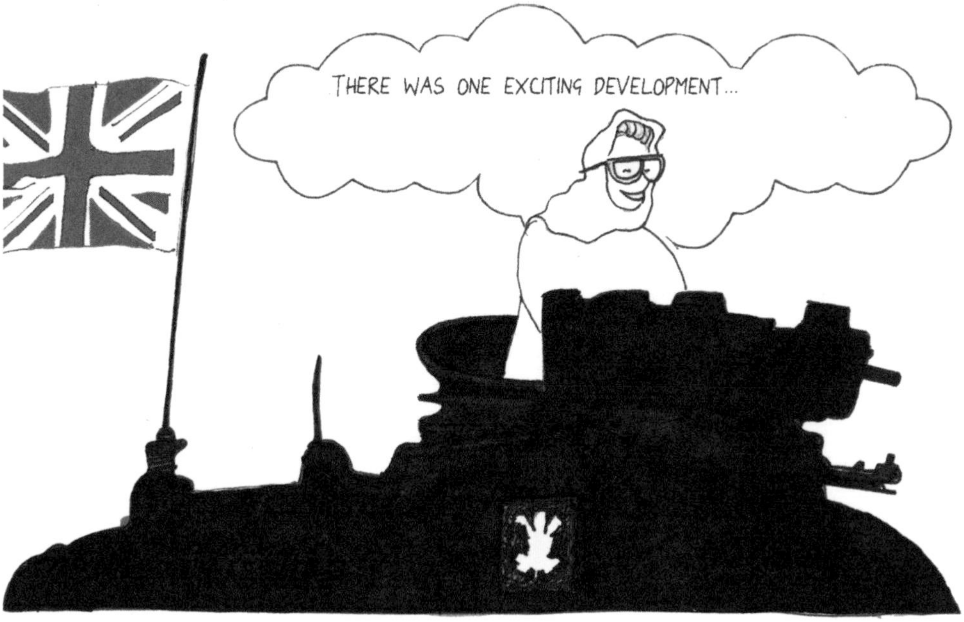
THERE WAS ONE EXCITING DEVELOPMENT...

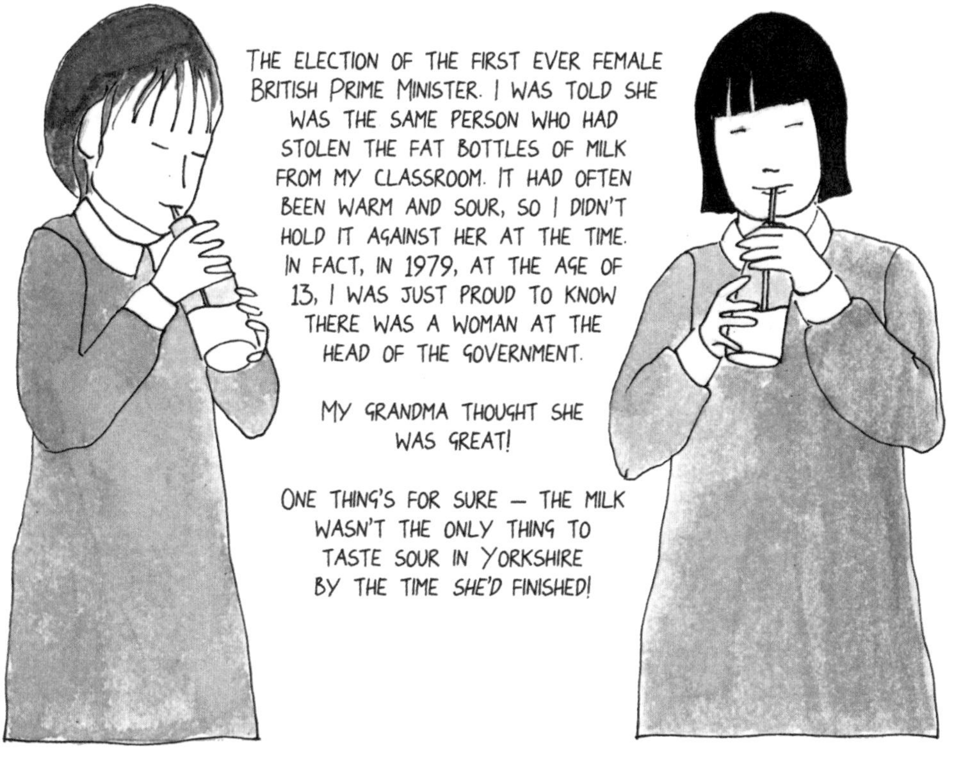
THE ELECTION OF THE FIRST EVER FEMALE BRITISH PRIME MINISTER. I WAS TOLD SHE WAS THE SAME PERSON WHO HAD STOLEN THE FAT BOTTLES OF MILK FROM MY CLASSROOM. IT HAD OFTEN BEEN WARM AND SOUR, SO I DIDN'T HOLD IT AGAINST HER AT THE TIME. IN FACT, IN 1979, AT THE AGE OF 13, I WAS JUST PROUD TO KNOW THERE WAS A WOMAN AT THE HEAD OF THE GOVERNMENT.
MY GRANDMA THOUGHT SHE WAS GREAT!
ONE THING'S FOR SURE – THE MILK WASN'T THE ONLY THING TO TASTE SOUR IN YORKSHIRE BY THE TIME *SHE'D* FINISHED!

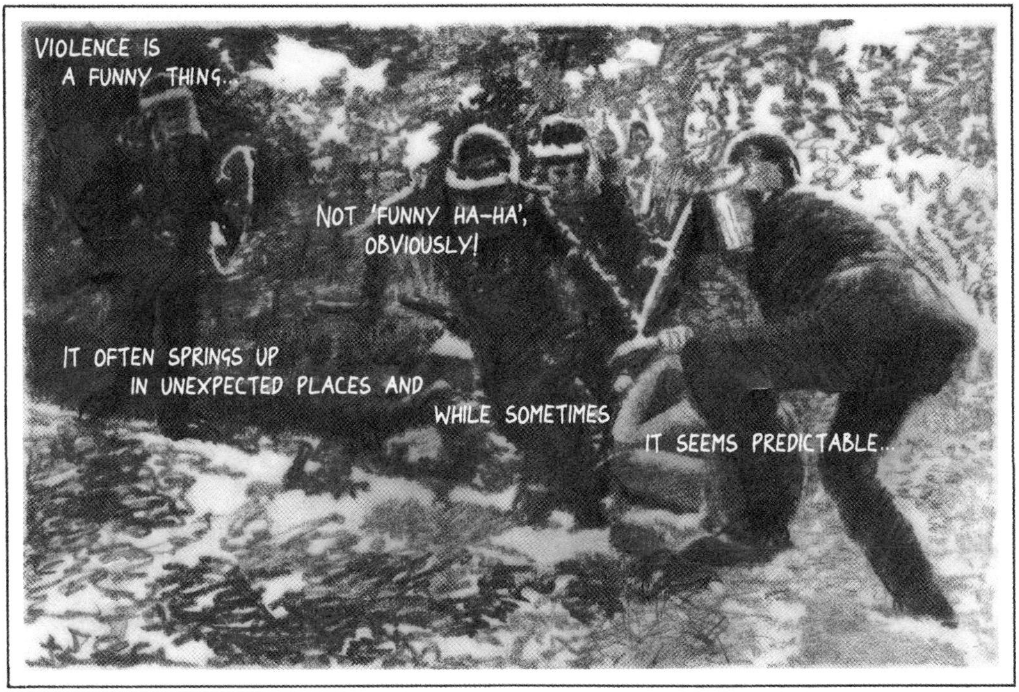
VIOLENCE IS A FUNNY THING...
NOT 'FUNNY HA-HA', OBVIOUSLY!
IT OFTEN SPRINGS UP IN UNEXPECTED PLACES AND
WHILE SOMETIMES
IT SEEMS PREDICTABLE...

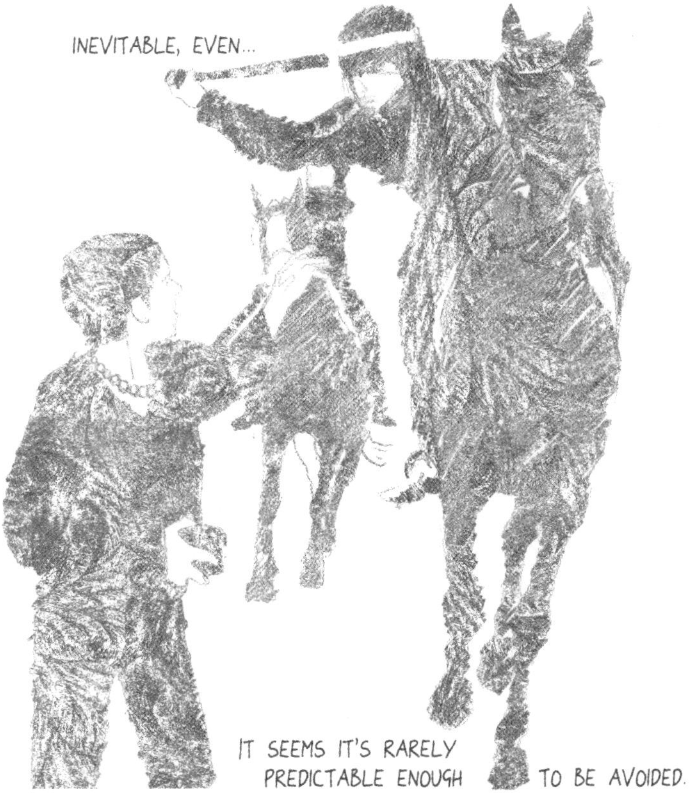
INEVITABLE, EVEN...
IT SEEMS IT'S RARELY PREDICTABLE ENOUGH
TO BE AVOIDED.

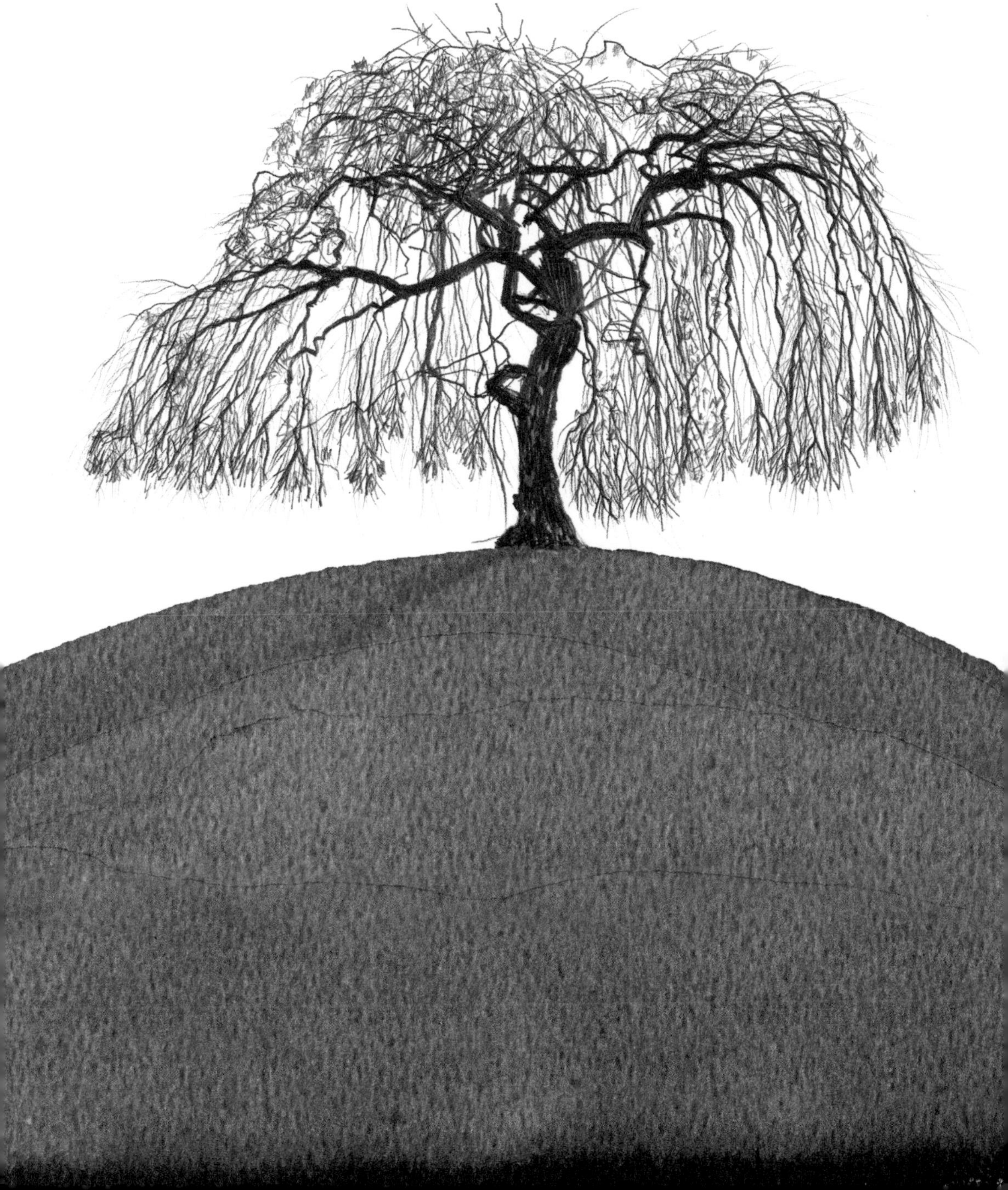

WHEN I WAS ABOUT 14, I WAS SENT TO SEE A PSYCHIATRIST.

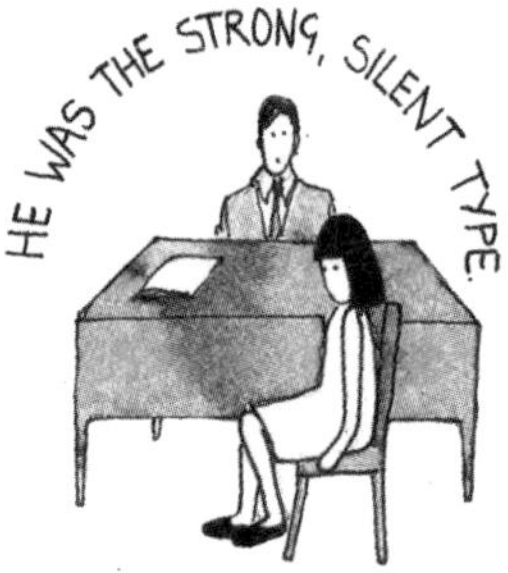
HE WAS THE STRONG, SILENT TYPE.

HE SAT BEHIND A DESK AND DIDN'T SPEAK.
I DIDN'T SAY MUCH EITHER.

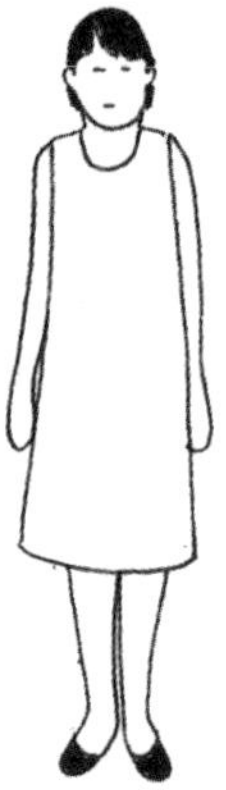

SO I WAS SENT TO SEE ANOTHER ONE.
I DIDN'T SAY MUCH MORE.

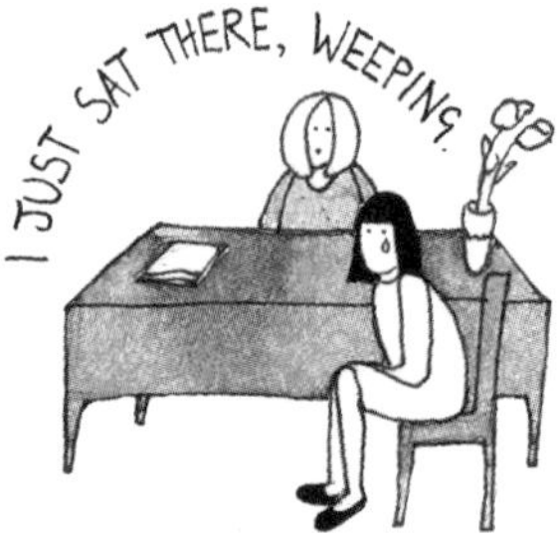
I JUST SAT THERE, WEEPING.

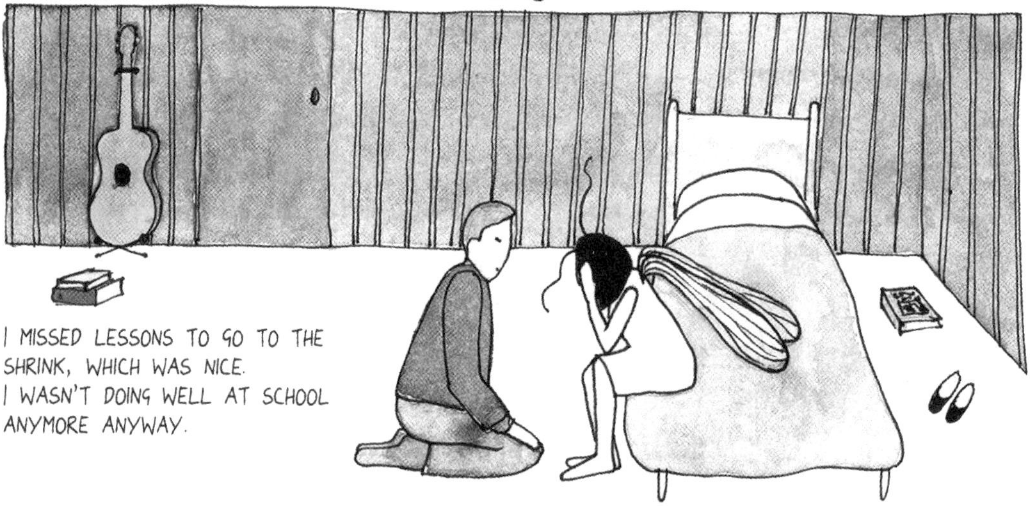

I MISSED LESSONS TO GO TO THE SHRINK, WHICH WAS NICE.
I WASN'T DOING WELL AT SCHOOL ANYMORE ANYWAY.

NO ONE COULD FIND ANYTHING SPECIFIC WRONG WITH ME, NOT SOMETHING THAT COULD BE TREATED BY A PSYCHIATRIST, ANYHOW. PEOPLE WERE KEEN TO WORK OUT WHAT THE PROBLEM WAS, BUT NO ONE GUESSED OR ASKED THE RIGHT QUESTIONS, EVEN WHEN THEY WERE BEING KIND, WHICH WASN'T OFTEN.

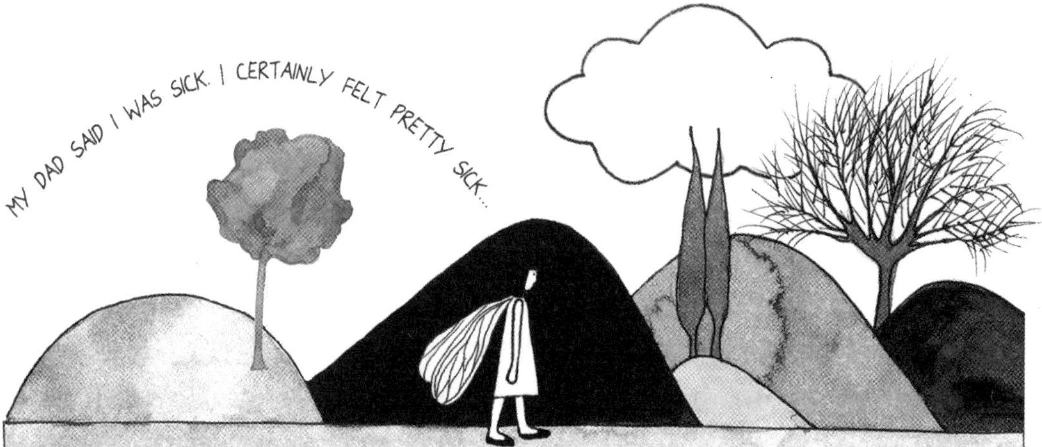
MY DAD SAID I WAS SICK. I CERTAINLY FELT PRETTY SICK...

BUT IT DIDN'T SEEM LIKE OTHER SICKNESSES I'D HAD – THIS MADE PEOPLE *REALLY* ANGRY!

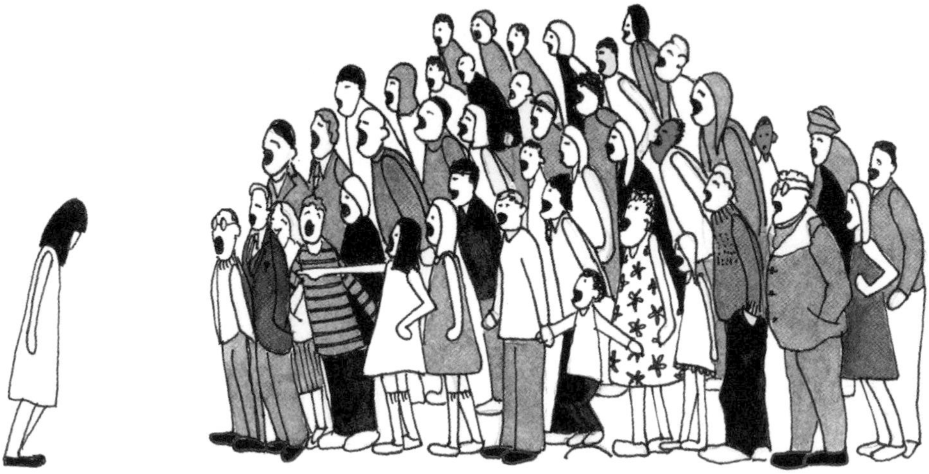

EVERYONE WAS IN AGREEMENT... THERE WAS A PROBLEM AND IT WAS LOCATED IN ME.

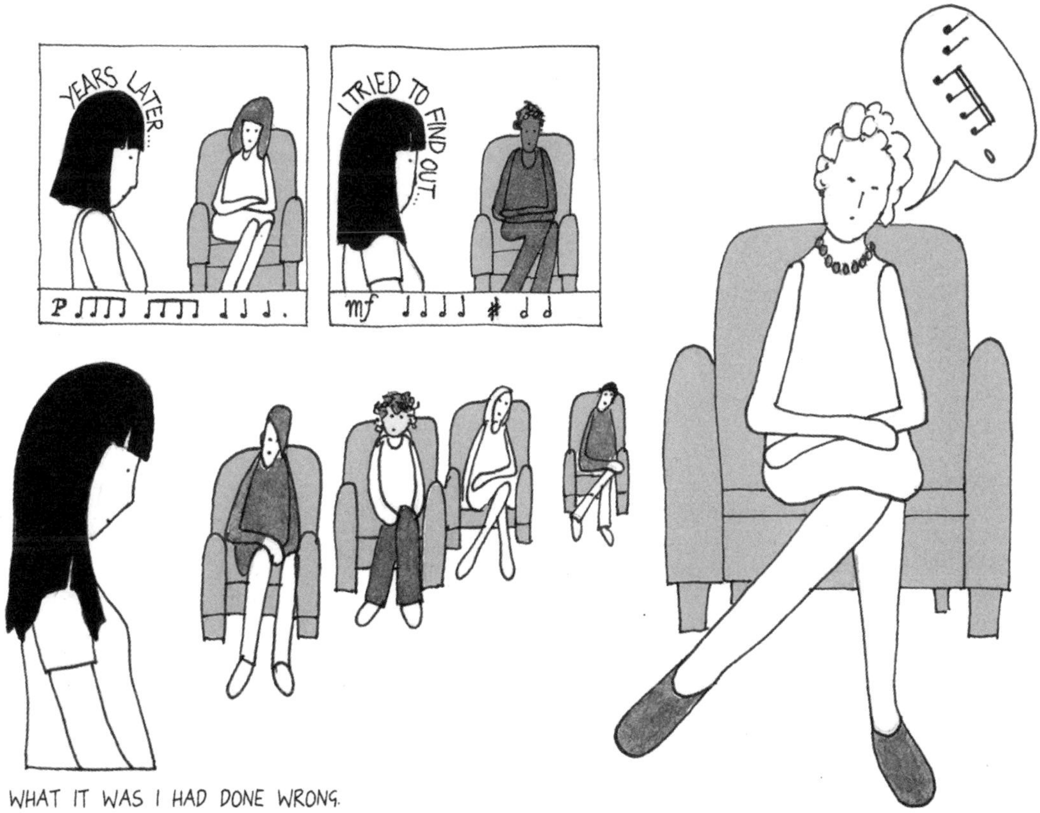
YEARS LATER...
I TRIED TO FIND OUT...

WHAT IT WAS I HAD DONE WRONG.

PEOPLE *DID* TRY TO HELP ME, BUT THIS CONSISTED MAINLY OF DEMONSTRATING CONCERN ABOUT MY STATE OF MIND, MY BEHAVIOUR, OR MY SCHOOL WORK. FROM THIS I UNDERSTOOD THAT I WAS EITHER MAD, BAD, OR THICK.

I WAS PUT ON A SPECIAL REPORTING SYSTEM AT SCHOOL.

	TUES 12TH FEB			WEDS 13TH FEB
GEOGRAPHY	DIDN'T SHOW UP, COULDN'T BE FOUND	ART		WORKED WELL
BIOLOGY	?	ART		WORKED QUIETLY
BIOLOGY	? NO HOMEWORK	MATHS		0/20
ENGLISH	SOME WORK DONE	ENGLISH		MORE TASKS COMPLETED
PHYSICAL EDUCATION	DIDN'T ARRIVE	HISTORY		ABSENT

> You have a lovely smile, you should smile more.

THE SILENT SHRINK KEPT ASKING ME HOW THINGS WERE AT HOME, THEN STARING AT ME FOR 40 MINUTES.

> You're just cheapening yourself, you know.

HOWEVER I LOOKED AT IT, IT SEEMED I WAS BOTH CAUSE AND EFFECT OF THE TROUBLE. A TROUBLE THAT COULDN'T BE NAMED. I KNEW THIS WASN'T RIGHT, OR FAIR, BUT IT WAS OUT OF MY HANDS.

> How are things at home?

A QUESTION I DIDN'T KNOW HOW TO ANSWER.

THE WORDS WOULD STICK IN MY THROAT.

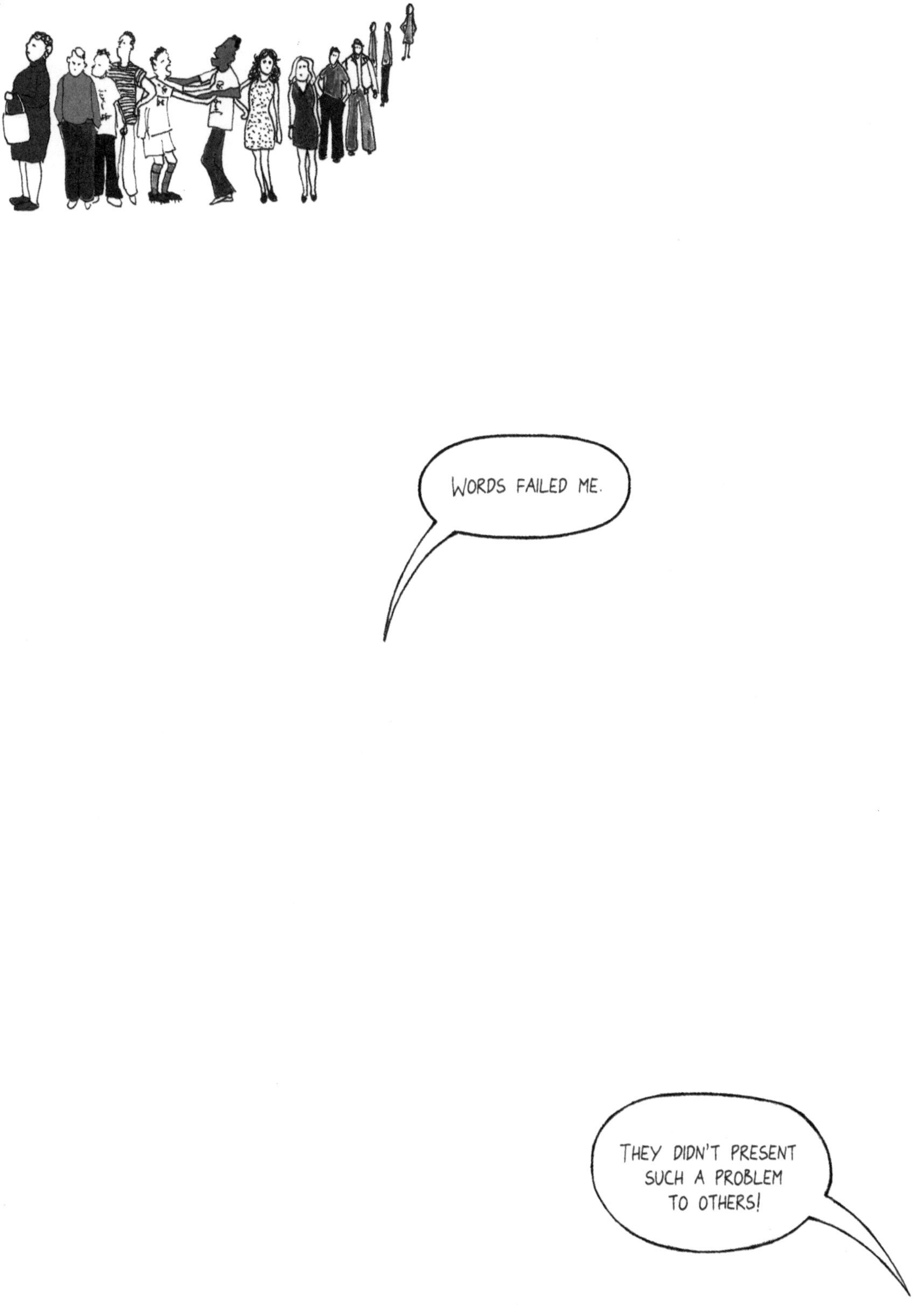
WORDS FAILED ME.
THEY DIDN'T PRESENT SUCH A PROBLEM TO OTHERS!

THE POP SONG *EMBARRASSMENT* BY MADNESS IS ABOUT THE RACIST, MISOGYNISTIC SHAMING OF A YOUNG GIRL WHO IS PREGNANT – CARRYING A MIXED RACE CHILD.

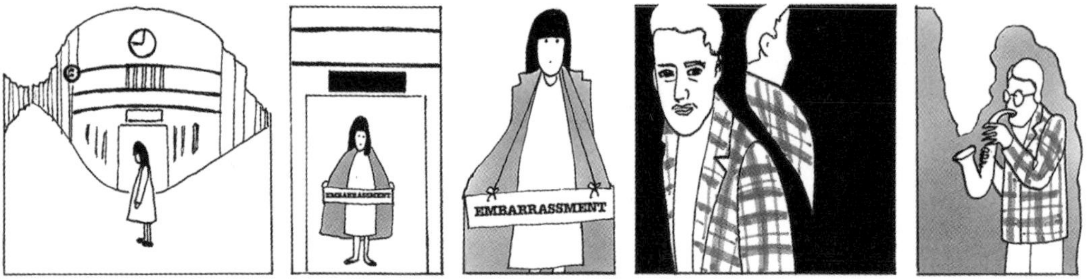
EMBARRASSMENT
EMBARRASSMENT

IT WAS SUNG BY GROUPS OF BOYS, AT SCHOOL AND ELSEWHERE, FOR THE PUBLIC HUMILIATION OF ME. HOW COULD I SHOW MY FACE, WHEN I'M A DISGRACE TO THE HUMAN RACE?

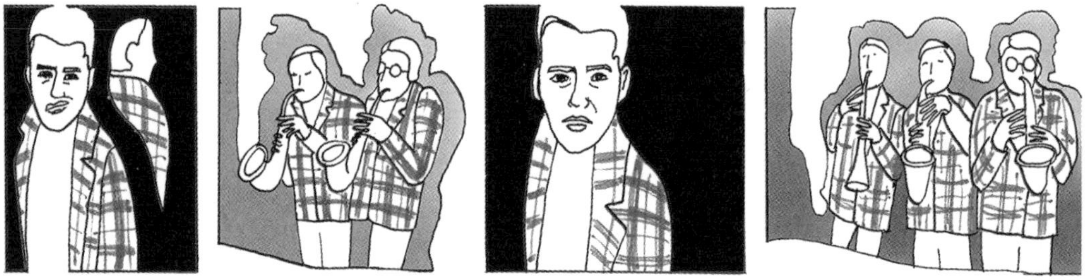

I'M FAIRLY SURE THEY WERE MISSING THE POINT OF THE SONG... BUT I SUPPOSE THEY FELT POWERFUL, JUSTIFIED – ALL TOGETHER, HATING.

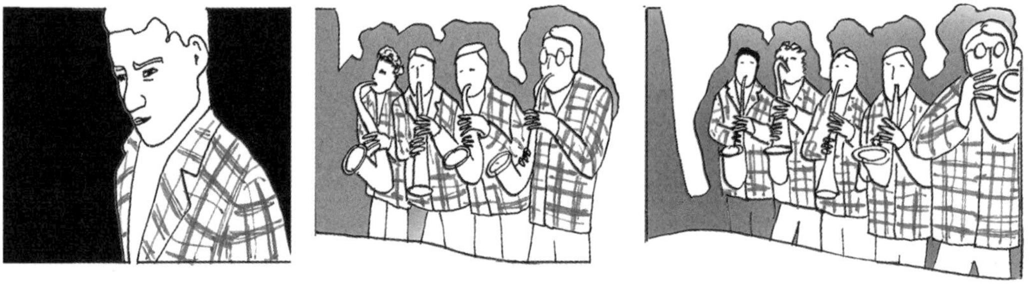

YOU'RE AN EMBARRASSMENT!

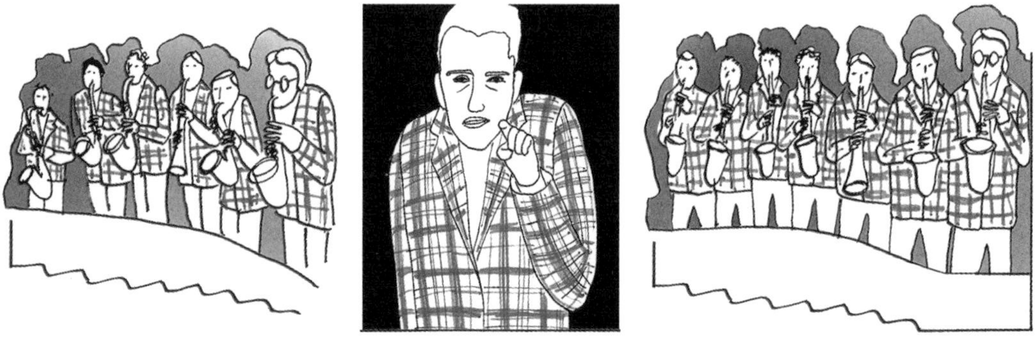

MADNESS WAS A POPULAR BAND IN 1980. I STILL CAN'T STAND THEM.

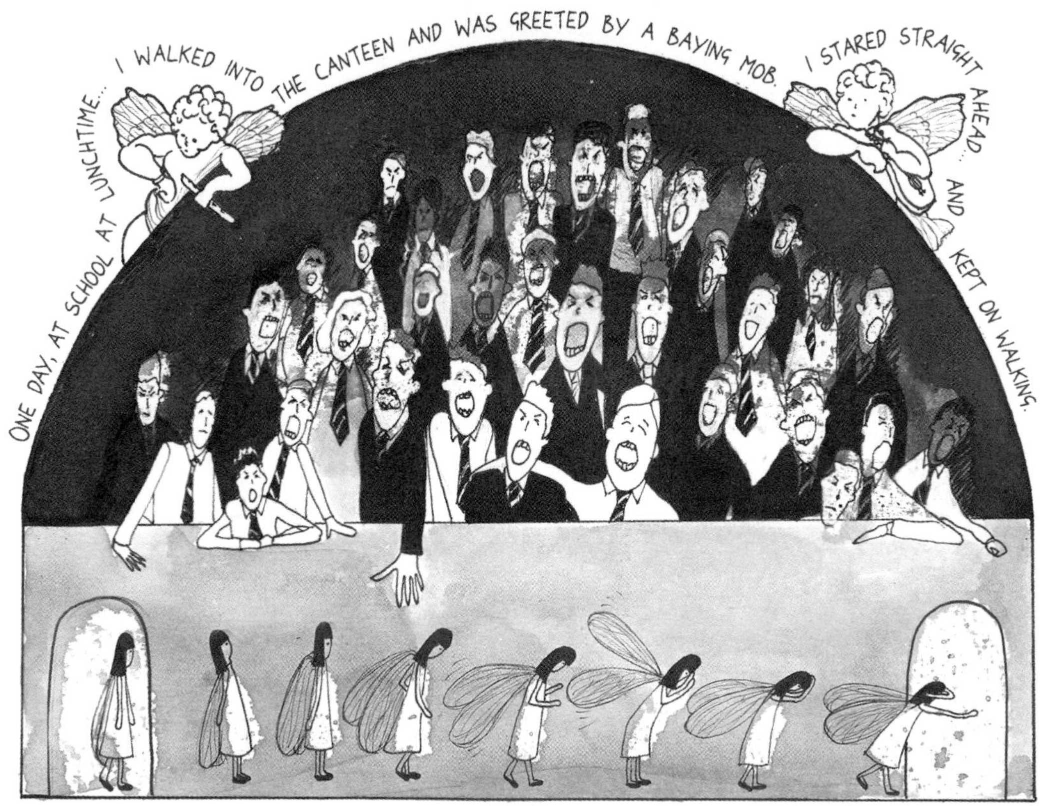
ONE DAY, AT SCHOOL AT LUNCHTIME... I WALKED INTO THE CANTEEN AND WAS GREETED BY A BAYING MOB. I STARED STRAIGHT AHEAD... AND KEPT ON WALKING.

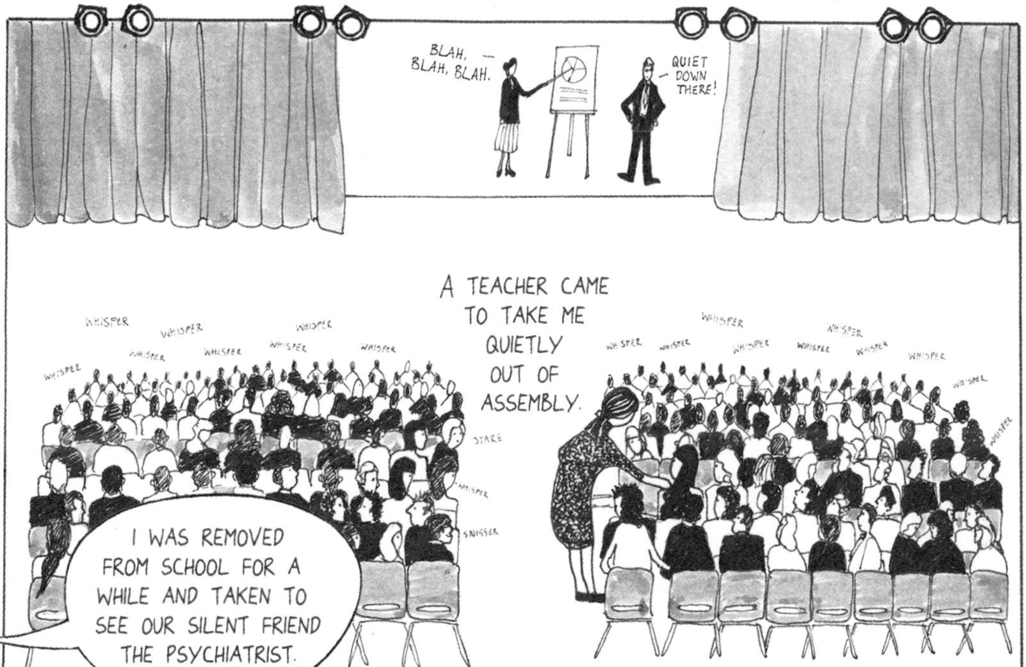
BLAH, BLAH, BLAH.
QUIET DOWN THERE!
A TEACHER CAME TO TAKE ME QUIETLY OUT OF ASSEMBLY.
I WAS REMOVED FROM SCHOOL FOR A WHILE AND TAKEN TO SEE OUR SILENT FRIEND THE PSYCHIATRIST.

SO I BECAME AN UNRELIABLE WITNESS AND A PERFECT VICTIM.

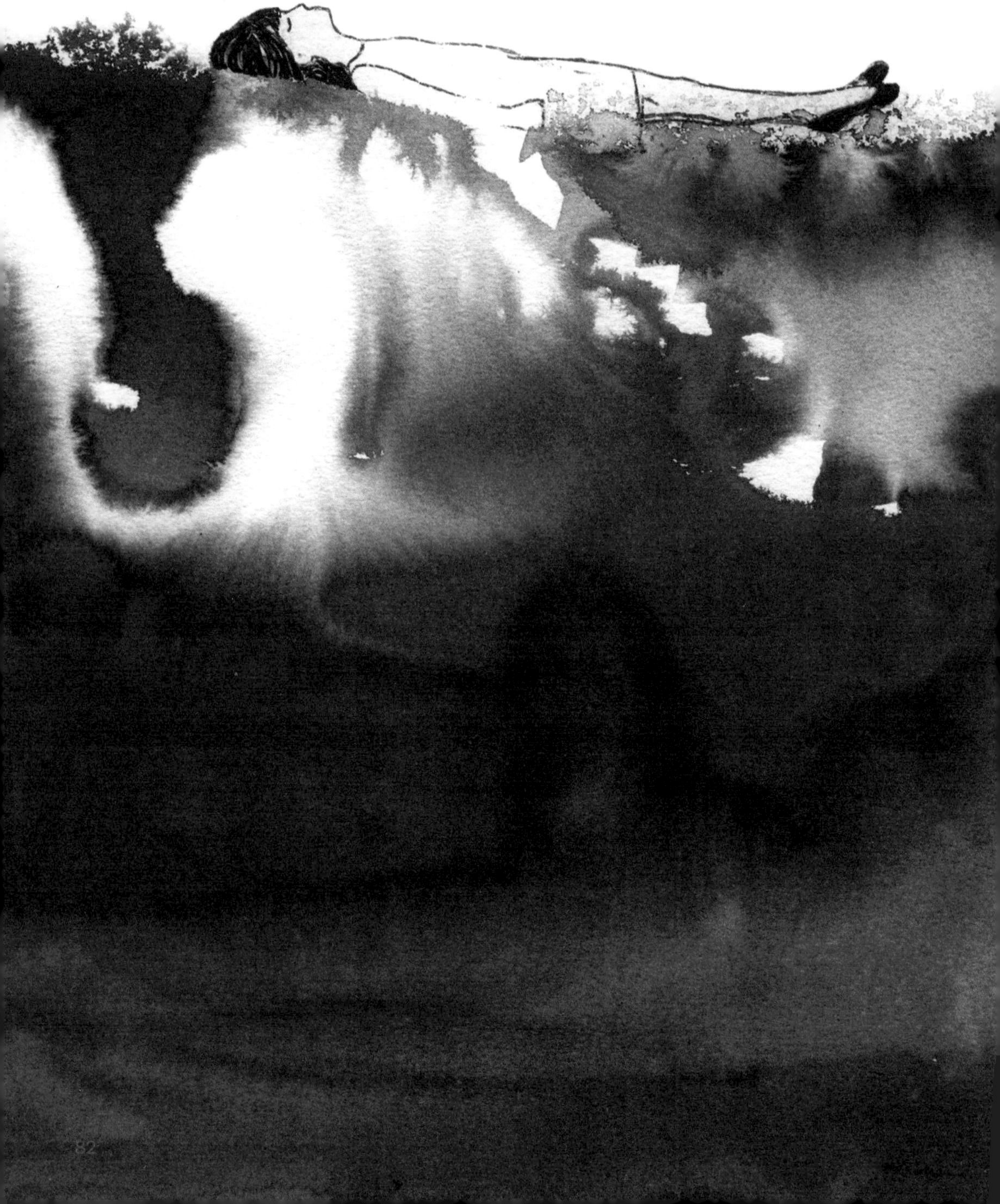

THEN ALONG CAME THEO. HE TOOK ONE LOOK AND KNEW I WAS THE ONE.

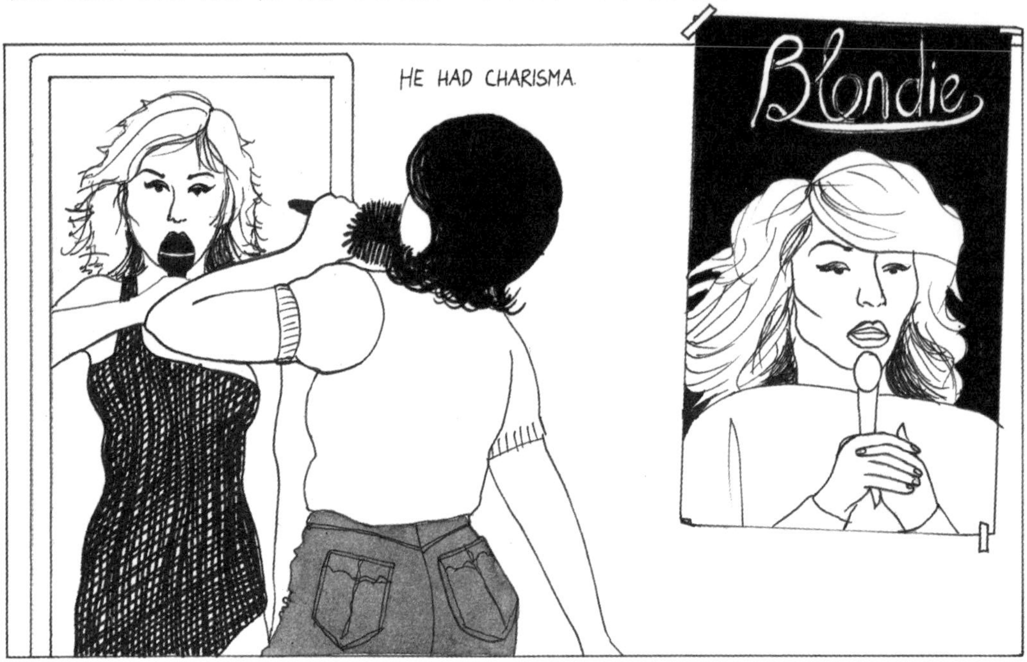
HE HAD CHARISMA.
Blondie

OTHER BOYS THOUGHT HE WAS COOL.
I THOUGHT HE LIKED ME, MAYBE EVEN LOVED ME.
HE EVEN HAD A PET NAME FOR ME!

HE WAS QUITE INTENSE...
HE USED TO ASK ME IF
I THOUGHT I MIGHT
DIE A VIOLENT
DEATH.

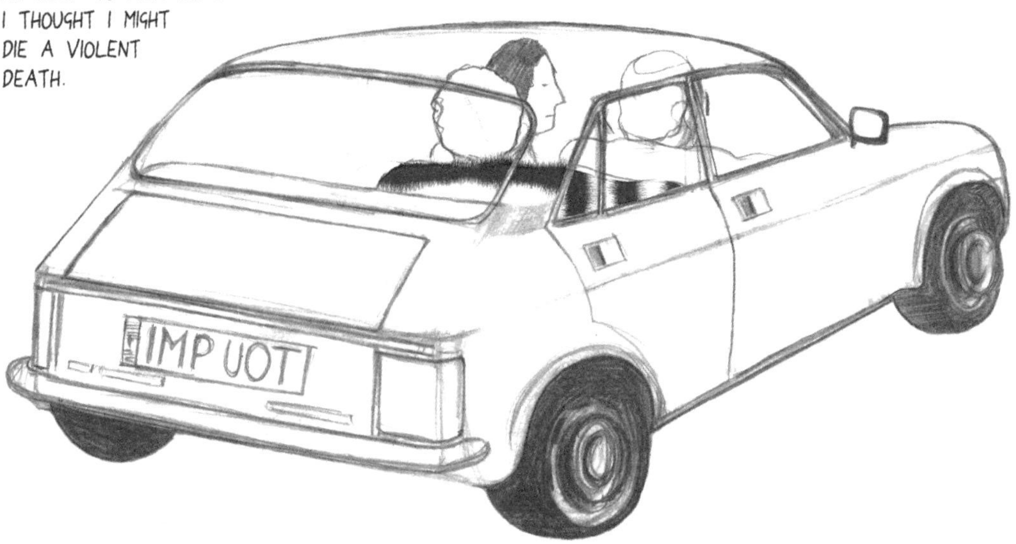
IMP UOT

BUT HE KNEW WHAT TO SAY AND WHEN TO SAY IT, TO GET WHAT HE WANTED.

THOSE WHO LIVE WITH POST-TRAUMATIC STRESS FIND SEEMINGLY RANDOM THINGS DEEPLY DISTRESSING.

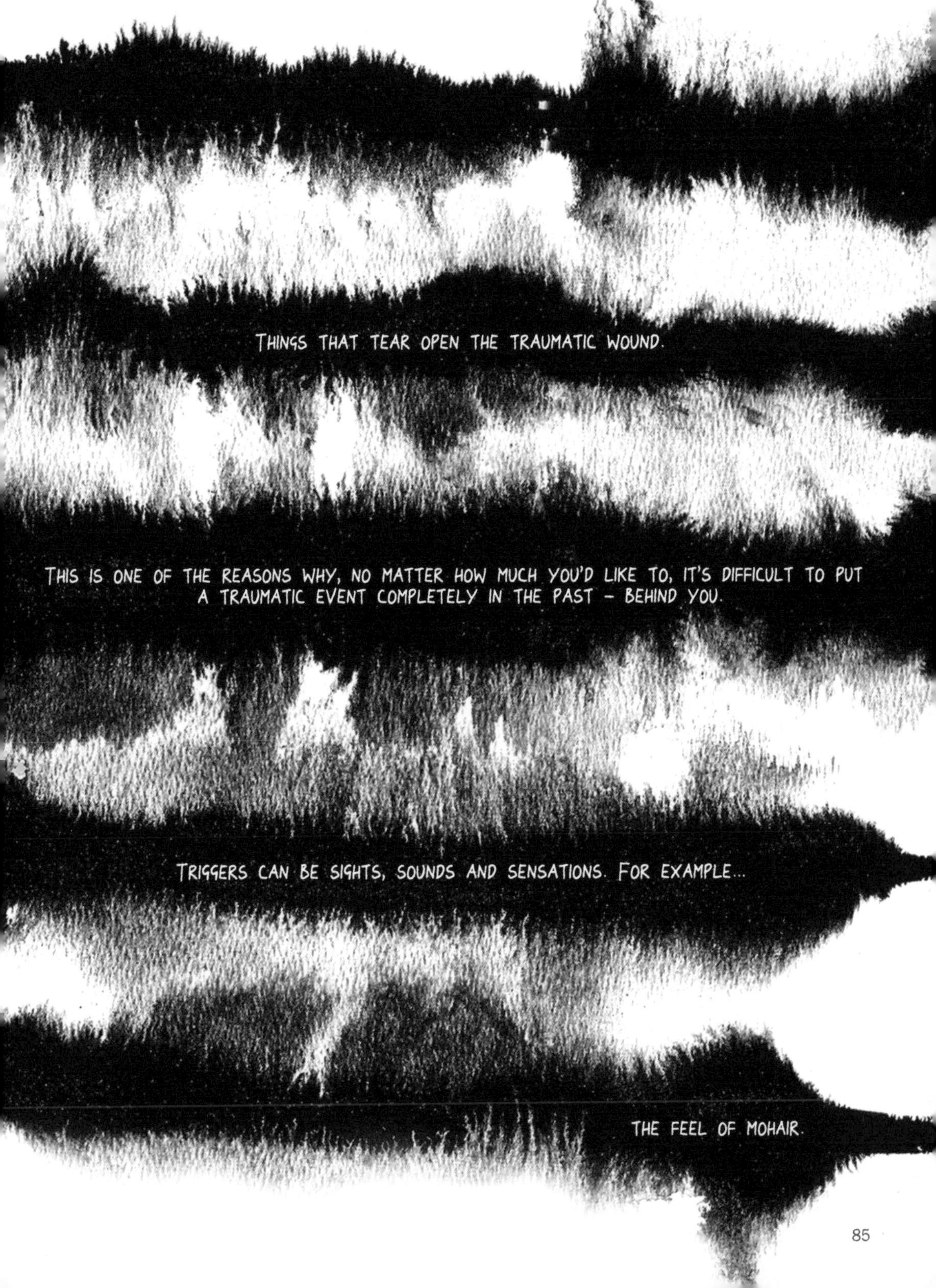
THINGS THAT TEAR OPEN THE TRAUMATIC WOUND.
THIS IS ONE OF THE REASONS WHY, NO MATTER HOW MUCH YOU'D LIKE TO, IT'S DIFFICULT TO PUT A TRAUMATIC EVENT COMPLETELY IN THE PAST - BEHIND YOU.
TRIGGERS CAN BE SIGHTS, SOUNDS AND SENSATIONS. FOR EXAMPLE...
THE FEEL OF MOHAIR.

I WASN'T SCARED AT ALL AT FIRST. HE MADE IT SEEM LIKE IT WAS ALL A BIG LAUGH...

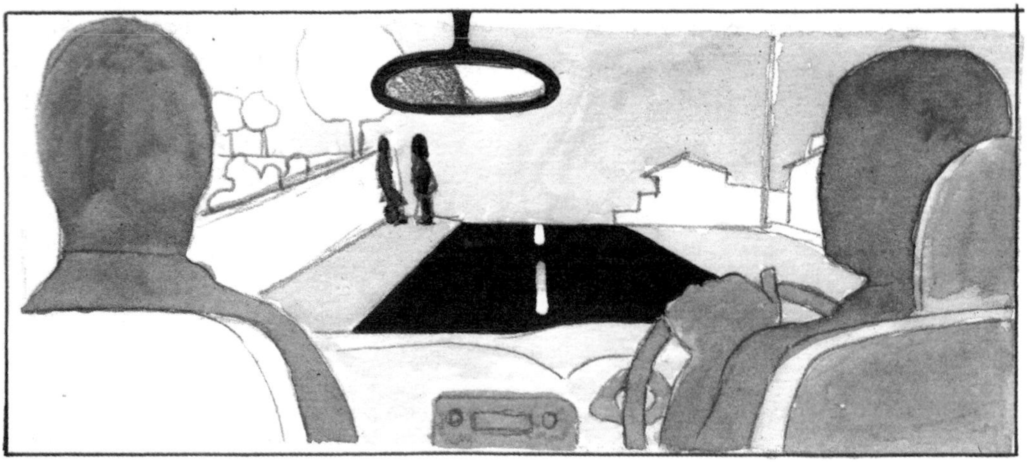

SO THAT I DIDN'T FEEL NERVOUS, OR UNCOMFORTABLE.

'COME FOR A RIDE WITH ME!'

HE SMILED AND TWINKLED AND PULLED MY ARM, LAUGHING ALL THE TIME.

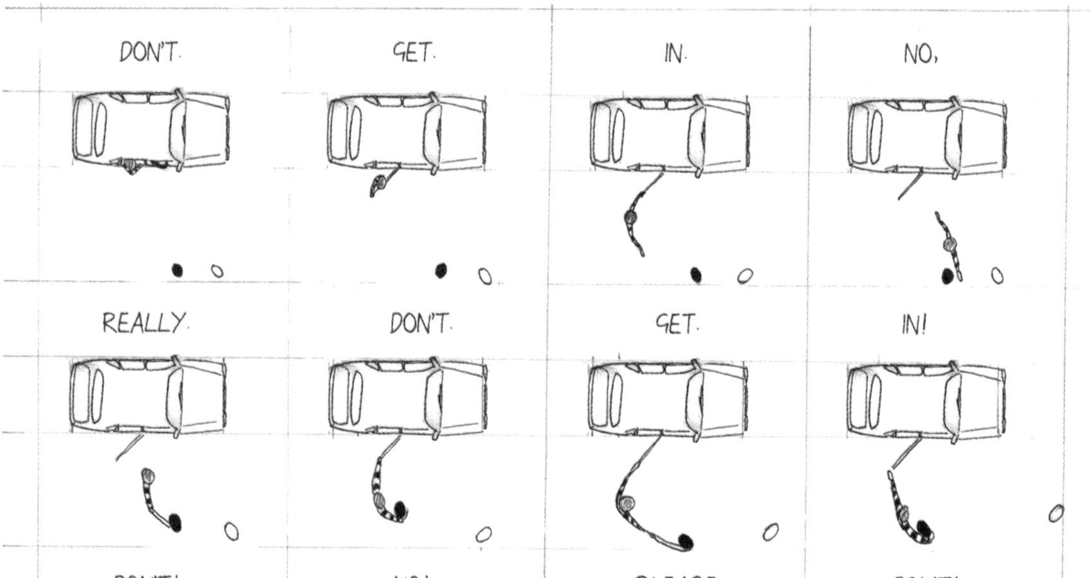

DON'T.
GET.
IN.
NO,
REALLY.
DON'T.
GET.
IN!
DON'T!
NO!
PLEASE,
DON'T!

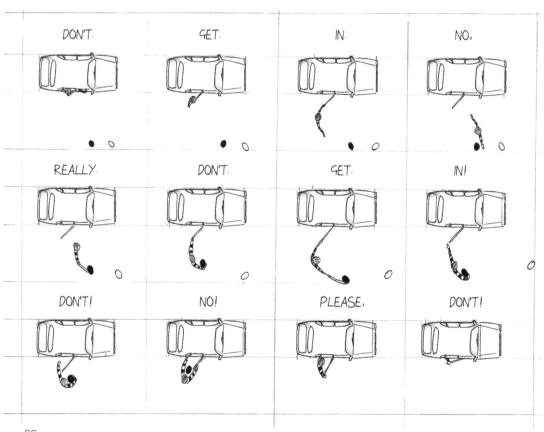

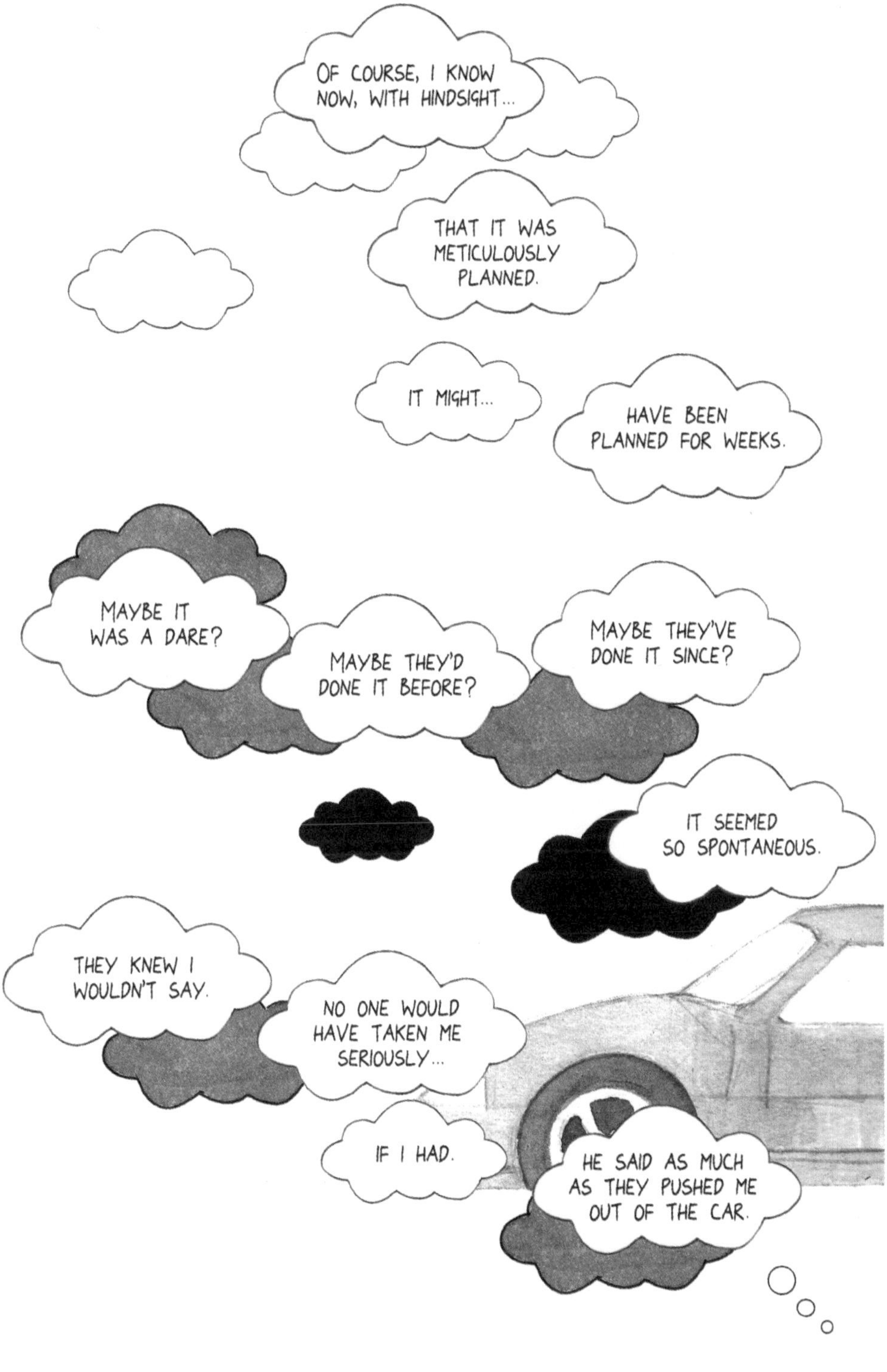
OF COURSE, I KNOW NOW, WITH HINDSIGHT...
THAT IT WAS METICULOUSLY PLANNED.
IT MIGHT...
HAVE BEEN PLANNED FOR WEEKS.
MAYBE IT WAS A DARE?
MAYBE THEY'D DONE IT BEFORE?
MAYBE THEY'VE DONE IT SINCE?
IT SEEMED SO SPONTANEOUS.
THEY KNEW I WOULDN'T SAY.
NO ONE WOULD HAVE TAKEN ME SERIOUSLY...
IF I HAD.
HE SAID AS MUCH AS THEY PUSHED ME OUT OF THE CAR.

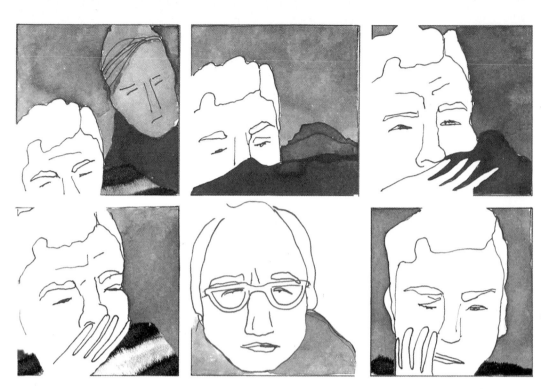

THAT DULL ACHE...
RAW, BREATHLESS HORROR.

MY FIRST RESPONSE WAS TO TRY TO PRETEND IT HADN'T HAPPENED.
IT CAN'T HAVE BEEN NOTICEABLE – NO ONE NOTICED ANYTHING.

I NOTICED SOMETHING.
A TORRENT OF WRETCHEDNESS, A GREAT WALL OF HEFTY SPACE I HAD TO PUSH THROUGH EACH DAY...
EVERY MINUTE.
A DEAFENING SILENCE, RINGING IN MY EARS AS I LURCHED FORWARD, ONWARD,
ONE FOOT IN FRONT OF THE OTHER.
HE CAME TO SEE ME A FEW DAYS AFTER, MAYBE TO JUST MAKE SURE.
I TOOK A SHOCKED SHARP BREATH WHEN I SAW HIM, STANDING THERE ON THE DOORSTEP, BUT I STILL
LET HIM IN.

HE WAS SUCH A NATURAL BASTARD, IT CAME EASILY TO HIM. I'M SURE HE'S STILL VERY PROUD OF IT.

HE EXPLAINED THAT HE HADN'T DONE ANYTHING WRONG. HE'D ONLY TAKEN WHAT WAS ALREADY HIS.
HE MADE SURE I UNDERSTOOD HE COULDN'T BE BLAMED...
AND NO ONE WOULD HAVE BLAMED HIM.

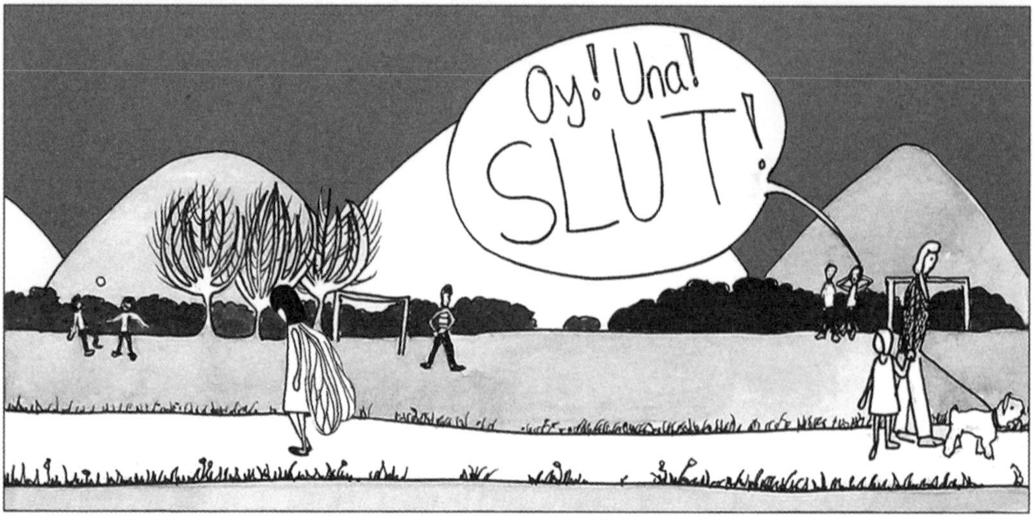
Oy! Una! SLUT!

I WAS BORN IN THE PRE-DIGITAL ERA – NO COMPUTERS, NO SMART PHONES, NO INTERNET.

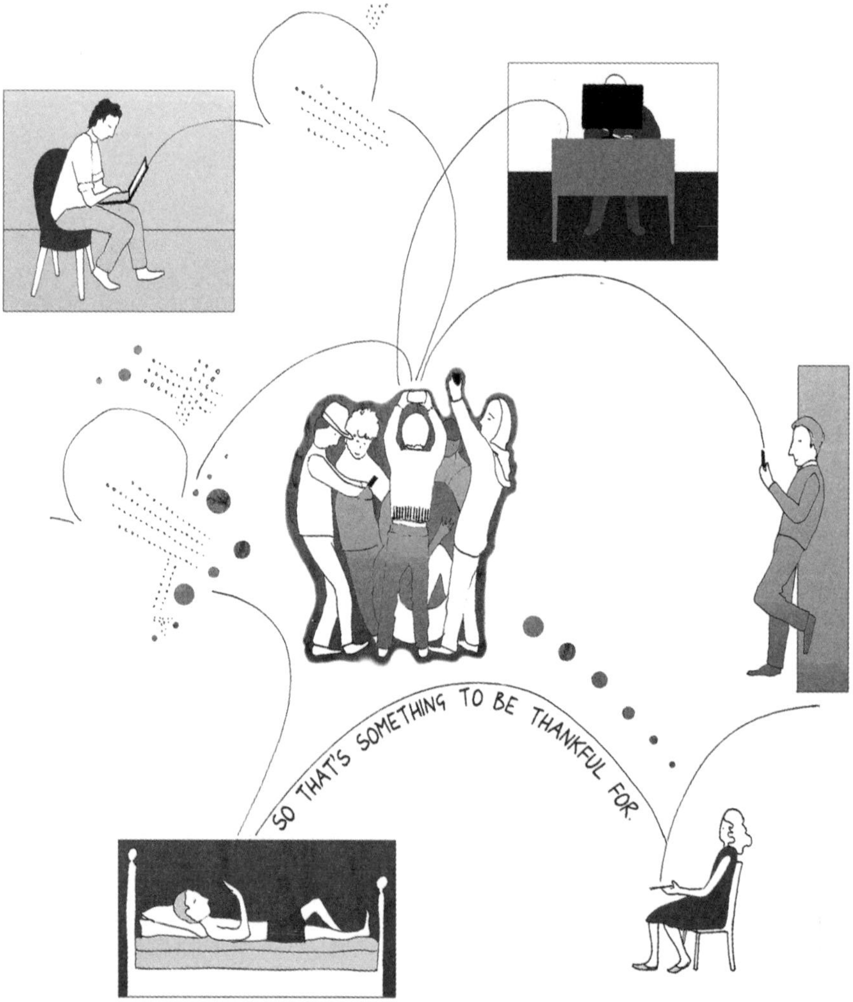
SO THAT'S SOMETHING TO BE THANKFUL FOR.

Yorkshire Post

January 1981

MAN, 40, DENIES RAPE

A 40-year-old man raped a young barmaid as she walked home early in the morning, it was alleged at Leeds Crown Court yesterday...

Barmaid tells of rape

A 27-year-old barmaid walked home alone at nights because she thought she was too plain to be attacked, a court heard yesterday...

Jury rejects rape claim

A 40-year-old man accused of raping a barmaid was found not guilty yesterday after telling Leeds Crown Court that everything he had done had been with her consent...

IT DIDN'T EVEN OCCUR TO ME TO REPORT IT, BUT IT DID OCCUR TO ME THAT...

THEY WOULDN'T HAVE DONE IT IF I HADN'T BEEN SUCH A SLUT.

I WAS SO ALONE.

THE THING ABOUT RECURRING NIGHTMARES IS THAT THEY DEVELOP OVER TIME. I FIRST STARTED HAVING MY DREAM WHEN I WAS ABOUT TEN YEARS OLD. I WAS BEING PURSUED BY SOMETHING UNSEEN...

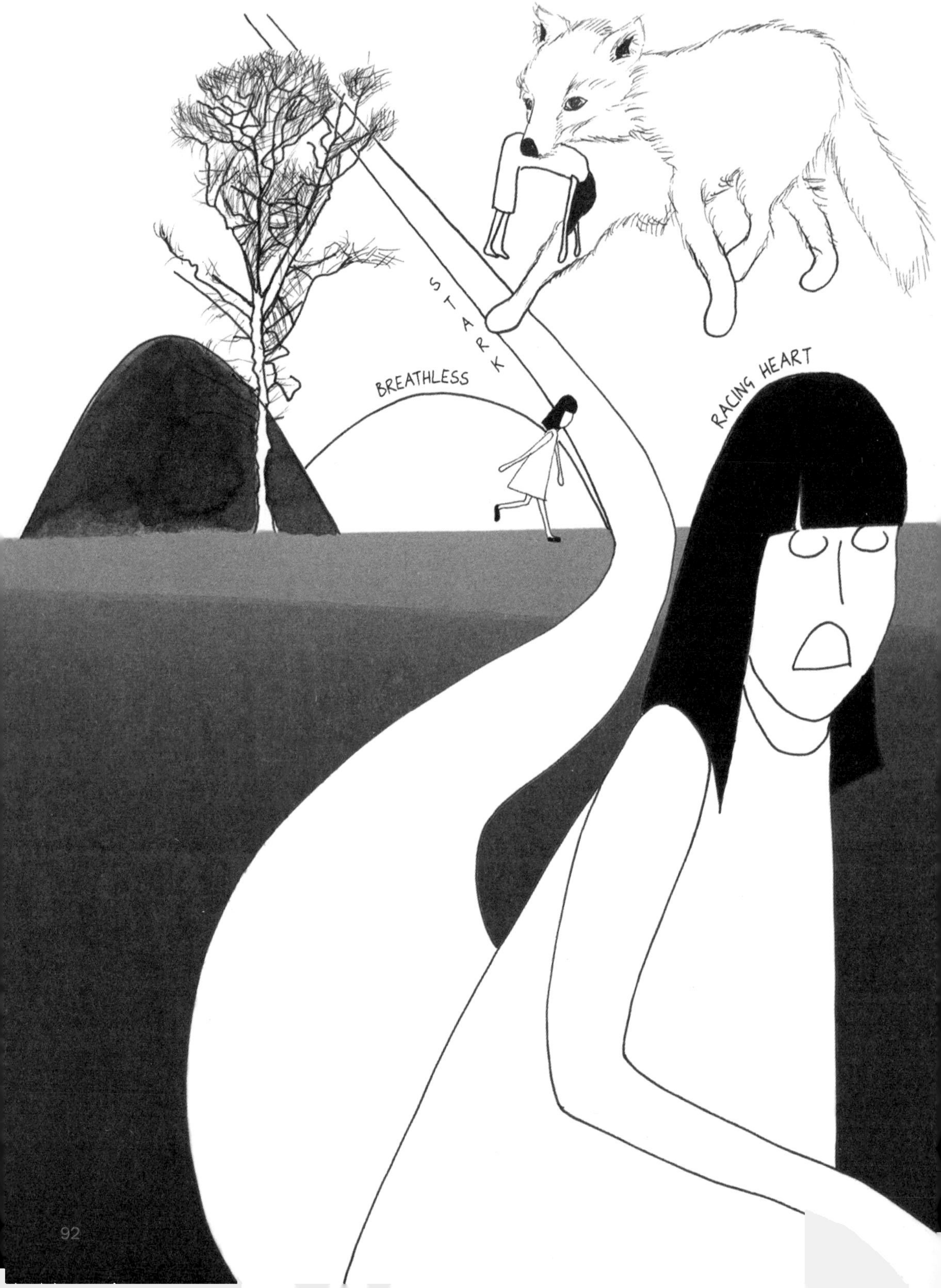
STARK
BREATHLESS
RACING HEART

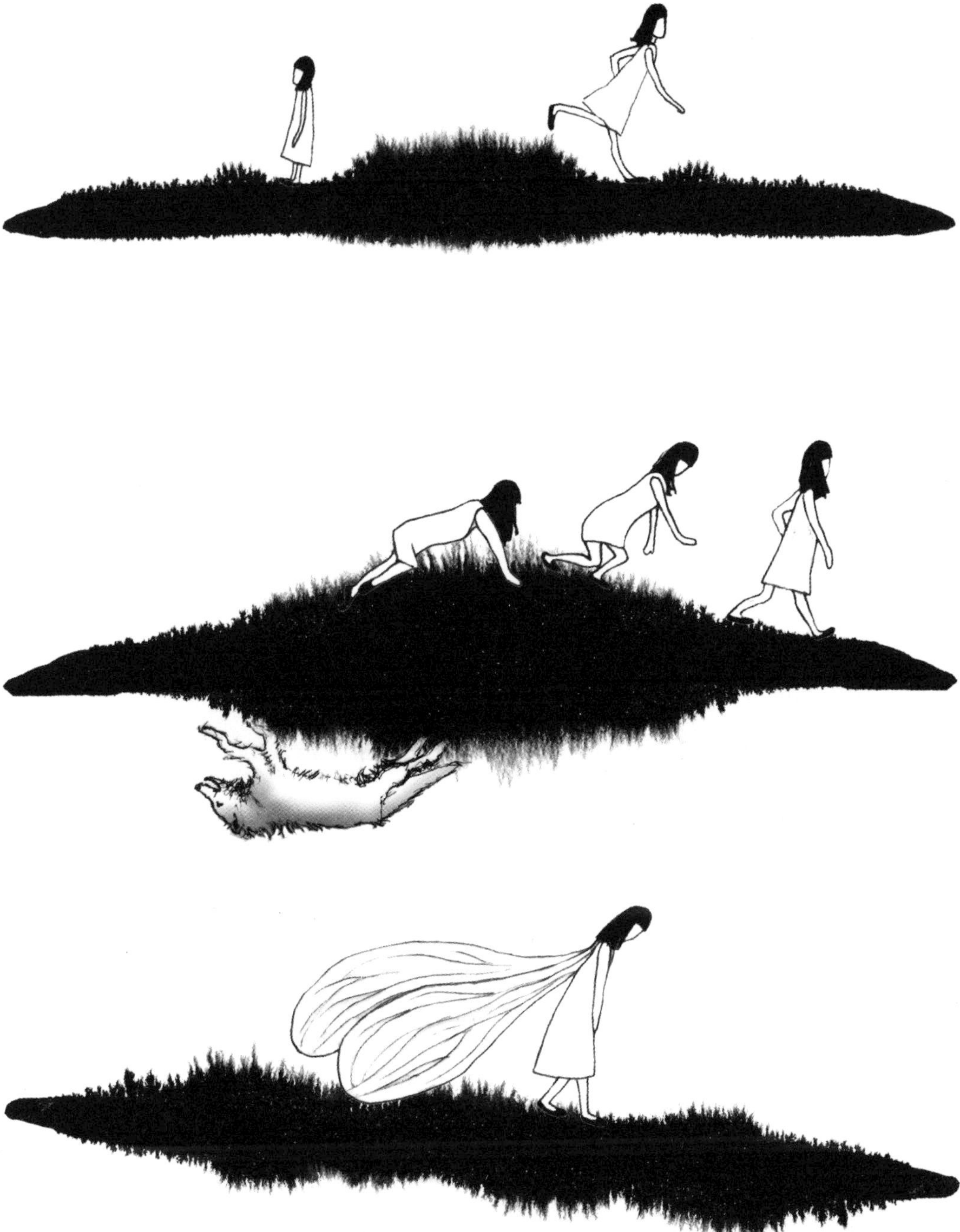

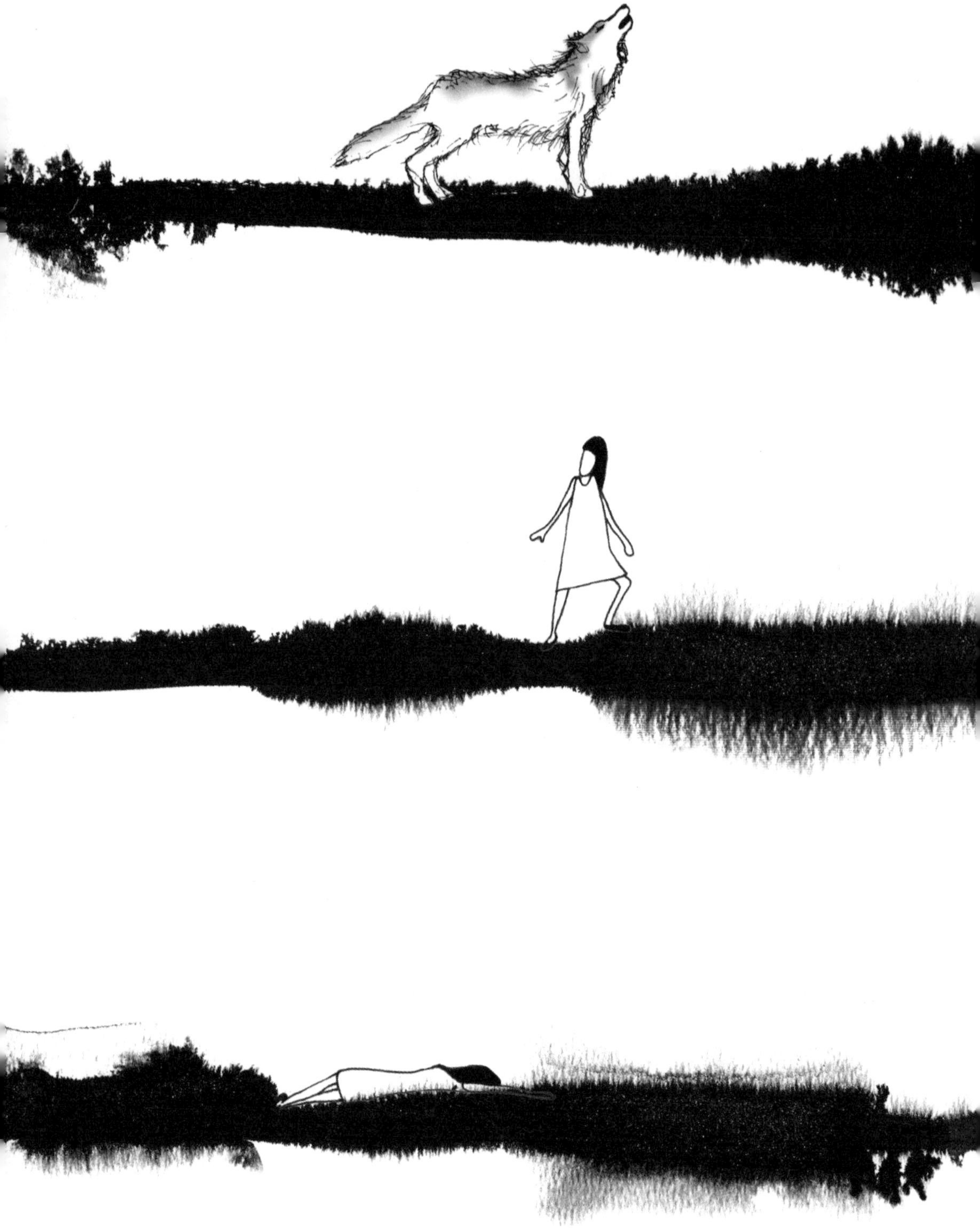

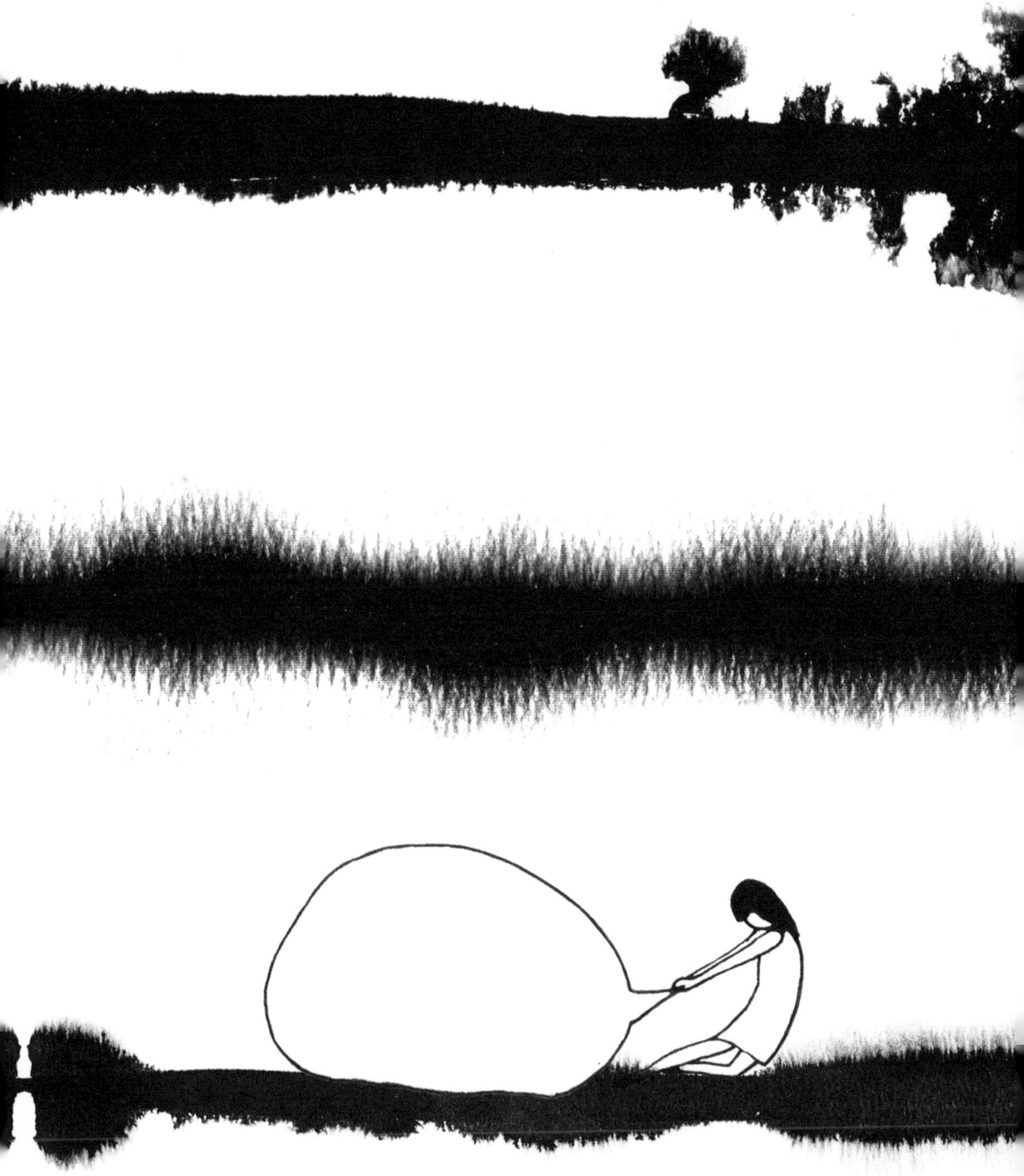

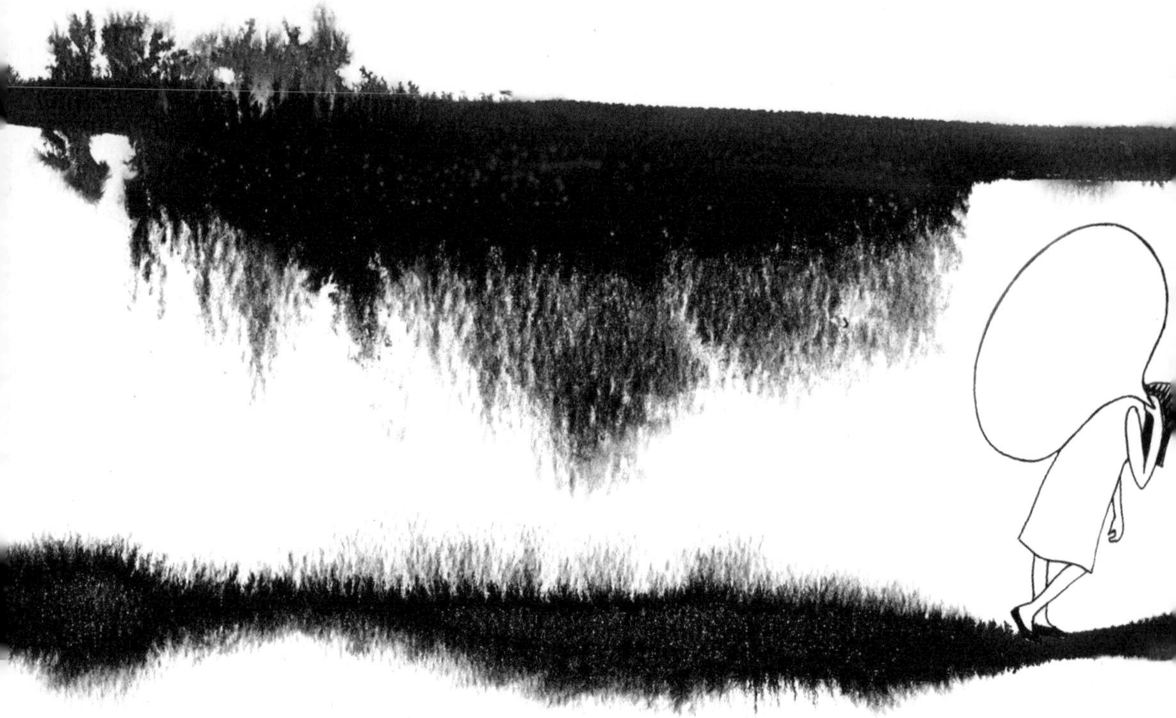

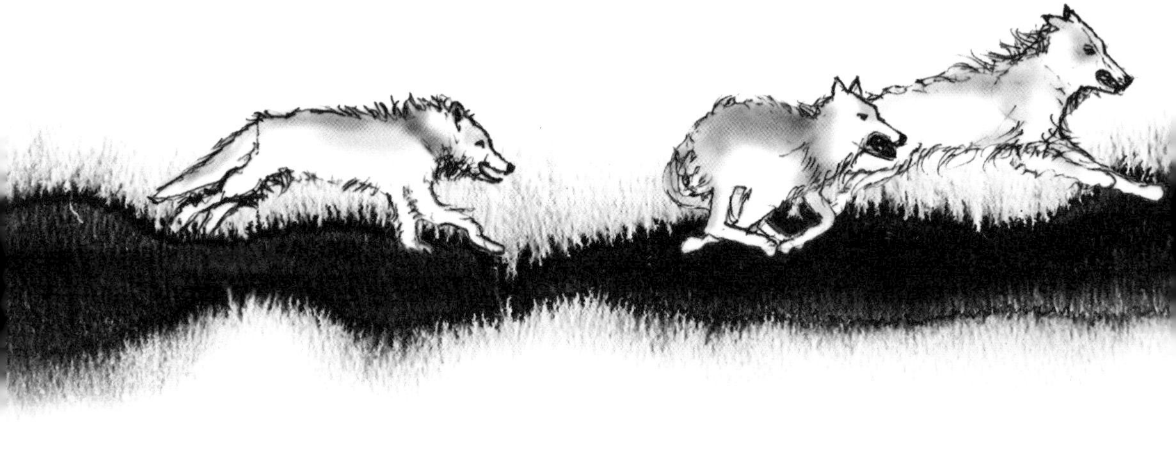

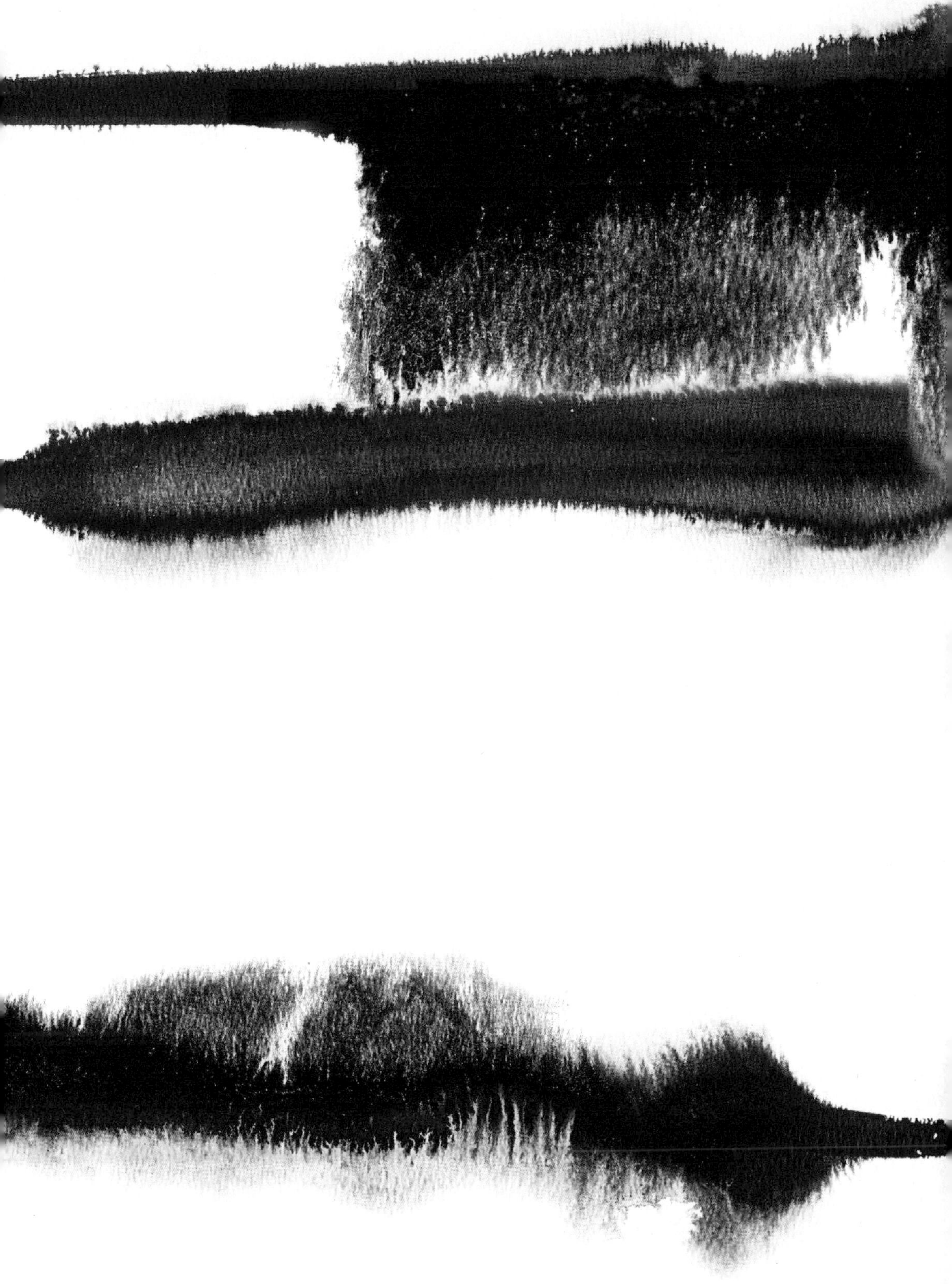

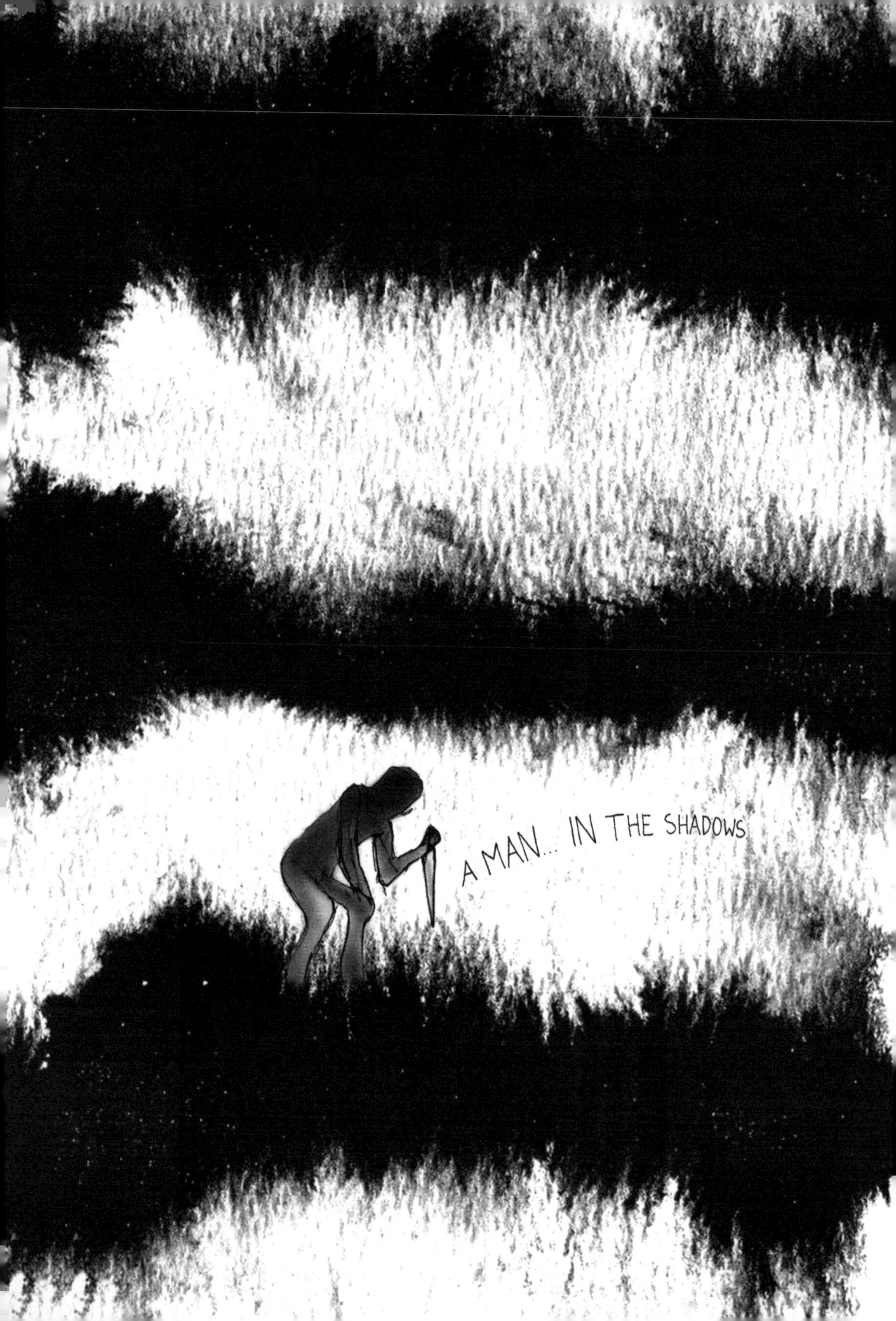
A MAN... IN THE SHADOWS.

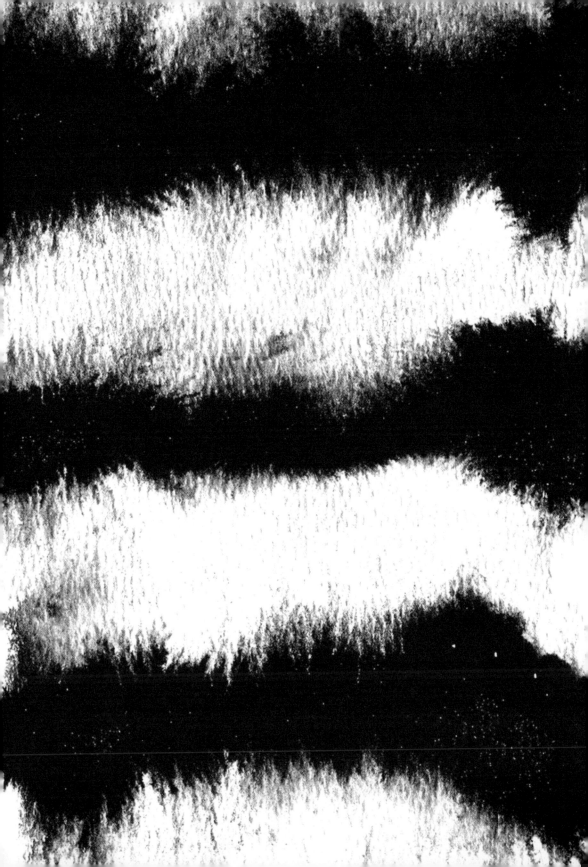

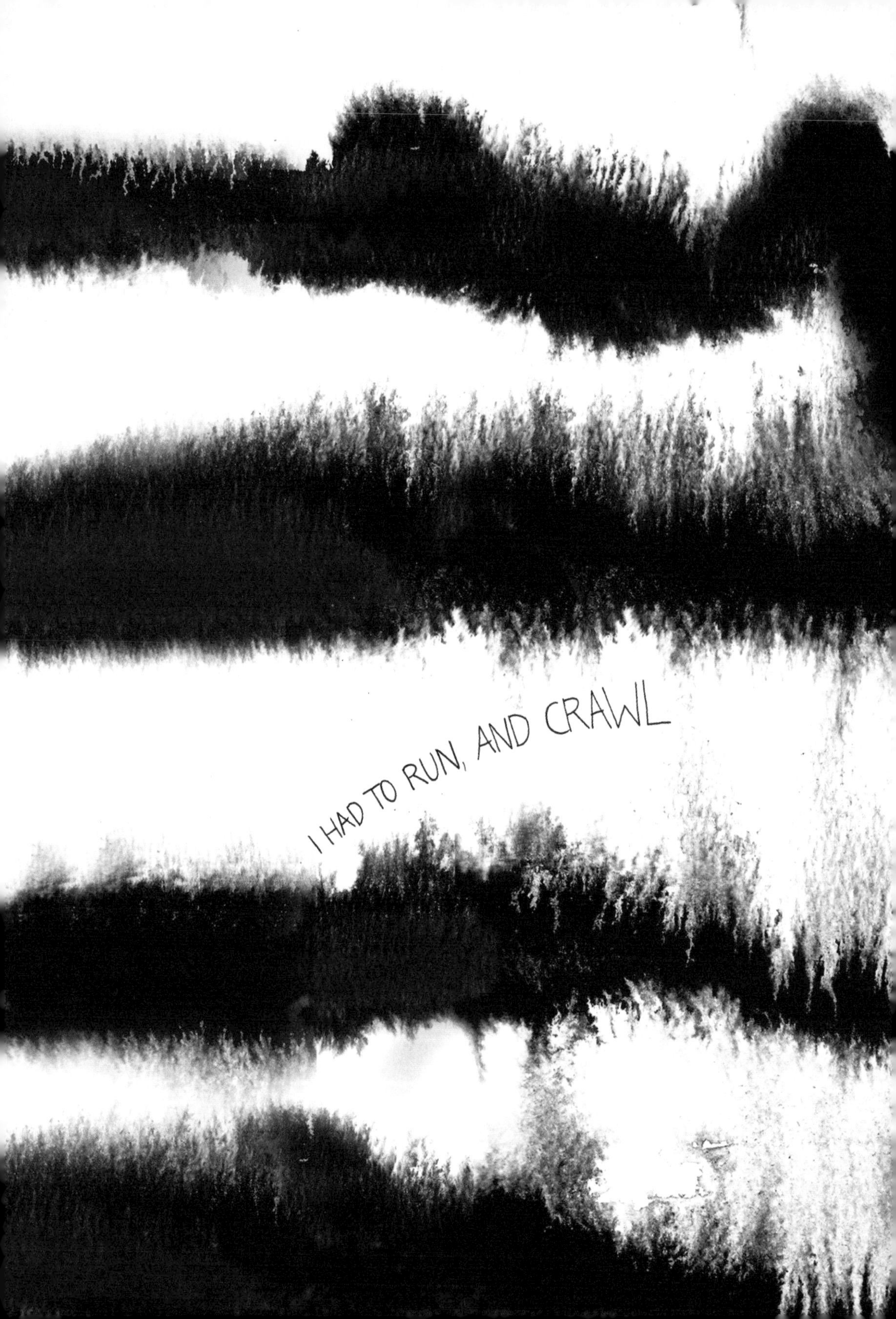

I HAD TO RUN, AND CRAWL

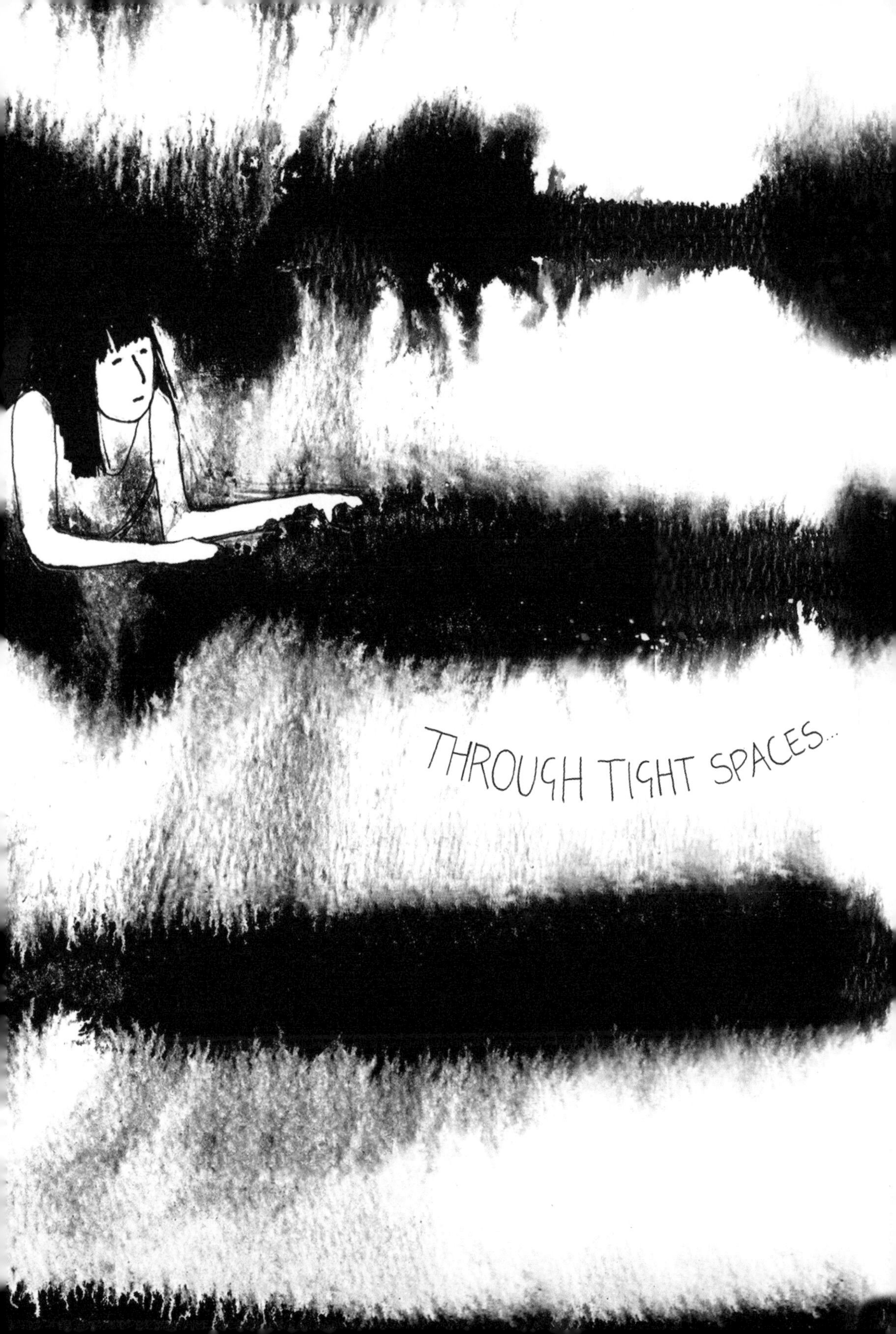
THROUGH TIGHT SPACES...

AFTER HAVING THE DREAM FOR A FEW YEARS, IT CHANGED – I WASN'T ALONE...

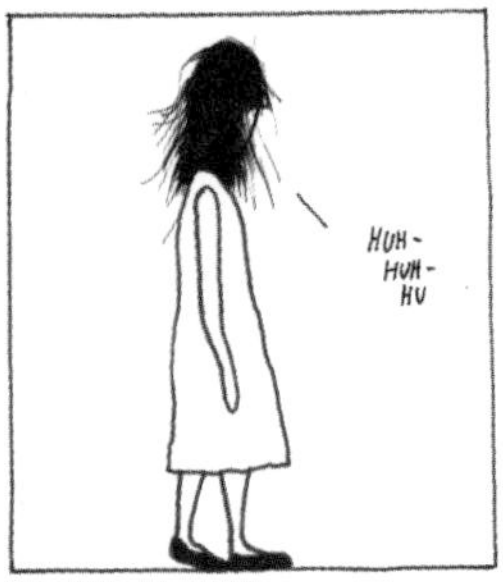

HUH-
HUH-
HU

I HAD MY SISTER WITH ME.

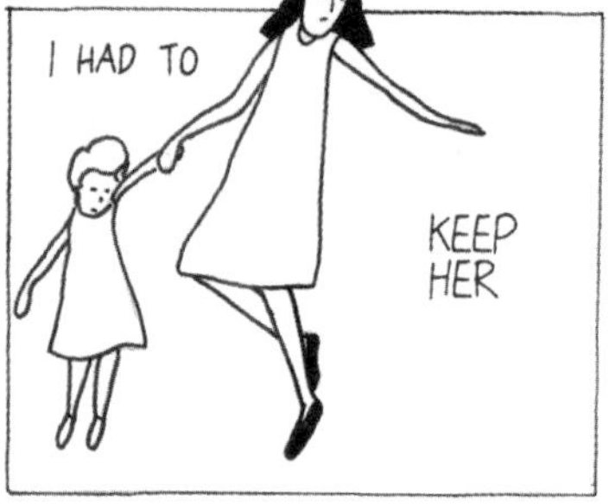

I HAD TO
KEEP HER

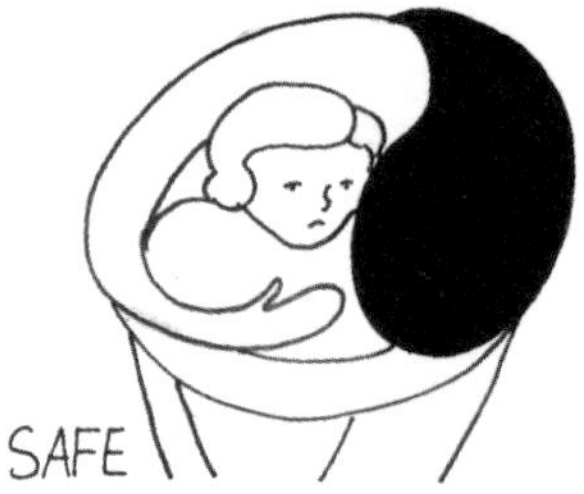

SAFE

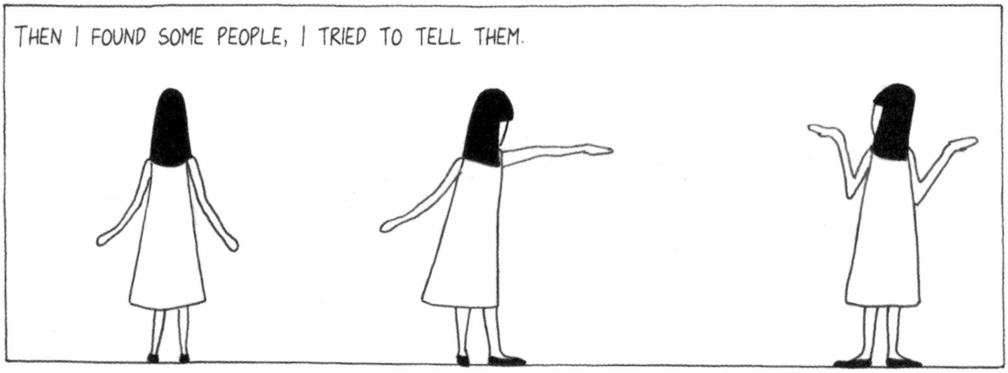

THEN I FOUND SOME PEOPLE, I TRIED TO TELL THEM.

THEY LISTENED BUT THEY DIDN'T SEEM TO HEAR. THEY JUST SHRUGGED AND CARRIED ON WITH WHAT THEY WERE DOING.

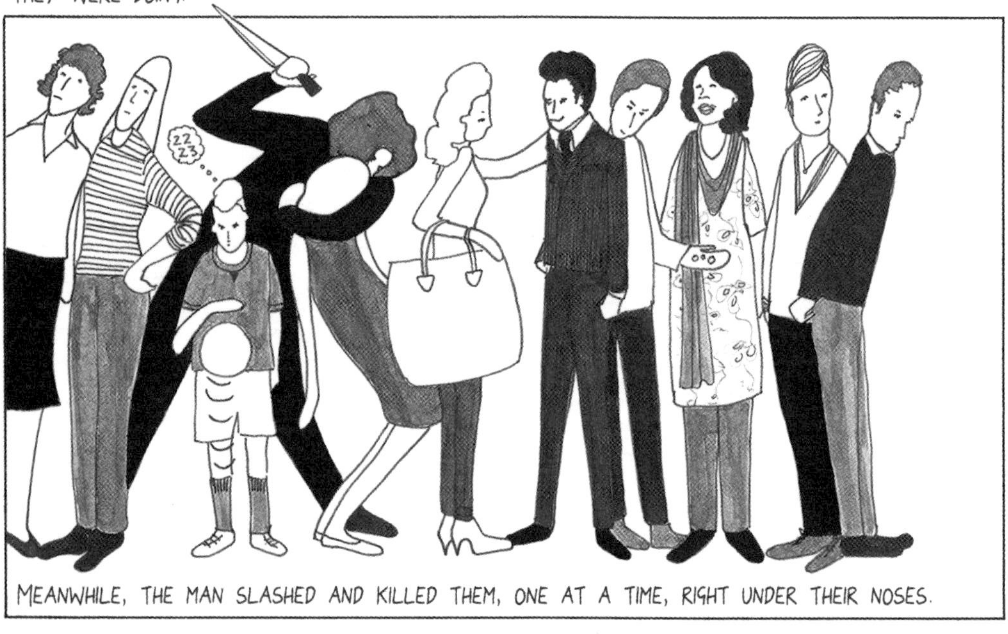

22
23
MEANWHILE, THE MAN SLASHED AND KILLED THEM, ONE AT A TIME, RIGHT UNDER THEIR NOSES.

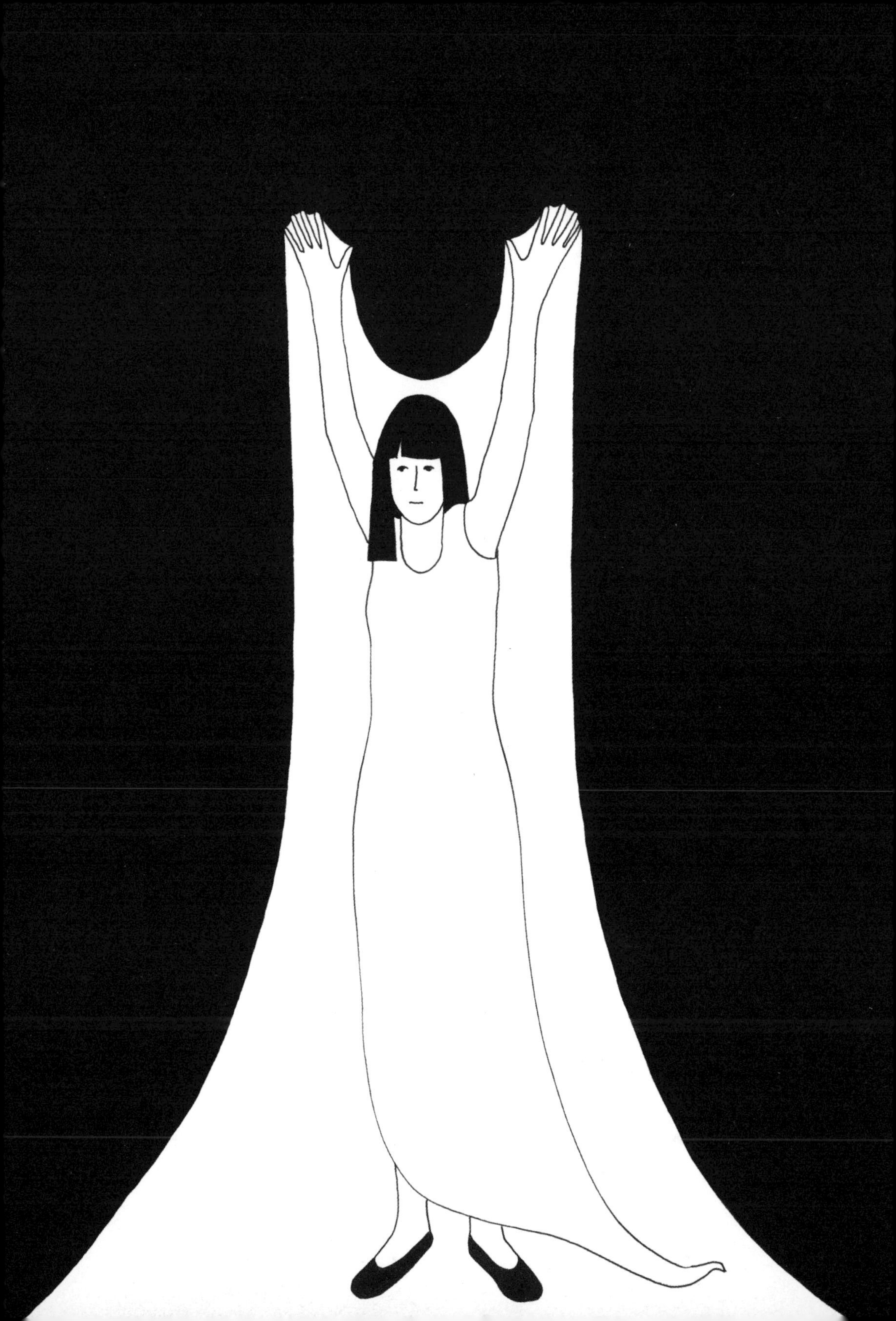

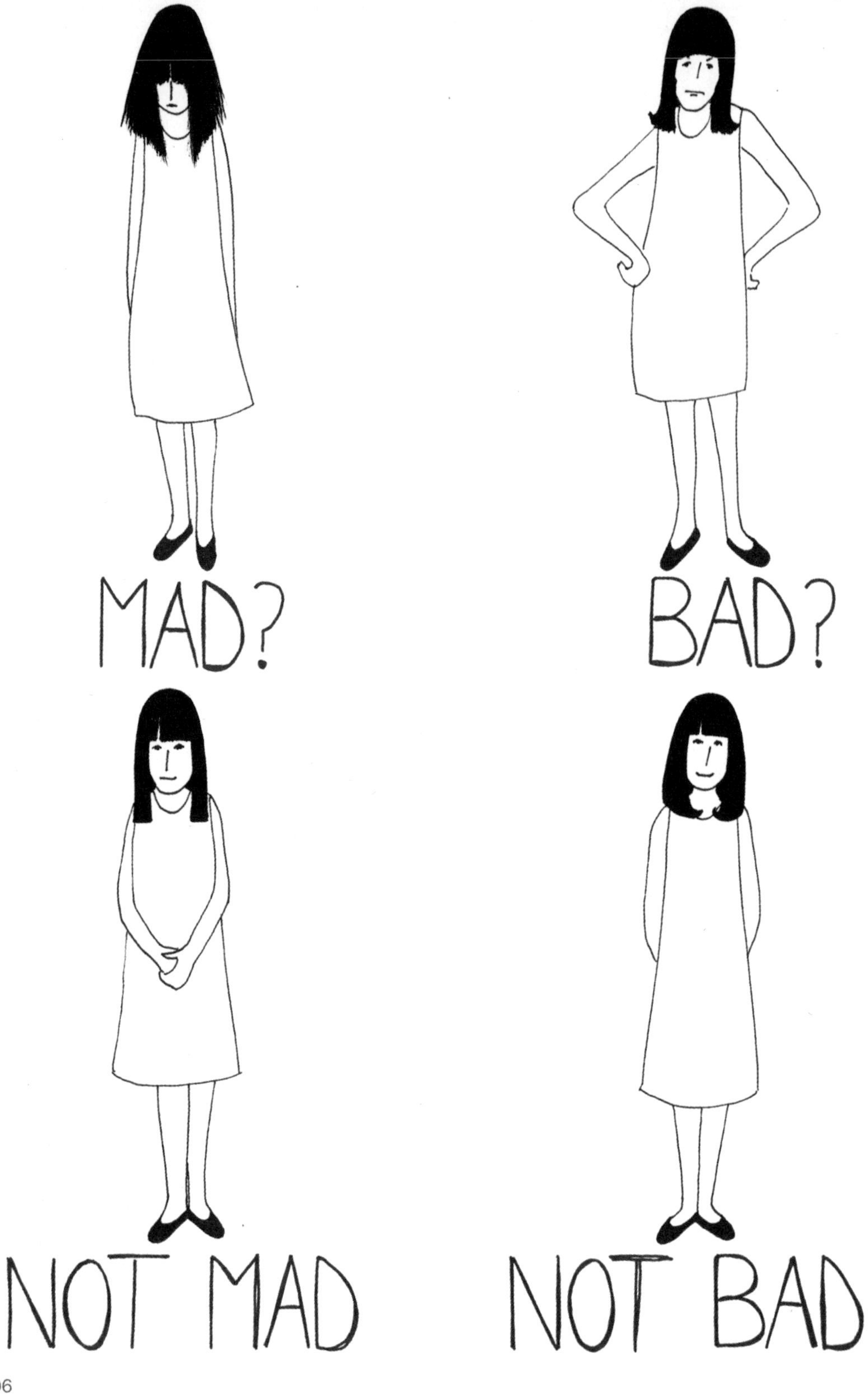
MAD?
BAD?
NOT MAD
NOT BAD

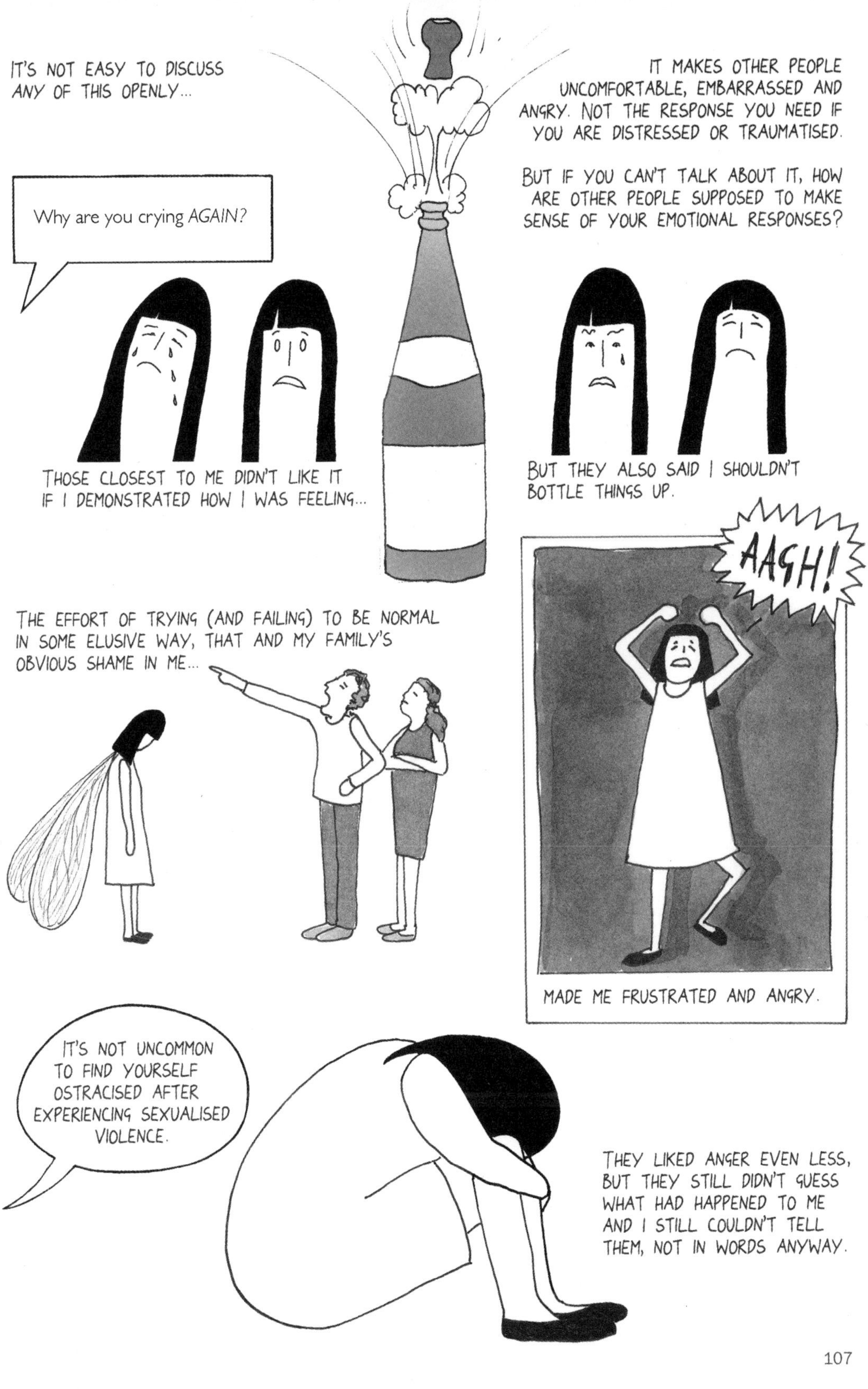
IT'S NOT EASY TO DISCUSS ANY OF THIS OPENLY...
IT MAKES OTHER PEOPLE UNCOMFORTABLE, EMBARRASSED AND ANGRY. NOT THE RESPONSE YOU NEED IF YOU ARE DISTRESSED OR TRAUMATISED.
BUT IF YOU CAN'T TALK ABOUT IT, HOW ARE OTHER PEOPLE SUPPOSED TO MAKE SENSE OF YOUR EMOTIONAL RESPONSES?
Why are you crying AGAIN?
THOSE CLOSEST TO ME DIDN'T LIKE IT IF I DEMONSTRATED HOW I WAS FEELING...
BUT THEY ALSO SAID I SHOULDN'T BOTTLE THINGS UP.
THE EFFORT OF TRYING (AND FAILING) TO BE NORMAL IN SOME ELUSIVE WAY, THAT AND MY FAMILY'S OBVIOUS SHAME IN ME...
AAGH!
MADE ME FRUSTRATED AND ANGRY.
IT'S NOT UNCOMMON TO FIND YOURSELF OSTRACISED AFTER EXPERIENCING SEXUALISED VIOLENCE.
THEY LIKED ANGER EVEN LESS, BUT THEY STILL DIDN'T GUESS WHAT HAD HAPPENED TO ME AND I STILL COULDN'T TELL THEM, NOT IN WORDS ANYWAY.

IF A PHYSICAL ASSAULT IS SEXUAL, THERE'S A WIDESPREAD PERCEPTION THAT THIS WILL BE SO DAMAGING AS TO PERMANENTLY AFFECT THE VICTIM'S MENTAL WELL-BEING.

CERTAINLY, BEING REPEATEDLY ASSAULTED, SHAMED AND BLAMED FOR IT, SHOOK ME TO THE CORE IN A UNIQUE WAY AND HAS NOT BEEN GREAT FOR MY MENTAL HEALTH, BUT IRRATIONAL? UNBALANCED? I'M NOT SO SURE ABOUT THAT.

THE IDEA THAT ONE IS LEFT DISTURBED IS DISTURBING IN ITSELF, BECAUSE IT'S HARD TO TAKE THE TESTIMONY OF THE MAD SERIOUSLY. TRAUMA IS NOT EASY TO DEAL WITH, EVEN WHEN SUPPORT IS AVAILABLE. UNFORTUNATELY, A LACK OF SUPPORT FROM FAMILY AND COMMUNITY CAN WORSEN THE EFFECTS OF TRAUMA.

THE HYSTERIC IS AN INTERESTING FIGURE; SHE HAS AS LITTLE CONTROL OVER HER OWN IMAGE AS A SLUT. IF SHE DISCLOSES ABUSE AND IS BELIEVED, SHE IS A DISTURBED VICTIM. IF SHE DISCLOSES AND IS NOT BELIEVED, SHE IS A DISTURBED LIAR.

I TRIED A LOT OF THINGS OVER THE YEARS TO DEAL WITH THE PAIN – RESPECTABLE MEDICAL ROUTES, SELF-HELP, *ALL* THE THERAPIES, SOME OF WHICH HELPED, THOUGH NOT ALWAYS FOR LONG AND...

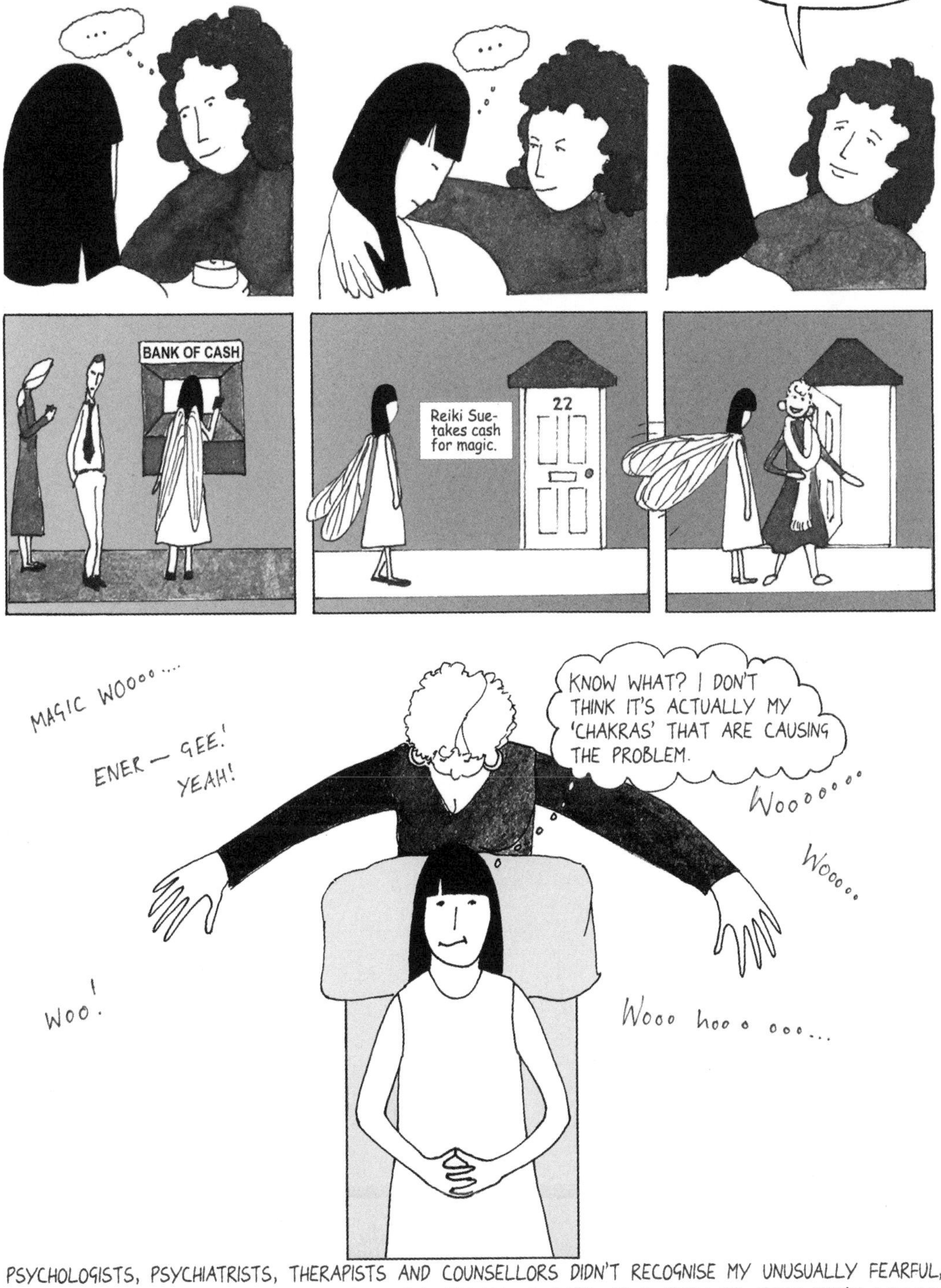

...
...
YOU SHOULD GO SEE REIKI SUE, SHE'S GREAT!
BANK OF CASH
Reiki Sue- takes cash for magic.
22
MAGIC WOOOO....
ENER — GEE! YEAH!
KNOW WHAT? I DON'T THINK IT'S ACTUALLY MY 'CHAKRAS' THAT ARE CAUSING THE PROBLEM.
Woooooo
Wooooo
Woo!
Wooo hooo ooo...

PSYCHOLOGISTS, PSYCHIATRISTS, THERAPISTS AND COUNSELLORS DIDN'T RECOGNISE MY UNUSUALLY FEARFUL, ANXIOUS VIGILANCE AS BEING A RESULT OF THE TRAUMA OF RAPE, OR IF THEY DID, THEY DIDN'T SAY SO.

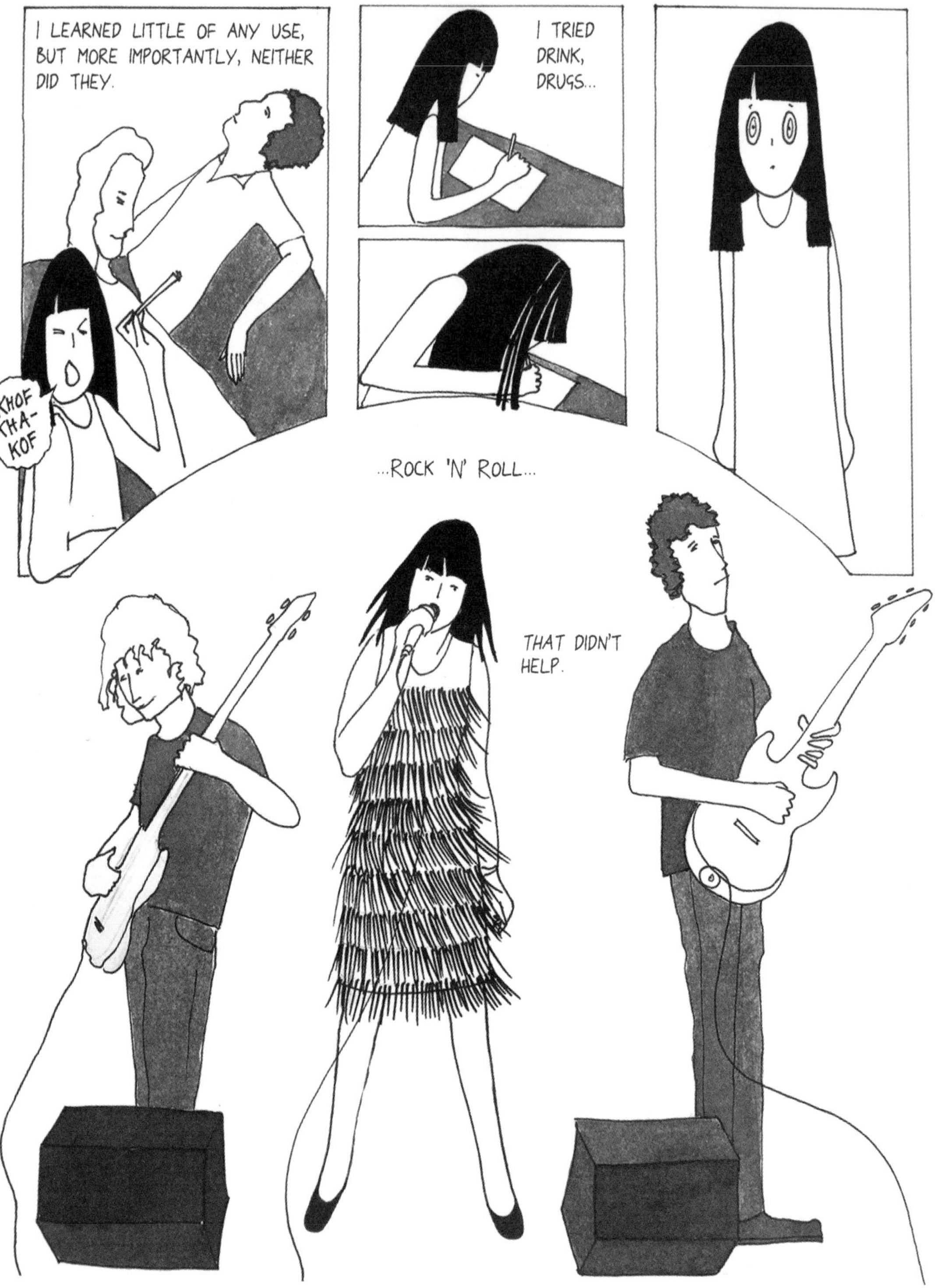
I LEARNED LITTLE OF ANY USE, BUT MORE IMPORTANTLY, NEITHER DID THEY.
KHOF KHA-KOF
I TRIED DRINK, DRUGS...
...ROCK 'N' ROLL...
THAT DIDN'T HELP.

NO ONE I TOLD SUGGESTED THAT I REPORT WHAT HAD HAPPENED TO THE POLICE.

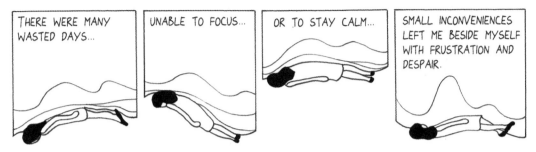

THERE WERE MANY WASTED DAYS...

UNABLE TO FOCUS...

OR TO STAY CALM...

SMALL INCONVENIENCES LEFT ME BESIDE MYSELF WITH FRUSTRATION AND DESPAIR.

IN BETWEEN TIMES I FUNCTIONED WELL ENOUGH TO KEEP PLODDING ON, ONE FOOT IN FRONT OF THE OTHER.

THE NEXT TRAIN DOES NOT STOP AT THIS STATION, PLEASE STAND BACK FROM THE PLATFORM...

BUT OCCASIONALLY I'D FIND MYSELF STANDING ON THE EDGE OF THE PLATFORM, THINKING.

THERE WERE TIMES I WAS SO CRIPPLED WITH ANXIETY AND PANIC, I JUST HAD TO LIE ON THE FLOOR.

OR I'D TRY TO...

HERE

ONLY TO PANIC AT THE WRONG MOMENT AND HAVE TO LEAVE. I'D MAKE MY WAY SLOWLY HOME, LEANING ON A WALL HERE, A BENCH THERE.

TING TING

THERE WERE DAYS I ONLY FELT OK IF I WAS SUBMERGED IN WATER, IN THE BATH...

SO I COULDN'T HAVE DONE ANY WORK THAT INVOLVED BEING CLOTHED OR UPRIGHT!

THINGS SETTLED DOWN FOR A WHILE...

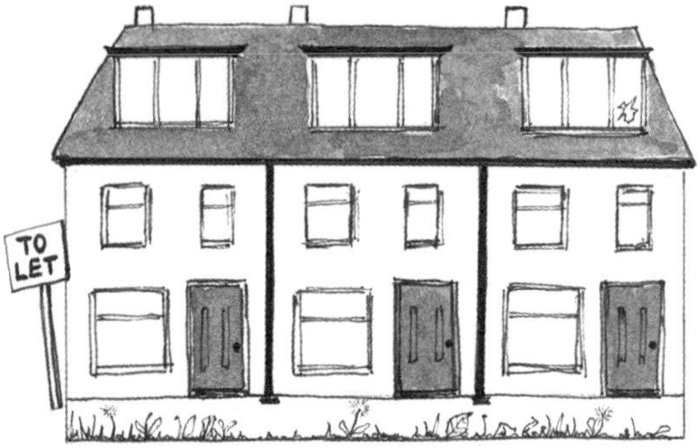
TO LET

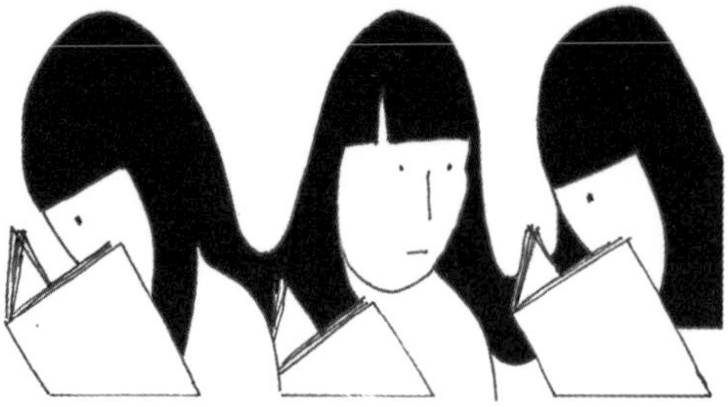

BUT SOMETHING... SOME *THING* KEPT BOTHERING ME.

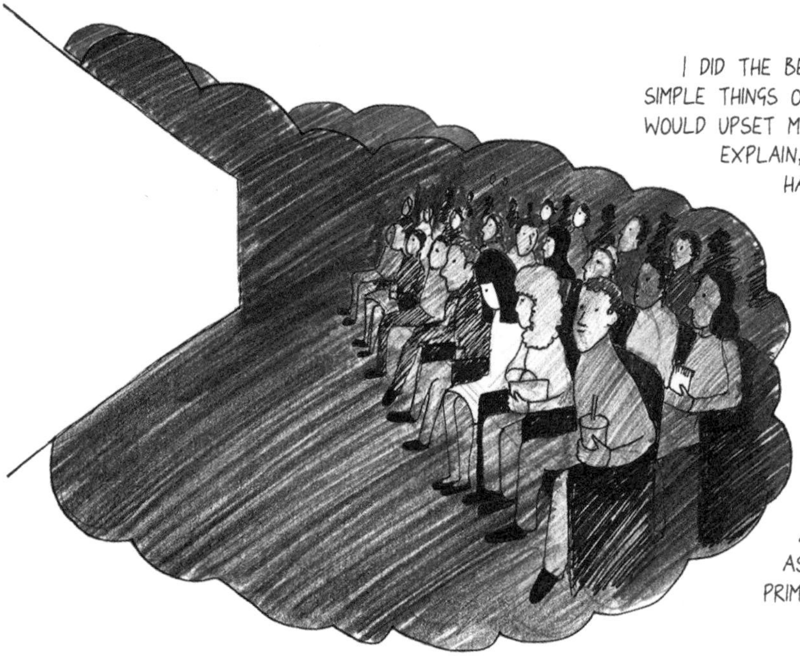

I DID THE BEST I COULD. HOWEVER, SIMPLE THINGS OTHER PEOPLE ENJOYED WOULD UPSET ME AT A LEVEL I CAN'T EXPLAIN, AND BECAUSE NO ONE HAD GUESSED WHAT HAD HAPPENED TO ME I COULDN'T EVEN TRY TO EXPLAIN IT.

FILMS, BOOKS, COMICS, TV DRAMAS, OPERAS, PAINTINGS, SONGS, JOKES... SO MANY CULTURAL FORMS USE THE RAPE AND MURDER OF WOMEN AS A NARRATIVE DEVICE, PRIMARILY FOR EXCITEMENT AND DRAMATIC EFFECT.

PERHAPS IT'S FELT THAT AUDIENCES RELATE TO THIS MUCH AS THEY DO ANY IMAGINARY HORROR, BECAUSE DESPITE ITS EVERYDAY NATURE, SEXUAL VIOLENCE STILL SEEMS LIKE A HYPOTHETICAL THING.

LIVING WITH A SENSITIVITY TO IT CAN BE A DAILY STRUGGLE.

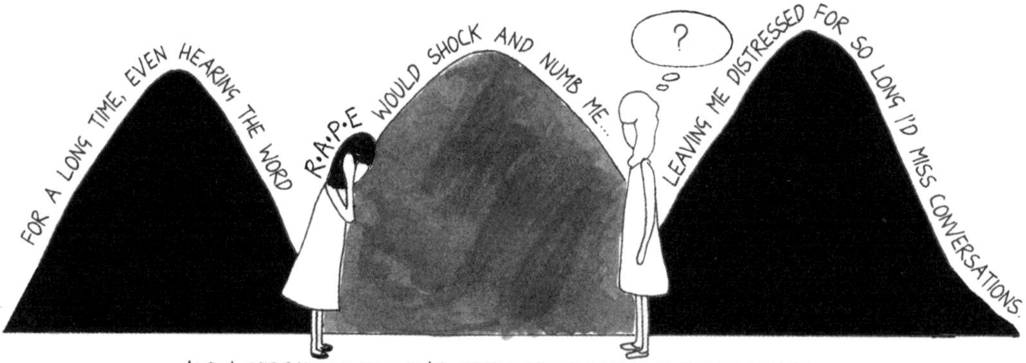
FOR A LONG TIME, EVEN HEARING THE WORD
R·A·P·E WOULD SHOCK AND NUMB ME...
?
LEAVING ME DISTRESSED FOR SO LONG I'D MISS CONVERSATIONS.

AND I CERTAINLY COULDN'T UTTER THAT WORD, NOT FOR YEARS.

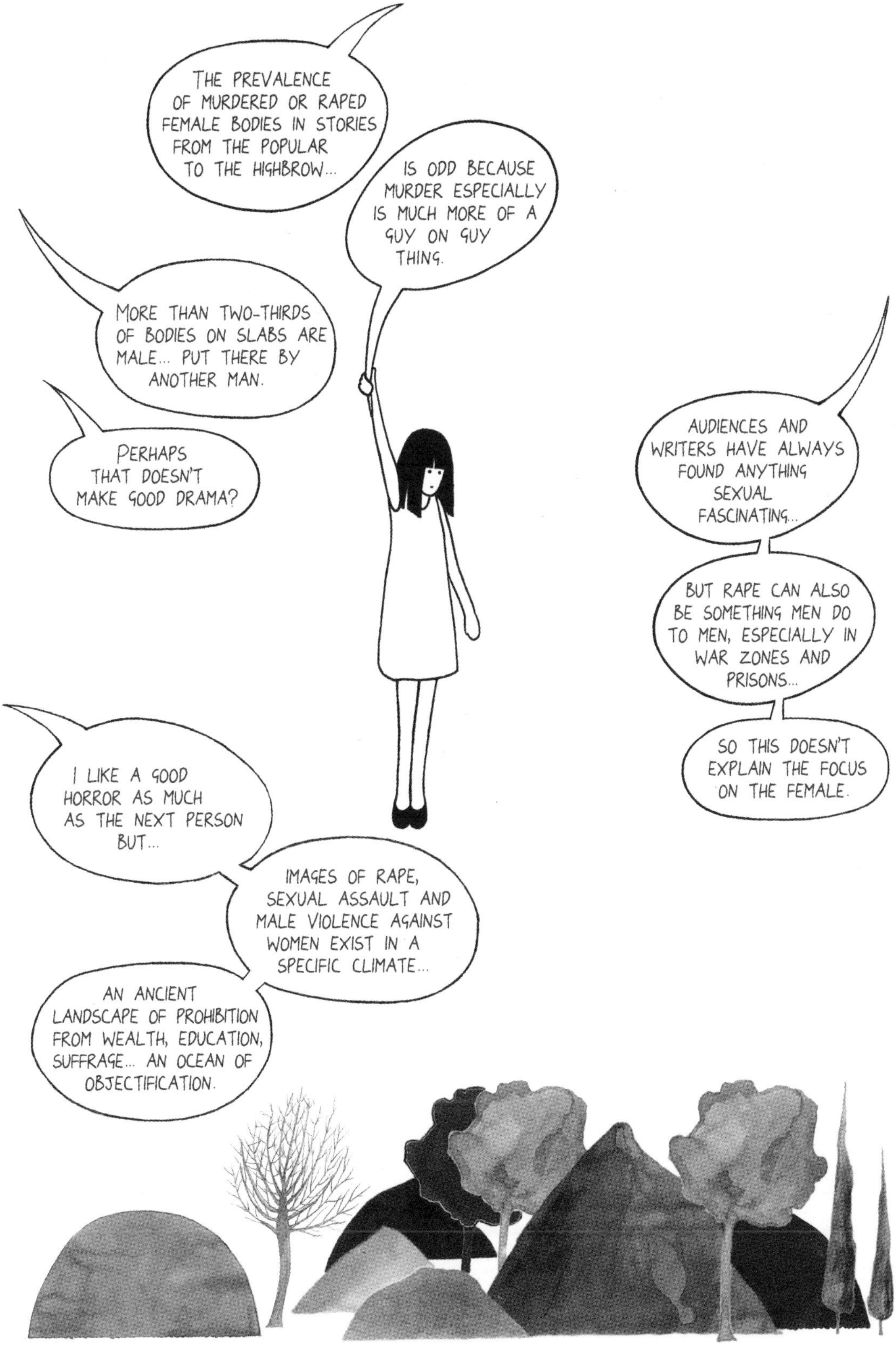

THE PREVALENCE OF MURDERED OR RAPED FEMALE BODIES IN STORIES FROM THE POPULAR TO THE HIGHBROW...
IS ODD BECAUSE MURDER ESPECIALLY IS MUCH MORE OF A GUY ON GUY THING.
MORE THAN TWO-THIRDS OF BODIES ON SLABS ARE MALE... PUT THERE BY ANOTHER MAN.
PERHAPS THAT DOESN'T MAKE GOOD DRAMA?
AUDIENCES AND WRITERS HAVE ALWAYS FOUND ANYTHING SEXUAL FASCINATING...
BUT RAPE CAN ALSO BE SOMETHING MEN DO TO MEN, ESPECIALLY IN WAR ZONES AND PRISONS...
SO THIS DOESN'T EXPLAIN THE FOCUS ON THE FEMALE.
I LIKE A GOOD HORROR AS MUCH AS THE NEXT PERSON BUT...
IMAGES OF RAPE, SEXUAL ASSAULT AND MALE VIOLENCE AGAINST WOMEN EXIST IN A SPECIFIC CLIMATE...
AN ANCIENT LANDSCAPE OF PROHIBITION FROM WEALTH, EDUCATION, SUFFRAGE... AN OCEAN OF OBJECTIFICATION.

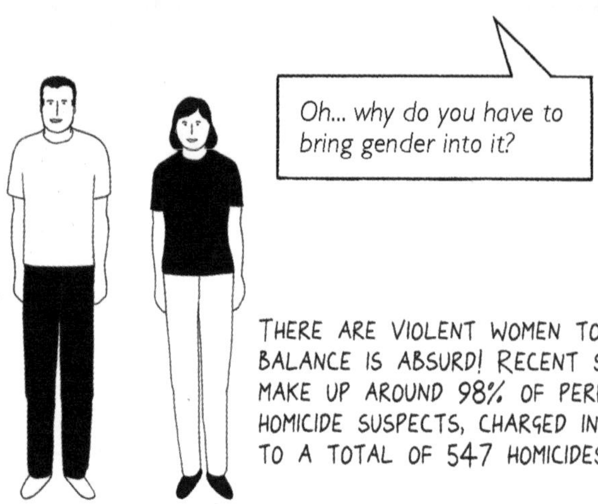
Oh... why do you have to bring gender into it?

IT'S UNAVOIDABLE!

A PERSON WHO HAS PHYSICAL, STRUCTURAL OR AUTHORITARIAN POWER OVER ANOTHER ABUSES THAT POWER TO SATISFY A SENSE OF ENTITLEMENT OR MALICE OR BOTH.

THERE ARE VIOLENT WOMEN TOO, BUT PRETENDING THERE'S SOME SORT OF BALANCE IS ABSURD! RECENT STATISTICS IN THE UK SHOW THAT MALES MAKE UP AROUND 98% OF PERPETRATORS OF SEXUAL OFFENCES, WHILE, OF HOMICIDE SUSPECTS, CHARGED IN THE YEAR 2011 TO 2012, AND RELATING TO A TOTAL OF 547 HOMICIDES – 210 WERE MALE AND 25 WERE FEMALE.

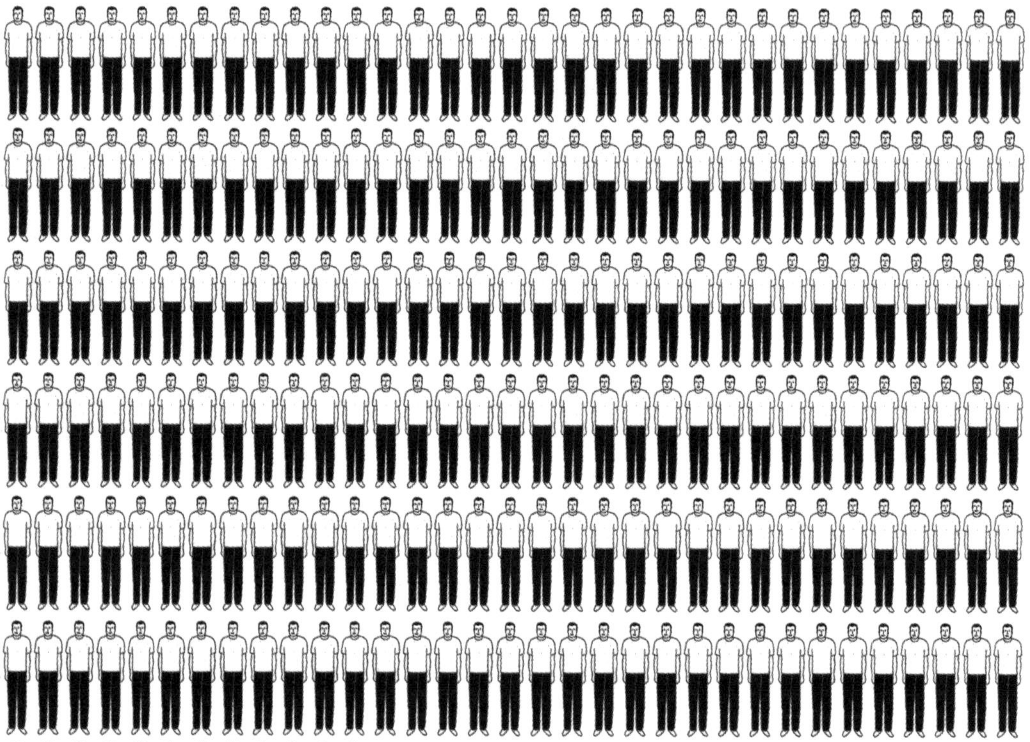

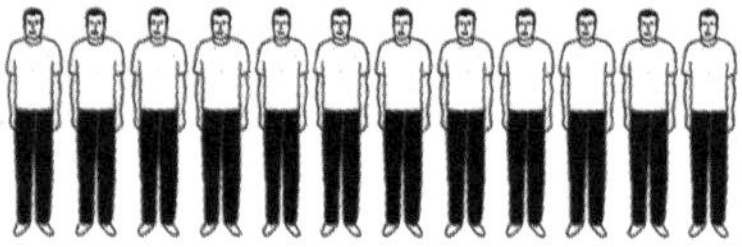

WHY IS THE IDEA THAT WOMEN AND GIRLS DESERVE WHAT THEY GET SO MUCH EASIER FOR SOCIETIES ACROSS THE GLOBE TO ACCEPT THAN THE FACT THAT VIOLENT MALES CAUSE MISERY TO MILLIONS WORLDWIDE, IN TIMES OF PEACE AND TIMES OF WAR?

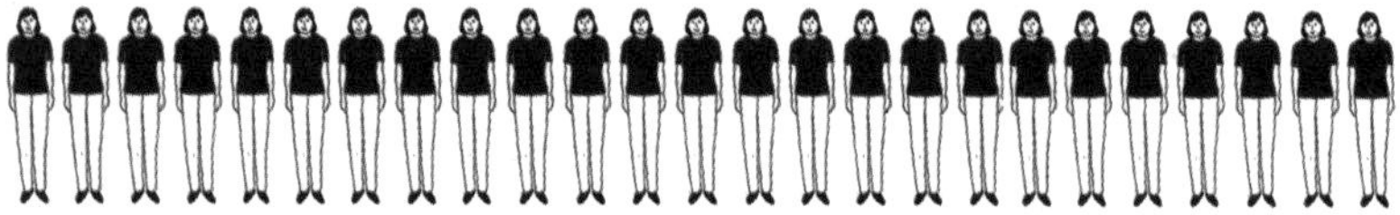

IF WE WERE TO AIM FOR SOME SORT OF EQUALITY, REDUCING THE LEVEL OF MALE VIOLENCE TO MATCH THE FEMALE ONE WOULD BE A MAJOR IMPROVEMENT.

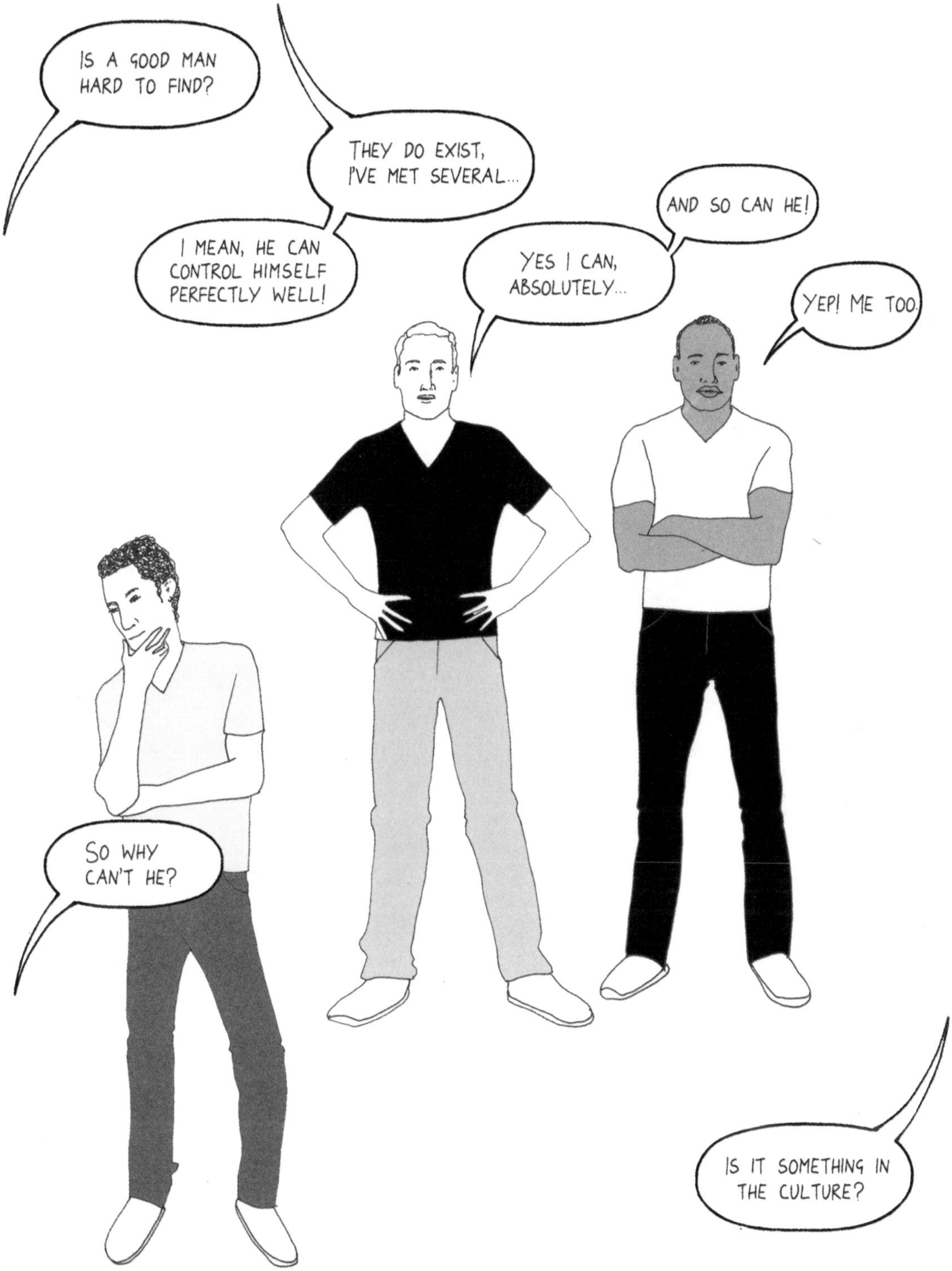
IS A GOOD MAN HARD TO FIND?
THEY DO EXIST, I'VE MET SEVERAL...
I MEAN, HE CAN CONTROL HIMSELF PERFECTLY WELL!
AND SO CAN HE!
YES I CAN, ABSOLUTELY...
YEP! ME TOO.
SO WHY CAN'T HE?
IS IT SOMETHING IN THE CULTURE?

THERE'S EVIDENCE THAT MEN WHO ASSAULT WOMEN AND GIRLS IN A NUMBER OF WAYS RESPOND WELL TO PEER PRESSURE FROM OTHER MEN. THEY DON'T TAKE ANY NOTICE OF WHAT WOMEN SAY, THAT'S FOR SURE!

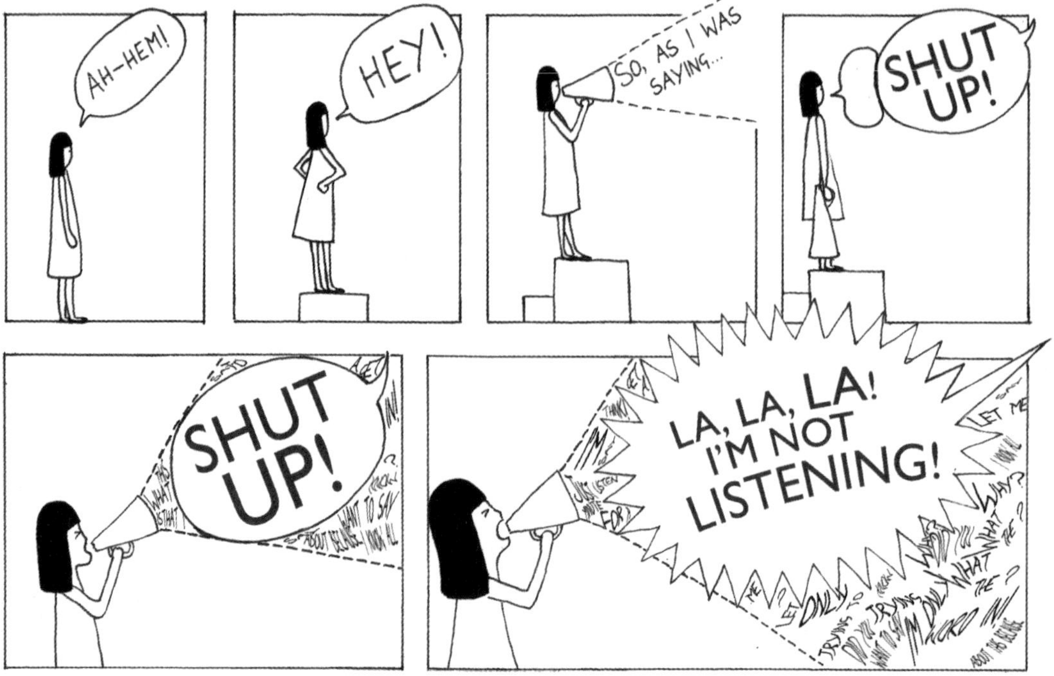
AH-HEM!
HEY!
SO, AS I WAS SAYING...
SHUT UP!
SHUT UP!
LA, LA, LA! I'M NOT LISTENING!
LET ME

BEFORE THE INVENTION OF THE INTERNET, ANYONE WANTING TO SHOUT A WOMAN DOWN WOULD NEED TO DO THIS FACE TO FACE. THIS WASN'T SO DIFFICULT. THOSE WHO ARE HOSTILE TO FEMINIST IDEAS CATCH A FREE RIDE WITH THE FOUR HORSEMEN OF GENDER VIOLENCE – SHAME, ISOLATION, DISBELIEF, RIDICULE.

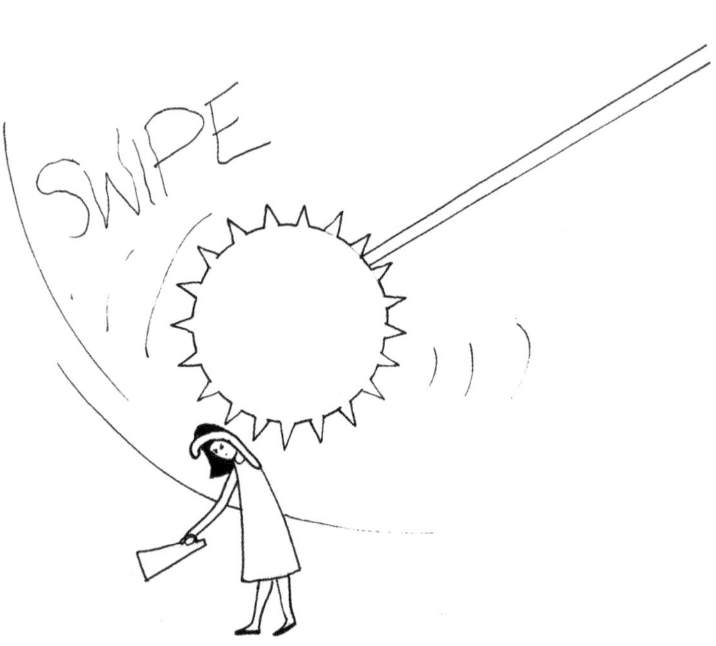
SWIPE

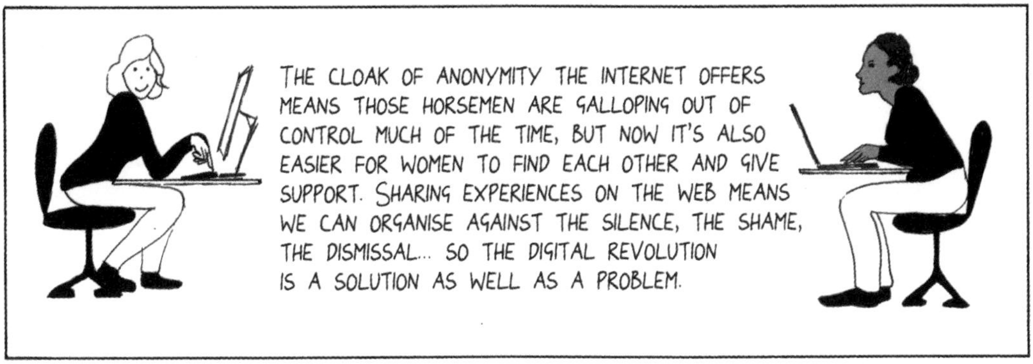
THE CLOAK OF ANONYMITY THE INTERNET OFFERS MEANS THOSE HORSEMEN ARE GALLOPING OUT OF CONTROL MUCH OF THE TIME, BUT NOW IT'S ALSO EASIER FOR WOMEN TO FIND EACH OTHER AND GIVE SUPPORT. SHARING EXPERIENCES ON THE WEB MEANS WE CAN ORGANISE AGAINST THE SILENCE, THE SHAME, THE DISMISSAL... SO THE DIGITAL REVOLUTION IS A SOLUTION AS WELL AS A PROBLEM.

THOSE EVERYDAY ACTS OF MISOGYNY HAVE ALWAYS BEEN AROUND, BUT NOW THEY ARE VISIBLE TO ALL.

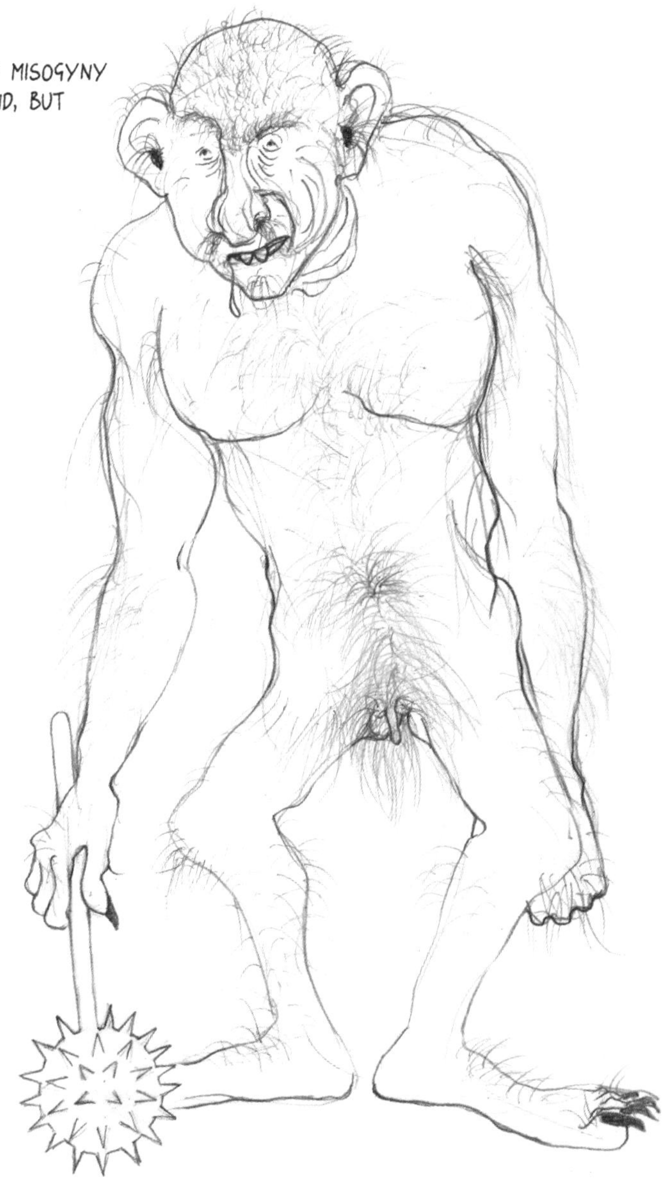

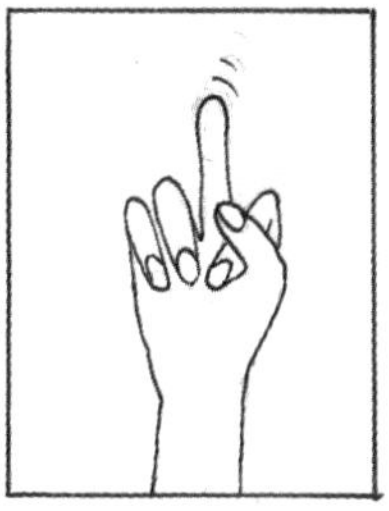

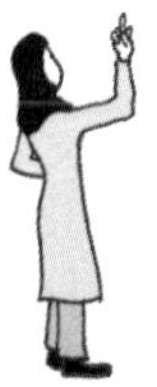

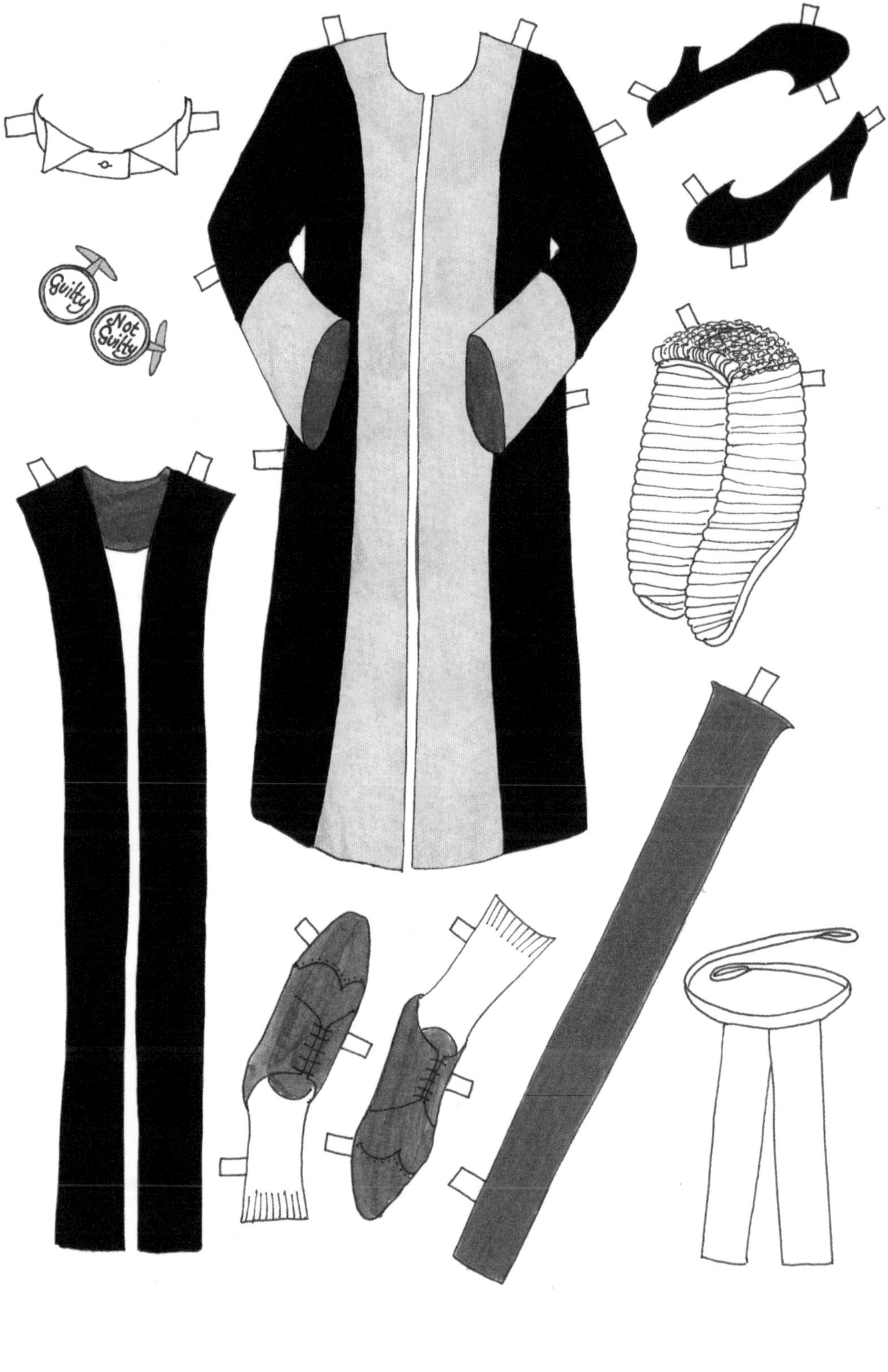
Guilty
Not Guilty

AFTER GROWING USED TO THE DISCOMFORT OF MY OWN SKIN, I KEPT MOVING FORWARD, SLIGHTLY OUT OF STEP, KEEPING IT TO MYSELF.

I GOT BETTER AT CONCEALING MY TRUE FORM, BUT THIS CREATURE... THIS MUTATION, HAD BECOME A PART OF ME.

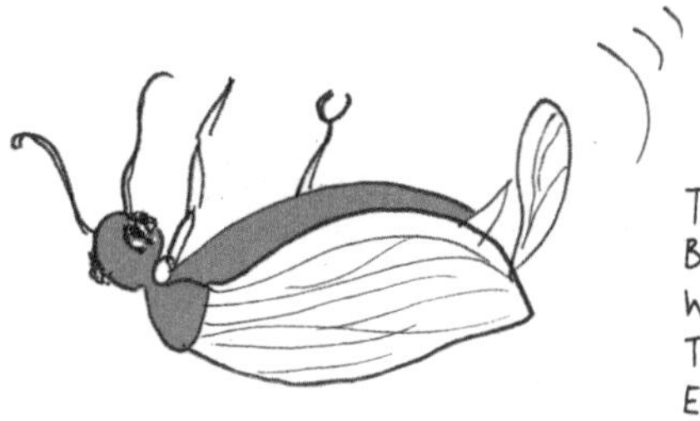

THERE WAS NO WAY BACK – I WAS STUCK WHERE THEY'D LEFT ME – TRYING TO RECOVER MY EQUILIBRIUM.

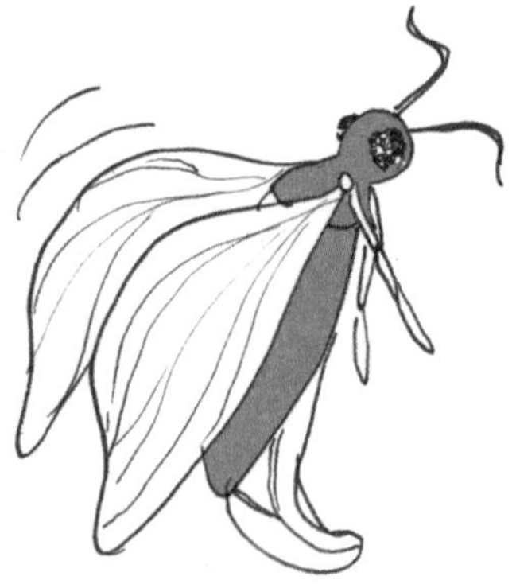

IT TOOK A LONG, LONG TIME TO FIND MY BALANCE AND I *STILL* DON'T HAVE JUSTICE.

WHERE IS JUSTICE?

NO ONE SHOULD HAVE TO WAIT 25 YEARS...

BUT SO MANY OF US DO.

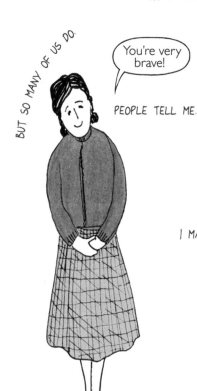

You're very brave!

PEOPLE TELL ME.

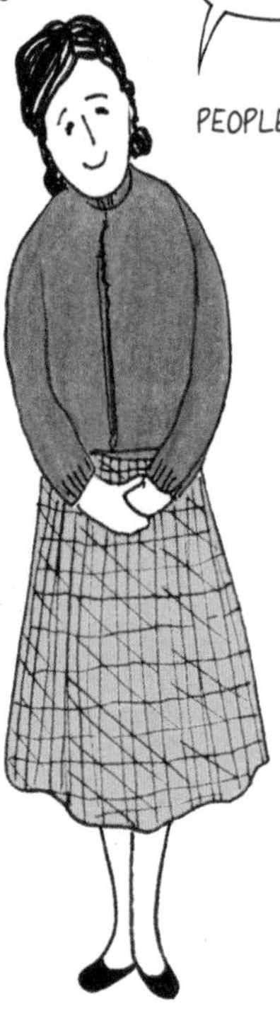

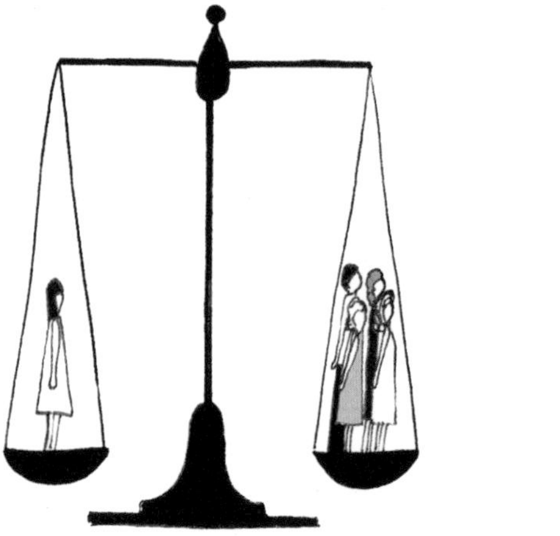

I MAY INDEED BE BRAVE, BUT MAYBE THAT'S MISSING THE POINT.

I HAVE TO WONDER WHY SO MUCH COURAGE IS *EXPECTED* OF GIRLS AND WOMEN IN THIS WORLD.

SO MUCH DAILY BRAVERY IN THE WORLD, AND YET...
HOW WOULD WE KNOW?

IT GOES UNSAID.

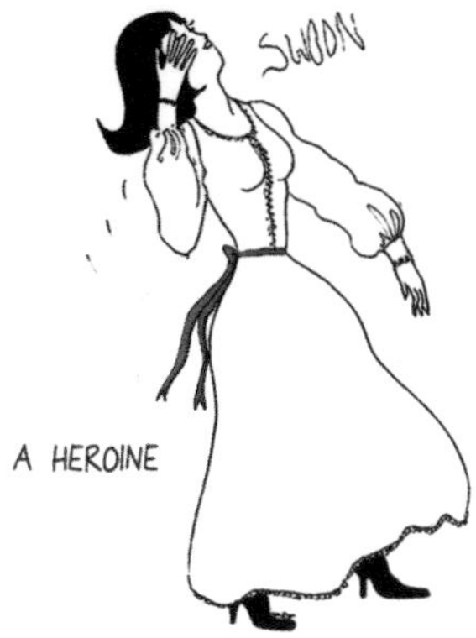
SWOON
A HEROINE

IMAGINE THE VOLUME, WERE WE TO
HEAR THE SOUND OF ALL THOSE
VOICES AT ONCE.

WE HAVE TO LISTEN FOR THEM...

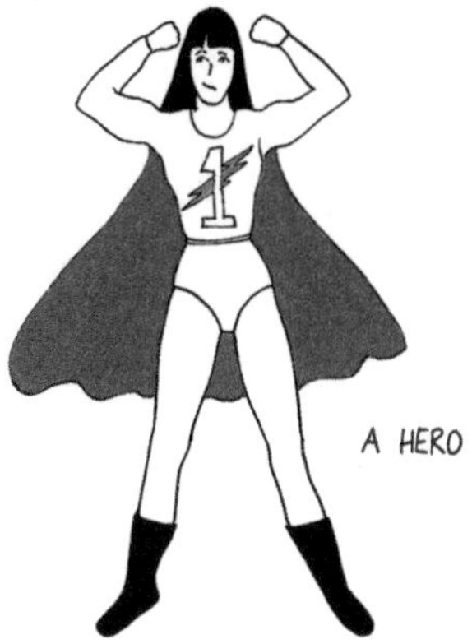
A HERO

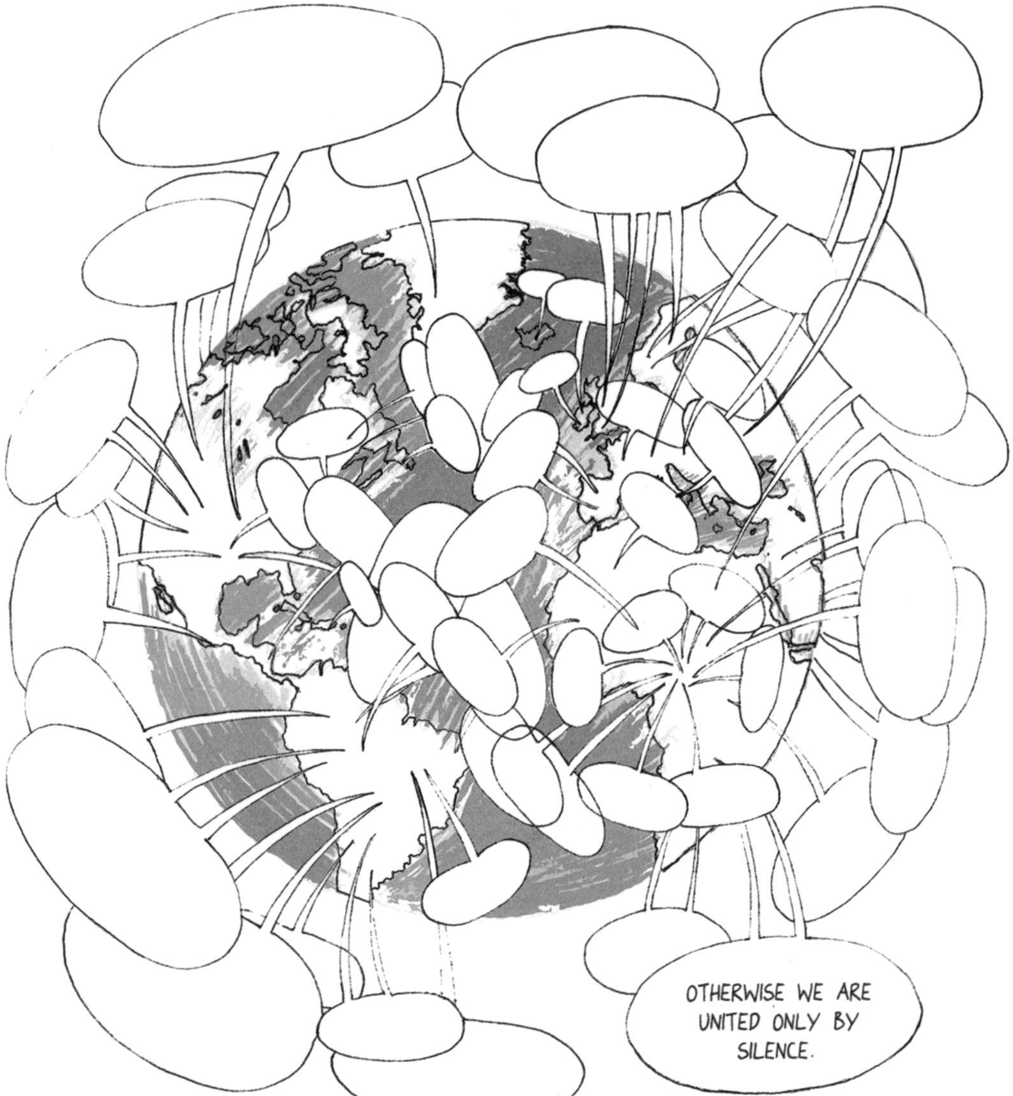
OTHERWISE WE ARE UNITED ONLY BY SILENCE.

WOMEN AND GIRLS ARE NOT JUST SEXUAL VICTIMS. THEY HAVE THEIR OWN SEXUALITY, NEEDS, DESIRES... BUT IF PROFESSIONALS IN THE JUSTICE SYSTEM AREN'T ABLE TO WORK OUT THE ISSUE OF CONSENT...

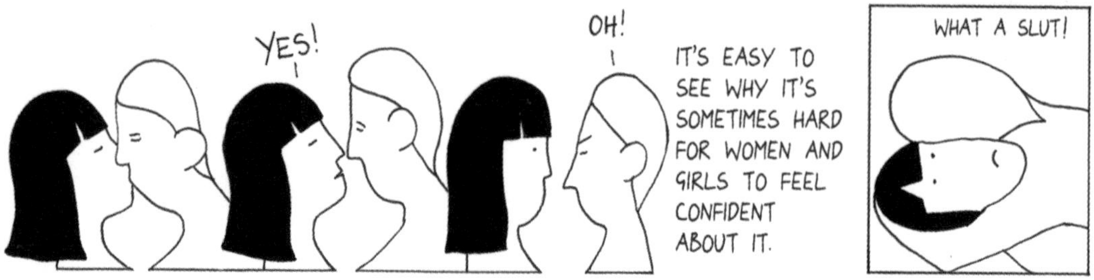
YES!
OH!
IT'S EASY TO SEE WHY IT'S SOMETIMES HARD FOR WOMEN AND GIRLS TO FEEL CONFIDENT ABOUT IT.
WHAT A SLUT!

I REPEATEDLY ENCOUNTERED A COMPLETE LACK OF INTEREST IN MY CONSENT, AND TOTAL UNINTEREST IN MY PLEASURE. WHAT A STRANGE THING THIS IS TO OVERLOOK!

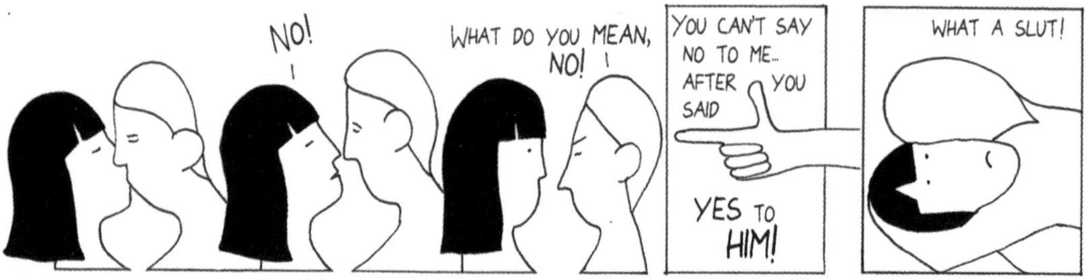
NO!
WHAT DO YOU MEAN, NO!
YOU CAN'T SAY NO TO ME... AFTER YOU SAID
YES TO HIM!
WHAT A SLUT!

WHETHER I SAID YES OR WHETHER I SAID NO, THE END RESULT WAS THE SAME.

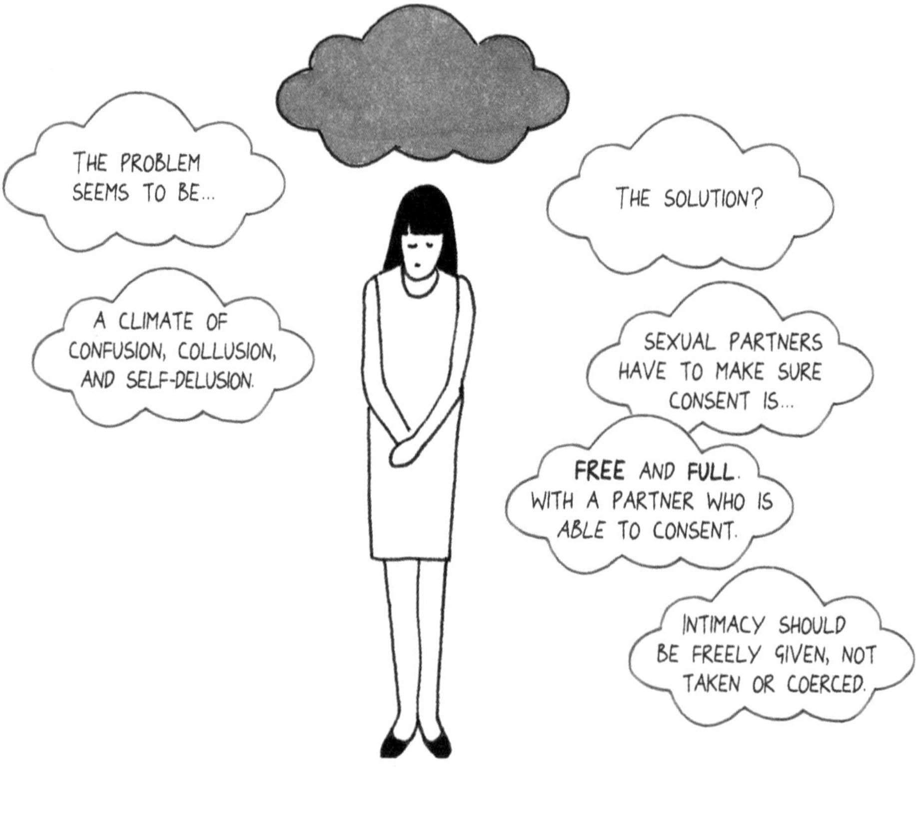
THE PROBLEM SEEMS TO BE...
A CLIMATE OF CONFUSION, COLLUSION, AND SELF-DELUSION.
THE SOLUTION?
SEXUAL PARTNERS HAVE TO MAKE SURE CONSENT IS...
FREE AND **FULL**. WITH A PARTNER WHO IS ABLE TO CONSENT.
INTIMACY SHOULD BE FREELY GIVEN, NOT TAKEN OR COERCED.

IN THE 1970S, JUSTICE FOR WOMEN AND GIRLS WAS NOTORIOUSLY HARD TO FIND.

IS IT EASIER TO FIND NOW?

NOT FOR SEXUALLY EXPLOITED GIRLS, IT ISN'T.

NO ONE SEEMS TO KNOW HOW TO STEP IN AND HELP.

IN 2010, A YOUNG GIRL FROM ROCHDALE SAID THAT QUITE A FEW PEOPLE CONTACTED SOCIAL SERVICES ABOUT HER SITUATION — HER SCHOOL, HER PARENTS — BUT HER MUM AND DAD WERE TOLD SHE WAS A PROSTITUTE AND THAT AS SHE WAS NEARLY 16, NOTHING WOULD BE DONE.

HER SITUATION — BEING ABUSED AND EXPLOITED BY GROUPS OF MUCH OLDER MEN — WAS DESCRIBED BY AUTHORITIES WHO MIGHT HAVE PROTECTED HER AS A 'LIFESTYLE CHOICE'.[10]

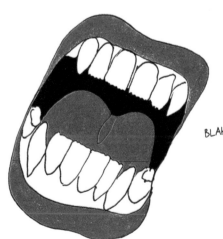

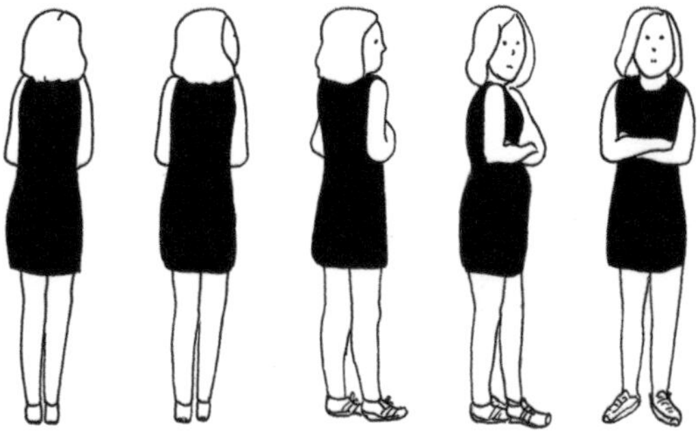

IT'S NO BETTER FOR ADULT WOMEN. DESPITE MUCH WORK TOWARDS IMPROVEMENTS TO THE CRIMINAL JUSTICE SYSTEM, SOME JUDGES AND JURY MEMBERS STILL NEED PERSUADING THAT RAPE AND SEXUAL ASSAULT ARE NOT TRIVIAL ISSUES THAT ARE AT LEAST PARTLY THE WOMAN'S FAULT. THIS ATTITUDE INFECTS THE SYSTEM AND LEADS TO MANY ACQUITTALS.

AS FAR AS MURDEROUS MALE VIOLENCE GOES, MORE THAN TWICE A WEEK, A POLICE OFFICER SOMEWHERE IN THE UK REASSURES A COMMUNITY THAT YET ANOTHER DEAD WOMAN IS AN ISOLATED INCIDENT.

Women who say no, don't always mean no...

THIS HAS ALL BEEN SAID A THOUSAND TIMES BEFORE.

BLAH BLAH BLAH BLAH BLAH BLAH BLAH!

HAS IT MADE ANY DIFFERENCE?

MAYBE A LITTLE.

BUT IT'S UNDERSTANDABLE IF IT'S HARD TO MUSTER THE COURAGE TO MAKE A DECISION TO REPORT.

SINCE RECENT REVELATIONS ABOUT THE SCALE OF SEXUAL VIOLENCE IN THE UK, REPORTING LEVELS ARE INCREASING BUT SUCCESSFUL PROSECUTIONS FOR SEXUAL ASSAULTS ARE UP AND DOWN.

COMPARING ACROSS SEX OFFENCES, RAPE OF A FEMALE HAS A LOWER CONVICTION RATE THAN RAPE OF A MALE, AND A LOWER CONVICTION RATE THAN FOR OTHER, NON-SEXUAL CRIMES.

IN 2011 IT WAS ONLY **39%**

CONVICTION RATES FOR CHILD SEXUAL OFFENCES ARE NOT EASY TO WORK OUT, DUE TO THE WAY DATA IS RECORDED. IN FACT, BECAUSE OF LOW REPORTING IT'S NOT EASY TO *REALLY* KNOW MUCH AT ALL.

WHAT DO WE KNOW?[11]

WE KNOW THAT VIOLENCE AGAINST WOMEN IS NOT RARE.
WE KNOW THAT MOST VICTIMS NEVER DISCLOSE AND DON'T REPORT.
WE KNOW THAT MOST ARE ASSAULTED BY SOMEONE THEY KNOW.

IN 2011 **NINE THOUSAND, NINE HUNDRED AND NINETEEN** DEFENDANTS WERE PROCEEDED AGAINST IN COURT FOR A RANGE OF SEXUAL OFFENCES. OF THESE:

FIVE THOUSAND, NINE HUNDRED AND SEVENTY-SEVEN

WERE FOUND GUILTY AT THE MAGISTRATES' OR CROWN COURT (SO AROUND HALF WENT TO PRISON). THE CONVICTION RATE MORE GENERALLY WAS 83%.

IN ADDITION TO THESE CASES THERE WERE:

FIFTY-THREE THOUSAND, FIVE HUNDRED AND THIRTY-NINE

SEXUAL ASSAULTS THAT WERE REPORTED BUT DIDN'T GET TO COURT. BROKEN DOWN, THERE WERE:

THIRTY-FOUR THOUSAND, FIVE HUNDRED AND FORTY-SEVEN

CASES OF RAPE AND SEXUAL ASSAULT AGAINST FEMALES.

THREE THOUSAND, FIVE HUNDRED AND FORTY-SEVEN

CASES OF RAPE AND SEXUAL ASSAULT AGAINST MALES.

FIVE THOUSAND, SEVEN HUNDRED AND SEVENTY-EIGHT

CASES OF SEXUAL ACTIVITY WITH A MINOR.

NINE THOUSAND, SEVEN HUNDRED AND NINETY-THREE

OTHER SEXUAL OFFENCES.

THEN THERE IS THE OCEAN OF SEXUAL CRIME THAT GOES UNREPORTED.

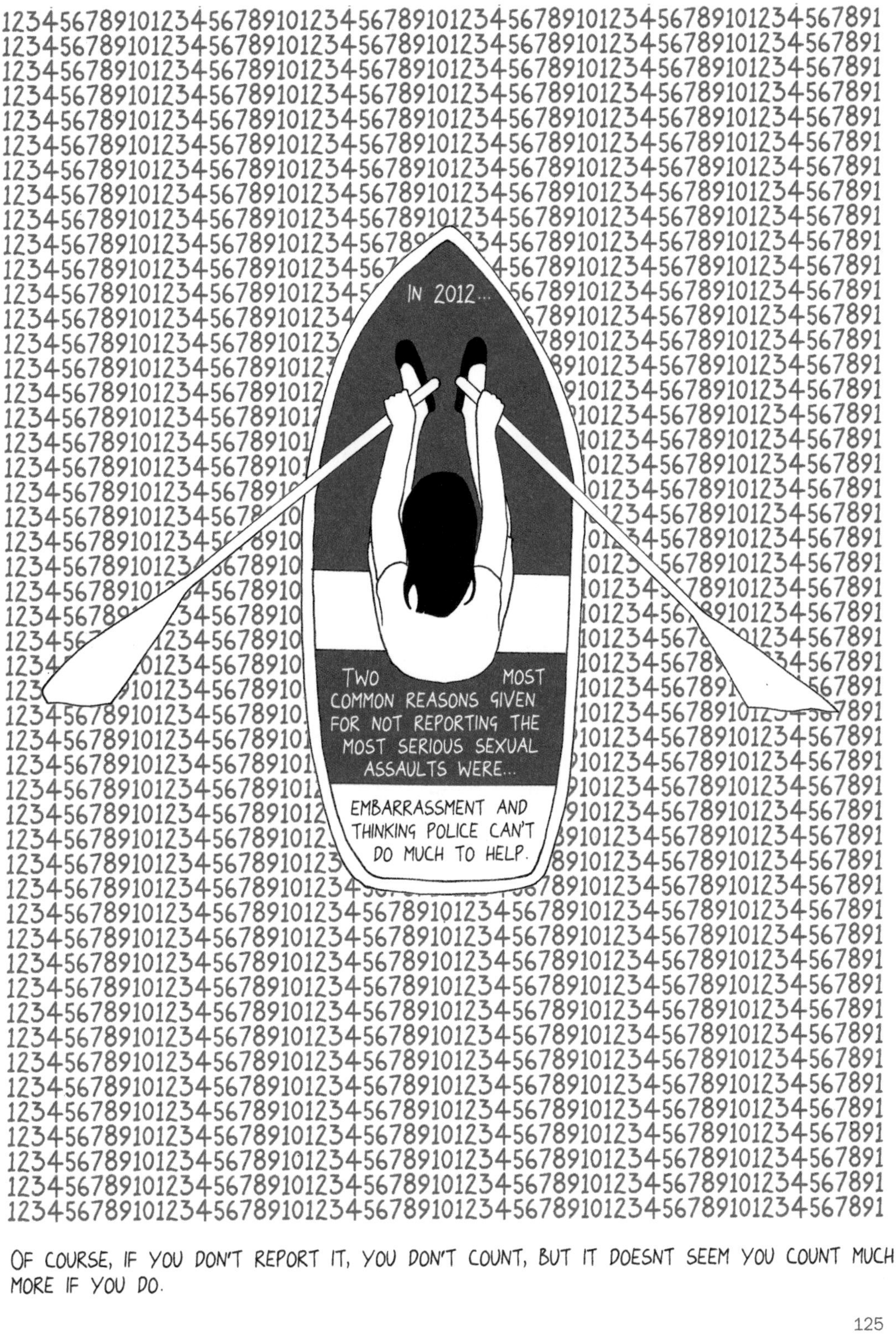
IN 2012...
TWO MOST COMMON REASONS GIVEN FOR NOT REPORTING THE MOST SERIOUS SEXUAL ASSAULTS WERE...
EMBARRASSMENT AND THINKING POLICE CAN'T DO MUCH TO HELP.

OF COURSE, IF YOU DON'T REPORT IT, YOU DON'T COUNT, BUT IT DOESN'T SEEM YOU COUNT MUCH MORE IF YOU DO.

THERE ARE A NUMBER OF THEORIES ABOUT WHAT CAUSES VIOLENT OFFENDING. PROMINENT AMONG THESE IS THE THEORY THAT THOSE WHO ARE ABUSED AS CHILDREN GO ON TO HARM OTHERS IN LATER LIFE. MAYBE THERE IS COMFORT IN THIS IDEA. AFTER ALL, OFFENDERS ARE JUST VICTIMS TOO – BUT IT ISN'T COMFORTING IF YOU ARE A PERSON WHO HAS BEEN ABUSED.

IN ANY CASE, THIS THEORY DOESN'T ADD UP WHEN YOU TAKE GENDER INTO ACCOUNT:

IF THE OVERWHELMING MAJORITY OF VIOLENT AND SEXUAL OFFENDERS ARE MALE, AND THE GREATER NUMBER OF THOSE THEY HURT IN BOTH CHILDHOOD AND ADULTHOOD ARE FEMALE, WELL...

HERE IS THE BREEDING PATTERN OF JUST SIX GENERATIONS OF RABBITS, DEMONSTRATED THROUGH THE FIBONACCI SEQUENCE, A MATHEMATICAL PATTERN THAT OCCURS IN NATURE. YOU CAN SEE HOW QUICKLY THE RABBITS MULTIPLY OVER A SHORT TIME.

SHOULDN'T WE BE DROWNING IN PREDATORY FEMALES BY NOW?
THERE MUST BE SOMETHING ELSE GOING ON.
PERHAPS IT'S SIMPLY THAT A NUMBER OF (MOSTLY) MEN JUST LIKE TO PREY ON OTHER PEOPLE?

RESEARCH UNDERTAKEN IN PRISONS SUGGESTS THAT CONVICTED SEX OFFENDERS, WHEN THEY ARE NOT UNDER PRESSURE TO JUSTIFY THEMSELVES FOR PAROLE OR COURT, TYPICALLY CLAIM THEY HAD HAPPY CHILDHOODS AND WERE NEVER ABUSED. THESE MEN DESCRIBE THE SAME CHILDHOOD EXPERIENCES AS MEN WHO SAY THEY WERE ABUSED IN CHILDHOOD BUT WHO HAVEN'T COMMITTED ANY SEX OFFENCES.

THE EXCUSES THAT PREDATORY MEN MAKE FOR THEIR BEHAVIOUR ARE GIVEN FURTHER CREDENCE BY SOCIETIES ALL OVER THE WORLD THAT ARE *DEEPLY* CONFUSED ABOUT SEX AND RESPECTABILITY.

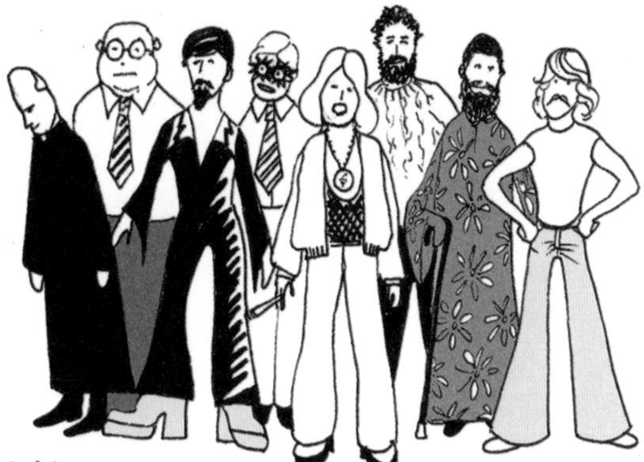

BECAUSE OF THIS CONFUSION, IN THE UK WE'VE ENDED UP WITH THE WHOLE OF THE 1970S ON TRIAL – BECAUSE JUSTICE IS STILL JUSTICE, EVEN IF IT'S 30 YEARS LATE.

A NUMBER OF MEN WHOM PEOPLE THOUGHT HIGHLY OF TURNED OUT TO BE NOT ALL THEY SEEMED. SEXUAL ASSAULT WAS AGAINST THE LAW IN THE 70S TOO, BUT THESE MEN KNEW THEY COULD GET AWAY WITH IT.

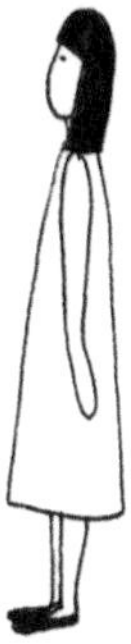

ONE YORKSHIRE MAN IN PARTICULAR HAS COMPELLED US TO FINALLY CONFRONT THE PROBLEM.

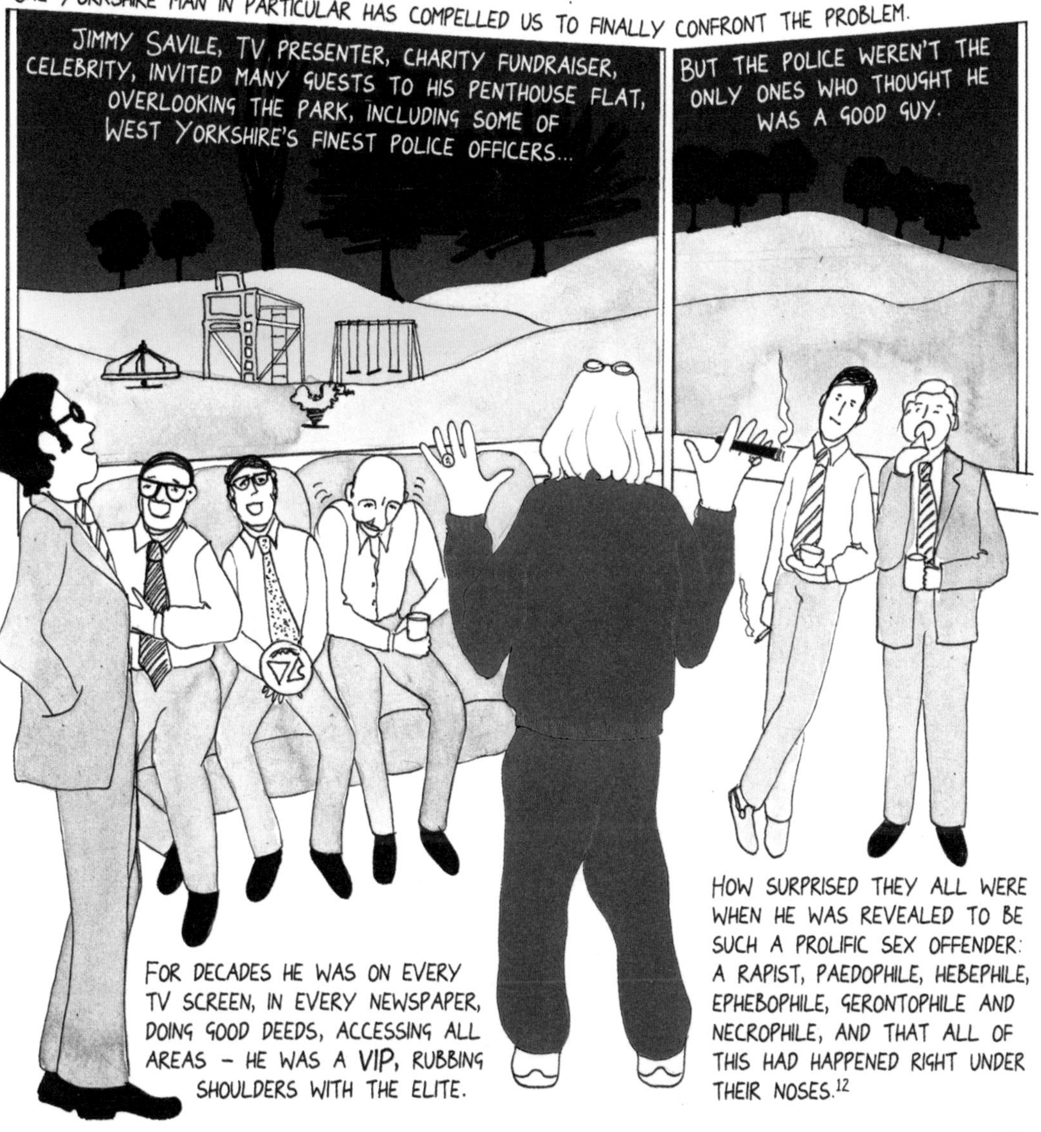
JIMMY SAVILE, TV PRESENTER, CHARITY FUNDRAISER, CELEBRITY, INVITED MANY GUESTS TO HIS PENTHOUSE FLAT, OVERLOOKING THE PARK, INCLUDING SOME OF WEST YORKSHIRE'S FINEST POLICE OFFICERS...
BUT THE POLICE WEREN'T THE ONLY ONES WHO THOUGHT HE WAS A GOOD GUY.
FOR DECADES HE WAS ON EVERY TV SCREEN, IN EVERY NEWSPAPER, DOING GOOD DEEDS, ACCESSING ALL AREAS – HE WAS A **VIP**, RUBBING SHOULDERS WITH THE ELITE.
HOW SURPRISED THEY ALL WERE WHEN HE WAS REVEALED TO BE SUCH A PROLIFIC SEX OFFENDER: A RAPIST, PAEDOPHILE, HEBEPHILE, EPHEBOPHILE, GERONTOPHILE AND NECROPHILE, AND THAT ALL OF THIS HAD HAPPENED RIGHT UNDER THEIR NOSES.[12]

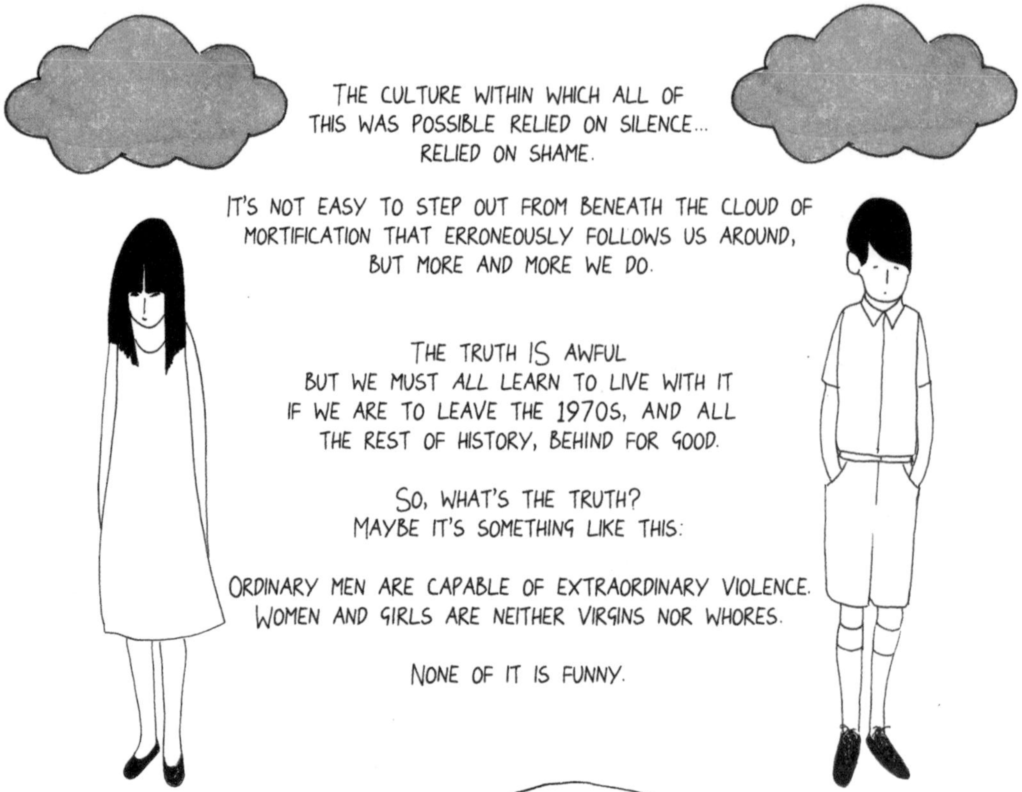
THE CULTURE WITHIN WHICH ALL OF THIS WAS POSSIBLE RELIED ON SILENCE... RELIED ON SHAME.
IT'S NOT EASY TO STEP OUT FROM BENEATH THE CLOUD OF MORTIFICATION THAT ERRONEOUSLY FOLLOWS US AROUND, BUT MORE AND MORE WE DO.
THE TRUTH *IS* AWFUL BUT WE MUST *ALL* LEARN TO LIVE WITH IT IF WE ARE TO LEAVE THE 1970S, AND ALL THE REST OF HISTORY, BEHIND FOR GOOD.
SO, WHAT'S THE TRUTH? MAYBE IT'S SOMETHING LIKE THIS:
ORDINARY MEN ARE CAPABLE OF EXTRAORDINARY VIOLENCE. WOMEN AND GIRLS ARE NEITHER VIRGINS NOR WHORES.
NONE OF IT IS FUNNY.

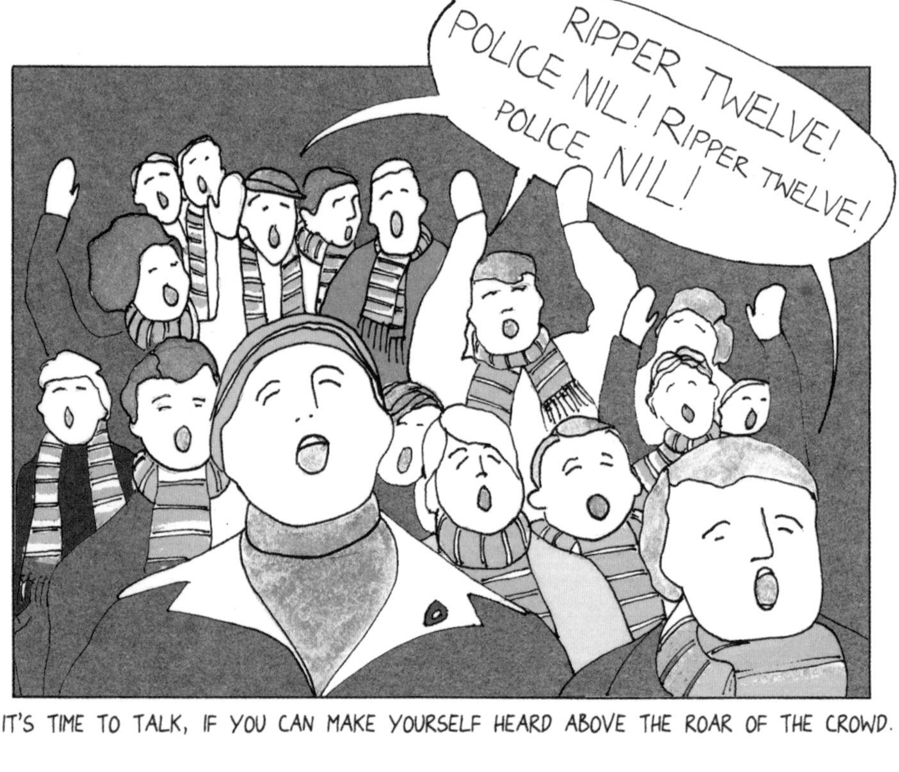
RIPPER TWELVE! POLICE NIL! RIPPER TWELVE! POLICE NIL!

IT'S TIME TO TALK, IF YOU CAN MAKE YOURSELF HEARD ABOVE THE ROAR OF THE CROWD.

IT'S GOOD TO TALK, BUT ACTION IS BETTER. IN THE UK AND AROUND THE WORLD, THE BULK OF THIS WORK IS DONE BY GROUPS OF WOMEN, WHO SCRAPE TOGETHER THE FUNDS AND GOODWILL TO RUN RAPE CRISIS CENTRES, REFUGES AND LEGAL ADVOCACY SERVICES.

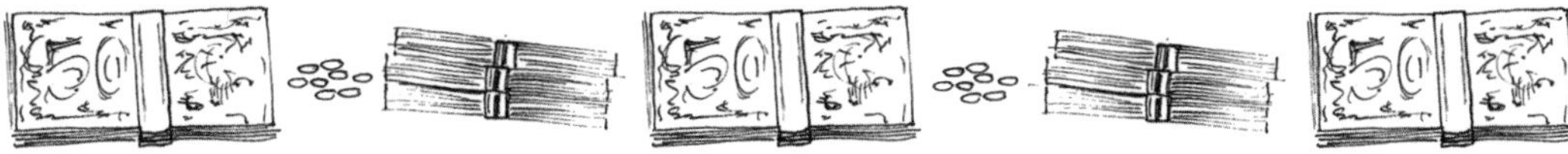

THEY HAVE TO FIGHT TO BE FUNDED BUT THEY STILL MANAGE TO CONSISTENTLY PROVIDE MUCH-NEEDED ACCESS TO JUSTICE, ALONG WITH PRACTICAL AND EMOTIONAL SUPPORT.

USUALLY, WHEN A PERSON IS INJURED, SYMPATHY AND COMFORT ARE ROUTINELY OFFERED, BUT GIRLS AND WOMEN ALL OVER THE WORLD OFTEN CAN'T *EVEN* COUNT ON THE SUPPORT OF THEIR OWN FAMILIES AFTER BEING ASSAULTED.

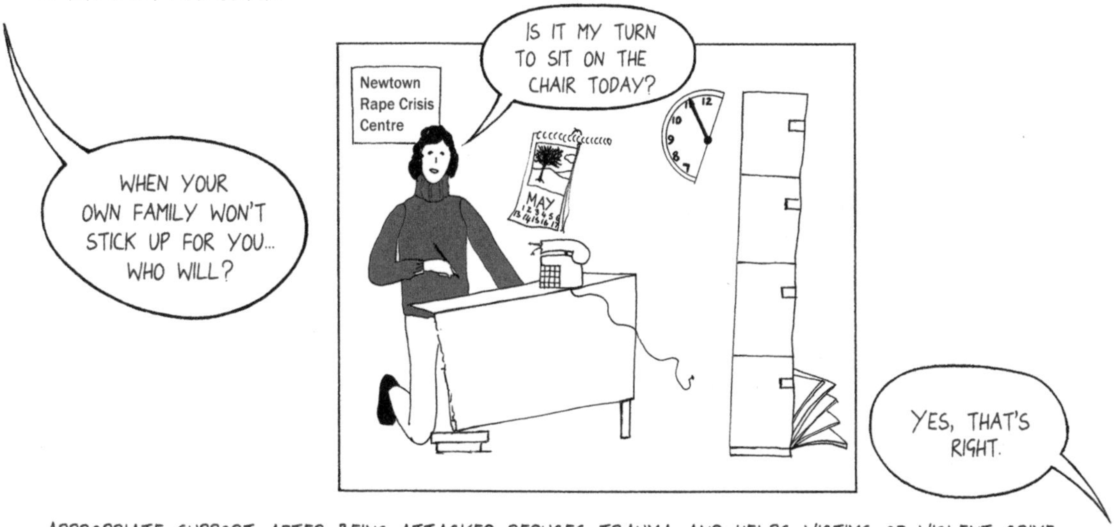
WHEN YOUR OWN FAMILY WON'T STICK UP FOR YOU... WHO WILL?
Newtown Rape Crisis Centre
IS IT MY TURN TO SIT ON THE CHAIR TODAY?
MAY
YES, THAT'S RIGHT.

APPROPRIATE SUPPORT AFTER BEING ATTACKED REDUCES TRAUMA AND HELPS VICTIMS OF VIOLENT CRIME TO RECOVER, SO FUNDING WOMEN'S SERVICES PROPERLY WOULD SAVE MONEY IN THE LONG RUN.

PEOPLE IN THE UK ARE NOT SHORT OF CASH, THEY'RE AMONG THE MOST PRIVILEGED PEOPLE IN THE WORLD, HAVING ENJOYED DECADES OF PEACE AND PROSPERITY, SO IT'S ODD THAT THEY NEGLECT SUCH ESSENTIAL SERVICES.

YOU'D THINK WE'D BE INTERESTED IN CATCHING CRIMINALS – BUT WE'VE LONG FOUND IT DIFFICULT TO GET OUR PRIORITIES RIGHT.

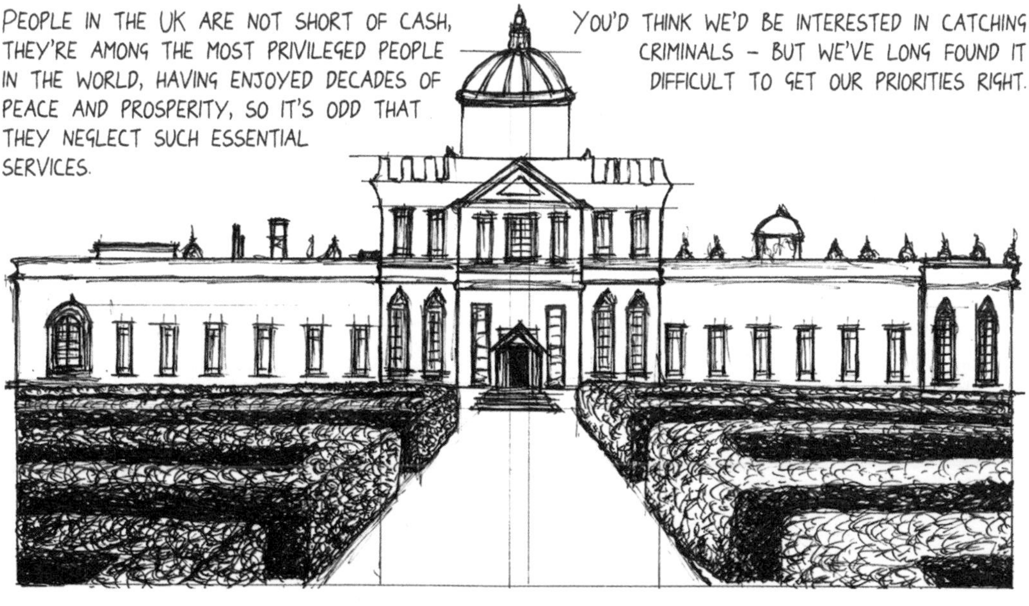

WOMEN ARE GOOD AT ORGANISING, CAMPAIGNING, HELPING ONE ANOTHER – EVEN WAR DOESN'T STOP THEM. IN A COUNTRY THAT WAS ONCE BRANDED THE RAPE CAPITAL OF THE WORLD:[13]

JULIENNE LUSENGE, PRESIDENT OF FEMALE SOLIDARITY FOR INTEGRATED PEACE AND DEVELOPMENT – A COALITION OF 40 WOMEN'S GRASSROOTS GROUPS IN EASTERN CONGO – PROVIDES SUPPORT TO SURVIVORS OF SEXUAL VIOLENCE, HELPING TO BRING THEIR CASES TO COURT AND CAMPAIGNING FOR REFORMS TO THE JUDICIAL SYSTEM IN CONGO.

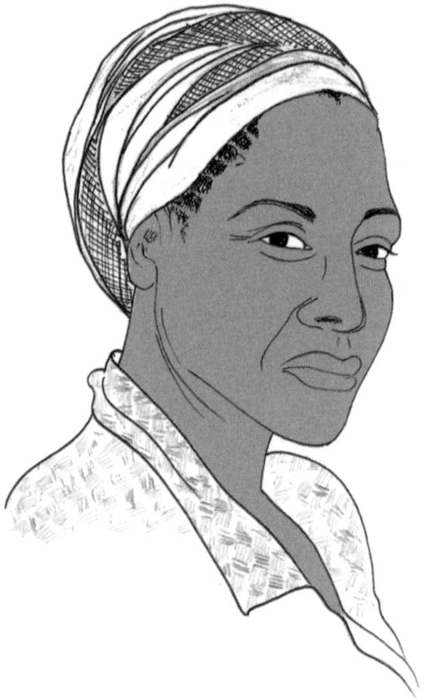

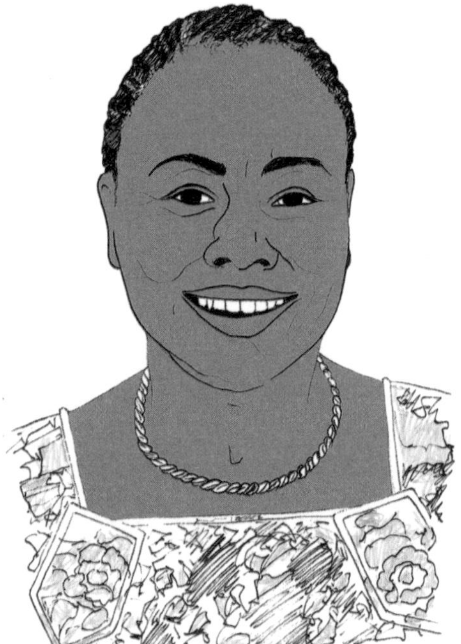

NEEMA NAMADAMU FOUNDED MAMAN SHUJAA, AN INITIATIVE THAT USES DIGITAL MEDIA TO AMPLIFY THE VOICES OF WOMEN DEMANDING PEACE IN EASTERN CONGO. THE ORGANISATION PROVIDES TRAINING TO WOMEN, WHO SHARE THEIR STORIES ONLINE.

SOLANGE LWASHIGA FURAHA IS EXECUTIVE SECRETARY OF THE SOUTH KIVU CONGOLESE WOMEN'S CAUCUS FOR PEACE. SOLANGE BRINGS FEMALE LEADERS FROM ACROSS THE REGION TOGETHER SO THAT WOMEN ARE INCLUDED IN PEACE TALKS AND CALLS ON CONGO TO RESPECT INTERNATIONAL COMMITMENTS TO GENDER EQUALITY.

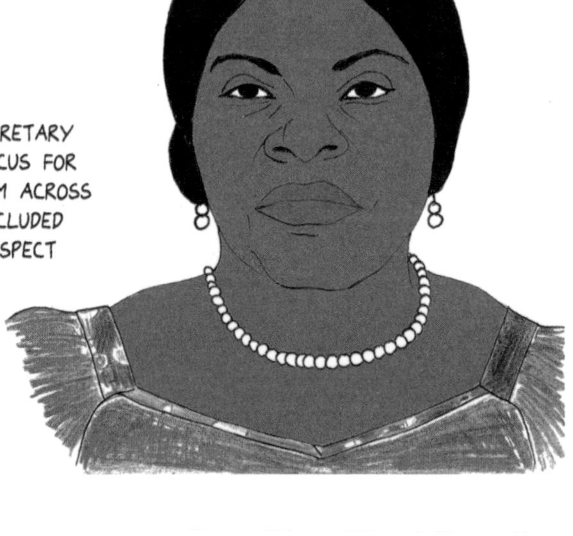

ACTIVISM IS COMMON BUT REVENGE IS RARE (OUTSIDE OF HOLLYWOOD FILMS). PEOPLE WHO SURVIVE SEXUALISED VIOLENCE TEND TO GO ABOUT THEIR LIVES, TAKING CARE OF THE EVERYDAY, SO ALTHOUGH THEY OFTEN DISPLAY SIGNS OF TRAUMA THAT ARE NOT DIFFICULT TO SPOT, THEY RARELY TAKE IT OUT ON OTHERS.

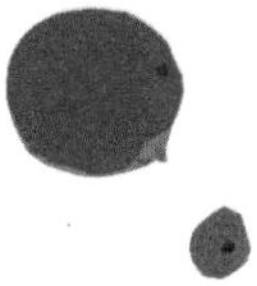

AUGUST 13TH, 2004, NAGPUR DISTRICT COURT, INDIA.

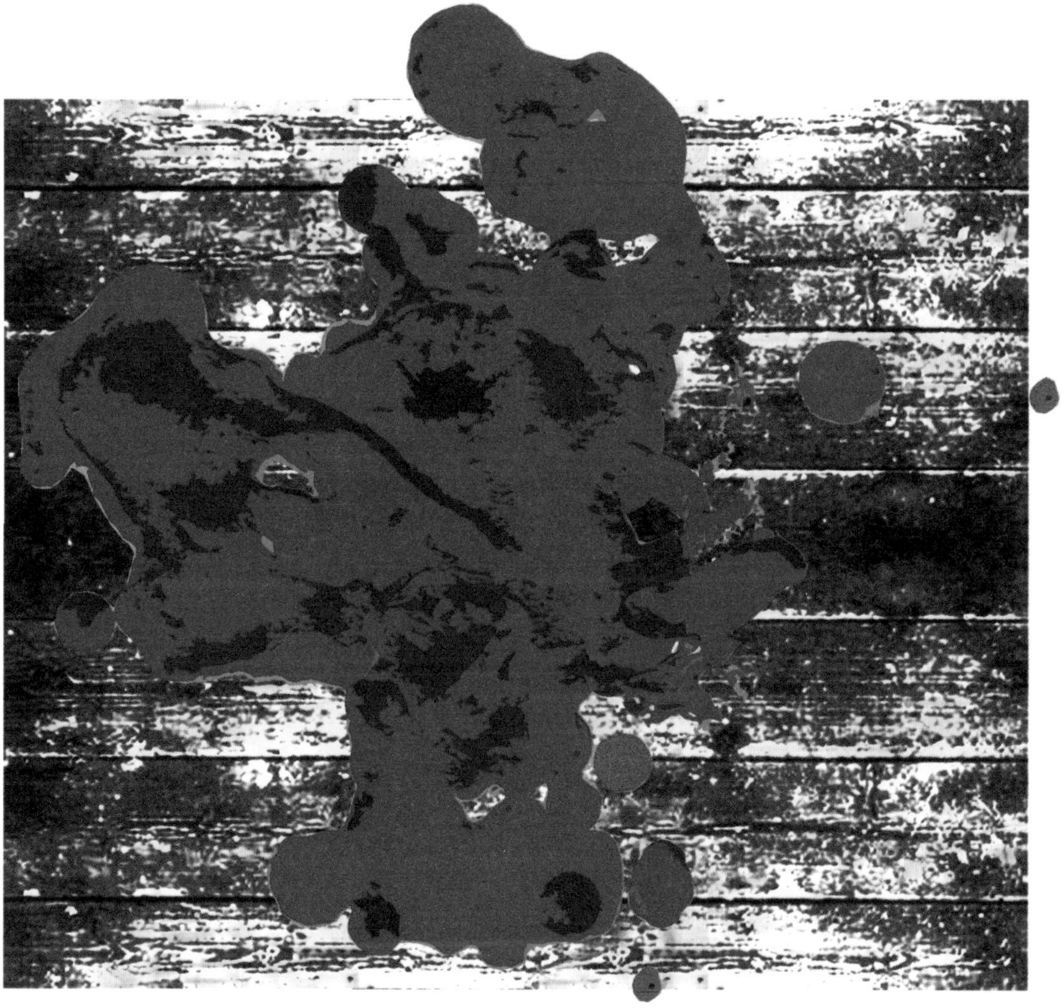

WHEN THE PEOPLE IN CHARGE OF THE CRIMINAL JUSTICE SYSTEM REPEATEDLY FAILED THEM AND LAUGHED AT THEIR PLIGHT, ONE GROUP OF 200 WOMEN IN NAGPUR, INDIA, TOOK THE LAW INTO THEIR OWN HANDS AND RID THEMSELVES OF A PROLIFICALLY VIOLENT MALE, WHO HAD BEEN MAKING THEIR EVERYDAY LIVES SUCH A MISERY, LEAVING A LARGE STAIN ON THE COURTHOUSE FLOOR.

THIS IS NOT A THING THAT *ANYONE* SHOULD NEED TO RESORT TO.

I THOUGHT ABOUT REVENGE. I USED TO FANTASISE ABOUT CHOPPING OFF THEO'S HEAD WITH AN AXE.

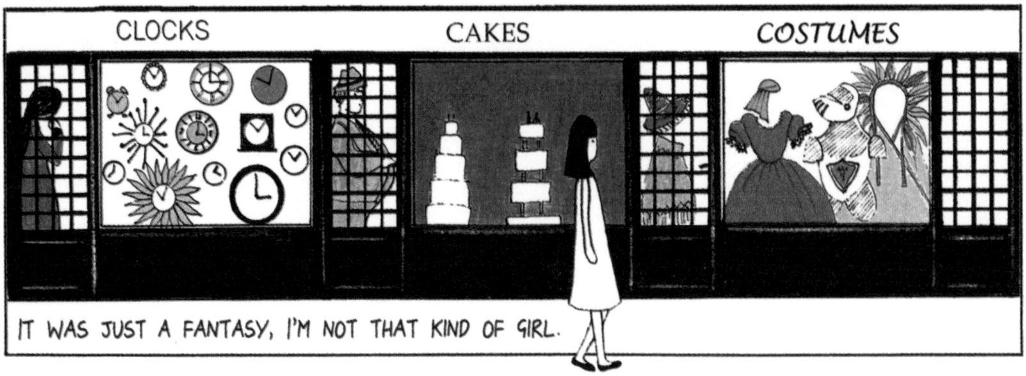
CLOCKS
CAKES
COSTUMES
IT WAS JUST A FANTASY, I'M NOT THAT KIND OF GIRL.

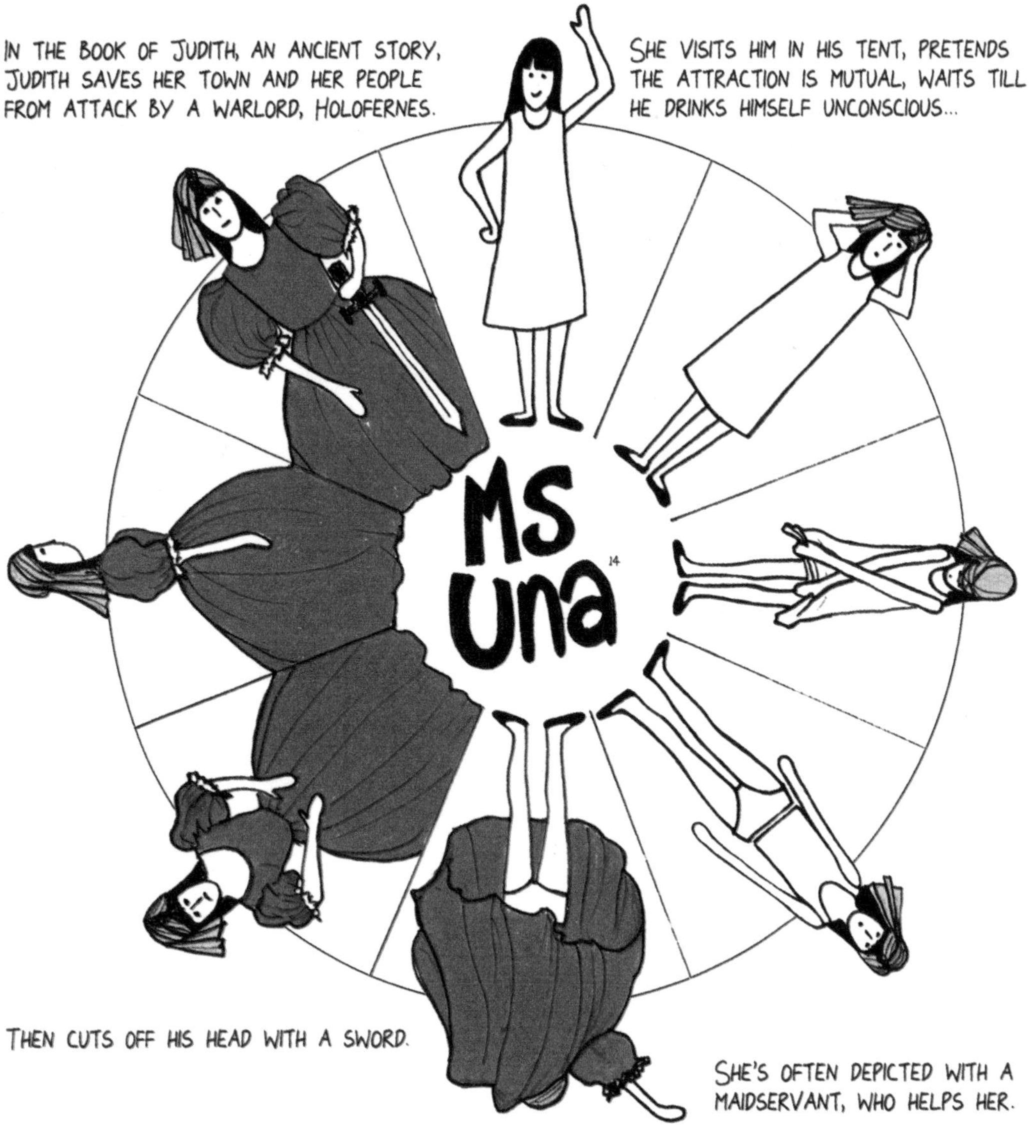
IN THE BOOK OF JUDITH, AN ANCIENT STORY, JUDITH SAVES HER TOWN AND HER PEOPLE FROM ATTACK BY A WARLORD, HOLOFERNES.
SHE VISITS HIM IN HIS TENT, PRETENDS THE ATTRACTION IS MUTUAL, WAITS TILL HE DRINKS HIMSELF UNCONSCIOUS...
Ms Una
THEN CUTS OFF HIS HEAD WITH A SWORD.
SHE'S OFTEN DEPICTED WITH A MAIDSERVANT, WHO HELPS HER.

ARTEMISIA GENTILESCHI WAS A WELL KNOWN ITALIAN BAROQUE PAINTER. SHE MADE TWO PAINTINGS OF JUDITH.

OTHER PAINTERS AT THE TIME PORTRAYED JUDITH AS A RATHER COY, SWEET-LOOKING GIRL, DELICATELY HOLDING THE HEAD OF HOLOFERNES ON A PLATE, SOMETIMES WEARING A PRETTY DRESS, SOMETIMES NUDE. EVEN CARAVAGGIO PAINTED JUDITH AS IF SHE WAS TRYING NOT TO GET HER DRESS DIRTY.

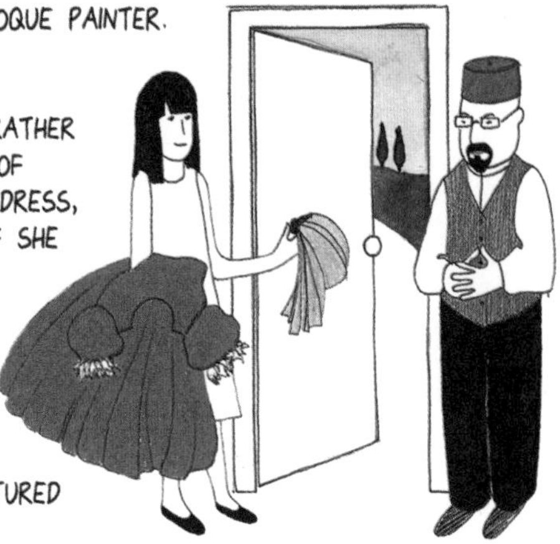

ARTEMISIA PAINTED HER FIRST JUDITH AT THE AGE OF SEVENTEEN, WHILE PARTICIPATING IN THE PROSECUTION OF THE MAN WHO RAPED HER WHEN HER FATHER LEFT HER IN HIS CARE. TO PROVE SHE WASN'T LYING, THE COURT TORTURED HER WITH THUMBSCREWS.

HER REPUTATION WAS DESTROYED BY THE SCANDAL AND SHE HAD TO MARRY AND MOVE TO A DIFFERENT AREA.

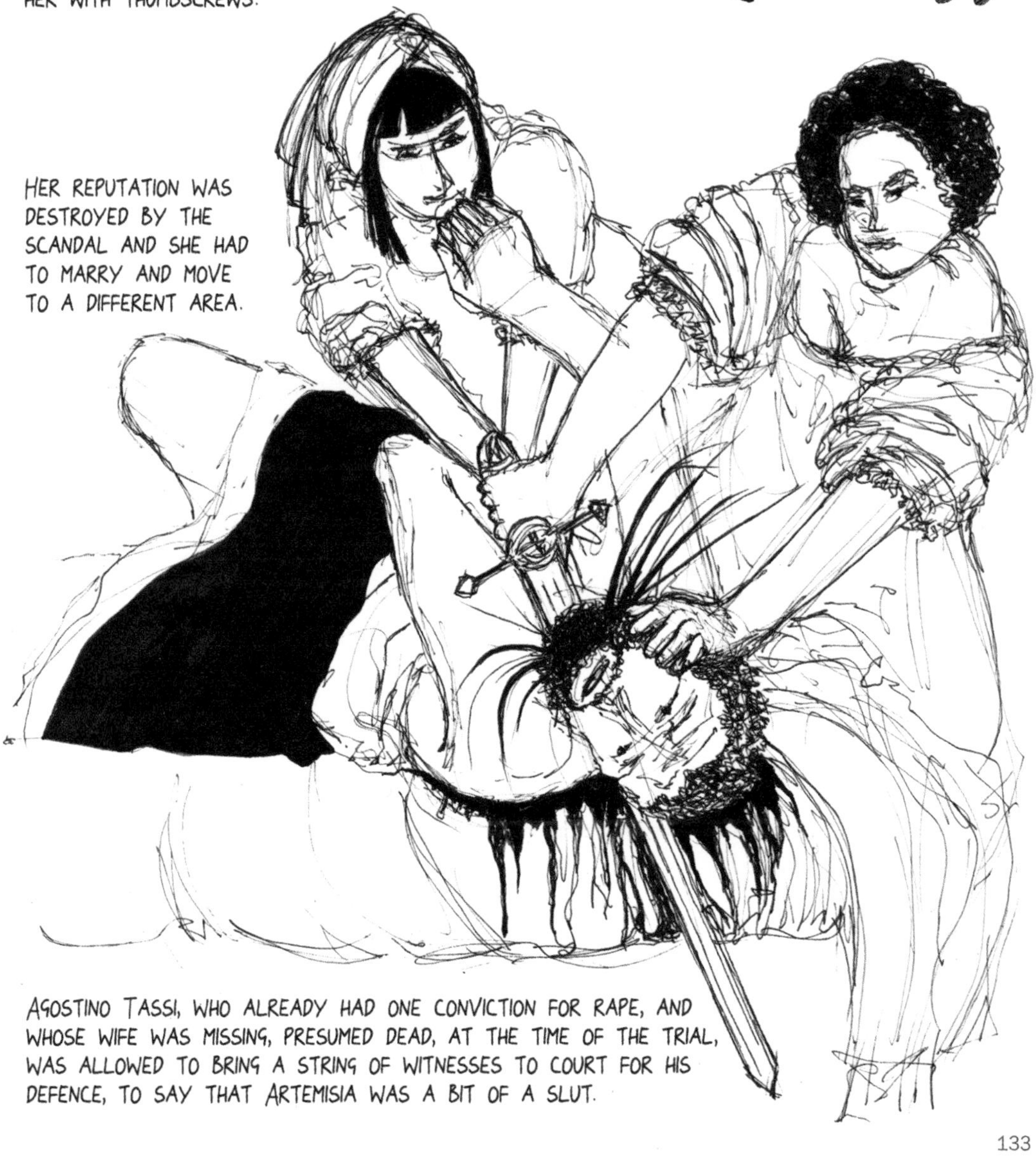

AGOSTINO TASSI, WHO ALREADY HAD ONE CONVICTION FOR RAPE, AND WHOSE WIFE WAS MISSING, PRESUMED DEAD, AT THE TIME OF THE TRIAL, WAS ALLOWED TO BRING A STRING OF WITNESSES TO COURT FOR HIS DEFENCE, TO SAY THAT ARTEMISIA WAS A BIT OF A SLUT.

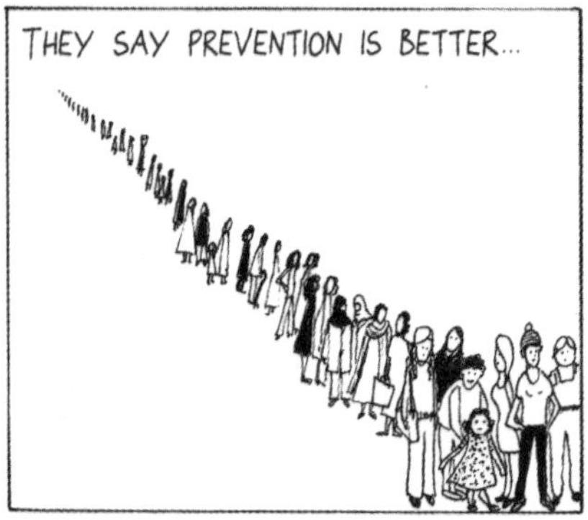
THEY SAY PREVENTION IS BETTER...

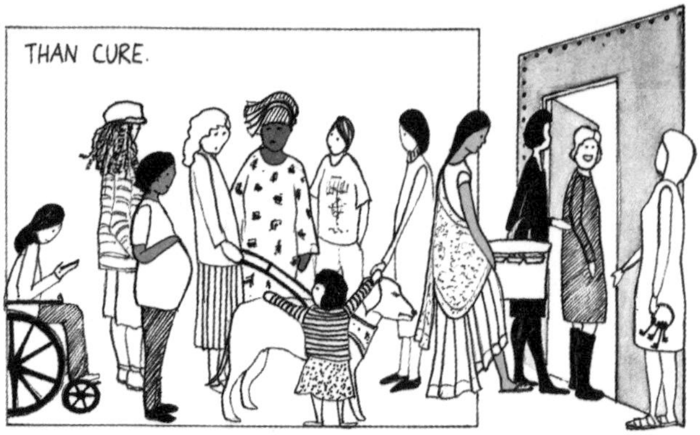
THAN CURE.

SO WE COULD TRY LOCKING AWAY ALL THE WOMEN AND ALL THE GIRLS, AS ADVISED, AD INFINITUM, BY EVERYONE, EVERYWHERE.

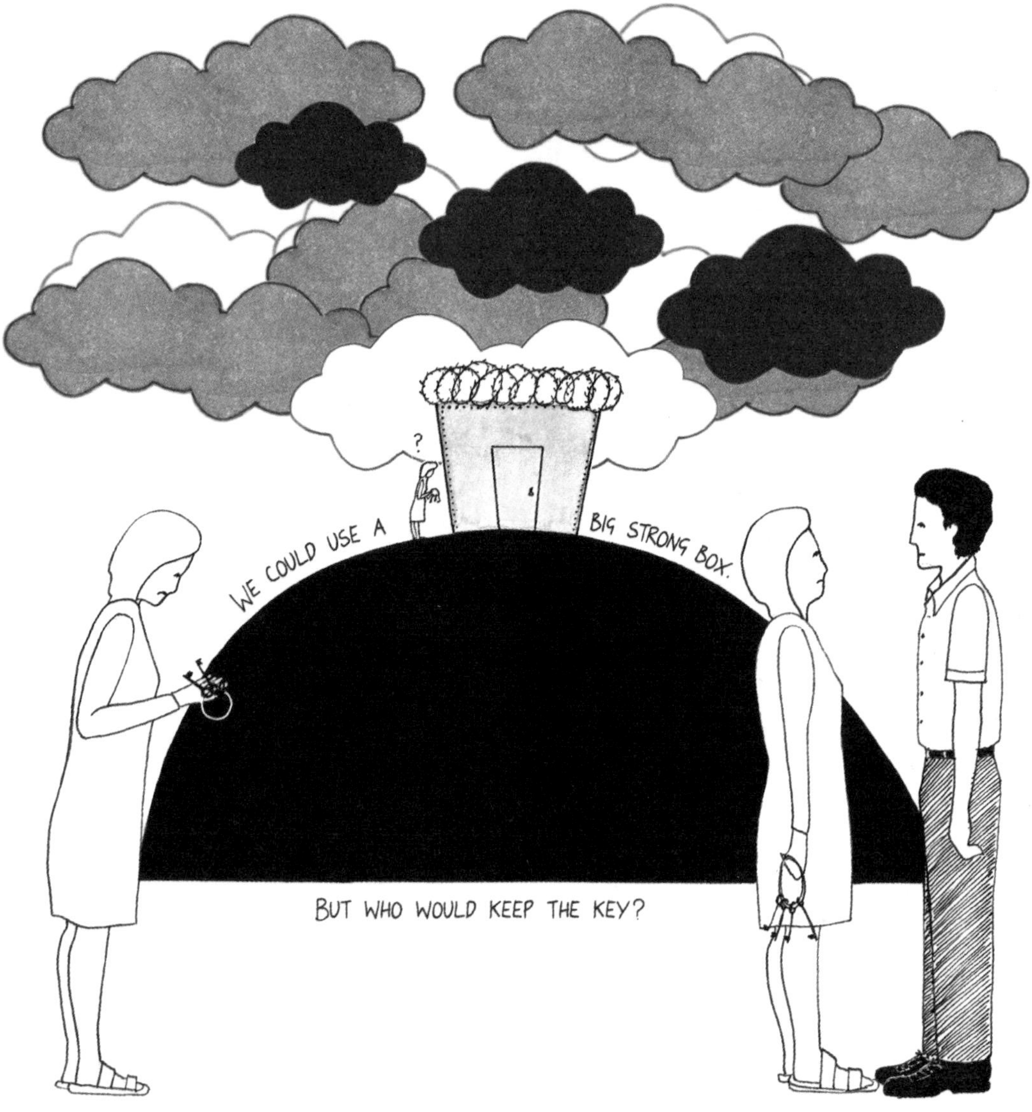
?
WE COULD USE A BIG STRONG BOX.
BUT WHO WOULD KEEP THE KEY?

OR MAYBE?

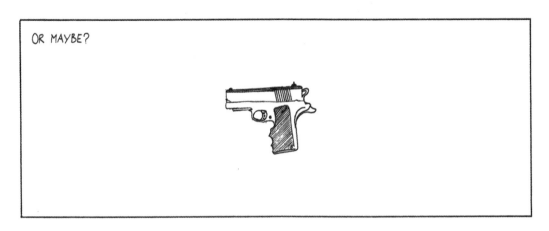

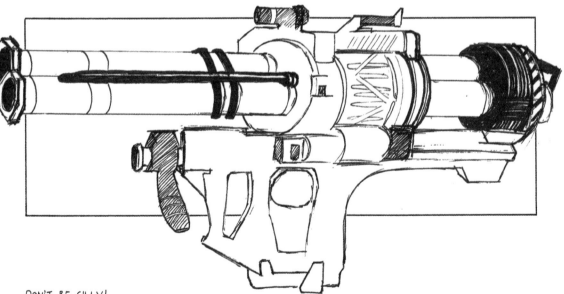

DON'T BE SILLY!
YOU HAVE TO PUT THE GUN DOWN SOME TIME.
PERHAPS IT'S SOMETHING ELSE THAT NEEDS TO CHANGE?

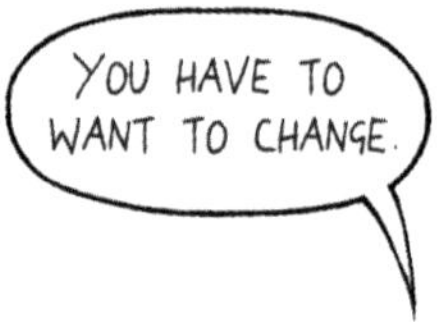
YOU HAVE TO WANT TO CHANGE.

SOME PEOPLE USE HUMOUR AS A DEFENCE MECHANISM, YOU KNOW.

I'VE HAD CONVERSATIONS...

WITH VARIOUS THERAPISTS...

HA!

IN WHICH MY INAPPROPRIATE LAUGHTER WAS MET WITH DISAPPROVAL. IT STRIKES ME AS ODD THAT UNDER THOSE CIRCUMSTANCES THEY FELT A NEED TO DIRECT ME TO TAKE MY EXPERIENCES MORE SERIOUSLY.

SURELY MENTAL HEALTH PROFESSIONALS REALISE HOW SERIOUS HUMOUR CAN BE?

SOME OF THE MOST SERIOUS THINKING IS DONE BY HUMOURISTS – IT'S NOT ALL FART JOKES AND GENTLE OBSERVATION, YOU KNOW.

A GOOD THERAPIST DOES AT LEAST UNDERSTAND ANGER BETTER THAN MOST PEOPLE, WHICH IS USEFUL...

BECAUSE I AM ANGRY–I'M MAD AS HELL! WOULDN'T YOU BE?

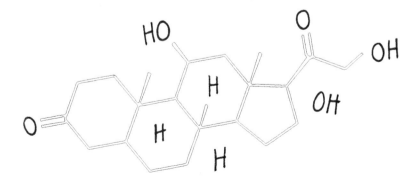

FROM A PURELY SCIENTIFIC POINT OF VIEW, LAUGHTER REDUCES THE STRESS HORMONE CORTISOL, SO IT'S A SHAME THEY DIDN'T GET MY JOKES, BECAUSE I COULD HAVE DONE WITH A LAUGH.

1970S COMEDIANS, THE FOUR BASIC TYPES.

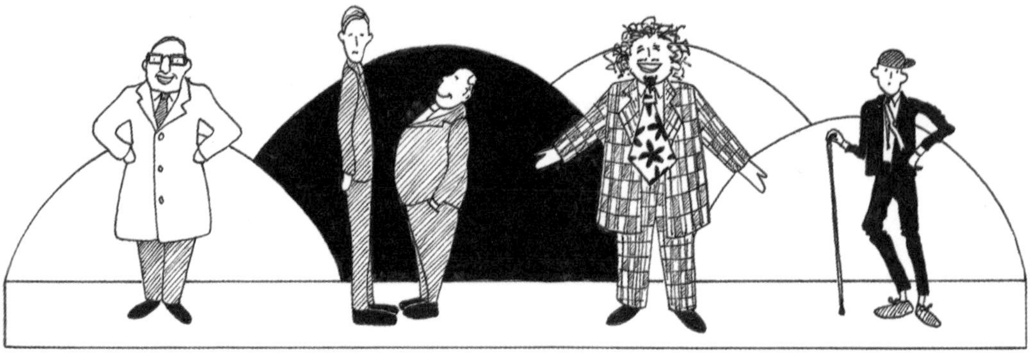

1970S FUNNY FEMALES, THE THREE BASIC TYPES.

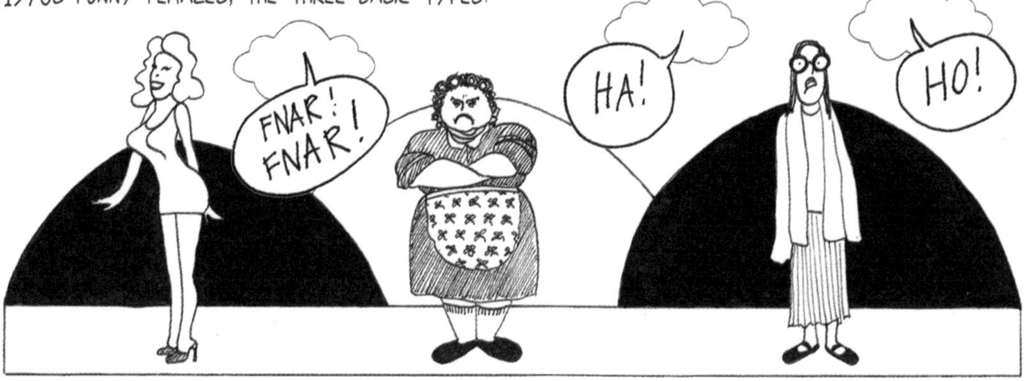
FNAR! FNAR!
HA!
HO!

THERE WAS A TIME IN THE 70S WHEN WOMEN WEREN'T MEANT TO BE FUNNY, WELL, NOT IN THAT WAY. THAT KIND OF THING WENT OUT OF FASHION, THANKFULLY.

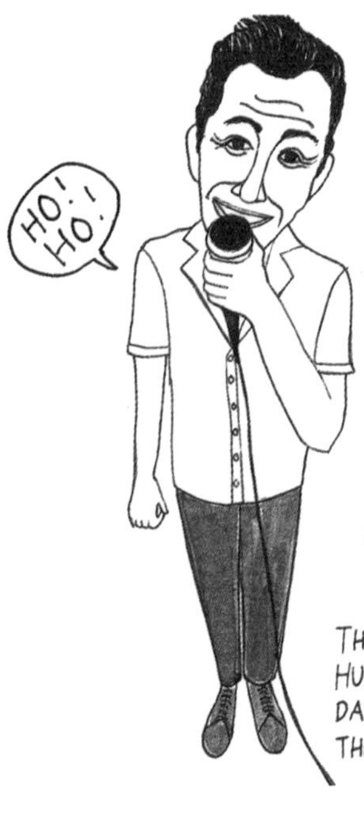
HO! HO!

MORE RECENTLY, YOUNG MEN WHO YOU'D THINK WOULD KNOW BETTER SEEM TO BELIEVE THAT MISOGYNY IS A HILARIOUS FORM OF IRONY.

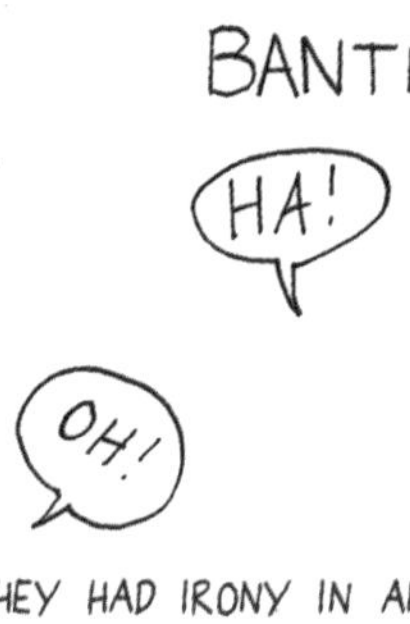
BANTER!
HA!
OH!

THEY HAD IRONY IN ANCIENT GREECE TOO; HUMOUR IS A PHILOSOPHICAL PROBLEM, DATING BACK TO ARISTOTLE, WHO DIDN'T THINK MUCH OF WOMEN EITHER.

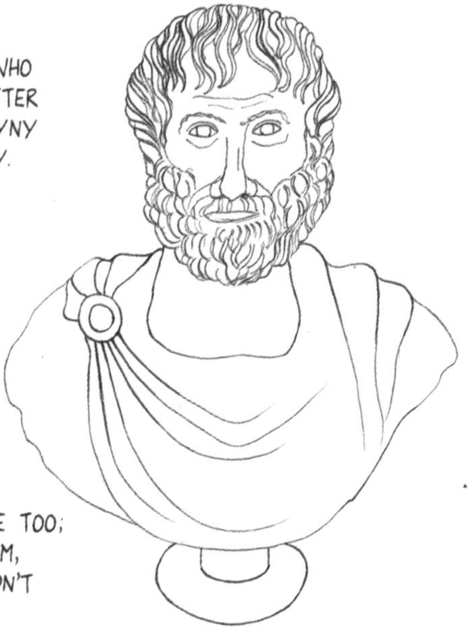

THERE WASN'T A LACK OF FEMINISM IN THE 70S – ON THE CONTRARY, IT WAS A BOOM PERIOD – BUT I SUFFERED FROM A LACK OF EXPOSURE TO IT. THIS UNDOUBTEDLY MADE MY SITUATION WORSE; BECOMING A WOMAN IS HARD WORK MADE HARDER, WITHOUT A LITTLE OF THE F WORD.

IT'S TAKEN FOR GRANTED THAT GIRLS WANT TO AND CAN BECOME WOMEN *IN THE PROPER WAY*. UNFORTUNATELY IT'S UP TO OTHER PEOPLE TO DECIDE IF WE GOT IT RIGHT...

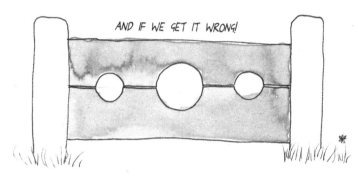

AND IF WE GET IT WRONG!

What, little me?

EVEN IF YOU ARE THE TYPE OF WOMAN TO WHOM THIS PROPERNESS COMES EASILY, DON'T KID YOURSELF, THERE ARE NO PRIZES WORTH WINNING. AND, IF YOU AREN'T? YOU CAN ALWAYS REBEL.

KISS, KISS, KISS FUN, FUN LIFE!

I'M SOMETIMES PAINTED AS HAVING BEEN REBELLIOUS IN MY YOUTH. THIS IS NONSENSE – ALTHOUGH I ADOPTED A STYLE OF DRESS THAT LOOKED REBELLIOUS, IT WAS ALL ON THE SURFACE.

PUNK EMERGED IN THE MID 70S, WHILE I WAS STILL INTO VAL DOONICAN. YOUNG PEOPLE BOUNCED AROUND MAKING A NOISE, REJECTING PROPERNESS AND OTHER HYPOCRISY AND SUDDENLY, WOMEN WERE ON STAGE, THRASHING GUITARS, SHOUTING, CALLING THEIR BANDS RUDE NAMES...

I'D LIKE TO PRETEND THIS MUSICAL MOVEMENT GAVE ME A CHANCE TO EMBRACE BEING AN OUTCAST, BUT I COULDN'T EMBRACE IT, I JUST WANTED TO BE *NORMAL*. INSTEAD OF LOVING *THE SLITS*, I LIKED BLONDIE!

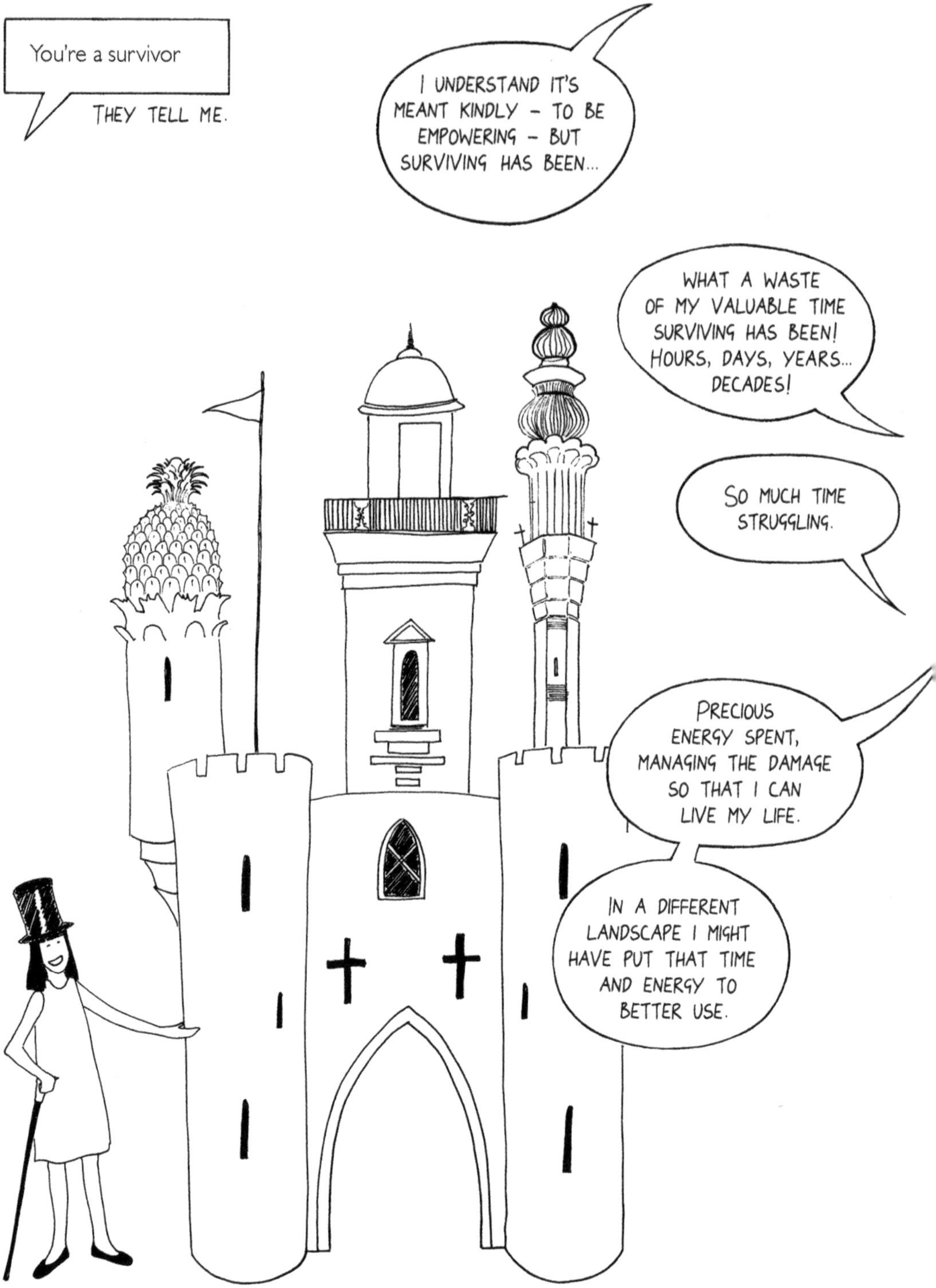
You're a survivor
THEY TELL ME.
I UNDERSTAND IT'S MEANT KINDLY – TO BE EMPOWERING – BUT SURVIVING HAS BEEN...
WHAT A WASTE OF MY VALUABLE TIME SURVIVING HAS BEEN! HOURS, DAYS, YEARS... DECADES!
SO MUCH TIME STRUGGLING.
PRECIOUS ENERGY SPENT, MANAGING THE DAMAGE SO THAT I CAN LIVE MY LIFE.
IN A DIFFERENT LANDSCAPE I MIGHT HAVE PUT THAT TIME AND ENERGY TO BETTER USE.

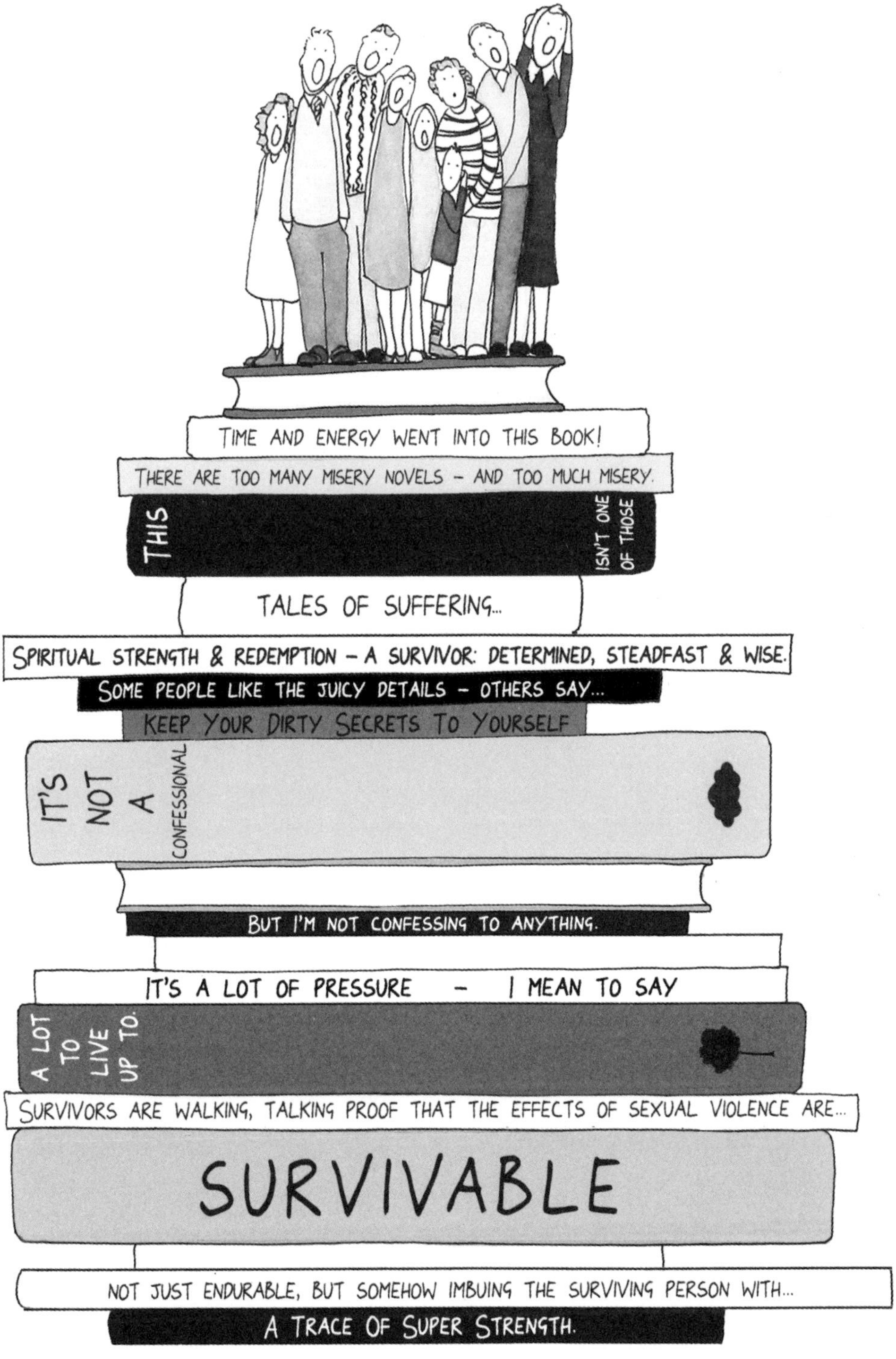

TIME AND ENERGY WENT INTO THIS BOOK!
THERE ARE TOO MANY MISERY NOVELS – AND TOO MUCH MISERY.
THIS
ISN'T ONE OF THOSE
TALES OF SUFFERING...
SPIRITUAL STRENGTH & REDEMPTION – A SURVIVOR: DETERMINED, STEADFAST & WISE.
SOME PEOPLE LIKE THE JUICY DETAILS – OTHERS SAY...
KEEP YOUR DIRTY SECRETS TO YOURSELF
IT'S NOT A CONFESSIONAL
BUT I'M NOT CONFESSING TO ANYTHING.
IT'S A LOT OF PRESSURE – I MEAN TO SAY
A LOT TO LIVE UP TO.
SURVIVORS ARE WALKING, TALKING PROOF THAT THE EFFECTS OF SEXUAL VIOLENCE ARE...
SURVIVABLE
NOT JUST ENDURABLE, BUT SOMEHOW IMBUING THE SURVIVING PERSON WITH...
A TRACE OF SUPER STRENGTH.

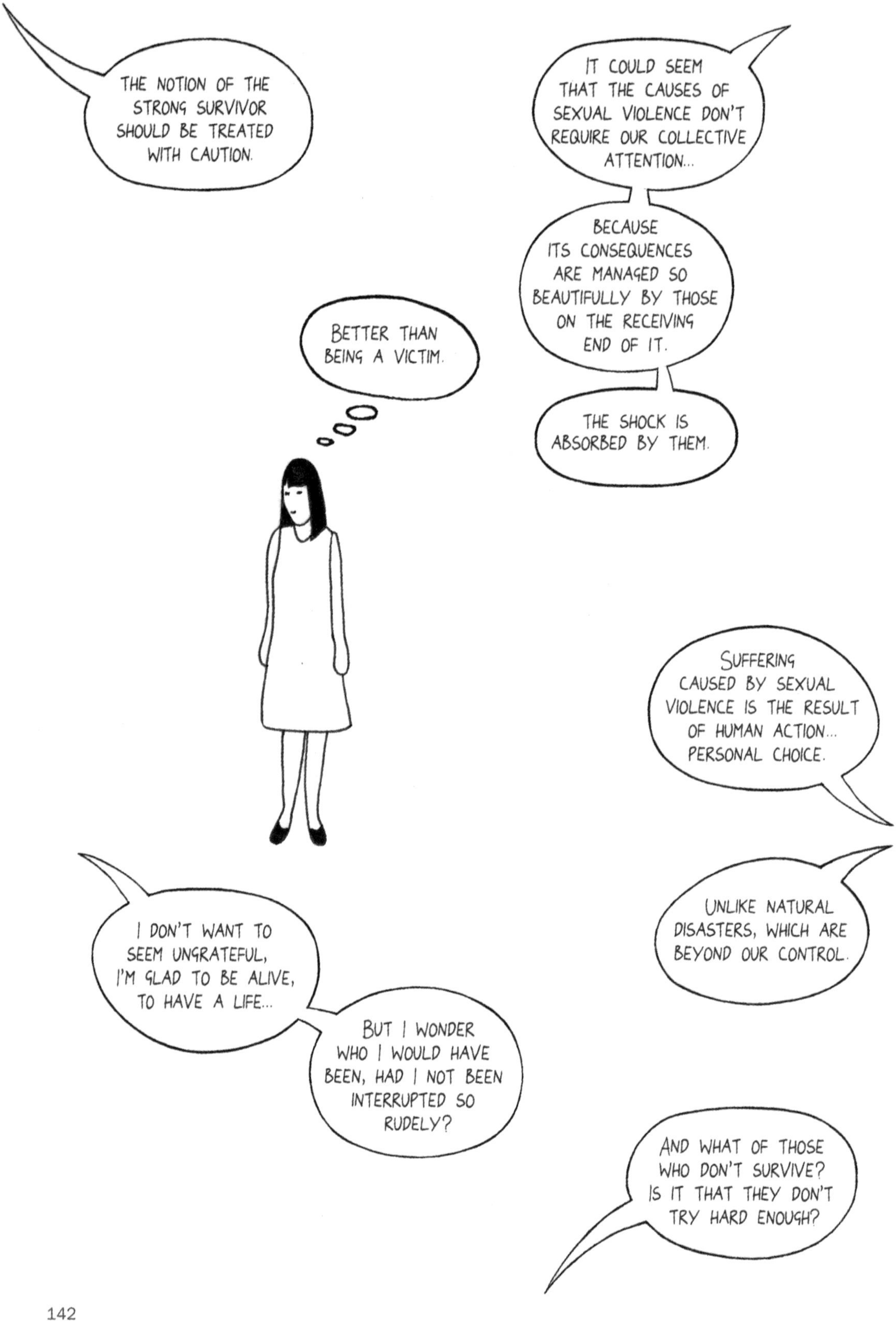
THE NOTION OF THE STRONG SURVIVOR SHOULD BE TREATED WITH CAUTION.
IT COULD SEEM THAT THE CAUSES OF SEXUAL VIOLENCE DON'T REQUIRE OUR COLLECTIVE ATTENTION...
BECAUSE ITS CONSEQUENCES ARE MANAGED SO BEAUTIFULLY BY THOSE ON THE RECEIVING END OF IT.
THE SHOCK IS ABSORBED BY THEM.
BETTER THAN BEING A VICTIM.
SUFFERING CAUSED BY SEXUAL VIOLENCE IS THE RESULT OF HUMAN ACTION... PERSONAL CHOICE.
UNLIKE NATURAL DISASTERS, WHICH ARE BEYOND OUR CONTROL.
I DON'T WANT TO SEEM UNGRATEFUL, I'M GLAD TO BE ALIVE, TO HAVE A LIFE...
BUT I WONDER WHO I WOULD HAVE BEEN, HAD I NOT BEEN INTERRUPTED SO RUDELY?
AND WHAT OF THOSE WHO DON'T SURVIVE? IS IT THAT THEY DON'T TRY HARD ENOUGH?

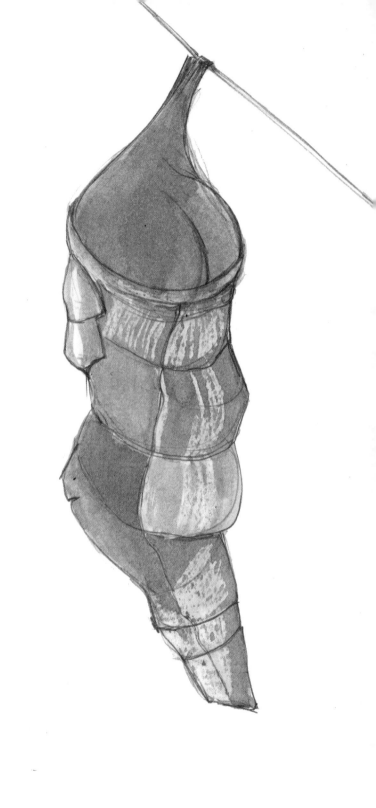

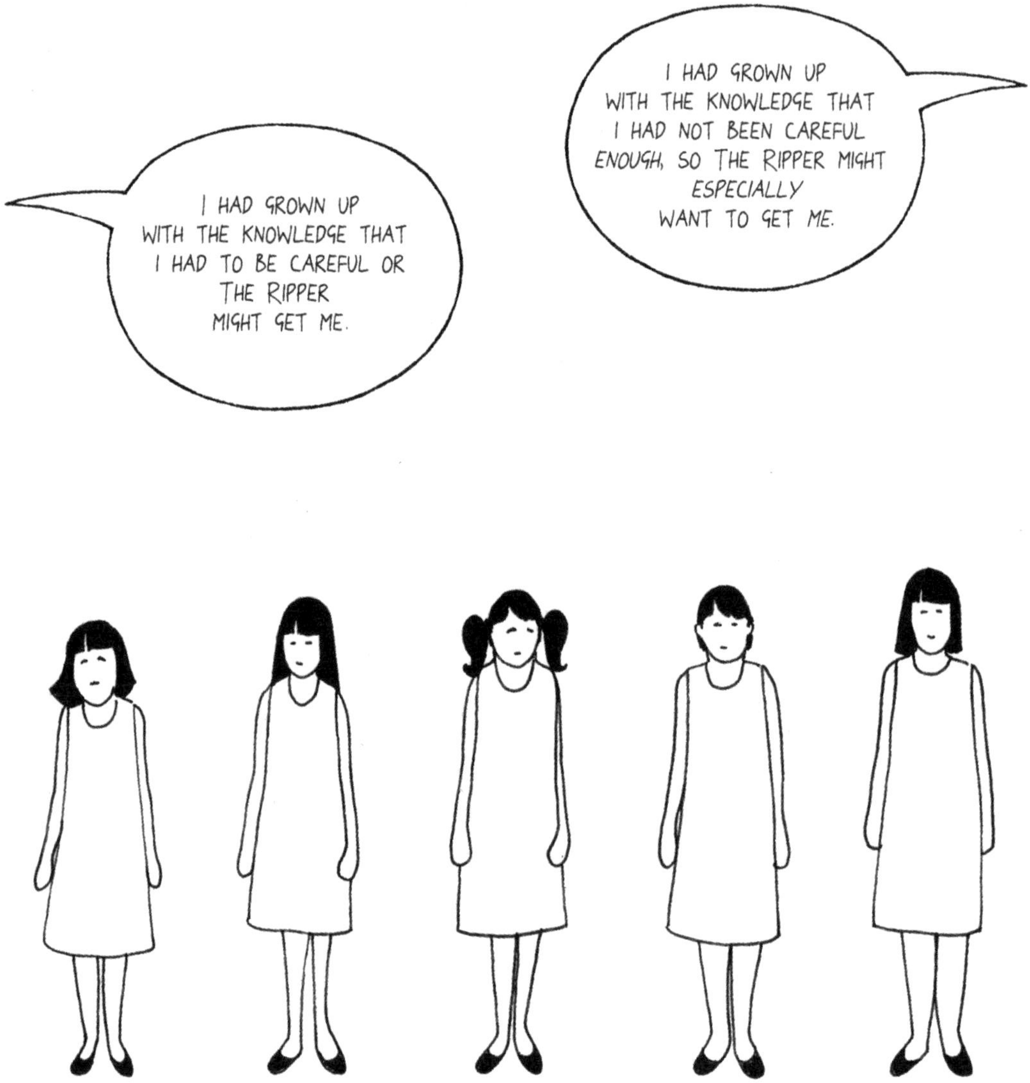
I HAD GROWN UP WITH THE KNOWLEDGE THAT I HAD TO BE CAREFUL OR THE RIPPER MIGHT GET ME.
I HAD GROWN UP WITH THE KNOWLEDGE THAT I HAD NOT BEEN CAREFUL *ENOUGH*, SO THE RIPPER MIGHT *ESPECIALLY* WANT TO GET ME.

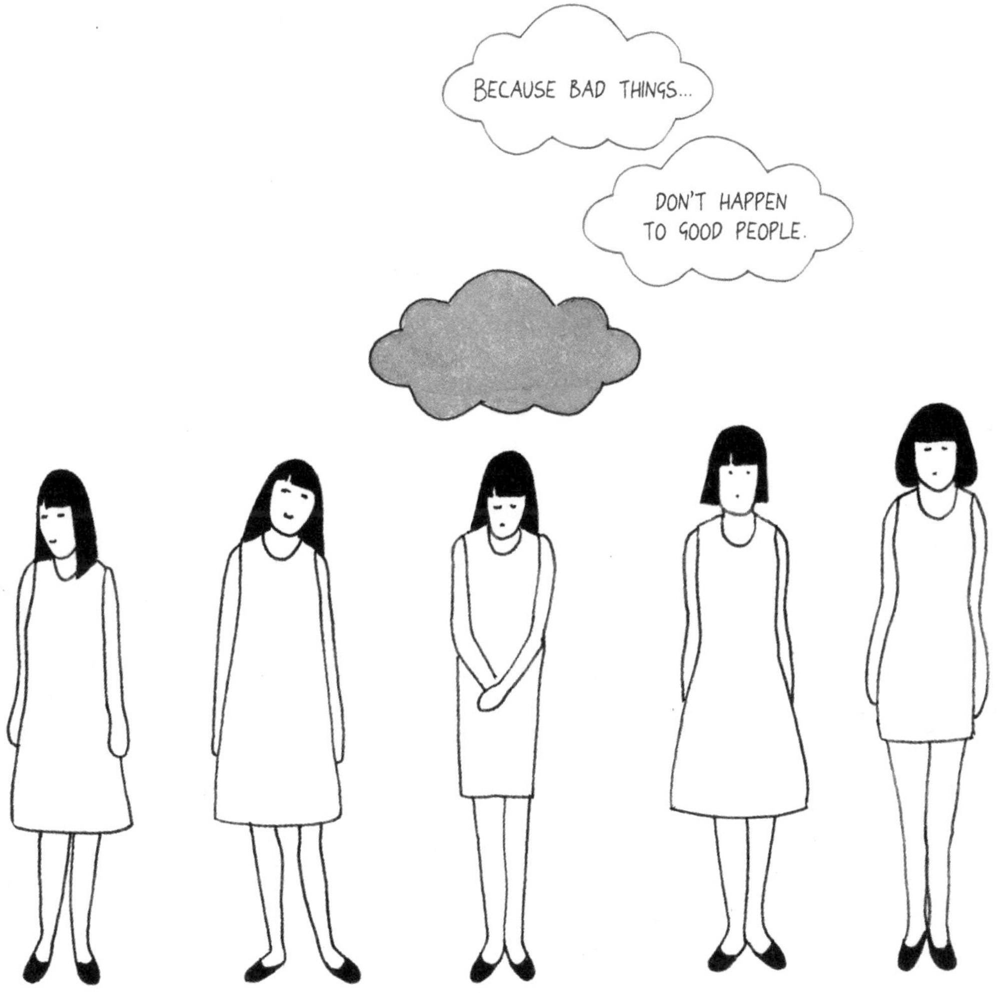
BECAUSE BAD THINGS...
DON'T HAPPEN TO GOOD PEOPLE.

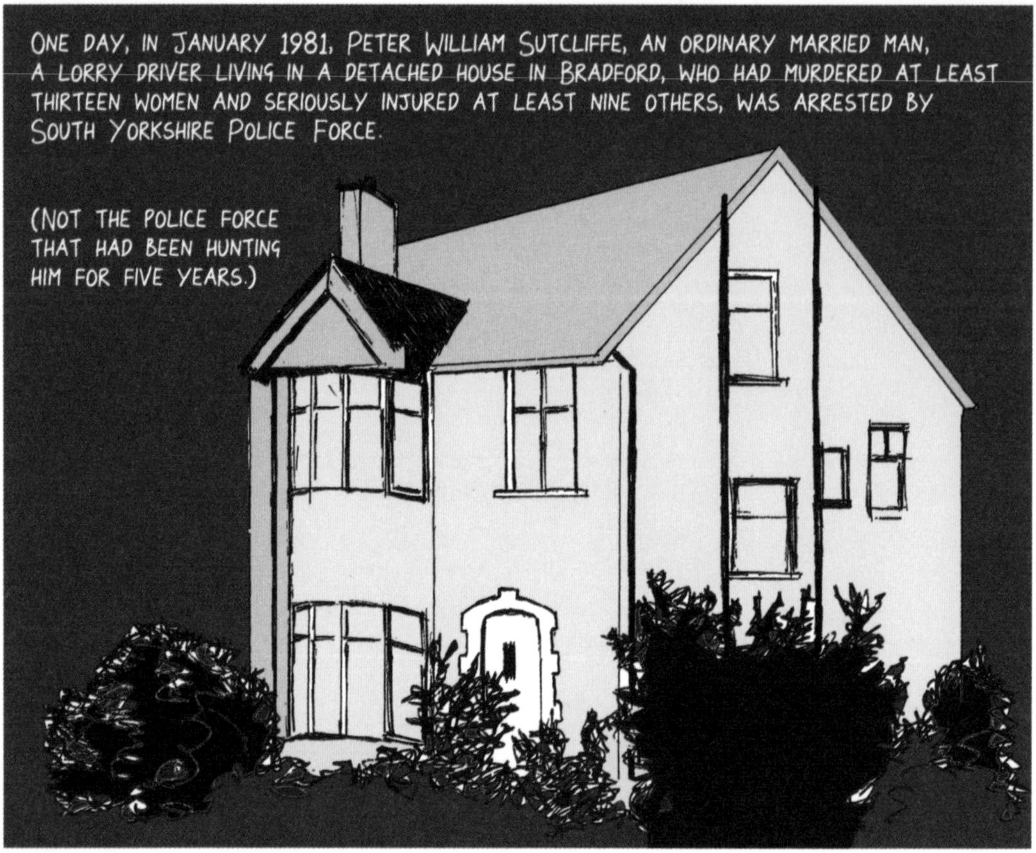
ONE DAY, IN JANUARY 1981, PETER WILLIAM SUTCLIFFE, AN ORDINARY MARRIED MAN, A LORRY DRIVER LIVING IN A DETACHED HOUSE IN BRADFORD, WHO HAD MURDERED AT LEAST THIRTEEN WOMEN AND SERIOUSLY INJURED AT LEAST NINE OTHERS, WAS ARRESTED BY SOUTH YORKSHIRE POLICE FORCE.
(NOT THE POLICE FORCE THAT HAD BEEN HUNTING HIM FOR FIVE YEARS.)

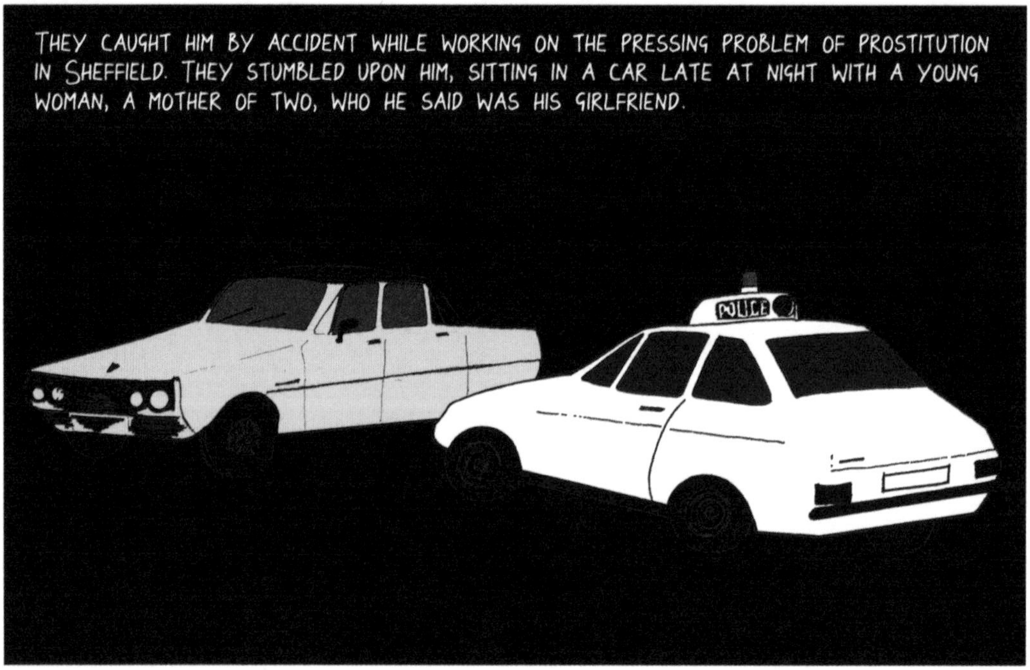
THEY CAUGHT HIM BY ACCIDENT WHILE WORKING ON THE PRESSING PROBLEM OF PROSTITUTION IN SHEFFIELD. THEY STUMBLED UPON HIM, SITTING IN A CAR LATE AT NIGHT WITH A YOUNG WOMAN, A MOTHER OF TWO, WHO HE SAID WAS HIS GIRLFRIEND.
POLICE

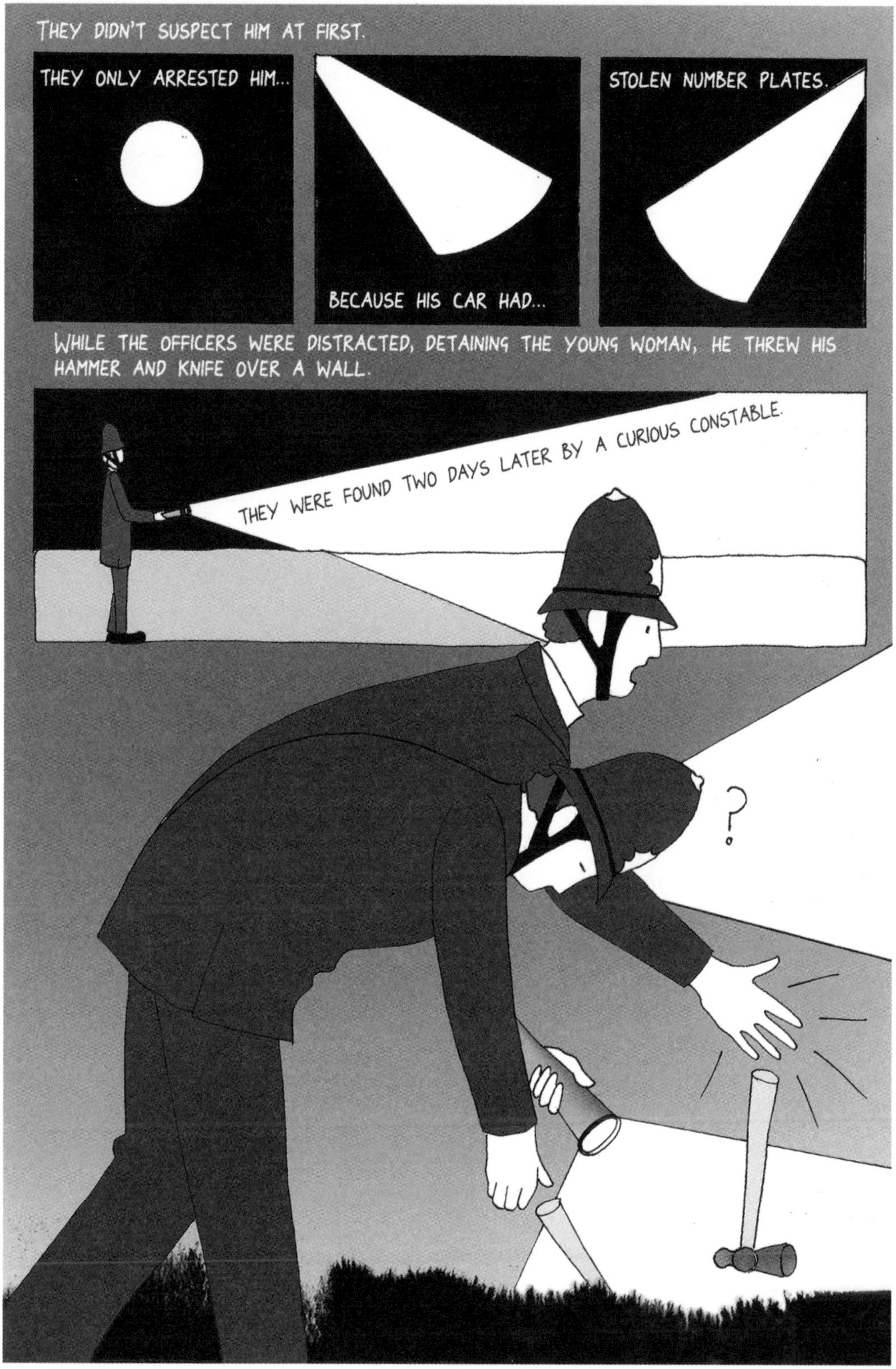
THEY DIDN'T SUSPECT HIM AT FIRST.
THEY ONLY ARRESTED HIM...
BECAUSE HIS CAR HAD...
STOLEN NUMBER PLATES.
WHILE THE OFFICERS WERE DISTRACTED, DETAINING THE YOUNG WOMAN, HE THREW HIS HAMMER AND KNIFE OVER A WALL.
THEY WERE FOUND TWO DAYS LATER BY A CURIOUS CONSTABLE.
?

BACK AT THE STATION, SUTCLIFFE SEEMED NERVOUS. HE KEPT CHANGING HIS STORY WHEN QUESTIONED. THE SOUTH YORKSHIRE OFFICERS DECIDED TO KEEP HIM FOR A WHILE, TO SEE WHAT HE WAS UP TO.

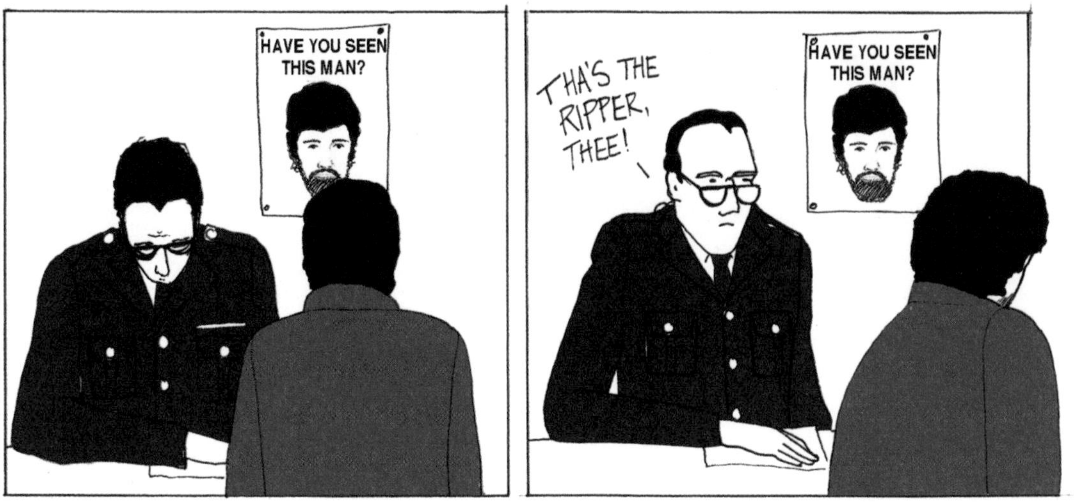
HAVE YOU SEEN THIS MAN?
THA'S THE RIPPER, THEE!
HAVE YOU SEEN THIS MAN?

AN OFFICER AT THE DESK JOKED WITH HIM THAT HE WAS THE YORKSHIRE RIPPER. HE DIDN'T REPLY.

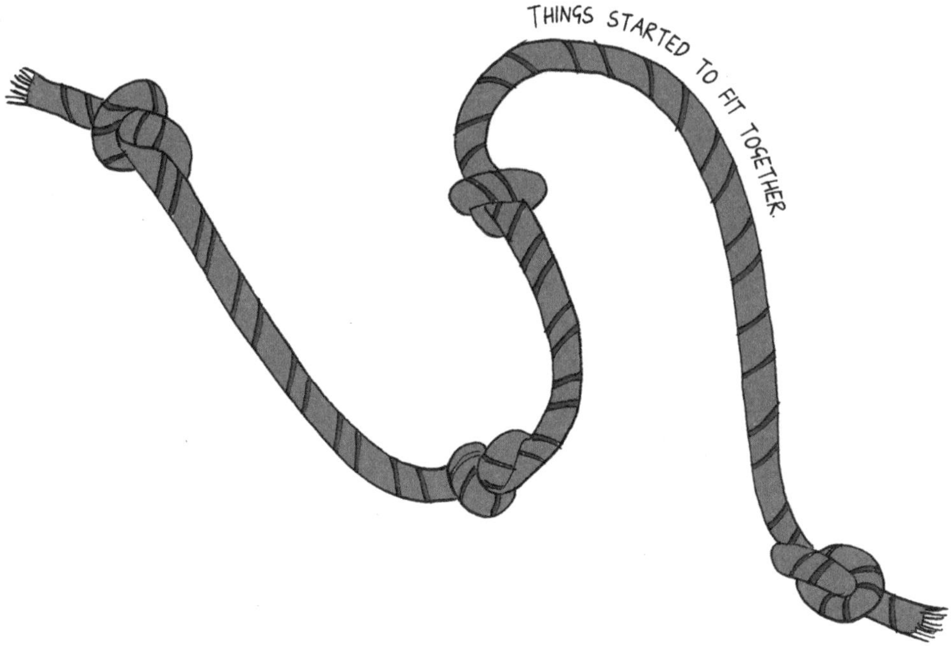
THINGS STARTED TO FIT TOGETHER.

HE DIDN'T HAVE A SATISFACTORY EXPLANATION AS TO WHY HE HAD A PIECE OF BLUE AND RED ROPE IN THE BOOT OF HIS CAR WITH KNOTS TIED IN IT AT ODD INTERVALS.
SOUTH YORKSHIRE PHONED WEST YORKSHIRE, TO SEE WHAT THEY HAD TO SAY.

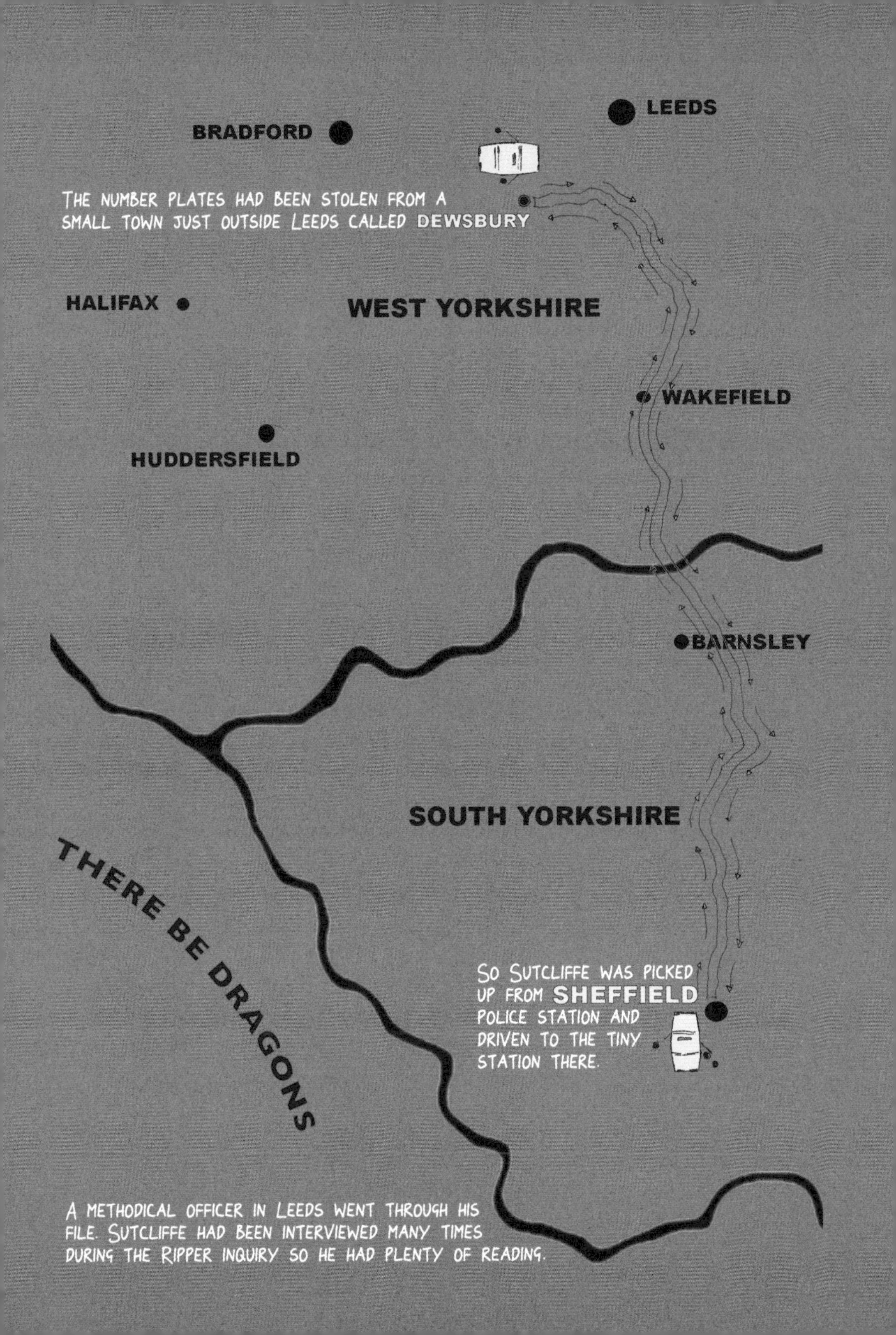
LEEDS
BRADFORD
THE NUMBER PLATES HAD BEEN STOLEN FROM A SMALL TOWN JUST OUTSIDE LEEDS CALLED DEWSBURY
HALIFAX
WEST YORKSHIRE
WAKEFIELD
HUDDERSFIELD
BARNSLEY
SOUTH YORKSHIRE
THERE BE DRAGONS
SO SUTCLIFFE WAS PICKED UP FROM SHEFFIELD POLICE STATION AND DRIVEN TO THE TINY STATION THERE.
A METHODICAL OFFICER IN LEEDS WENT THROUGH HIS FILE. SUTCLIFFE HAD BEEN INTERVIEWED MANY TIMES DURING THE RIPPER INQUIRY SO HE HAD PLENTY OF READING.

EVENTUALLY, HE STARTED TO TALK.

THEY PAID CLOSE ATTENTION TO WHAT HE TOLD THEM.

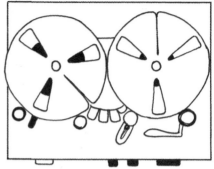

THEY LISTENED CAREFULLY, MAKING NOTES.

GOD TOLD ME TO KILL PROSTITUTES

HE SAID.

THAT SEEMED REASONABLE...

AFTER ALL, EVERYONE HAD BEEN READING THE SAME PAPERS...

RIPPER'S NEW VICTIM

ALL THE GREAT STORIES: THE COLUMNS, THE OPINIONS, THE EDITORIALS.

THE RIPPER HAD EVEN BEGUN TO DEVELOP A FAN BASE.

'I reckon your boys are letting you down, George; they can't be much good, can they?'

MAD?

BAD?

NOT MAD

NOT BAD

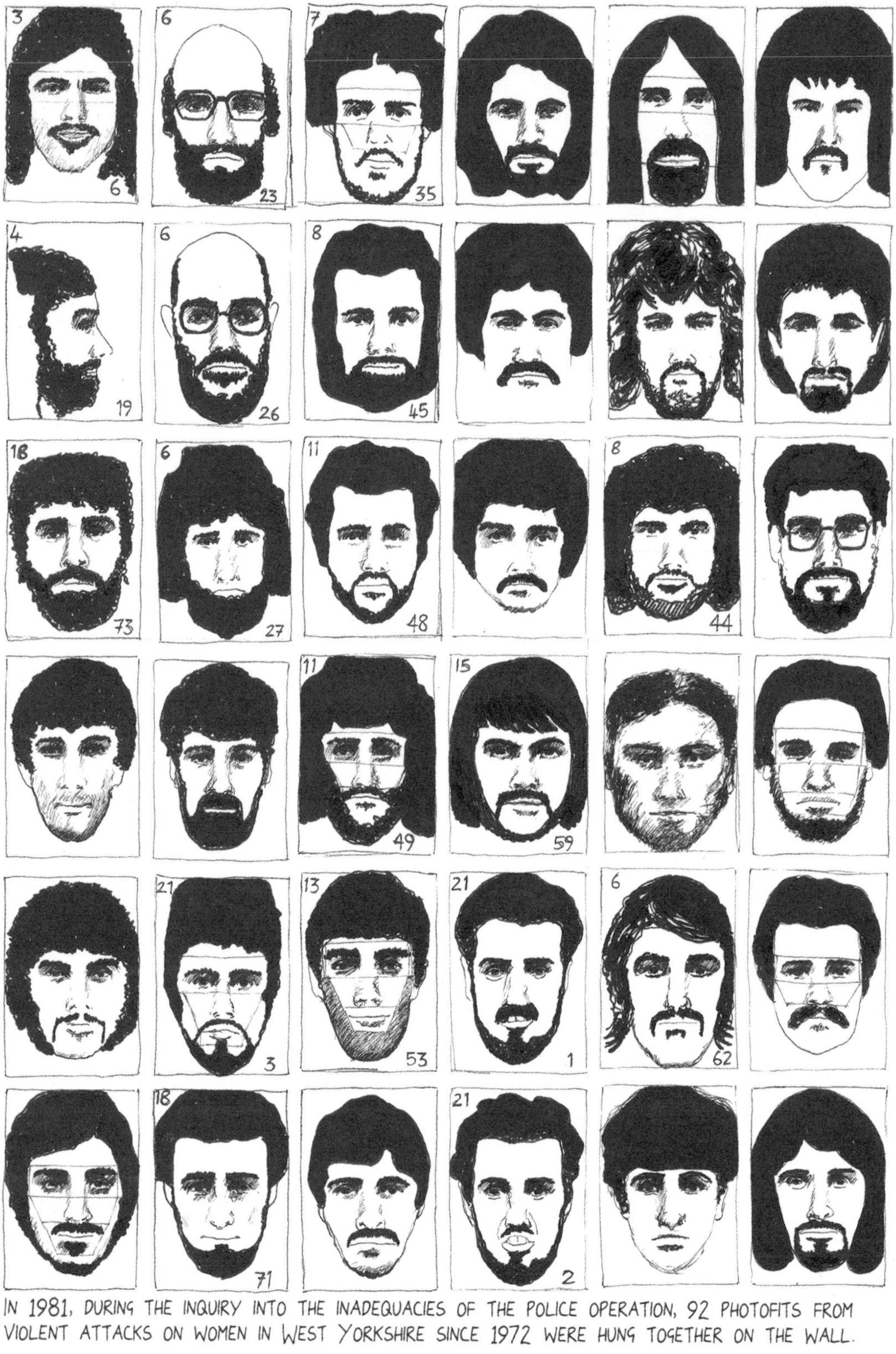
3
6
6
23
7
35
4
19
6
26
8
45
18
73
6
27
11
48
8
44
11
49
15
59
21
3
13
53
21
1
6
62
18
71
21
2

IN 1981, DURING THE INQUIRY INTO THE INADEQUACIES OF THE POLICE OPERATION, 92 PHOTOFITS FROM VIOLENT ATTACKS ON WOMEN IN WEST YORKSHIRE SINCE 1972 WERE HUNG TOGETHER ON THE WALL.

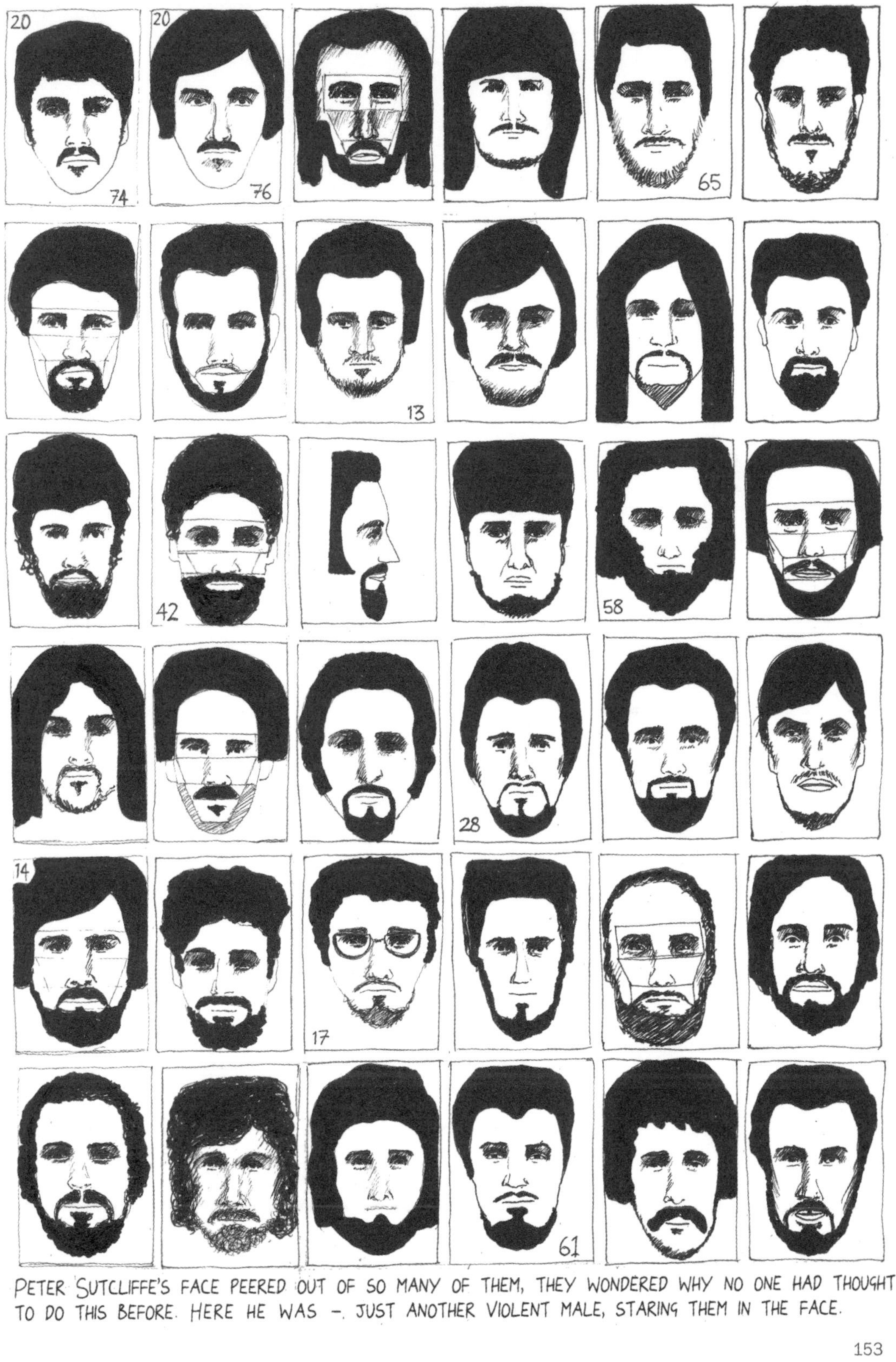
20
74
20
76
65
13
42
58
28
14
17
61

PETER SUTCLIFFE'S FACE PEERED OUT OF SO MANY OF THEM, THEY WONDERED WHY NO ONE HAD THOUGHT TO DO THIS BEFORE. HERE HE WAS – JUST ANOTHER VIOLENT MALE, STARING THEM IN THE FACE.

THE REVIEW TEAM WERE ABLE TO ADD ANOTHER THIRTEEN VICTIMS TO THE THIRTEEN MURDERS AND
SEVEN ATTEMPTED MURDERS WITH WHICH HE'D BEEN CHARGED AND FOUND GUILTY.

AFTER HE WAS CAUGHT, HIS NEIGHBOURS SAID HOW SURPRISED THEY WERE — WHAT
A LOVELY MAN HE'D SEEMED. A TEENAGE GIRL TOLD REPORTERS HOW HE'D GIVEN HER A MARS BAR
FOR CLEARING THE SNOW FROM HIS DRIVEWAY.

MISTAKES WERE MADE, THAT MUCH WE KNOW.
OFFICERS OF ALL RANKS INVOLVED IN THE INVESTIGATION FOUND IT HARD TO LIVE WITH THEIR FAILURE.
LESSONS WERE LEARNED, THOUGH NOT ALWAYS FOR LONG.

AT LEAST HE WAS OFF THE STREETS.
PEOPLE WERE RELIEVED — NOW WE WERE SAFE AGAIN.

THE YORKSHIRE RIPPER.

TWENTY-FIVE CHILDREN HAD BEEN LEFT WITHOUT A MOTHER BECAUSE OF HIM.

THERE WERE MANY, MANY THEORIES ABOUT WHY HE HAD DONE IT.

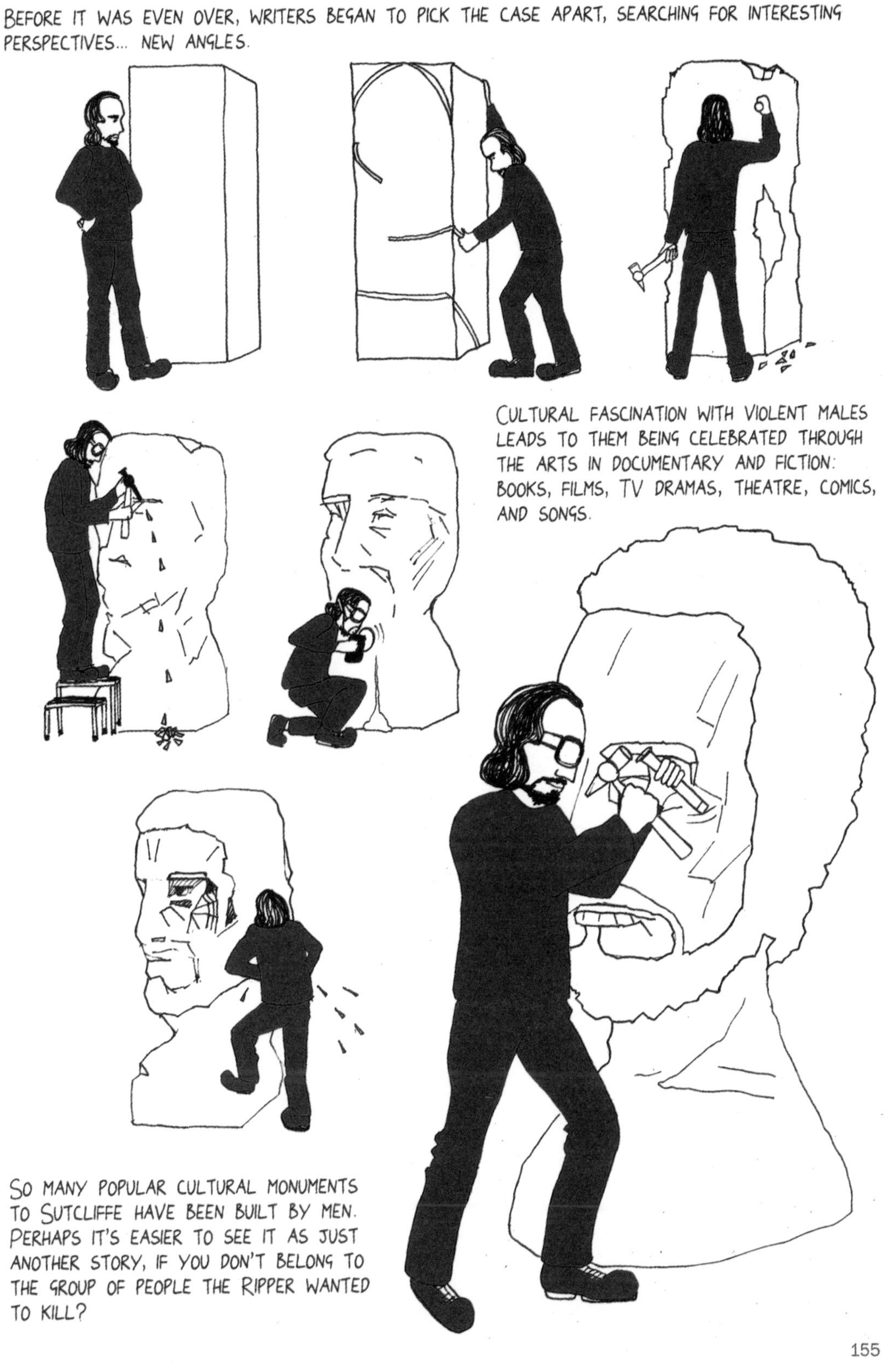
BEFORE IT WAS EVEN OVER, WRITERS BEGAN TO PICK THE CASE APART, SEARCHING FOR INTERESTING PERSPECTIVES... NEW ANGLES.
CULTURAL FASCINATION WITH VIOLENT MALES LEADS TO THEM BEING CELEBRATED THROUGH THE ARTS IN DOCUMENTARY AND FICTION: BOOKS, FILMS, TV DRAMAS, THEATRE, COMICS, AND SONGS.
SO MANY POPULAR CULTURAL MONUMENTS TO SUTCLIFFE HAVE BEEN BUILT BY MEN. PERHAPS IT'S EASIER TO SEE IT AS JUST ANOTHER STORY, IF YOU DON'T BELONG TO THE GROUP OF PEOPLE THE RIPPER WANTED TO KILL?

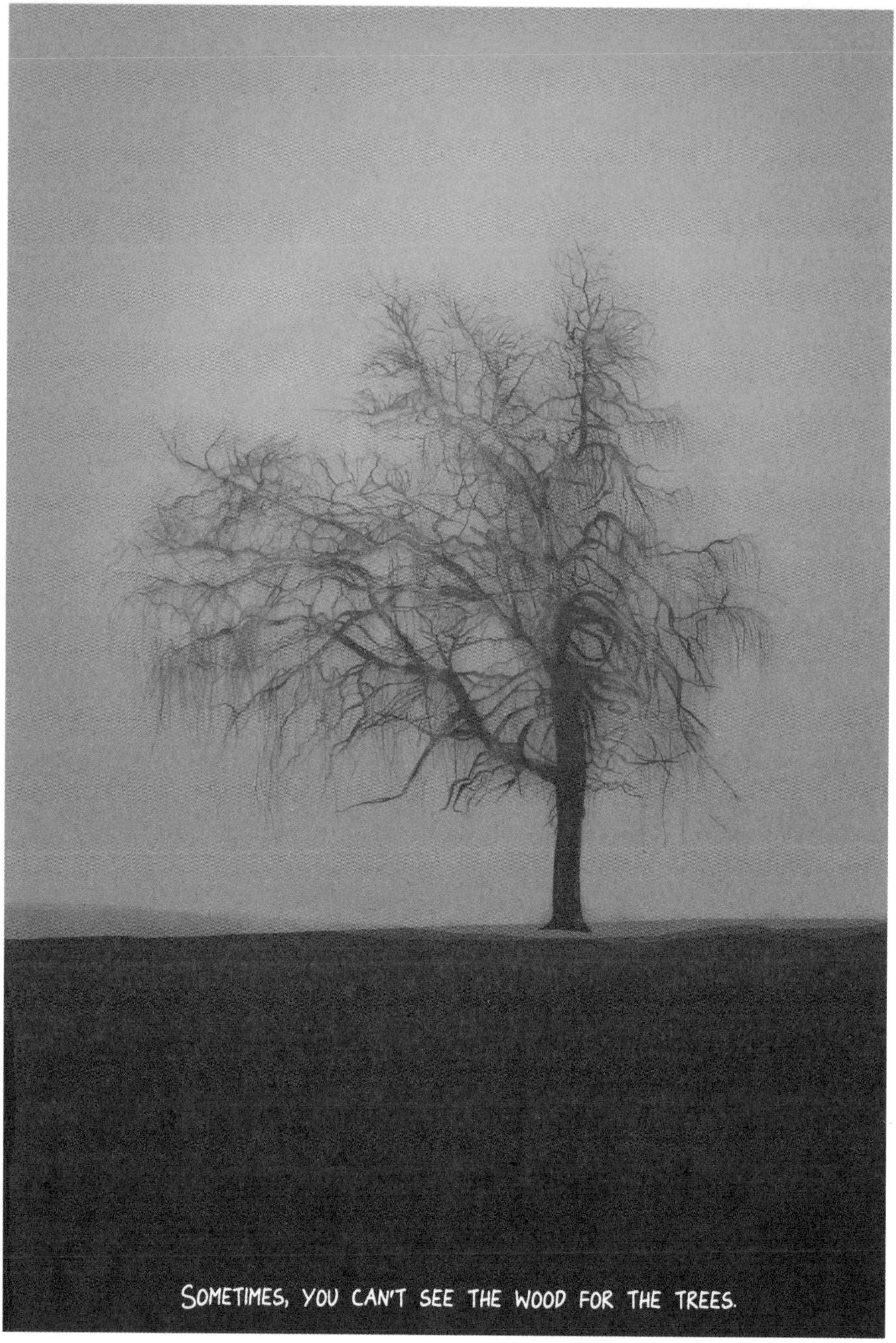
SOMETIMES, YOU CAN'T SEE THE WOOD FOR THE TREES.

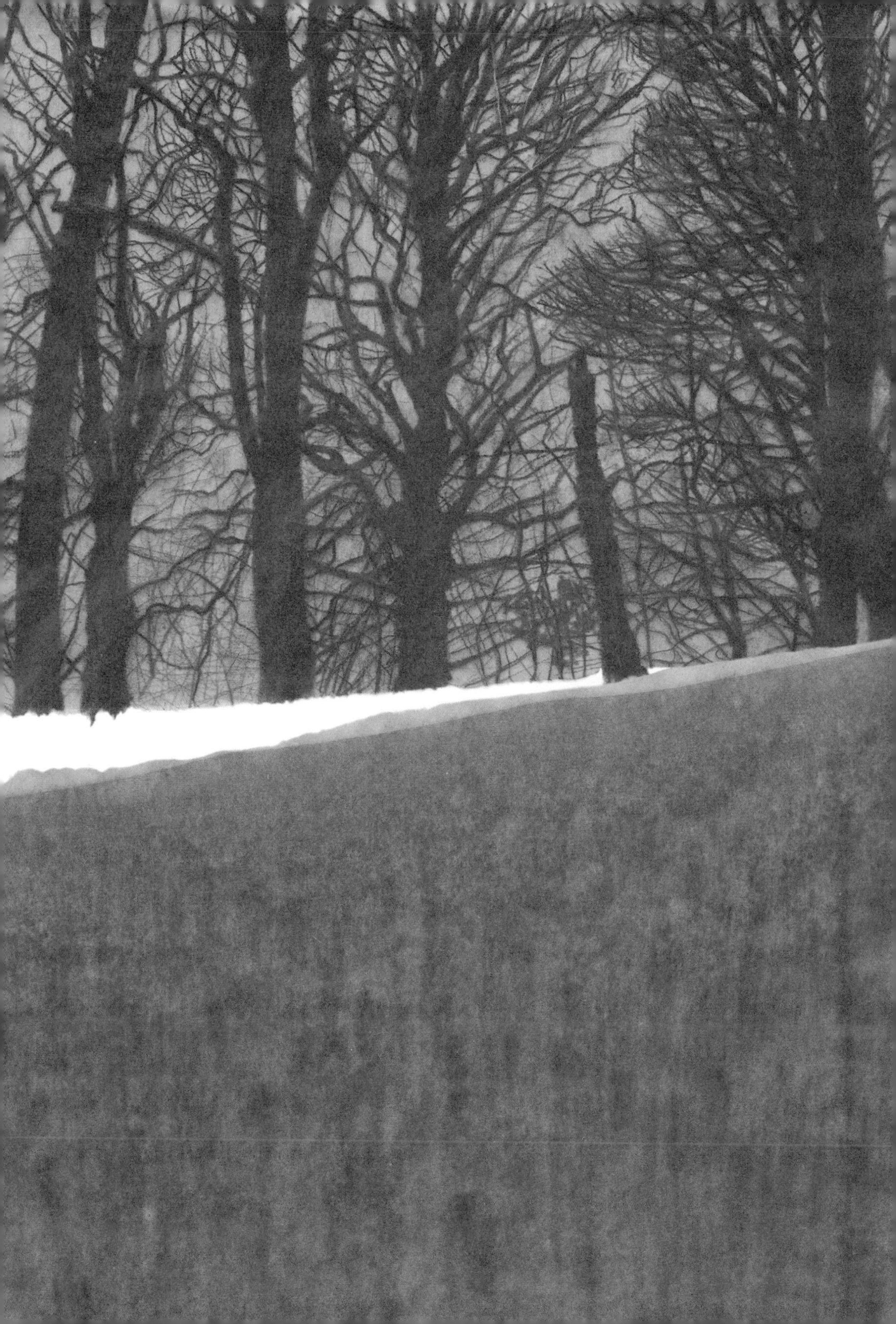

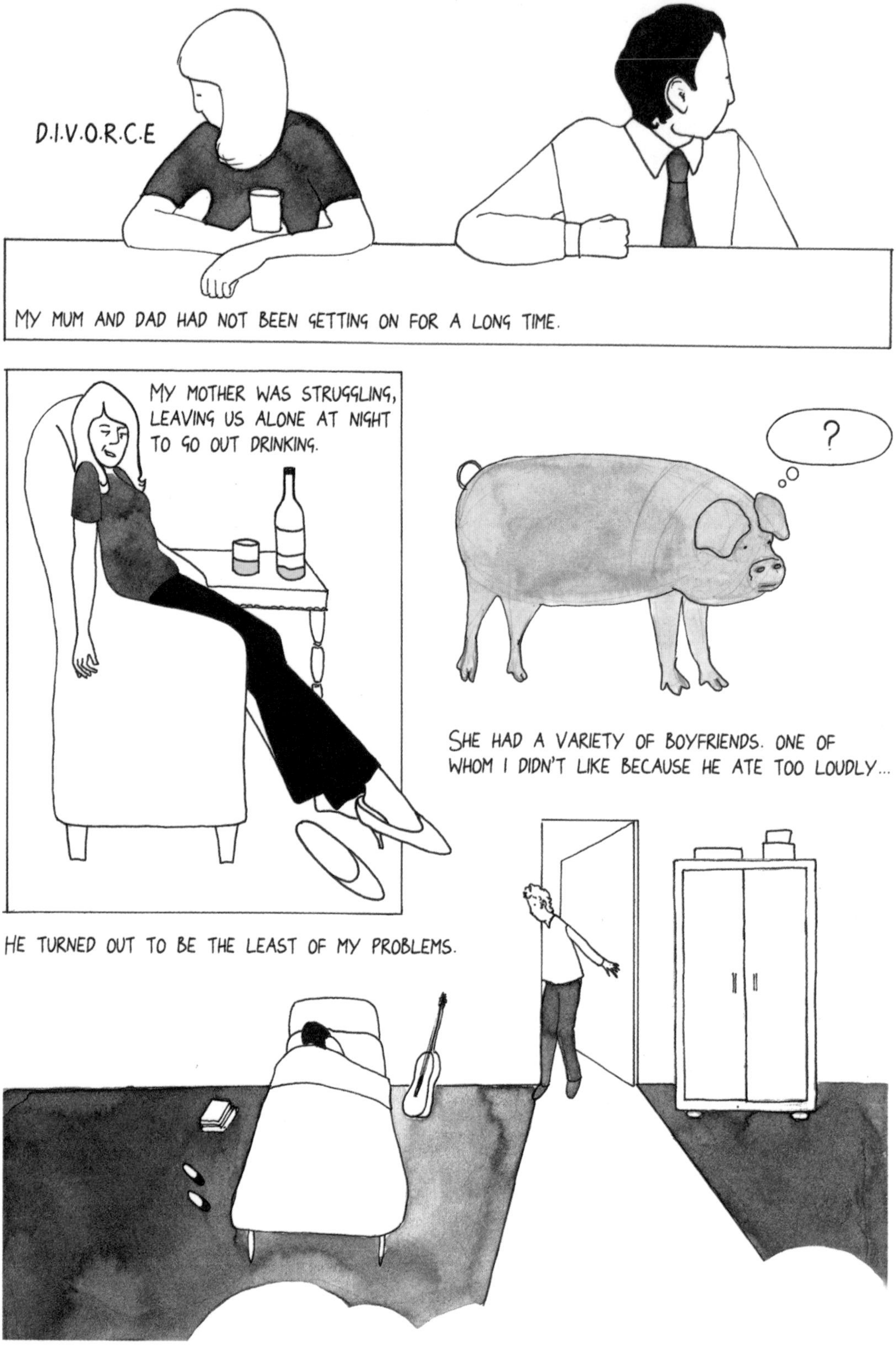
D.I.V.O.R.C.E
MY MUM AND DAD HAD NOT BEEN GETTING ON FOR A LONG TIME.
MY MOTHER WAS STRUGGLING, LEAVING US ALONE AT NIGHT TO GO OUT DRINKING.
?
SHE HAD A VARIETY OF BOYFRIENDS. ONE OF WHOM I DIDN'T LIKE BECAUSE HE ATE TOO LOUDLY...
HE TURNED OUT TO BE THE LEAST OF MY PROBLEMS.

THEN THERE WAS THE STRANGELY SMILING, HOSTILE ONE. HE GAVE HER BLACK EYES – SHE TOOK TO WEARING DARK GLASSES. I DIDN'T LIKE HIM EITHER.

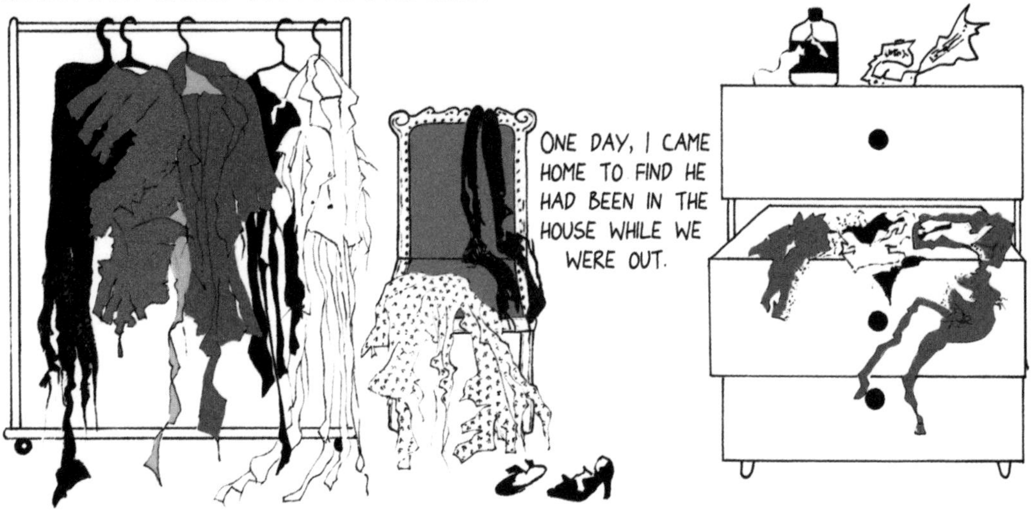
ONE DAY, I CAME HOME TO FIND HE HAD BEEN IN THE HOUSE WHILE WE WERE OUT.

USING A KNIFE AND SCISSORS, HE HAD CUT AND SLASHED AND STABBED ALL MY MOTHER'S THINGS. HER CLOTHES, HER SHOES, HER UNDERWEAR... ANYTHING HE COULD FIND THAT WAS HERS, HE DESTROYED.

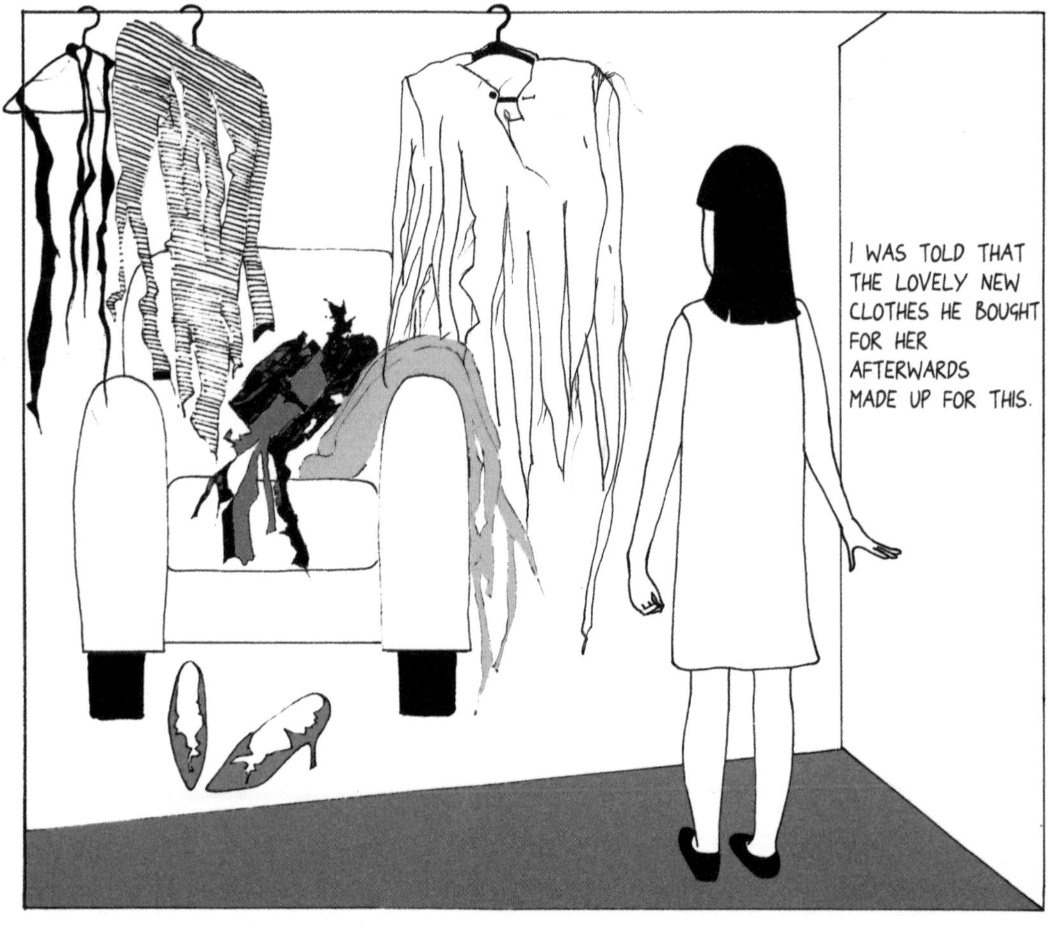
I WAS TOLD THAT THE LOVELY NEW CLOTHES HE BOUGHT FOR HER AFTERWARDS MADE UP FOR THIS.

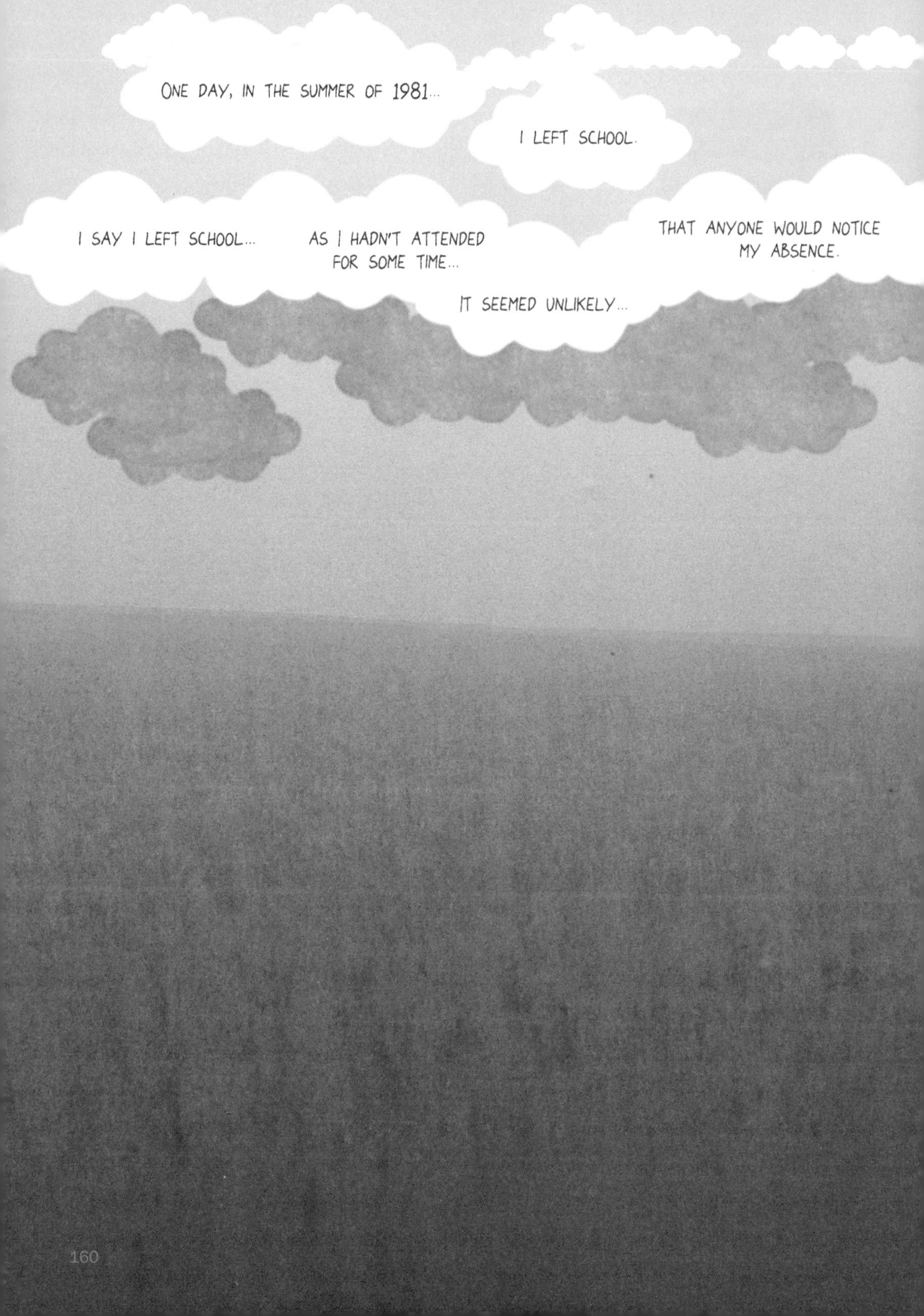
ONE DAY, IN THE SUMMER OF 1981...
I LEFT SCHOOL.
I SAY I LEFT SCHOOL...
AS I HADN'T ATTENDED FOR SOME TIME...
IT SEEMED UNLIKELY...
THAT ANYONE WOULD NOTICE MY ABSENCE.

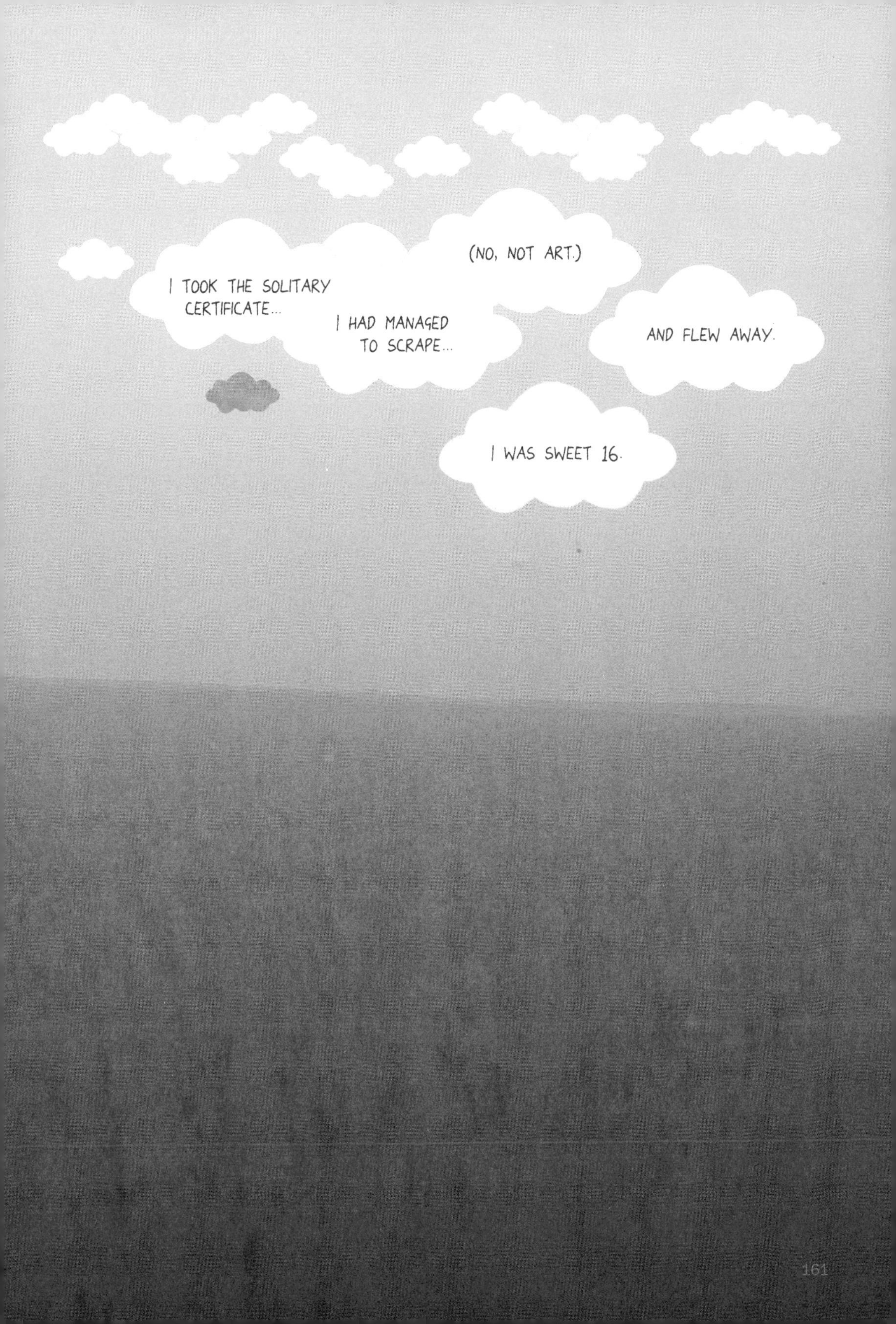
I TOOK THE SOLITARY CERTIFICATE...
I HAD MANAGED TO SCRAPE...
(NO, NOT ART.)
AND FLEW AWAY.
I WAS SWEET 16.

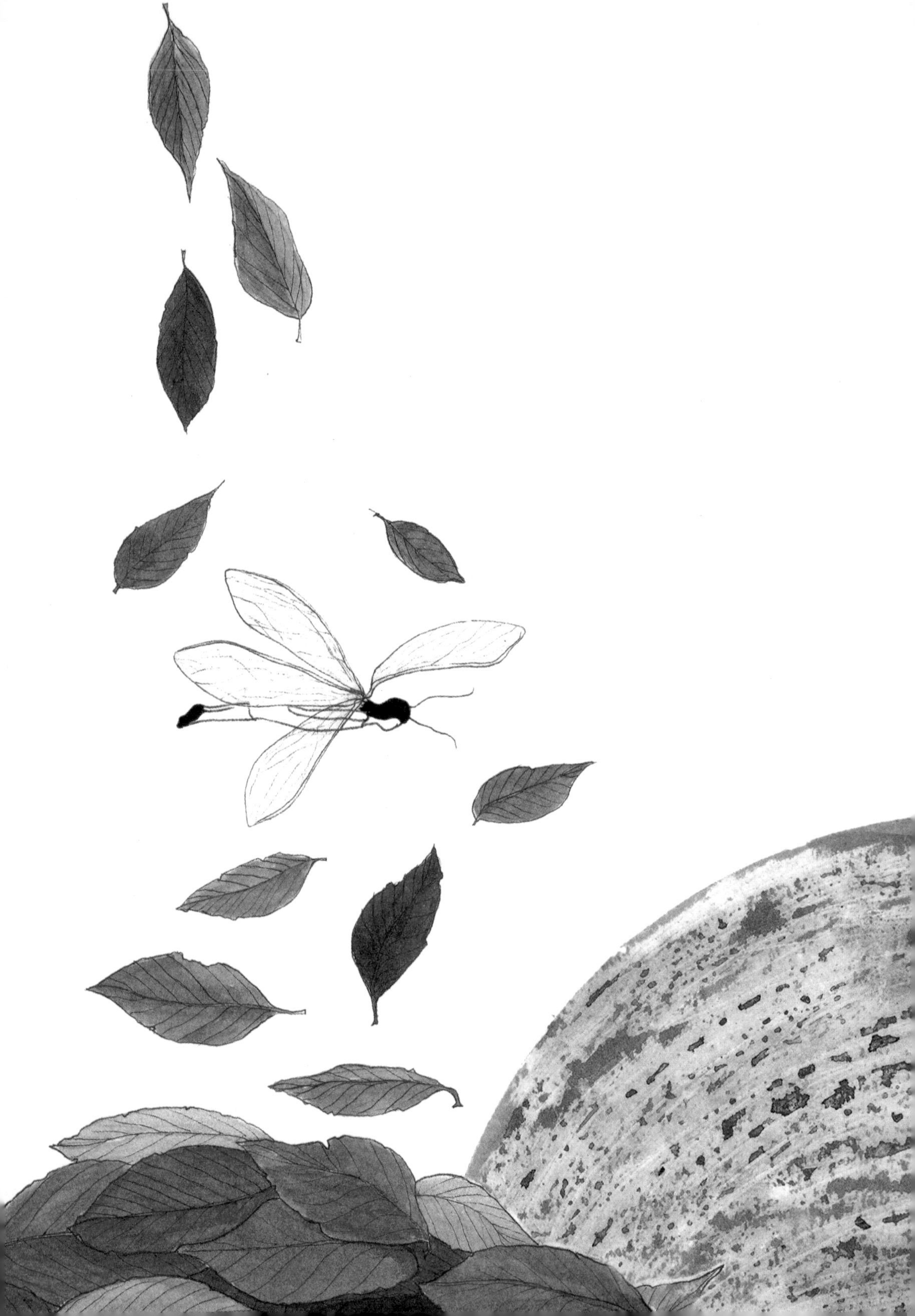

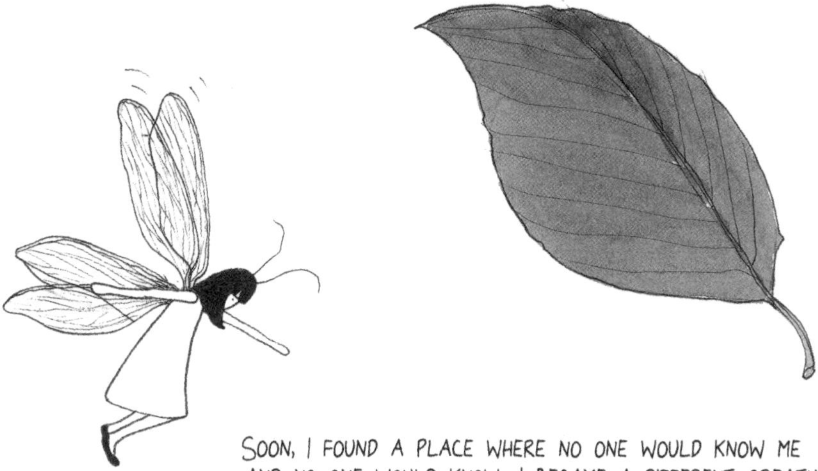

SOON, I FOUND A PLACE WHERE NO ONE WOULD KNOW ME
AND NO ONE WOULD KNOW. I BECAME A DIFFERENT CREATURE.

IT WASN'T EASY TO HIDE. MORE THAN ONCE THE REPUTATION
I HAD SO CARELESSLY LOST CAME TO FIND ME.

BECAUSE PEOPLE LOVE A GOOD STORY.

AND SO I LEFT MY NAME BEHIND,
THE LAST THING I HAD THAT WAS TRULY MINE.

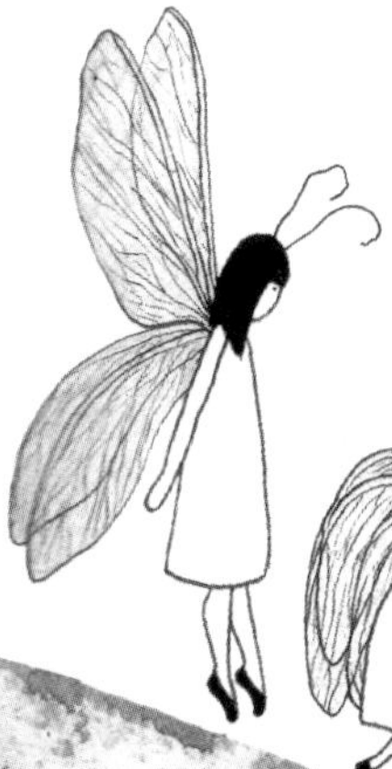

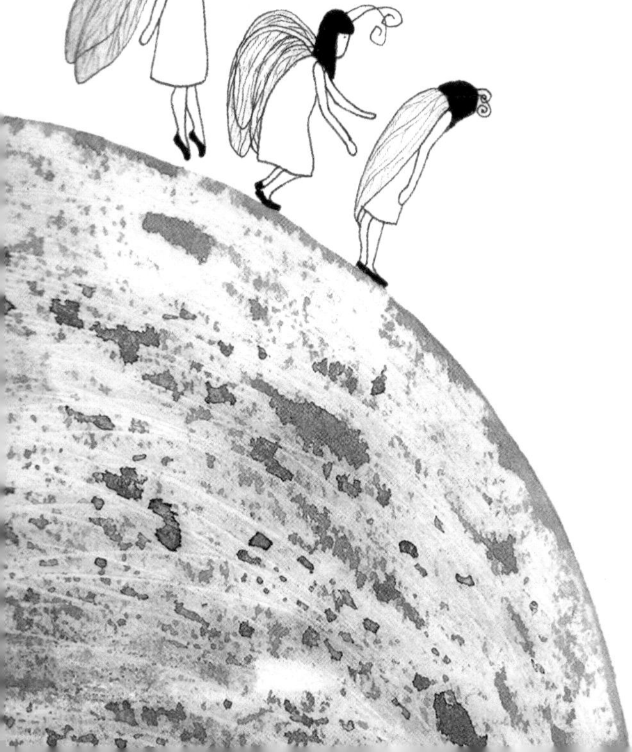

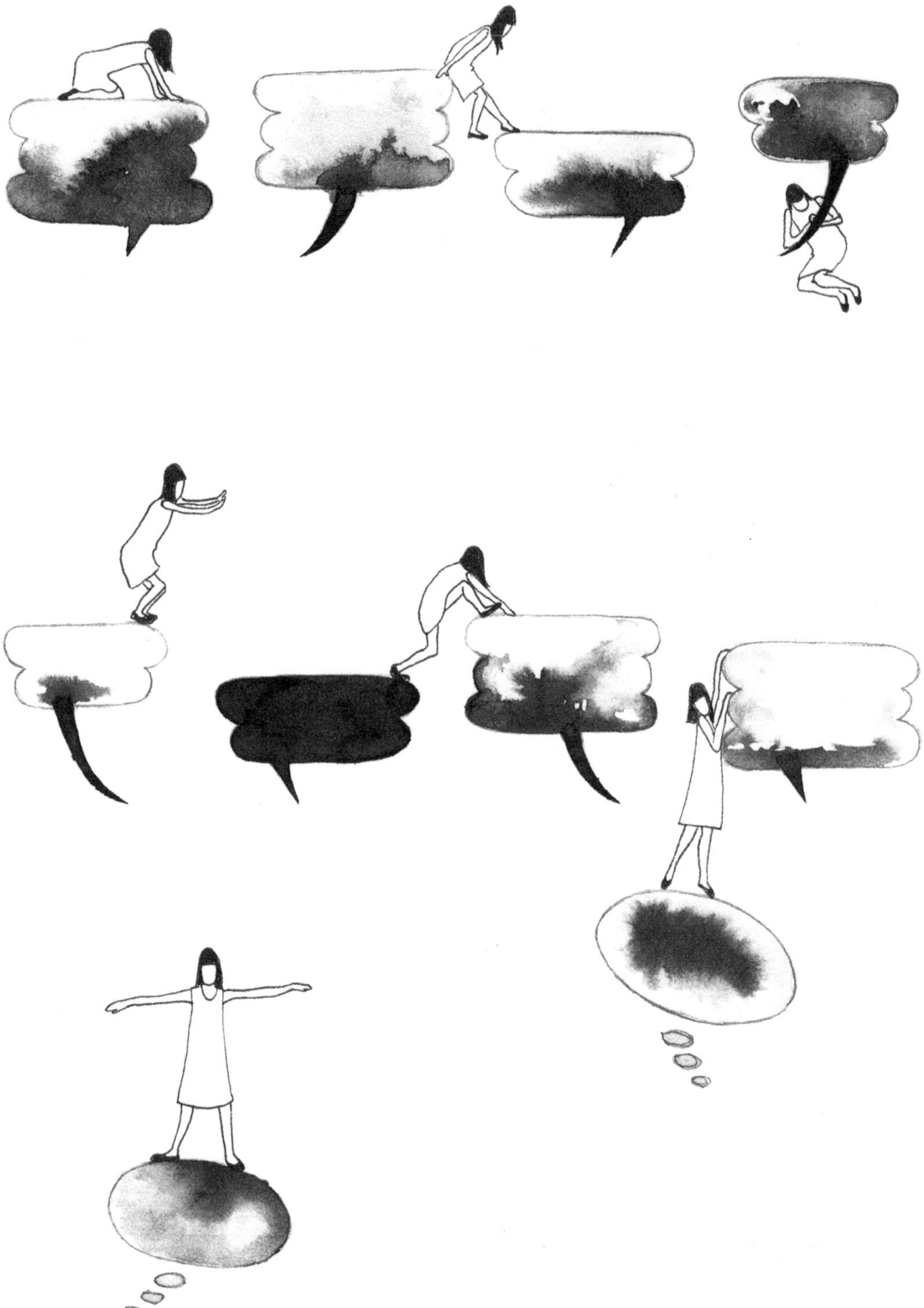

THERE'S NO DOUBT WE NEED A RELIABLE SYSTEM OF JUSTICE, BUT WE CAN'T BLAME THE JUSTICE SYSTEM FOR THE THINGS IT THINKS AND DOES, IF IT JUST THINKS AND DOES THE SAME THINGS AS EVERYONE ELSE.

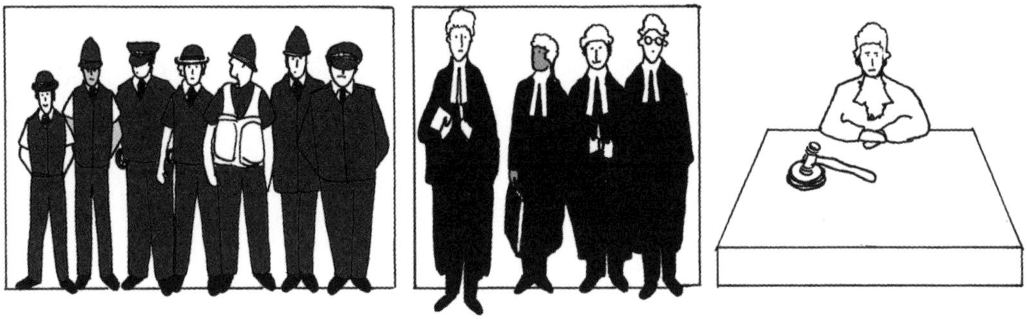

THOSE ARE PEOPLE, BEHIND THE UNIFORMS AND ROBES, AND WHEN THEY MANAGE TO BRING A CASE TO COURT, TWELVE PEOPLE, PEOPLE LIKE YOU AND I, CHOSEN AT RANDOM, GET THE LAST WORD.

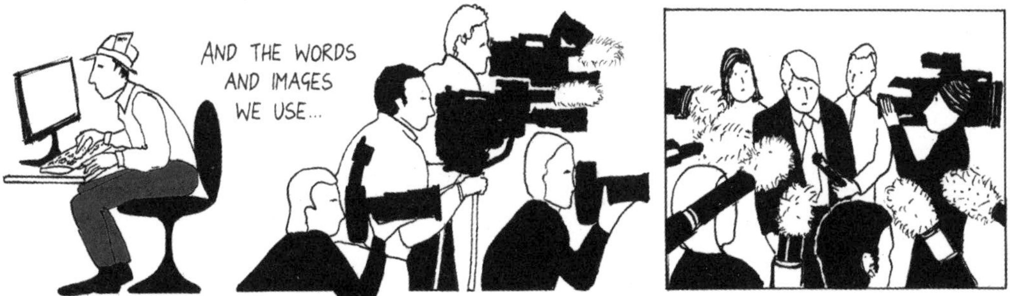
AND THE WORDS AND IMAGES WE USE...

ARE ALL PART OF THE SAME LANDSCAPE.

CHANGE TAKES TIME, I HEAR YOU SAY.

WE'VE HAD A FEW THOUSAND YEARS. HOW MUCH LONGER BEFORE WE ARE RID OF THIS DEAD WEIGHT?

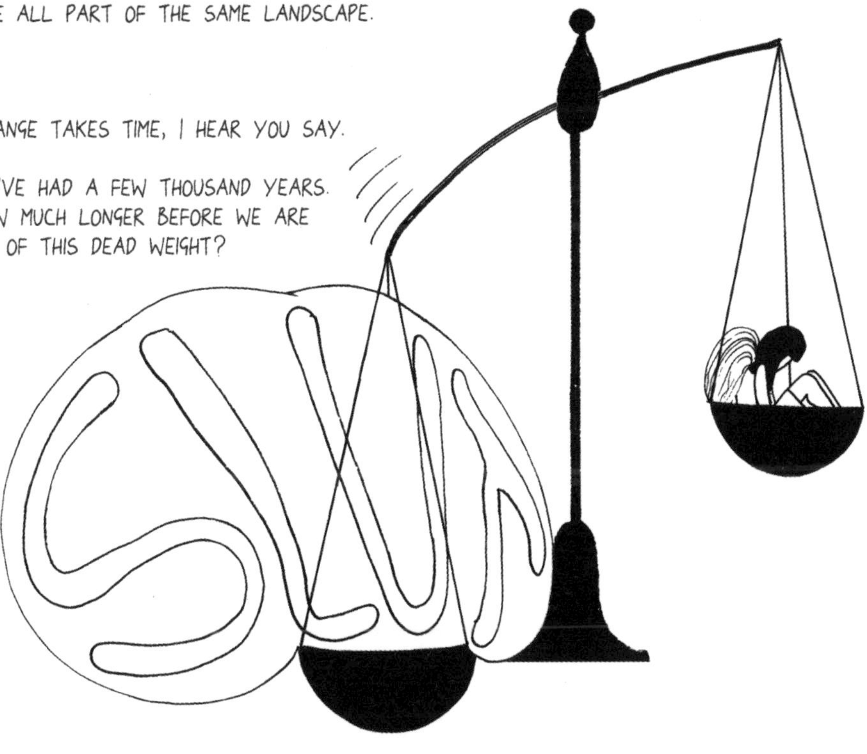

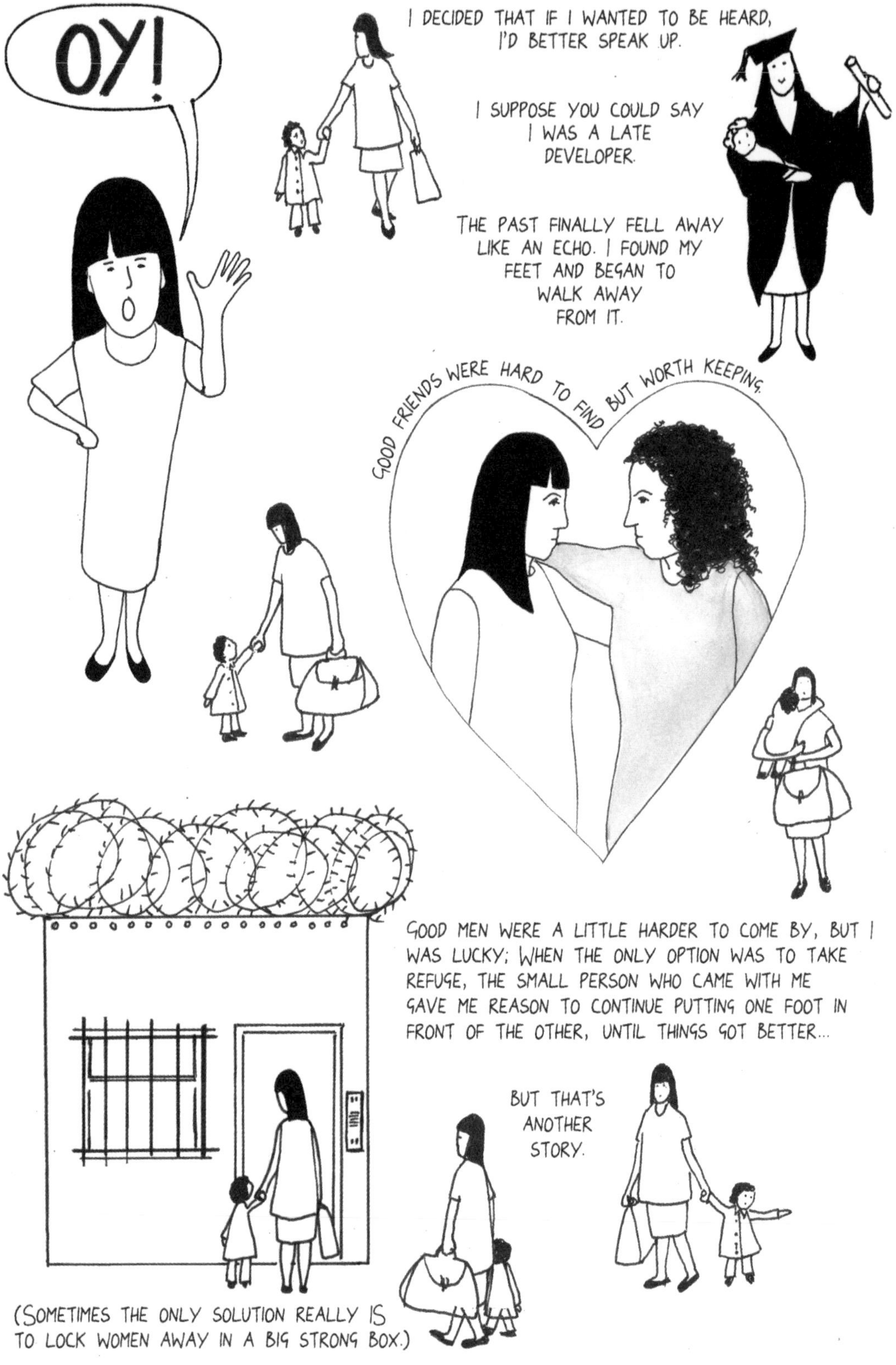

OY!
I DECIDED THAT IF I WANTED TO BE HEARD, I'D BETTER SPEAK UP.
I SUPPOSE YOU COULD SAY I WAS A LATE DEVELOPER.
THE PAST FINALLY FELL AWAY LIKE AN ECHO. I FOUND MY FEET AND BEGAN TO WALK AWAY FROM IT.
GOOD FRIENDS WERE HARD TO FIND BUT WORTH KEEPING.
GOOD MEN WERE A LITTLE HARDER TO COME BY, BUT I WAS LUCKY; WHEN THE ONLY OPTION WAS TO TAKE REFUGE, THE SMALL PERSON WHO CAME WITH ME GAVE ME REASON TO CONTINUE PUTTING ONE FOOT IN FRONT OF THE OTHER, UNTIL THINGS GOT BETTER...
BUT THAT'S ANOTHER STORY.
(SOMETIMES THE ONLY SOLUTION REALLY IS TO LOCK WOMEN AWAY IN A BIG STRONG BOX.)

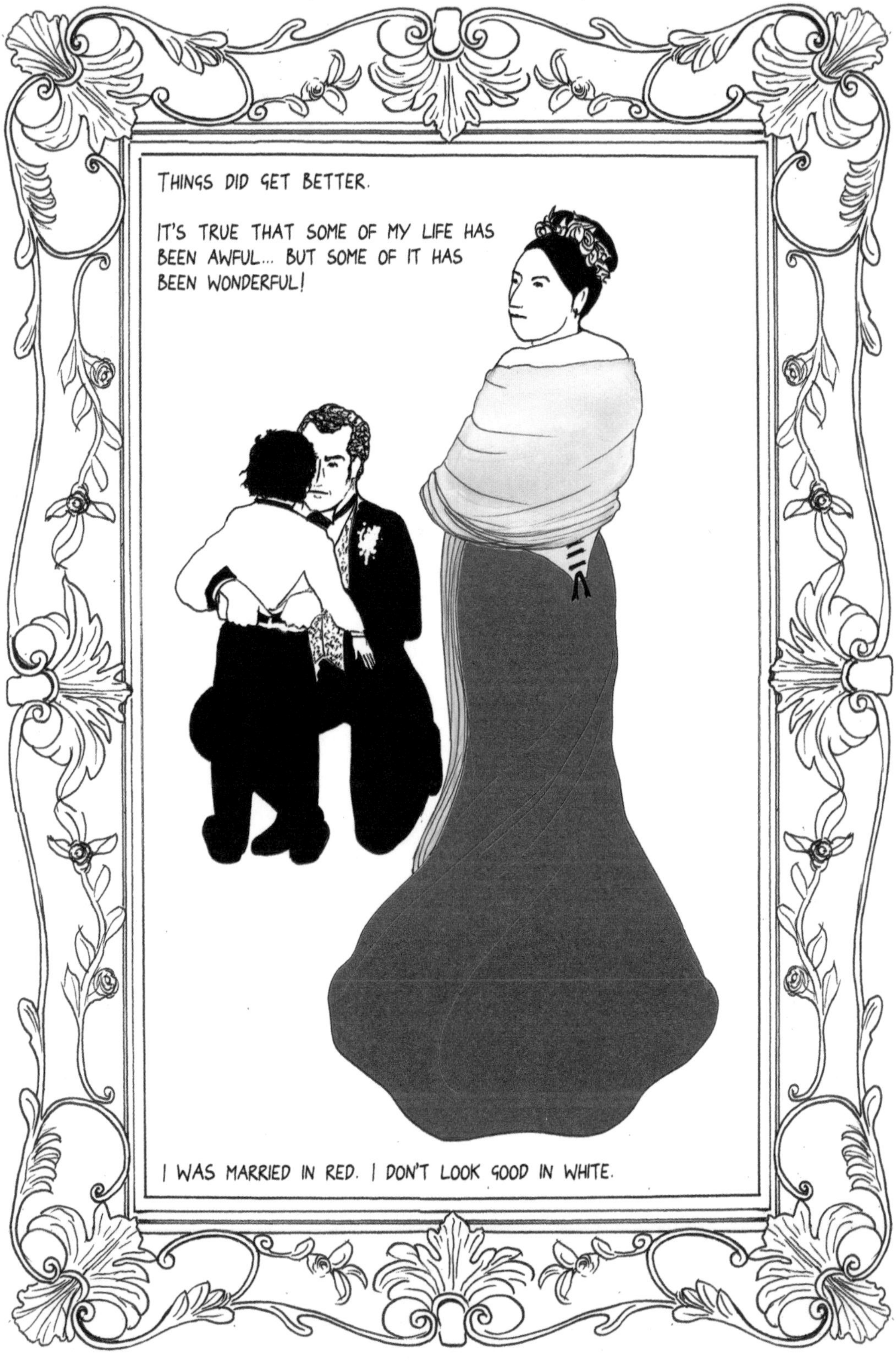
THINGS DID GET BETTER.
IT'S TRUE THAT SOME OF MY LIFE HAS BEEN AWFUL... BUT SOME OF IT HAS BEEN WONDERFUL!
I WAS MARRIED IN RED. I DON'T LOOK GOOD IN WHITE.

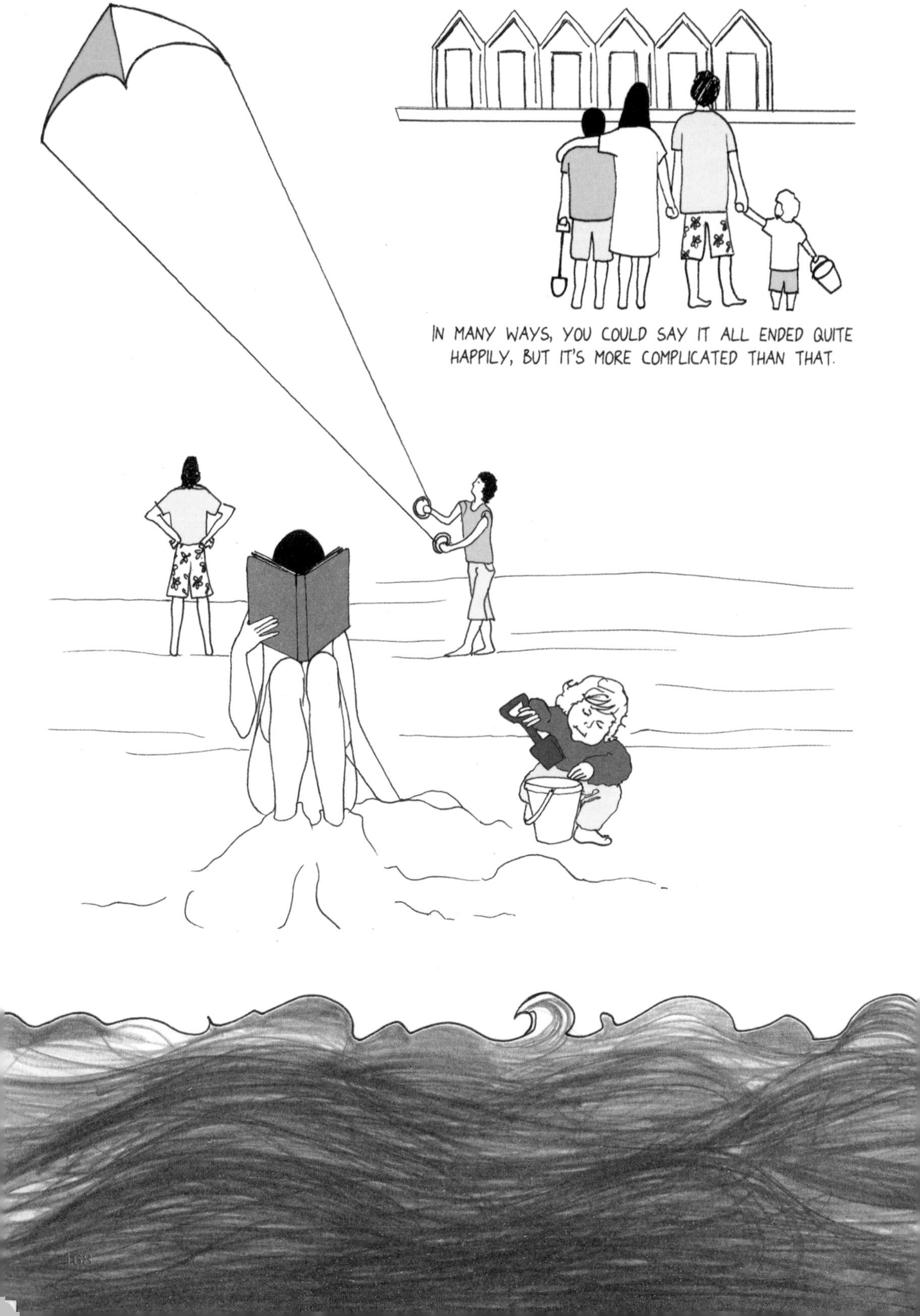
IN MANY WAYS, YOU COULD SAY IT ALL ENDED QUITE HAPPILY, BUT IT'S MORE COMPLICATED THAN THAT.

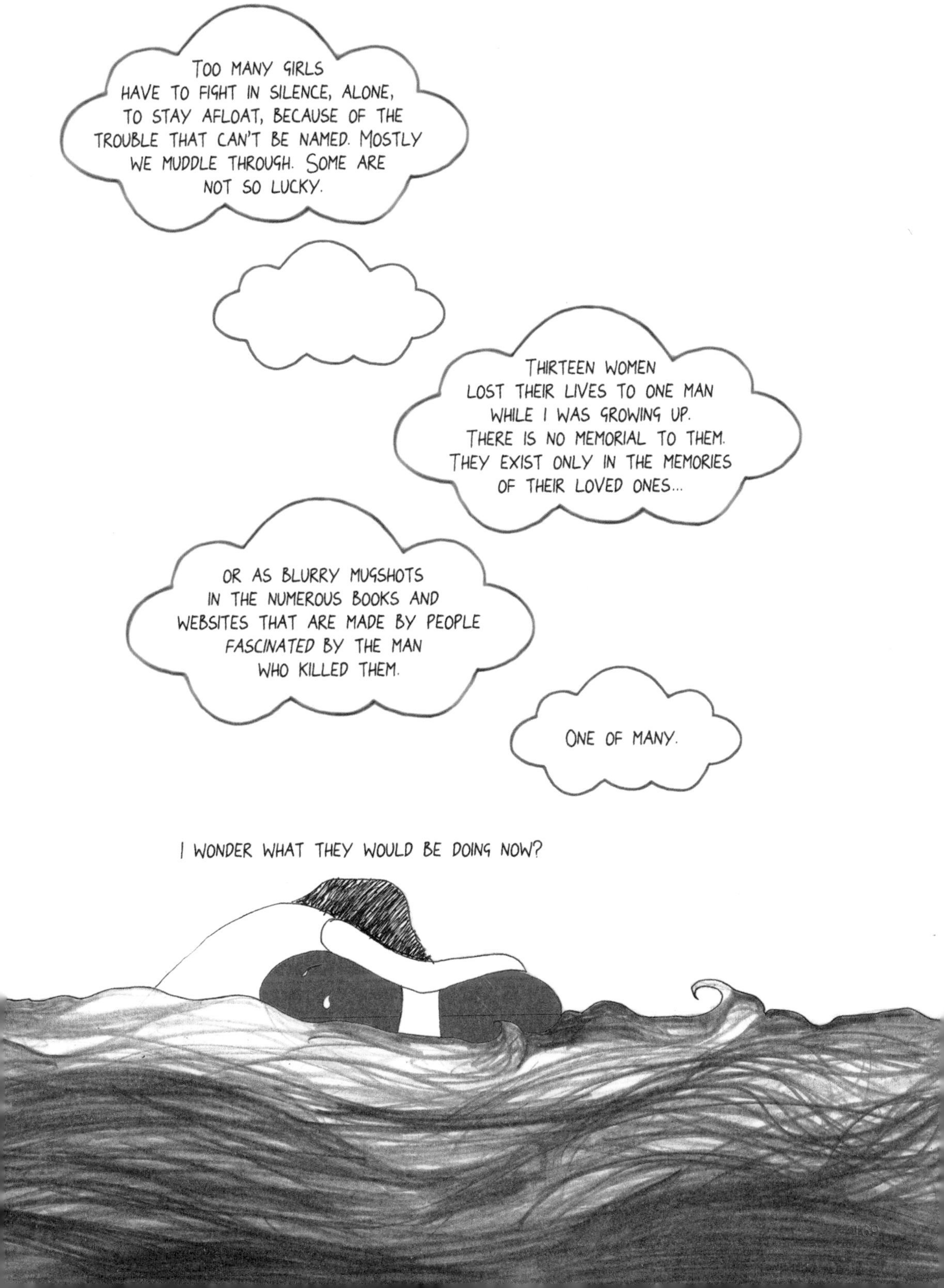
TOO MANY GIRLS HAVE TO FIGHT IN SILENCE, ALONE, TO STAY AFLOAT, BECAUSE OF THE TROUBLE THAT CAN'T BE NAMED. MOSTLY WE MUDDLE THROUGH. SOME ARE NOT SO LUCKY.
THIRTEEN WOMEN LOST THEIR LIVES TO ONE MAN WHILE I WAS GROWING UP. THERE IS NO MEMORIAL TO THEM. THEY EXIST ONLY IN THE MEMORIES OF THEIR LOVED ONES...
OR AS BLURRY MUGSHOTS IN THE NUMEROUS BOOKS AND WEBSITES THAT ARE MADE BY PEOPLE FASCINATED BY THE MAN WHO KILLED THEM.
ONE OF MANY.
I WONDER WHAT THEY WOULD BE DOING NOW?

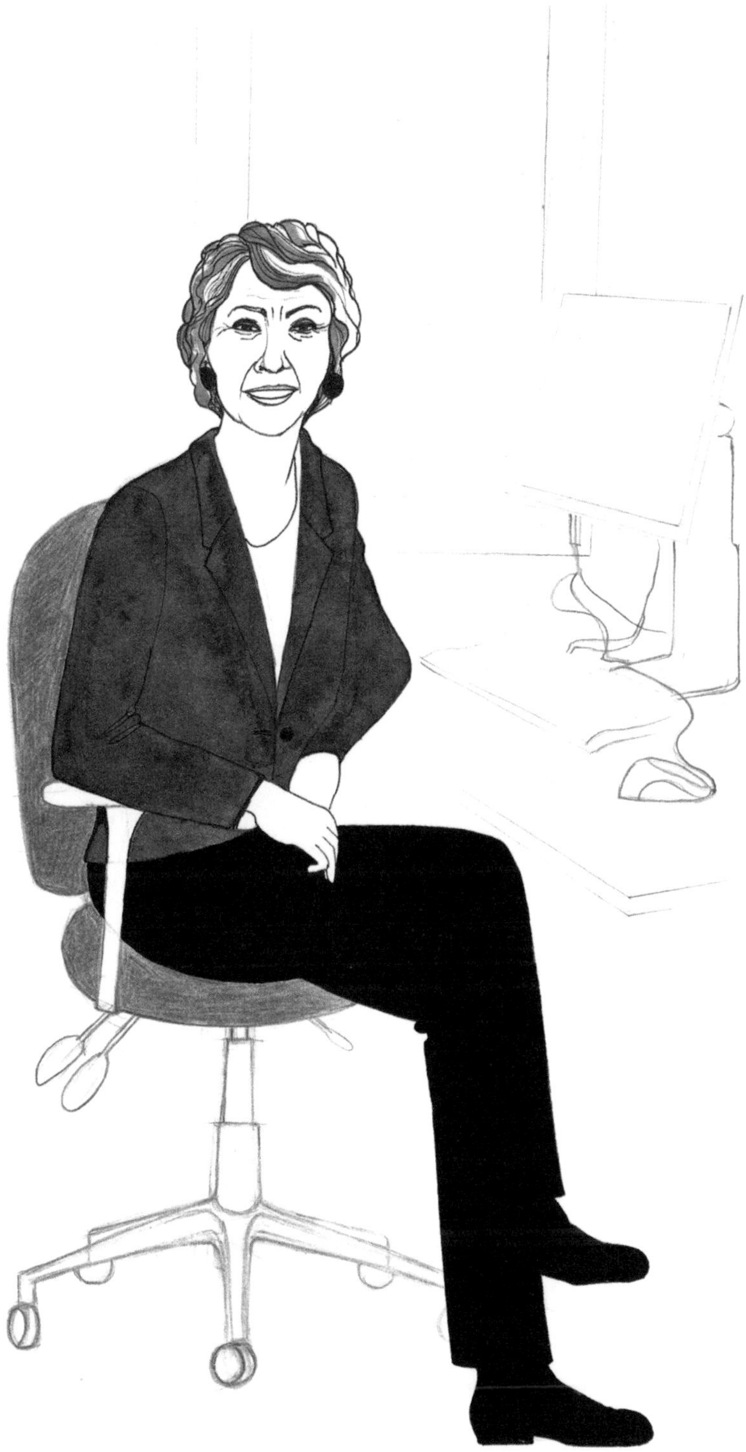

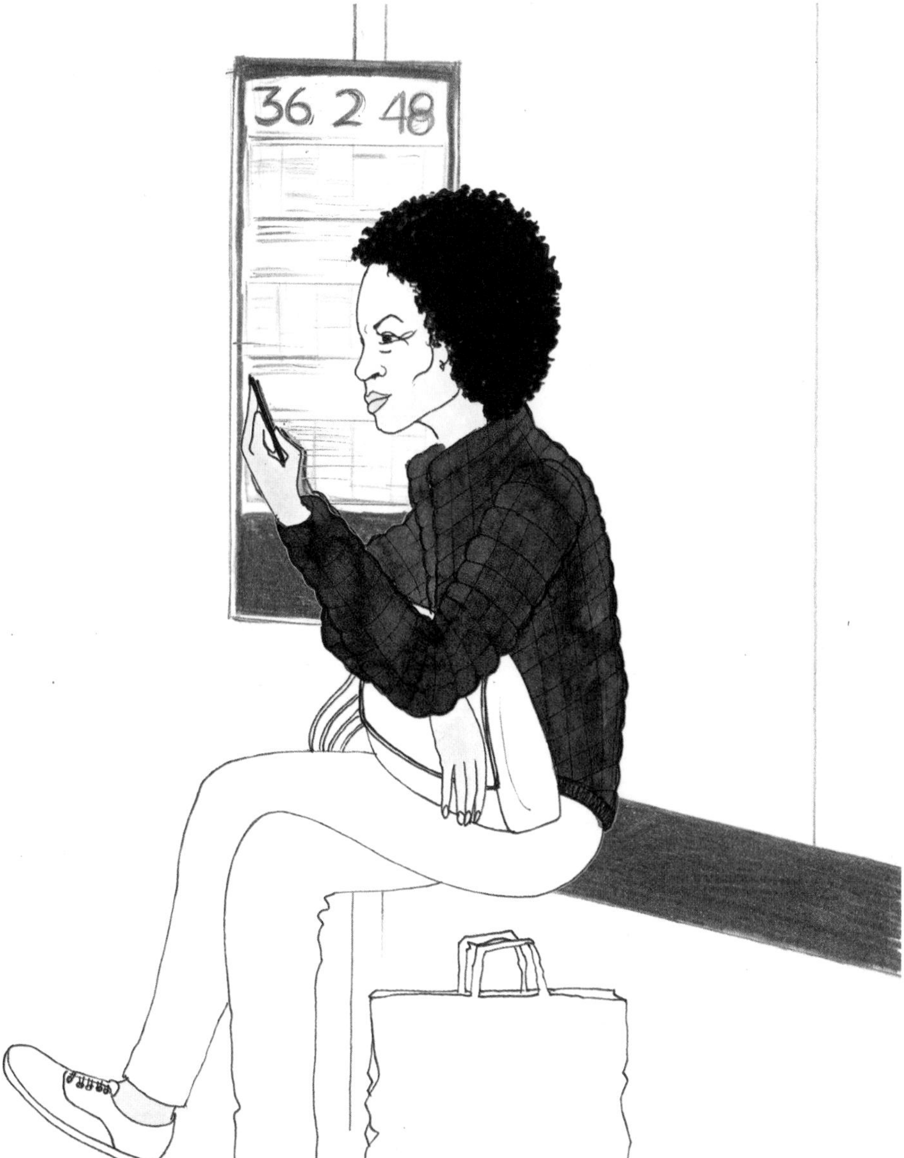
36 2 48

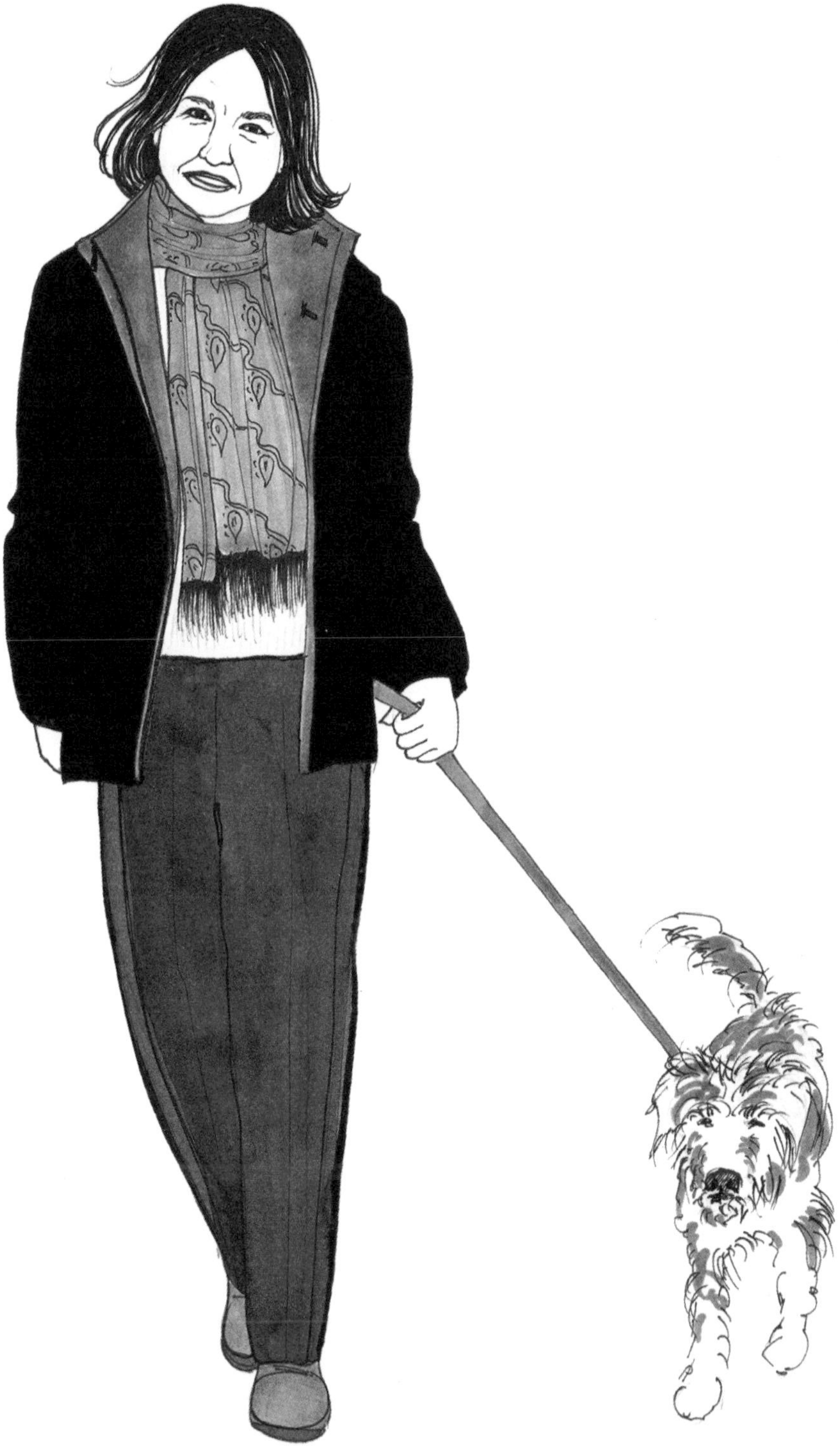

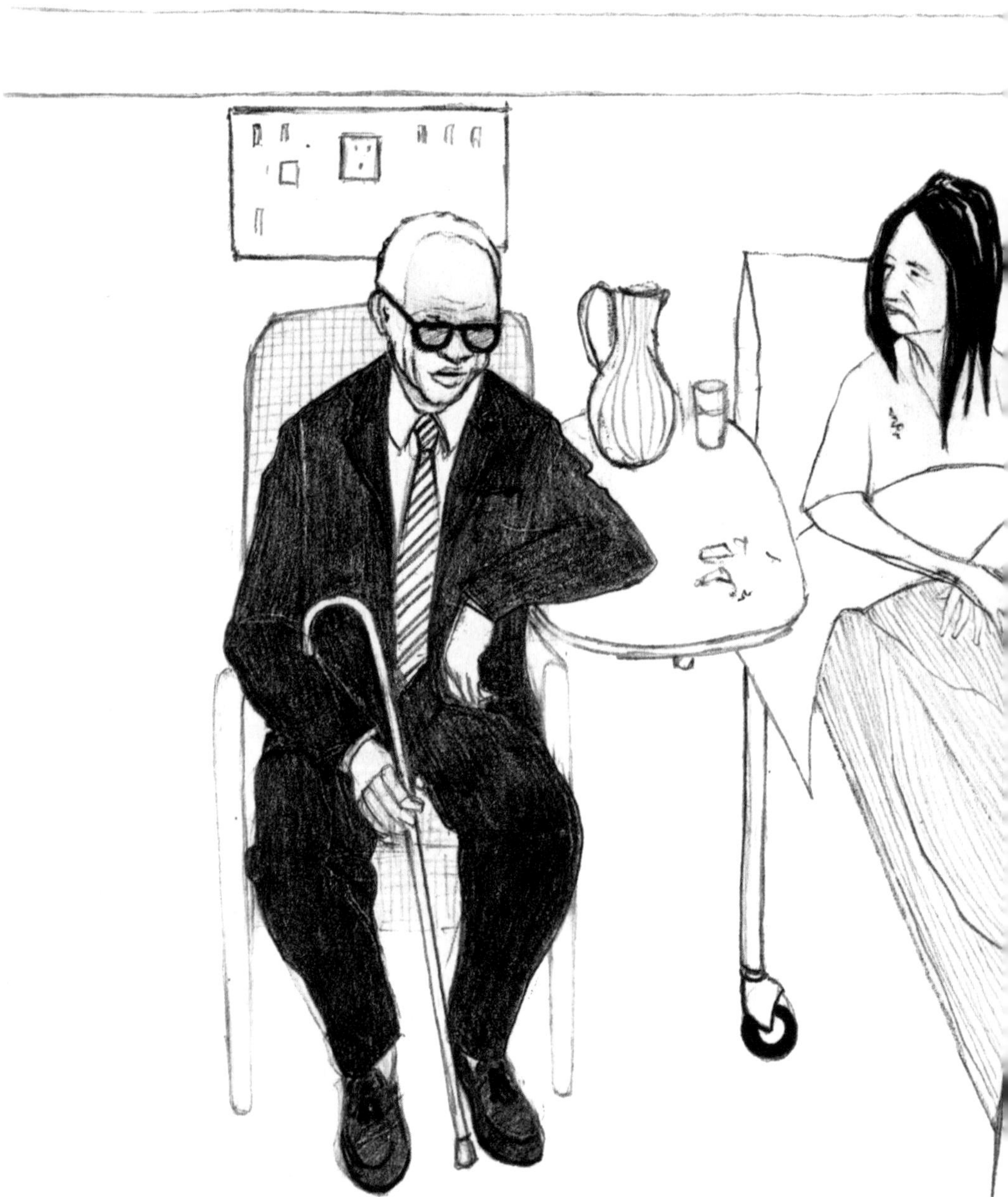

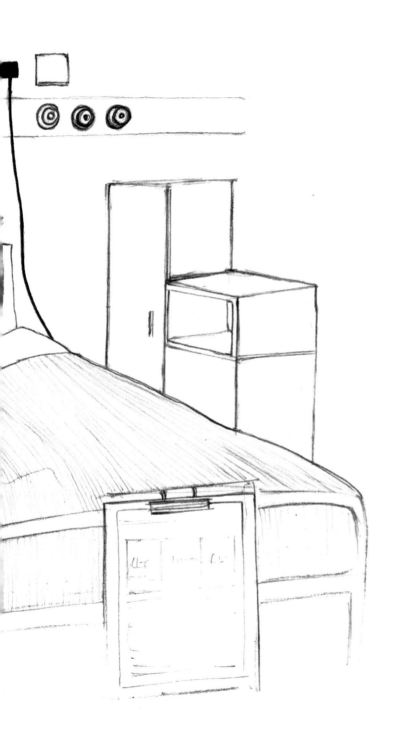

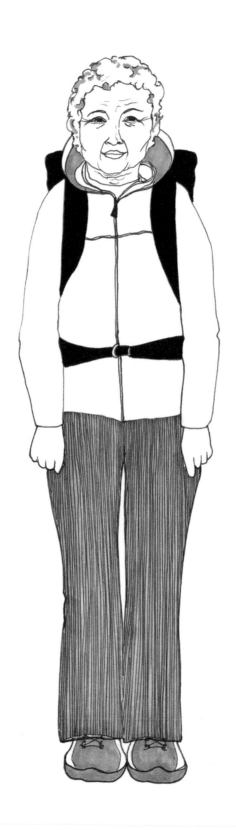

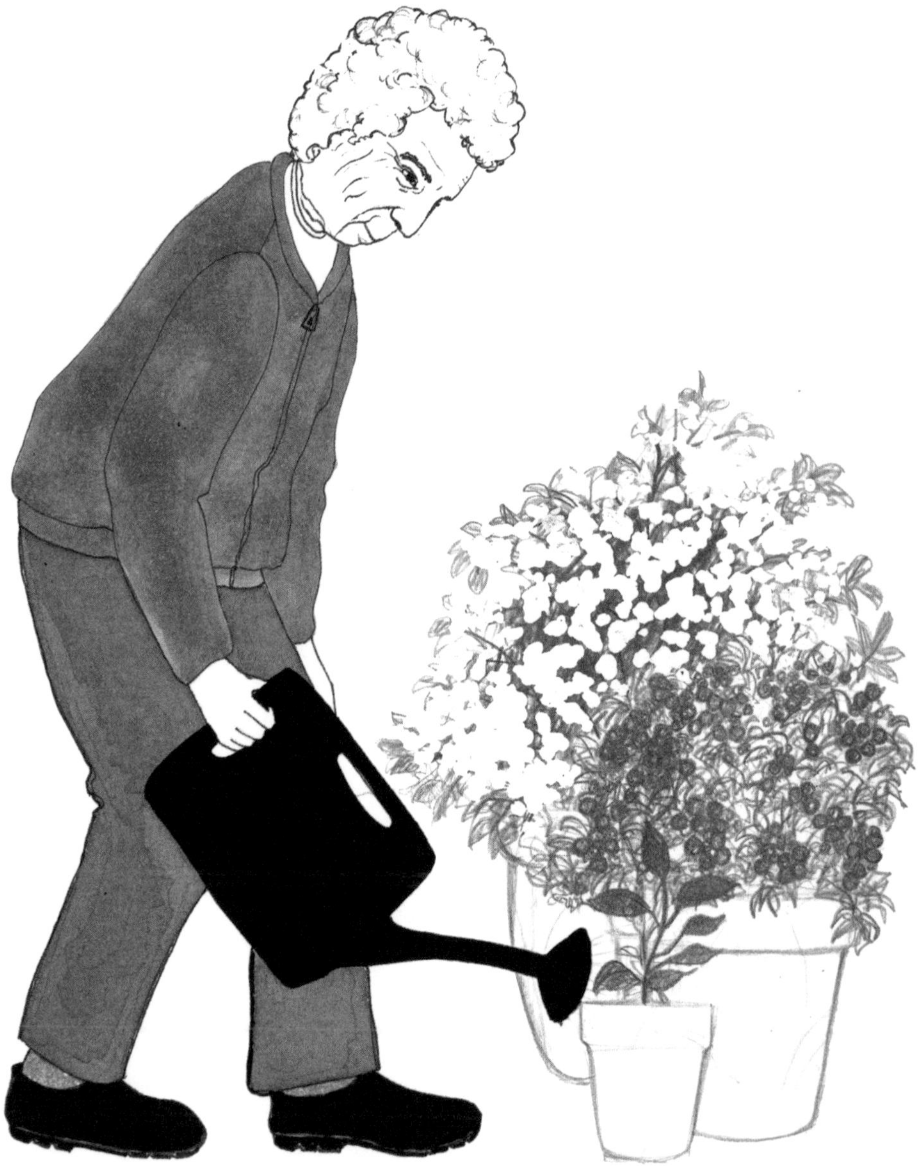

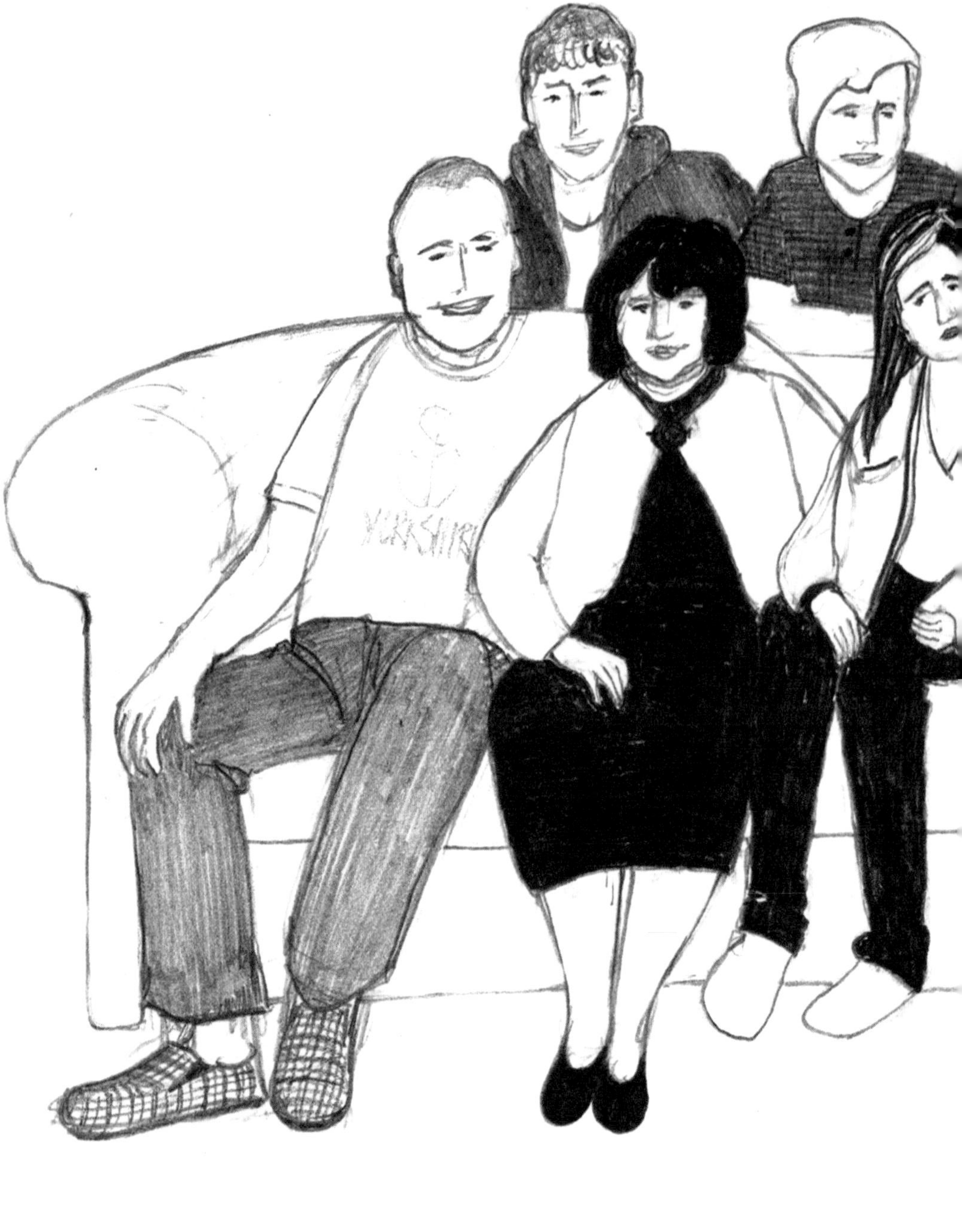

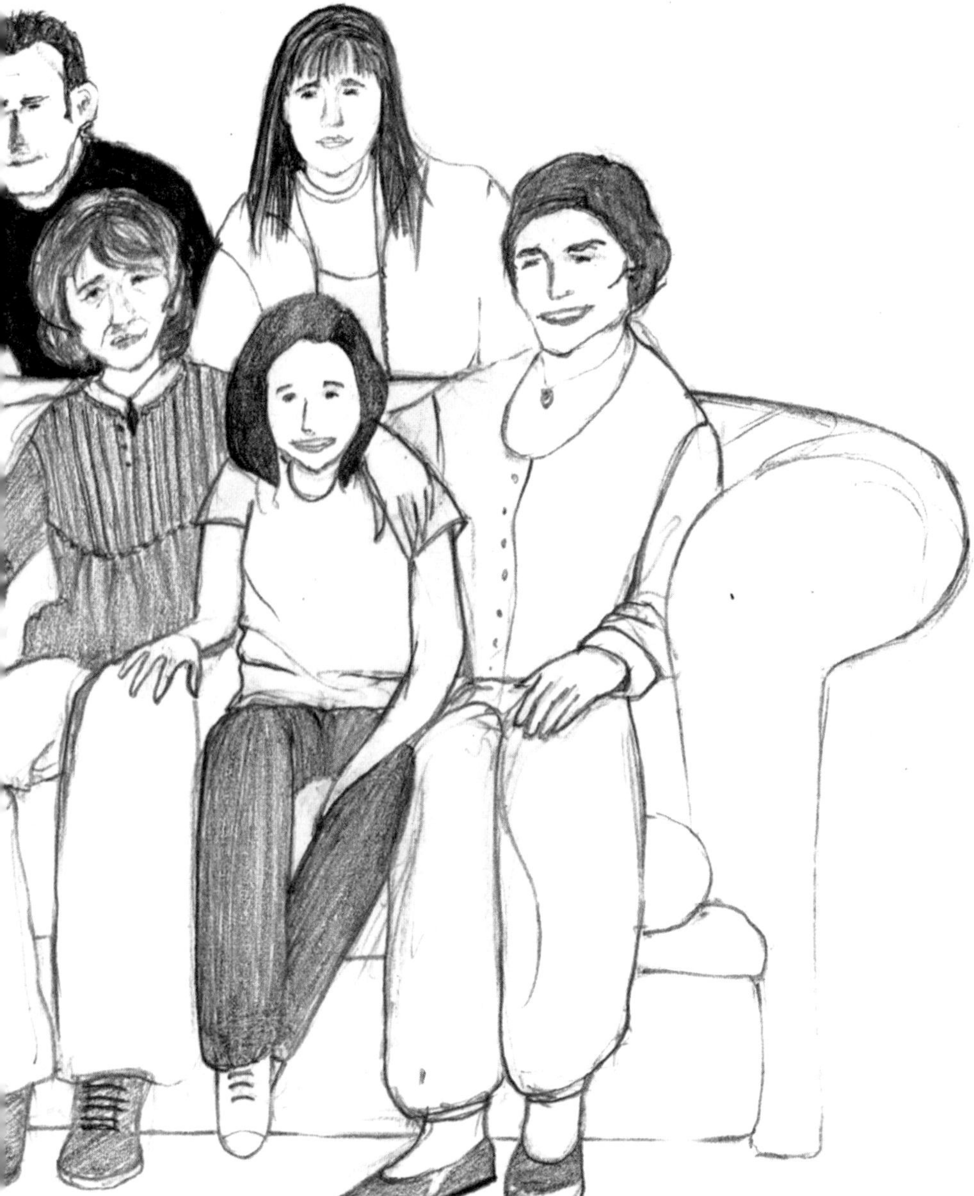

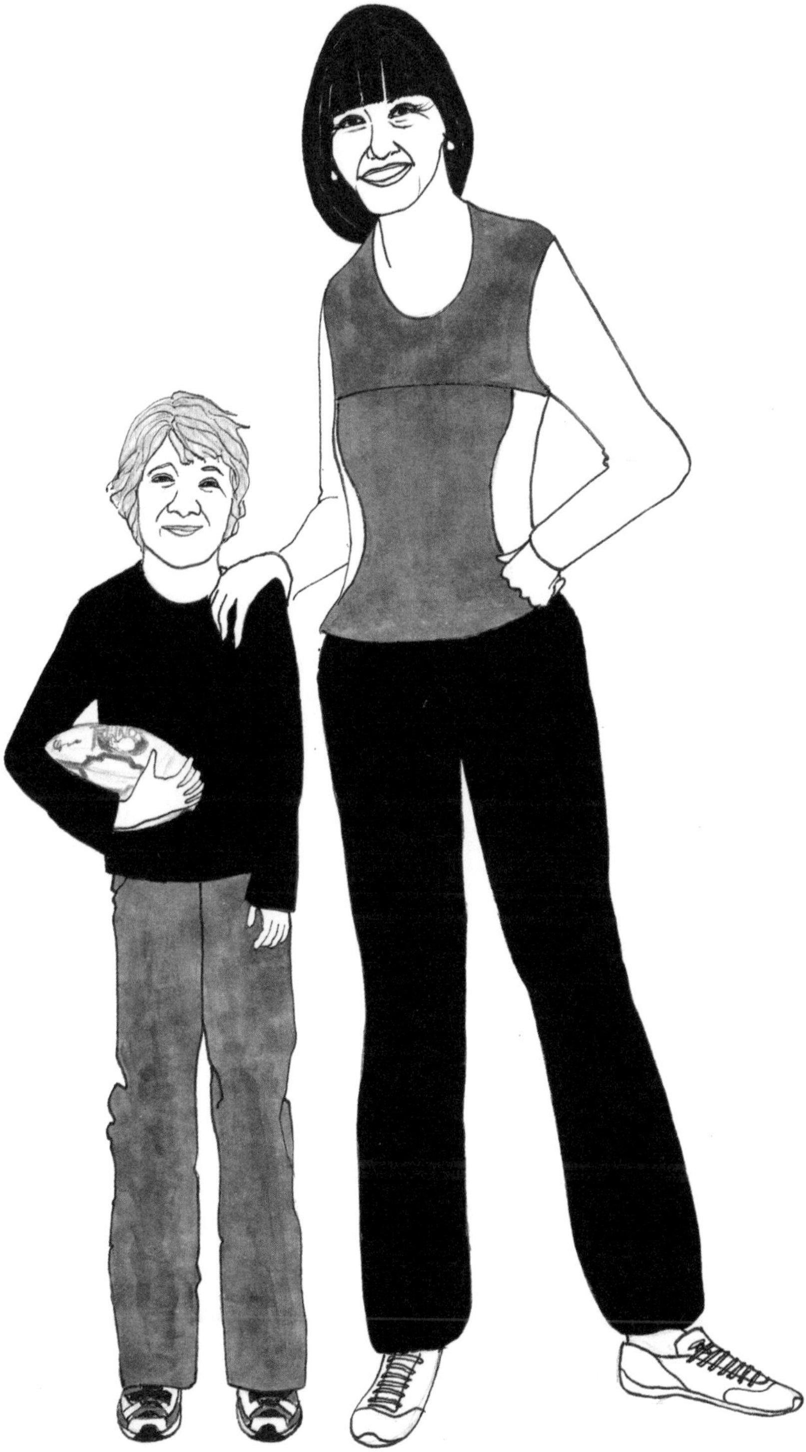

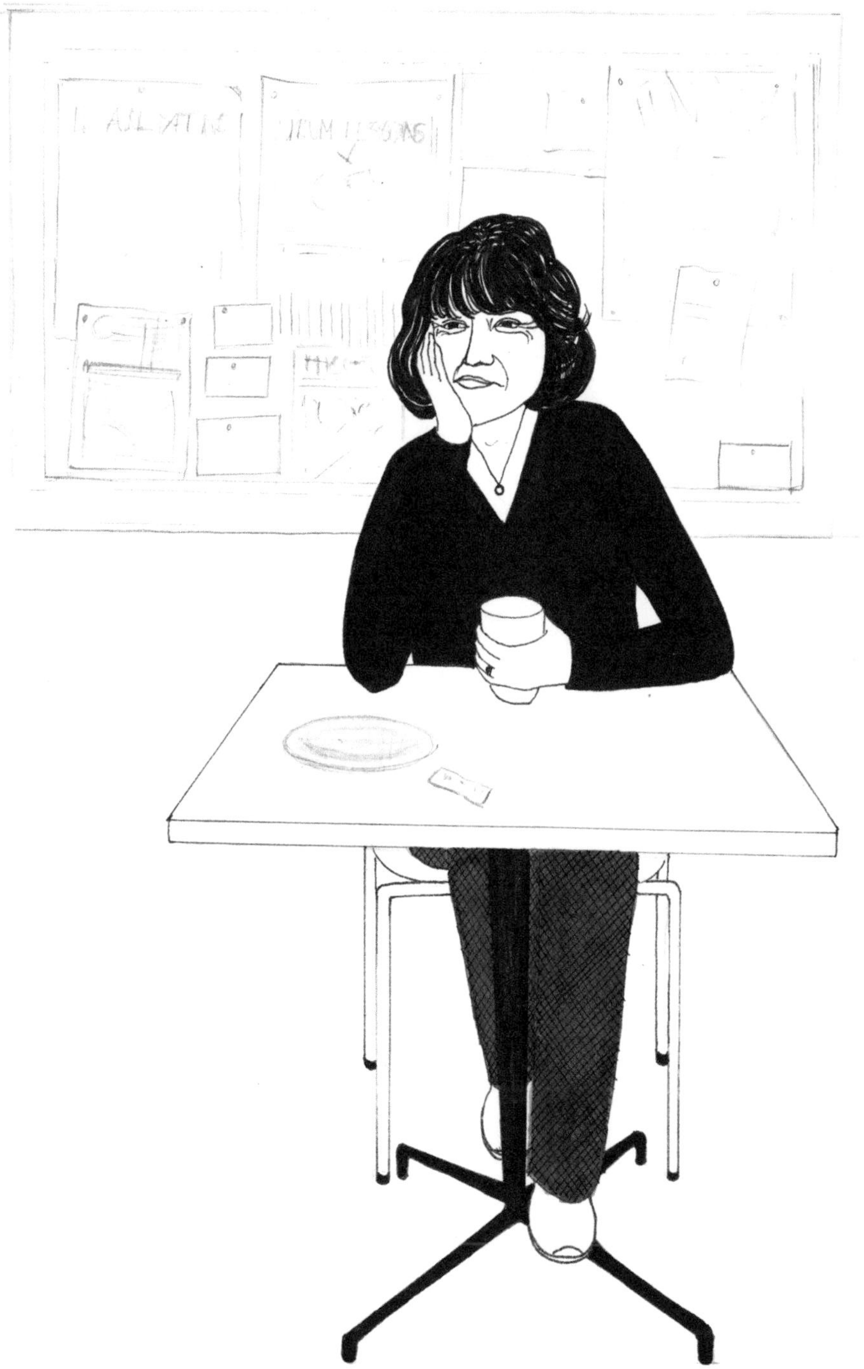

AFTERWORD:

In 2004, I read a book that I should have read 15 years earlier, when it was first published – *Misogynies* by Joan Smith. It was mind-blowing. I had read other books on sexual violence and feminism but suddenly, in this collection of essays, was the confirmation I needed that the hostility, hatred and disgust directed towards me as a child was *not* in my head, and that I might be perfectly justified in feeling angry about it. Two essays in particular, 'Crawling From The Wreckage' and 'There's Only One Yorkshire Ripper', reminded me so strongly of the things said around me and to me when I was growing up that I felt moved to contact the author to tell her how much her work had meant to me.

In this book, I have tried to build on some of Smith's arguments around the victim-blaming culture of the Ripper inquiry, drawing on research in related texts and archived newspapers and on my own experience of the period in question.

Central to Smith's essay, 'There's Only One Yorkshire Ripper', is the idea that the reason West Yorkshire Police so spectacularly failed to identify and apprehend Peter Sutcliffe has less to do with old-fashioned policing methods and more to do with old-fashioned attitudes towards women. An insistence that the killer was targeting prostitutes (as this was surely reasonable) meant that evidence that didn't fit with this idea was ignored. Indeed, it is now widely recognised that one crucial piece of evidence from a teenage girl, early in the investigation, if followed up, might have prevented almost all of the deaths and injuries which were to follow. The police did not know how to listen; they did not know how to take women seriously and they did not know how to see beyond their own entrenched ideas about them. This may not have changed much, but the will to change is there – something in the culture is shifting as I write. However, between 1975 and 1981, the years of my growing from the ages of 10 to 16, becoming a woman, no person crossed my path who contradicted prevailing social attitudes, reflected by police and press. I am aware *now* of the feminist activism that took place off my radar during this time-frame, but I could draw no comfort from it. Living in a small, conservative suburb, as I did, the people around me believed what they were told, trusted authority and read the same newspapers. No one told me about Reclaim the Night, or Andrea Dworkin and Susan Brownmiller.

In the Preface to Michael Bilton's 2003 book *Wicked Beyond Belief: The Hunt For the Yorkshire Ripper*, it is proposed that the murders were motiveless and that society is at the mercy of such a killer. This represents the conventional view. In Joan Smith's writing, it is proposed that the concept of the Ripper as being *sui generis*, a person outside the culture, without context, is flawed and stands in the way of understanding why misogynistic violence happens. The idea that there is something embedded deep within the culture that produces eruptions of gendered violence and allows them to flourish, rather than their being random and motiveless, is becoming mainstream, and is what drives this book. When I began it, I was attempting to make sense of myself. I wondered what effect it had had on me, growing into an adult during this notorious period of vicious misogyny, while experiencing a daily reality that had to be somehow made sense of within it. In order to survive, I internalised much of the unhelpful and contradictory *non*sense that I heard, simply because I was a child. It has taken me a lifetime to be free of these ideas.

Blaming the victim is an act of refuge and self-deception. It allows the blamer to sit in judgment, imagining some mystical justice that means bad things happen only to bad people, thus ensuring their own safety. A similar mysticism shrouds the idea of the monstrous man, the lunatic, the cloaked figure in the shadows. As Smith says, there is a strong impulse to assign an identity to an unknown violent male – an insubstantial figure can be turned into someone *known* – with disastrous results (Smith, p.166). This is a disaster mainly because it directs the collective gaze away from the ordinariness of male violence. It is interesting that a common line of argument against this ordinariness is that not all men are violent. Not all parents are abusive either, but groups of parents cannot be heard complaining loudly about being victimised when they are asked to alter their behaviour or habits to help protect *all* children in our societies.

While we puzzle and argue over what to do and who is right, millions of ordinary people live with everyday experiences that they cannot process properly, because they cannot speak about them freely due to a set of outdated and confused taboos. Muddled thinking around gendered violence allows us to turn away from potential solutions and has long prevented us from understanding, on a global scale, what this violence does to our societies. I have no neat answers, but I have tried to present an interesting set of questions in this book in various forms.

When I began drawing, I didn't plan to show the work to anyone, so it is odd to be sharing it with the world now. Many of the earliest drawings will forever remain private, but some of the early, quite abstract drawings are included here. They can be understood as functioning on a more unconscious, symbolic level than the more conventional narrative panels. I think they communicate something that words perhaps cannot. The varied visual approaches and experiments within the book demonstrate the journey of learning how to make a graphic narrative by *making* one. I hope this is a good book, but perhaps not a *worthy* one. Neither was it therapeutic, but it has been freeing. I like to think of this as my tapestry: like Philomela, who wove her own story after her tongue was cut out, this is my communication, my contribution, as one among many.

Una
June 2015

ACKNOWLEDGEMENTS:

With thanks to Michael, always at my side: I couldn't have done any of it without you. Thanks to Deborah, my precious friend; Corinne, my editor, ever patient and thoughtful; Marion, for being there; Becky, for leaping in; Mum, for all the babysitting; Griselda, for the sage advice; Roger, for the critique; Jacky, for the encouragement; Joan, for the inspiration; and Sally, for helping me to reach the end of the story.

BIBLIOGRAPHY:

News Sources

Yorkshire Post and *Yorkshire Evening Post* from 16 August 1975 to 31 March 1981, available on microfilm at Leeds Central Library and the British Library Newsroom, London.

Media Sources

Left for Dead by the Yorkshire Ripper (2014). TV movie. Directed by Katinka Newman. London: Brite Spark Films. (*For interview with Tracy Browne.*)

Bates, L. (28 Dec 2012). '2012: the year when it became okay to blame victims of sexual assault'. *Independent*. [Online]

Statistical Sources

UK, Office for National Statistics (2013). Statistical Bulletin. *Crime Statistics, Focus on: Violent Crime and Sexual Offences*, 2011/12. [Online and PDF] Available from: www.ons.gov.uk.

UK, Home Office (2012). Statistical Bulletin, Smith, K. (ed), S. Osborne, I. Lau and A. Britton. *Homicides, Firearm Offences and Intimate Violence, 2010/11 – Supplementary Volume 2 to Crime in England and Wales 2010/11*. [PDF] Available from www.gov.uk.

UK, Ministry for Justice, Home Office and Office for National Statistics (2013). *An Overview of Sexual Offending in England and Wales*. [PDF] Available from www.gov.uk, www.justice.gov.uk, www.homeoffice.gov.uk/rds/index.htm, and www.ons.gov.uk.

Books

Bilton, M. (2003). *Wicked Beyond Belief – The Hunt for the Yorkshire Ripper*. London: Harper Collins.

McCann, R. (2004). *Just a Boy – The True Story of a Stolen Childhood*. 2nd edition. London: Random House.

Smith, J. (1989). 'There's Only One Yorkshire Ripper'. In Smith, J., *Misogynies* (1989). Revised paperback edition 1996. London: Vintage.

Smith, J. (1989). 'M'learned Friends'. In Smith, J., *Misogynies, ibid.*

Hesse-Honegger, C. (2001). *Heteroptera: The Beautiful and the Other, or Images of a Mutating World*. Germany: Scalo Verlag Ac.

1. Page 23. A senior detective involved in Kiszco's conviction, Detective Superintendent Dick Holland, was invited, fresh from this triumph, to work with Assistant Chief Constable George Oldfield in the hunt for the hammer killer. Detectives Holland and Oldfield were close friends, trusting one another to work the same 'old' West Yorkshire methods (Bilton, 2003, p.91). In his book about the case, Michael Bilton, who was also a friend of Holland's (*ibid*, p.xii) describes the pair as two big fish (*ibid*, p.147). On p.89 of Bilton's book, there is a description of an internal investigation in the 1970s of a sexual assault on two young girls by a uniformed police officer. Oldfield and Holland were the investigating officers. Oldfield persuaded the girls' parents to keep the case out of court despite having determined that the officer was guilty. Holland later rationalised this as being better for the girls, 'in case they break down in court, which might ruin their lives'. Holland recalls 'another investigator might have done it by the book and it would have gone all the way to court' (*ibid*, p.89). In extensive interviews in the book, Holland is quoted as saying that political correctness never was his strong point (when talking about gypsies) and he makes comments about ex-coal-miner colleagues as being 'thick' detectives (*ibid*, p.148). This, in a book that seems designed to rescue Holland's reputation. Holland was a frustrated scientist, who enjoyed working with colleagues from forensic labs (*ibid*, p.147). In 1995 he was charged, along with his retired colleague Ronald Outteridge, a forensic scientist, with perverting the course of justice owing to their having suppressed forensic evidence that would have proved Stefan Kiszco innocent of the murder of Lesley Molseed. The case never went before a jury because magistrates ruled that too much time had passed for the officers to receive a fair trial.

2. Page 28. Discussions of the five-pound-note débâcle appear in Smith, 1989, p.165, and Bilton, 2003, p.278. Michael Bilton describes the narrowing of the search for the five-pound note from almost 6,000 to 240 employees in a chapter of his book titled 'Swamped by Paper'. On p.278 he notes that Sutcliffe was no.76 on the list of 240 created in collaboration with the Bank of England, and that paperwork relating to his being interviewed (twice) about the banknotes was missing or misplaced, resulting in his being left out of resulting investigations. The chaos of 1970s record-keeping systems is often blamed for the incompetency of the Ripper inquiry; however, Joan Smith, 1989, states that, although there is some truth in this, it comes nowhere near the heart of the matter. For Smith, the police did little more than stumble around in a Jack-the-Ripper-style fog of their own making.

3. Page 31. The girl is Tracy Browne, speaking to a constable at Keighley police station. Both quotes can be found in Bilton, 2003. p.140. Tracy also describes the frustration of going to the police station with her mother only to be dismissed and sent away in a Brite Spark Films documentary by Katinka Newman, 2014.

4. Page 36. I have not used the word 'rape' to describe this incident, even though that is what it was. This is because I didn't name it as rape until many years later. It's impossible to explain why. I can only say that Terry was not interested in whether I consented, or whether I was old enough to consent. He also didn't care whether I was hurt or shocked or whether I cried, which I did.

5. Page 62. In 'There's Only One Yorkshire Ripper', 1989, Joan Smith describes the contents of an 18-page dossier, produced by West Yorkshire police in 1979 and circulated to other police forces in the UK and around the world. The

dossier not only demonstrates the mess the investigation was in; it contains numerous references to the 'prostitutes or women of loose morals' on whom the killer is supposed to have concentrated. The victims of the attacks are grouped into two rigid categories – loose or innocent – without evidence, merely according to the say-so of the officers involved. This, in spite of a surviving victim, shown in the image on page 63 of this book, having rejected Sutcliffe's approaches in no uncertain terms. ('Do you fancy it?' 'Not on your life!': Smith, pp.171–5.)

6. Page 64. This list of the women's imagined moral infringements is adapted from the list in Smith, 1989, p.175.

7. Page 68. Police statement made by West Yorkshire detective Jim Hobson, quoted in Smith, 1989, p.175.

8. Page 70. These statements are paraphrased from text in Bilton, 2003, p.216.

9. Page 71. This is a reversal of Joan Smith's well-known statement that what began with jokes ended in murder (Smith, 1989, p.viii).

10. Page 123. Quotes are from Bates, 2012. Victim-blaming is not a phenomenon confined to the past. In an article for the *Independent* newspaper, Laura Bates, founder of Everyday Sexism, describes a series of contemporaneous victim-blaming episodes in life, the media and the judicial system, including the quoted comments from the Rochdale sexual exploitation cases. There have been independent inquiries into Child Sexual Exploitation in a number of towns in the UK, including Rochdale, Oxford and Rotherham. It is widely acknowledged that adult women have a difficult time persuading the authorities that sexualised violence is not their fault, but it seems

incredible that young girls are also routinely blamed for what adult men do. Maggie Blyth, chair of Oxfordshire Safeguarding Board, writing about her report for the Home Office in 2015, states that police, social workers and health workers in Oxford failed to look past the troubled teenager to the abuse. Blyth does not accept the excuse that the depth of the failure to protect children was because Child Sexual Exploitation was not widely recognised at the time, and points out that one does not need training in CSE to know that there is something wrong if a 12-year-old is sleeping with a 25-year-old.

11. Page 124. Figures are from the Office for National Statistics. See bibliography.

12. Page 127. Throughout the 1970s and '80s, Jimmy Savile used his social position to gain access to a number of hospitals and other institutions, including Broadmoor High Security Hospital, where difficult and dangerous patients are detained. He was photographed there with Peter Sutcliffe, the Yorkshire Ripper, and was said to have visited him frequently.

13. Page 130. The drawings are adapted from photographs by award-winning photographer Pete Muller for the International Campaign to Stop Rape & Gender Violence In Conflict.

14. Pages 132–3. Ms Una refers to the 1970s children's TV programme *Mr Benn* (McKee, Zephyr Films, 1971), in which the eponymous character travelled through history by changing his costume. The costume shop was owned by a welcoming but inscrutable man, inexplicably wearing a fez.

RESOURCES:

Amnesty International. Campaigning on sexual and reproductive rights. http://amnesty.org.uk

Barnardos. Campaigning for policy change around the issue of Child Sexual Exploitation. www.barnardos.org

Counting Dead Women. Documenting deaths by male violence. http://kareningalasmith.com

The End Violence Against Women Coalition. A broad range of campaigns around VAW. www.endviolenceagainstwomen.org.uk

The Everyday Sexism Project. Documenting everyday experiences. http://everydaysexism.com

Everyday Victim Blaming. A collaborative blog collecting women's personal stories. http://everydayvictimblaming.com

International Campaign to Stop Rape & Gender Violence in Conflict. Co-ordinated effort for change. http://stoprapeinconflict.org

Justice for Women. Challenging discrimination in criminal justice. www.justiceforwomen.org.uk

National Society for the Prevention of Cruelty to Children (NSPCC). Children's charity fighting to end child abuse. http://nspcc.org.uk

The Rape Crisis Network. For support, legal advocacy and counselling. www.rapecrisis.org.uk

The Samaritans. Listening and support, around the clock. http://samaritans.org

Women's Aid. Working to end domestic abuse. www.womensaid.org.uk

FURTHER READING:

If you'd like to know more about the issues raised in this book, in addition to the books listed in the bibliography I recommend the following:

Brownmiller, S. (1986). *Against Our Will: Men, Women and Rape*. Harmondsworth: Penguin.

Dworkin, A. (2002). *Heartbreak: The Political Memoir of a Feminist Militant*. New York: Basic Books.

Gloeckner, P. (2000). *A Child's Life and Other Stories*. Berkeley: Frog Books.

Morrison, B. (1987). *The Ballad of The Yorkshire Ripper*. London: Chatto & Windus.

Rhys, J. (1966). *Wide Sargasso Sea*. London: André Deutsch; London: Penguin Essentials.

Tanenbaum, L. (2000). *Slut! Growing Up Female With a Bad Reputation*. New York: Harper Perennial.

UK, The Children's Commissioner for England. *Inquiry into Child Sexual Exploitation in Gangs and Groups (CSEGG)*. Available from www.childrenscommissioner.gov.uk/info/csegg.

UK, Home Office (2006). *Sir Lawrence Byford report into the police handling of the Yorkshire Ripper case*. [PDF] Available from www.gov.uk.

MORE FROM MYRIAD

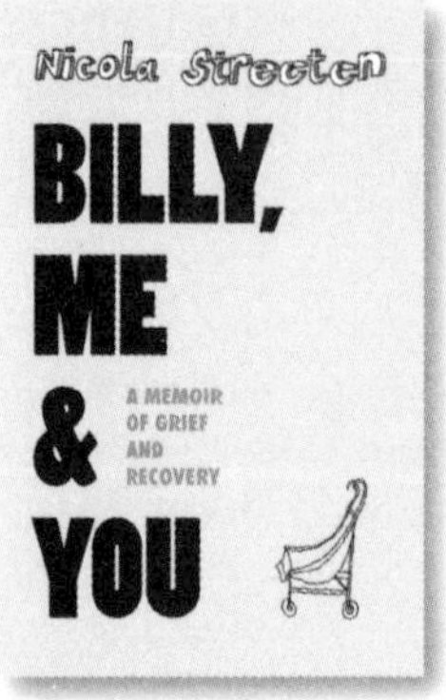
Nicola Streeten
BILLY, ME & YOU
A MEMOIR OF GRIEF AND RECOVERY

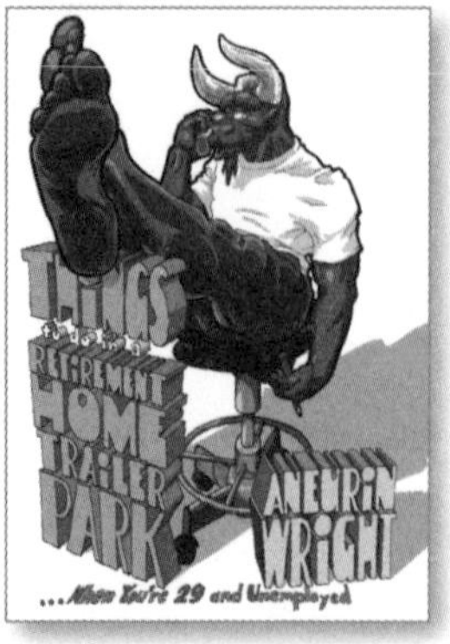
THINGS
RETIREMENT HOME TRAILER PARK
ANEURIN WRIGHT
...When You're 29 and Unemployed

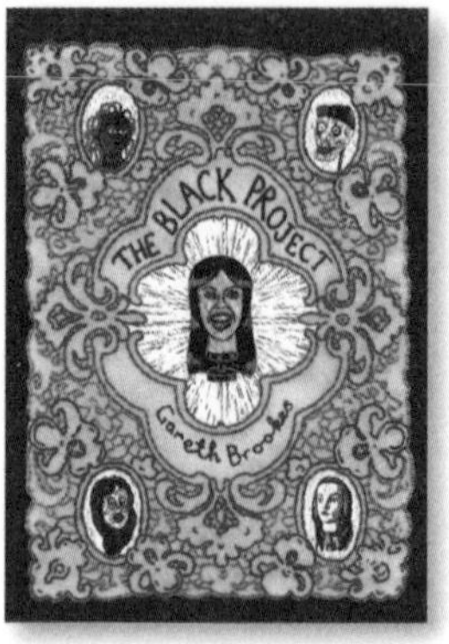
THE BLACK PROJECT
Gareth Brookes

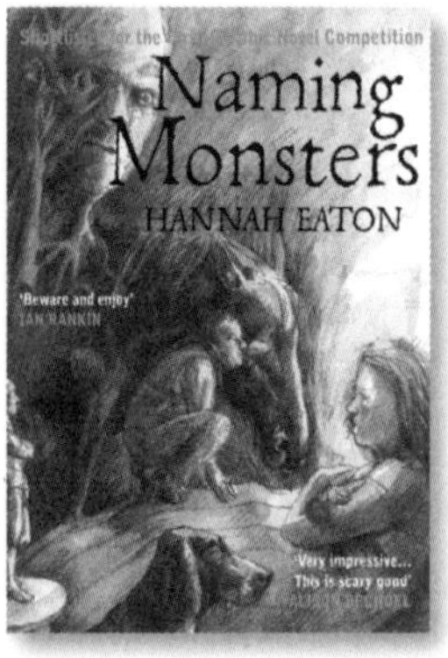
Naming Monsters
HANNAH EATON
'Beware and enjoy'
IAN RANKIN
'Very impressive... This is scary good'

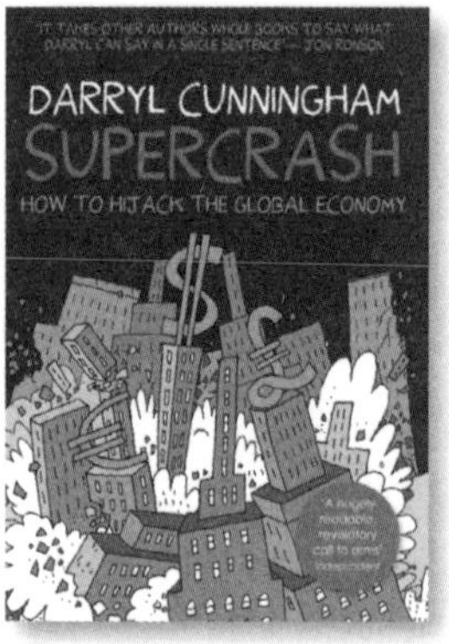
DARRYL CUNNINGHAM
SUPERCRASH
HOW TO HIJACK THE GLOBAL ECONOMY

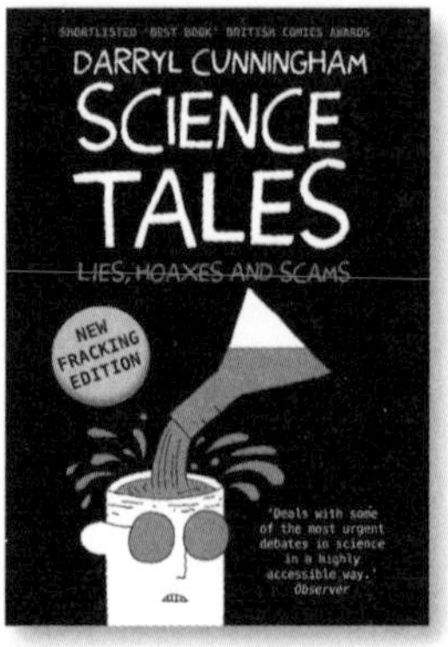
DARRYL CUNNINGHAM
SCIENCE TALES
LIES, HOAXES AND SCAMS
NEW FRACKING EDITION
'Deals with some of the most urgent debates in science in a highly accessible way.'
Observer

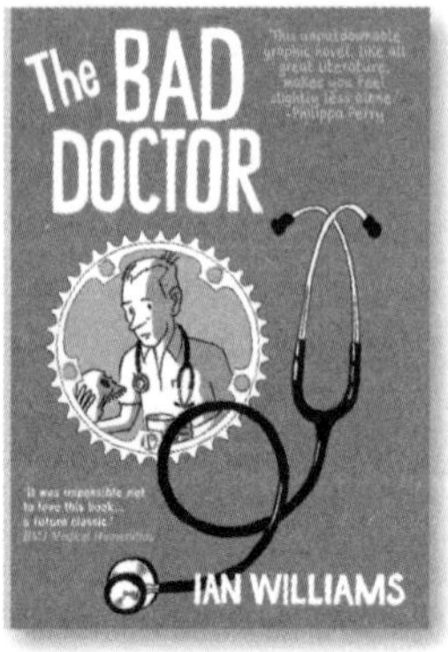
The BAD DOCTOR
IAN WILLIAMS

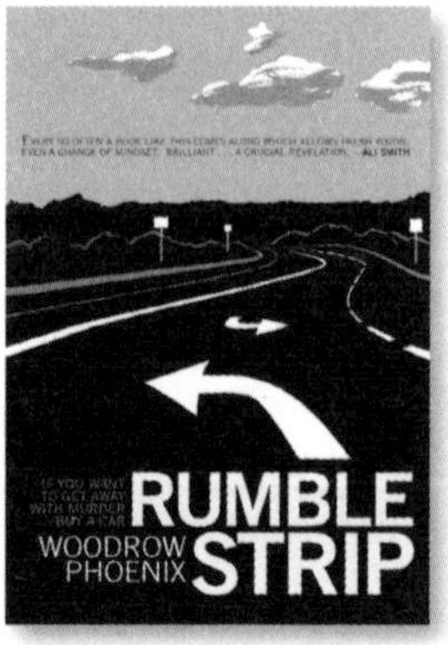
RUMBLE STRIP
WOODROW PHOENIX

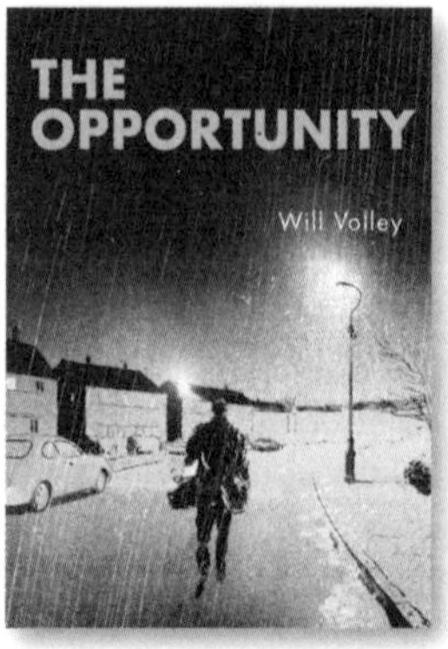
THE OPPORTUNITY
Will Volley

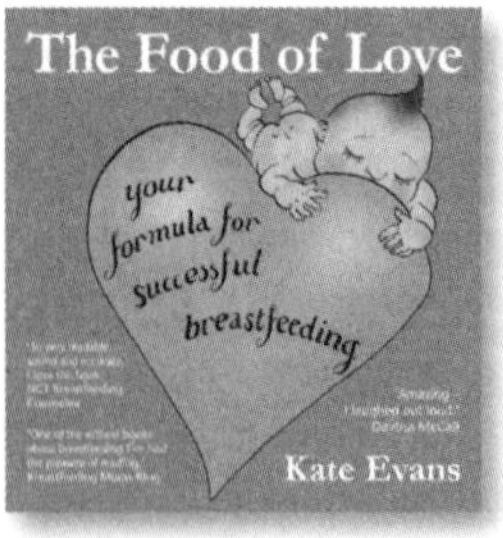
The Food of Love
your formula for successful breastfeeding
Kate Evans

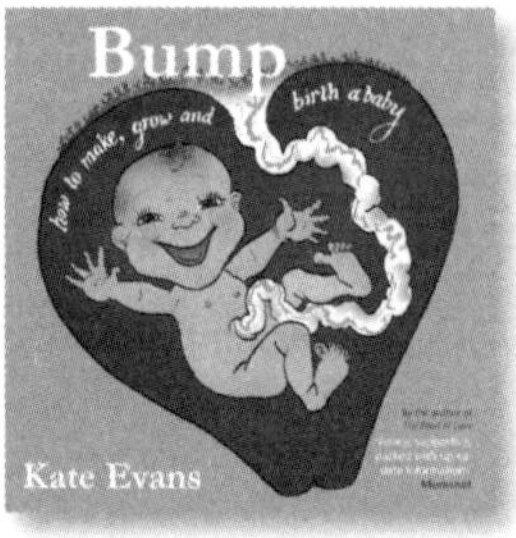
Bump
how to make, grow and birth a baby
Kate Evans

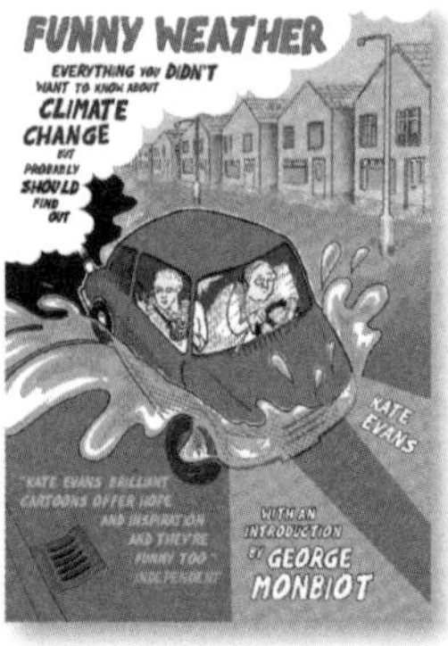
FUNNY WEATHER
EVERYTHING YOU DIDN'T WANT TO KNOW ABOUT CLIMATE CHANGE BUT PROBABLY SHOULD FIND OUT
KATE EVANS
WITH AN INTRODUCTION BY GEORGE MONBIOT